GARDEN OF DREAMS

HOLLYWOOD LEGENDS SERIES
CARL ROLLYSON, GENERAL EDITOR

GARDEN OF DREAMS

The Life of

Simone Signoret

PATRICIA A. DEMAIO

University Press of Mississippi • Jackson

www.upress.state.ms.us

The University Press of Mississippi is a member of the Association of American
University Presses.

Copyright © 2014 by Patricia A. DeMaio
All rights reserved
Manufactured in the United States of America

First printing 2014

∞

Library of Congress Cataloging-in-Publication Data

DeMaio, Patricia A.
Garden of dreams : the life of Simone Signoret / Patricia A. DeMaio.
pages cm — (Hollywood legends series)
Includes bibliographical references and index.
ISBN 978-1-60473-569-7 (hardback) — ISBN 978-1-61703-936-2 (ebook)
1. Signoret, Simone, 1921–1985. 2. Actors—France—Biography. I. Title.
PN2638.S47D46 2014
791.43′028′092—dc23
[B]   2013029852

British Library Cataloging-in-Publication Data available

To my parents,
James and Helen DeMaio

CONTENTS

GARDEN OF DREAMS

Introduction

It's miraculous when life brings you parts that seem to grow better each year; stronger, laden with the memories and personal experiences that have put lines on your face . . . . for the stars, those scars are killers; they creep stealthily in prior to the expulsion from the garden of dreams.
—SIMONE SIGNORET

The incomparable Simone Signoret was never expelled from the garden of dreams. While her contemporaries struggled to secure meaningful roles after forty, the legendary French actress aged in the course of playing groundbreaking roles, appearing for over four decades in film and television. While she did not age gracefully, her transition from the young and beautiful femme fatale to the svelte woman of the world, and then to the aged matron—wrinkled, fat, and formless—was almost seamless on screen, where she never lost that earthy sensuality that made sex appeal and glamour seem superficial and trite. "Signoret has more depth and uniqueness," director Peter Glenville noted, than the "sprightly prettiness" of others.

Simone, fluent in three languages, won a Best Actress Academy Award in 1960 for her work in the British independent film *Room at the Top*, giving her a backdoor entrance to Hollywood after she was blacklisted for her association with communists during the McCarthy era. She was the first French actress to win the Oscar, as well as an array of nominations and other awards from Hollywood. She received a Golden Globe nomination, a Golden Laurel, and the National Board of Review Award in 1960 for *Room at the Top*. In 1966, she was nominated for an Academy Award and a Golden Globe for *Ship of Fools*. She also won the Emmy as Best Actress for Bob Hope's Chrysler Theater Presents production, *A Small Rebellion*. And then, Simone quietly disappeared from Hollywood, even as her international career soared.

3

Why wasn't Simone Signoret a more prominent figure in Hollywood? That was the question I asked five years ago, while watching *Ship of Fools* for the first time. Though the question would prove to be inconsequential in the context of her complex life, it was pertinent at the time because I was unfamiliar with the artist contemporaries described as "no skim milk actress." Indeed, if not for the dramatic and authentic interaction between Signoret as La Condesa, and Oskar Werner, as Dr. Schumann, the ship's physician, and their poignant love story, I would have turned off *Ship of Fools*, my reaction mirroring the sentiment of critic Pauline Kael, who wrote, "Everything is staccato, loud, crude . . . . But everyone will 'buy' the doomed lovers right out of *One Way Passage*." Ironically, a film I disliked set into motion a five-year journey that was always intriguing and rewarding—and sometimes very frustrating.

Anyone who has studied Simone in any depth quickly discovers that she was an extraordinarily intelligent, charming, gifted, and complex woman with an uncanny ability to re-invent herself—especially when the odds were stacked against her. As many have noted, she had multiple lives. Her marriage of thirty-six years to Yves Montand formed the core from which films, social activism, writing, translation, stage, and television emerged. These "lives" are so intricately interwoven, it is nearly impossible to separate them without doing a disservice to the entire life.

The first sign that I was researching a difficult subject appeared while I was reading Simone's autobiography, *Nostalgia Isn't What It Used to Be*. The book is witty, entertaining, and informative—particularly from a historical perspective. However, it wasn't long before I discovered that it isn't about Simone. Instead, the book is about her husband, Yves Montand, and their life together. The focus, however, is trained on Montand's experiences rather than hers. In contrast, *You See, I Haven't Forgotten*, Yves Montand's biography, devotes only a few chapters to Simone, leading me to wonder about their unique relationship. If he was the center of her life, was she the center of his? What would happen if I tried to separate them, just a little, in order to gain a closer perspective on Simone as both actress and woman?

Establishing chronology was a major challenge, because Simone purposely left gaps in her autobiography. She enjoyed storytelling and often mixed up events, allowing one story to lead to others, so that unraveling them was like peeling an onion, with one layer endlessly revealing another. Unraveling the story was the first great challenge in allowing the young Simone Kaminker to emerge as Simone Signoret. Yet, it paled in comparison to other challenges. The lack of chronology in *Nostalgia* has created many myths.

Discovering the depth of Simone's personal outlook on stardom was of great importance to my research. She always made it clear that she considered herself an anti-star who abhorred publicity, particularly if its aim was to invade her privacy or that of her family. This view was itself the result of a deep-seated philosophy. Simone believed that she could separate her two lives—woman and actress—and was successful in maintaining that separation for a time by creating a public persona and a script for the story of her life. This strategy was obvious when she spoke of her early life in interviews. Her stories were so well crafted that she rarely deviated from her established line—and she always avoided commentary that dove beneath the surface. Each interview mirrored others, and it was a challenge to find any that revealed more detail than her script allowed. She usually avoided the temptation to psychoanalyze, particularly with regard to her parents, their relationship, and her relationship with them. If she were asked questions that she thought intrusive, particularly questions about her political beliefs, she had no difficulty shutting down an interviewer by simply stating that her political beliefs were no one's business. Rather than cite redundant materials, I sought out sources that went beneath the surface.

Another persona Simone established was as half of the ideal couple. This image was more important to her than any other. She worked hard to cultivate it and was largely successful in doing so for the first ten years of her marriage to Yves Montand. But, as she learned after he and Marilyn Monroe had a well-publicized affair, it became impossible to keep the two "zones" she had created—the woman and the actress—separate. Indeed, two were inextricable, and "the slices of life stained with the blood of yesterday's tears" would create the deep well she drew from for powerful, unparalleled dramatic performances.

❧

Some film treatments in this book are longer than others. Many of Simone's films are not available in the United States and so, I utilized films that clearly paralleled Simone's life at the time. While the Marilyn Monroe and Yves Montand affair created a turning point in her life, it was not the sole cause of Simone's emotional wounds. There were other controversies. Books written by Simone's grandson, Benjamin Castaldi, and her daughter, Catherine Allégret, give conflicting versions of Yves Montand's overall behavior towards his wife. As neither Simone nor Montand can weigh in on the controversy, I handle the material carefully, reporting it as family members do in their books. I would have preferred to skip the entire episode, but it was impossible to relate the story of Simone's rapid physical decline and alcoholism without addressing this source of anguish, which far outweighed the Marilyn Monroe intrusion. While the Montand-Monroe affair embarrassed Simone, contrary to myth, it was not the sole reason for Simone's physical decline.

Interviews for this biography were problematic. As the French journalist and author Catherine David noted in her book, *Simone Signoret*, Simone is a "wonderful subject . . . . But a taboo one . . . protected by an impalpable aura of silence," which prevented David from obtaining interviews with Simone's colleagues, friends, and family members. Unfortunately, that protective aura is still in place more than twenty-five years after Simone's death. Jean-Pierre Kaminker was the only relative willing to discuss Simone and their early life together. Her cousin Robert Kaminker provided insight on André Kaminker, Simone's father. Her daughter, the actress Catherine Allégret, would not grant an interview or give permission to quote from correspondence I discovered. Most of Simone's surviving friends and colleagues did not grant interviews. Among those who granted interviews, some individuals did not want to be quoted. Most of these politely declined, others had more to say. "Enough has been written about Simone . . . let her rest in peace . . . everything you need to know about her is in *Nostalgia* . . . I will not participate in a Hollywood story," I was told.

I was forced to combat this aura of silence by relying heavily on Simone's autobiography, *Nostalgia Isn't What It Used To Be*, on the sequel, *The Next Day, She Smiled*, which has never been translated into English, and on accounts of her life as described in books written by her daughter, Catherine Allégret, her grandson, Benjamin Castaldi, and by a few friends of the family. The biography of Yves Montand, *You See, I Haven't Forgotten*, also played a prominent role, as did news articles, taped interviews, reference books, and films. I discovered new information about Simone's attempt to break into Hollywood during the McCarthy era at the Harry Ransom Research Center at the University of Texas, Austin, as well as at the Margaret Hennick Library at the Academy of Motion Picture Arts and Sciences, and in the Hedda Hopper FBI files. Although I was disappointed by the paucity of interviews I was able to obtain, after putting together various pieces of the puzzle, I was surprised by the emergence of a unique, contemporary, and provocative story.

"To continue . . . the big thing . . . the only thing, I ever really wanted," Simone said, of her career. And she did continue. She continued on
screen, and she emerged as a best-selling author, a translator, a respected
social activist, and a loyal wife, mother, and grandmother. She reached
her peak as an actress with her receipt of an Oscar, and then pushed
Hollywood aside in favor of international stardom in films with real life
stories rather than formulaic treatments of an artificial one.

"In life I haven't done all I would have liked to do," she said shortly
before her death in 1985, "but I've never done anything I didn't want to
do." She was right. The cinema was Simone's garden of dreams. However, since few films could ever be as rich, fertile, and provocative as her
life, I rather thought of Simone Signoret herself as the garden of dreams,
and I am pleased to present this first American biography of the grand
French actress.

PART I

THE LONG FOUR-YEAR NIGHT

CHAPTER 1

A Secret Desire

SHE NEVER FELT A CALLING TO A PARTICULAR VOCATION AND WAS conflicted about what she wanted to do when the time came for making this decision. While she enjoyed writing essays and stories in school, she couldn't yet imagine herself as an author; that would come later in life. Beyond that, there was only one thing that compelled her, something that had such a subtle genesis she couldn't remember exactly when it started. She wanted to become a Hollywood star. And because America seemed remote to a teenager growing up in Paris, she carefully devised a plan to get there, a plan inspired by all the stories she'd read in the movie star magazines she could get her hands on, stories about pretty young girls who were discovered while working as waitresses or secretaries.

Her fantasy unfolded at Studio Harcourt in Paris, where Marlene Dietrich had her glamorous portrait taken. Simone couldn't help but admire the subtle lighting that accentuated the actress's cheekbones or the shadows cast by her luxurious eyelashes. Harcourt was the photographer of the stars, and if she could get a job there as a sales clerk, Simone reasoned, a director was bound to notice her and approach. "Mademoiselle, would you like to be in the movies," he would ask. Simone worked out the details of this scene so thoroughly, she would have to feign surprise if it actually happened.

Simone kept abreast of the latest news from Hollywood and felt so close to the stars that when Jean Harlow died on June 7, 1937, she grieved as though the actress had been a close friend. The teen star Deanna Durbin was the envy all the girls when her first kiss on the silver screen inspired headlines. Everyone knew the story of Carole Lombard's car accident and scar, and that the French actress Simone Simon was discovered in a restaurant. There was a delicious rumor circulating about Simon: Her secretary claimed the actress gave men a gold key to her boudoir. It wasn't true of course, but the rumor only added to the mystique of Hollywood, where in the fantasies of a teenager, eyelashes grew longer than anywhere else in the world.

Simone continued the dream in the privacy of her bedroom, where she stole moments in front of the mirror, playing Annabella when she fell in love with Tyrone Power in *Suez*, and Danielle Darrieux's Youki in *Port Arthur*. Since Darrieux was a particular favorite, Simone tried to imitate the star's hairstyle during a lunch break, heating her curling iron on the gas flame in the bathroom to achieve the desired effect. Much to the dismay of her Latin teacher, Simone returned to class reeking of singed hair. However, the embarrassment she endured was worthwhile, because those tiny sausage curls were all the rage in movie star magazines in the late 1930s.

Simone carefully nurtured her dream. "But I never said at home, 'Ah-la-la, I would really love to act.' I didn't dare," she explained.[2] It wasn't that her parents were against the performing arts, but they shared a typically bourgeoisie belief that acting was a childish fantasy and not the most honest way to earn a living. Simone was expected to concentrate her energy on passing two baccalaureate exams before leaving high school: the "pre-bac," which covered math, sciences, and languages, and then in the last year, the philosophy or "philo bac," an exam required for entrance to the university.

"I was not a particularly model pupil," she was quick to admit, "but I was strong in English," which helped her score sixteen out of twenty points on the pre-bac exam. Indeed, Simone's English was so strong that her language teacher took pity on his student's weaker command of the German language, questioning Simone on pages from Goethe in English, rather than German. "I translated without difficulty into French!" Simone declared triumphantly. She passed, with her score balancing out a miserable performance—only four out of thirty points—on the physics and chemistry exam.

She despised math and science. However, her attitude about these subjects was not regarded as cause for concern, because in the polite bourgeoisie society of the 1930s greater emphasis was placed on the arts and humanities. This was particularly true in the very "scholastic environment"[3] of the Kaminker household, where exposure to literature, art, music (particularly opera), history, and languages was of utmost importance. Simone's father, André Kaminker, was a renowned linguist, and her mother, Georgette, was "a delicate reader" of the French author Marcel Proust.

Simone certainly had potential and was "singled out for her literary abilities"[4] and intellectual interests by teachers, her brother Jean-Pierre explained. She was an avid reader and enjoyed writing essays. As a child, she took piano lessons and was intimately familiar with Wagner operas and Greek mythology, favorites of her father. While academics were important, social skills played an important role in a young women's education. In high school, Simone was envious of the male students, who studied interesting subjects and read books she couldn't wait to get her hands on. However, these interests had to wait. It was more important that young ladies learn how to serve tea, hold a fork with pinky finger extended, and walk skillfully on tiptoes so as not to disrupt a visit with the clatter of shoes.

Young men talked about careers; young women talked about marriage and families. And absolutely no one talked about acting. That subject was about as inappropriate in conversation as discussing one's desires to be wealthy, beautiful, or in love, Simone explained later in life. During those awkward adolescent years, Simone was so convinced acting was a taboo, she would rather have cut out her tongue than give voice to her desire.[5] She tried to wish it away, and she worried, as she got older, that there must be something wrong with her, because in spite of her best efforts, the dream only grew stronger. Finally, unable to ignore it, the teenager decided to give in. Acting could not be a vocation, but it could be her "secret desire."

However, it was not the best-kept secret. Her younger brothers Alain and Jean-Pierre, aged seven and five, respectively, were witnesses to their sixteen-year-old sister's flair for the dramatic. Jean-Pierre recalled watching Simone "at play with her friends in a sketch of her own creation in the living room or rooms of the family apartment. She excelled as well and with a great deal of mischief in telephone mystifications,"[6] elaborately crafted but never malicious prank calls to unsuspecting victims.

She brought home many friends, who all seemed to enjoy the free-spirited environment of the Kaminker household—which she noted was nothing like their formal homes, where servants waited on guests when the girls hosted teas. Though the Kaminker family could well afford to have servants, they did not, and Georgette seemed to hold the belief that children should not be waited on. This belief was so firmly ingrained that Simone followed it later when she became a parent. But at the time, she couldn't decide what mortified her most: guests making their own sandwiches, or her mother's lectures about hygiene—particularly those delivered on inclement days, when Georgette required guests to remove their boots, because it was unsanitary to have "humid feet.". While this statement may have been true, it was nonetheless embarrassing. Yet, Simone discovered that her friends were unfazed by her mother and thought her home was far more fun than their own.

But for Simone these little mortifications were symptoms of a deeper angst. Home was a reminder of the ever-widening abyss separating her parents. As her father, André, gained prominence as a conference interpreter, he traveled extensively and was never home. This absence was a sore point for Simone's mother, Georgette—particularly since her husband imposed his love of ostentatious status symbols on the family and then left his wife to her own devices. As André's career advanced, he moved the family to ever-larger apartments, causing Simone to feel that her family lacked roots and security.[7]

The family lived first on Rue de Sablonville, and then, when Simone was old enough to enter school, they moved to a larger apartment on Rue Jacques Dulard. After the birth of a second child, Alain, in 1930, when Simone was nine years old, the Kaminkers moved to an apartment on Rue Peronnet. Jean-Pierre was born in 1932, and three years later they were on the move again—this time to a luxury apartment on Avenue du Roule, their fourth residence in ten years. Yet, in all the moves, they never left Neuilly-sur-Seine, an upper-middle class suburb on the right bank of the Seine known for its beautiful churches, synagogues, ornate homes, and exclusive schools. Georgette was not happy there, and with every move, tensions between husband and wife were played out through passive-aggressive actions, behavior that was especially pronounced after their last move.

The eight-story luxury apartment at 73 Avenue du Roule, on the corner of Rue d'Orléans, boasted a lobby and seven floors of spacious apartments. There were two apartments per floor, each residence equipped with all the modern conveniences and amenities for residents. Servants used a stairwell located in the rear of the building. Each apartment enjoyed a view of the neatly tree-lined Avenue du Roule from large, ornate wrought iron balconies that spanned the front of the building. The lobby was elegantly appointed with mirrors, a grand staircase, and a tiny hydraulic elevator, the latest advancement in technology. However, the lift never arrived fast enough for Simone, who was always anxious to escape the ever-watchful concierge, who could not hide her disdain for the Kaminkers.

It was clear to the concierge that the Kaminkers were not like other families in the building. Among other things, they were unable to hold on to their maids because no one ever cleaned thoroughly enough to satisfy Georgette. Simone observed that housekeeper departures occurred with clocklike regularity and often without notice, usually during the third week of employment. When she arrived from school and had to wait longer than usual for her mother to answer the door because she was busy with chores, Simone knew another housekeeper had quit.

The apartment was more than adequate for the three children and Georgette's mother, Henriette Signoret, who had come to live with the Kaminkers in 1932 after her husband, Charles, passed away. They shared four bedrooms, a kitchen, a dining room, a large living room, a smaller den, a bathroom, and their sizable balcony. They lived on the top floor, and Georgette was so worried that her sons might fall eight stories to their deaths, she encased the balcony in wire mesh.

Despite their luxurious surroundings, the residence was far from chic. Georgette showed no interest in decorating yet another apartment, so no one bothered to put up wallpaper, even though the walls had been prepped with salmon-colored sizing that reminded Simone of the lining in clothing. They had oriental carpets in storage, but Georgette preferred to use older carpets left behind by previous tenants. Georgette never seemed to have time to purchase shades for the ceiling light fixtures.[9] The appearance of austerity in the midst of luxury was the most conspicuous sign of discord in the Kaminker marriage.

Simone tended to side with her mother when it came to disagreements between her parents, which were usually fueled by the moves and by André's frequent absences—ostensibly for work, though work apparently was his escape from his wife's contrariness. The relationship festered, finally reaching a climax during Simone's adolescence when things, she said, "went from bad to worse," a view she never elaborated.[10]

"Simone lived through the conflict that existed between her parents when our father announced his intention of getting a divorce," Jean-Pierre explained. The announcement "set off such a reaction in his wife that he gave up on the idea."[11] Instead, André immersed himself further in his work and travel. He provided more than adequate financial support for his family and visited periodically, often bringing gifts for the children. But Simone resented such gestures because she was old enough to see them for what they were: a pay-off from a guilty absentee father.

Clearly, there had been a time when her parents were happy and in love. However, their love story held little interest for Simone, who felt it was "too long a story" to share. What impressed her most was not their romance, but rather the social conscience her mother exhibited when they lived in Germany during the occupation of the Rhineland after World War I. Georgette spoke of the large requisitioned houses and plentiful stock of food made available to officers in the French occupation army. The German family that owned the Kaminkers' requisitioned house was forced to live in the attic. Georgette felt sorry for their children and made sure they had an adequate supply of milk. But this was not a common practice. Simone would never forget her mother's dark stories about the evils of occupation. Yet, her youngest brother, Jean-Pierre, had an entirely different recollection: "At every age, I heard my mother speak with unrestrained emotion about the years of Wiesbaden as the too short years of happiness."

٭ᴗ

André Kaminker was thirty-three years old in 1920, when he re-enlisted for another tour of duty in the French army after serving three years of mandatory service before Word War I and then four years during the war. As an officer of the French forces occupying the Rhineland, he was assigned to the restitution service in Wiesbaden, responsible for the recovery of works of art and other valuables confiscated by the Germans during the war. Georgette Signoret, who was twenty-four years old at the time had moved to Wiesbaden with her second cousin Rosa, a young war widow, because the Occupation provided many opportunities for national service as France attempted to recover. Georgette signed an ad hoc agreement to serve as secretary to the occupation army and was given the rank of sergeant.[12]

After work, Georgette and Rosa often stopped at a local brasserie popular with Belgian and French officers. One day, a Belgian officer, Georges, noticed the two women sitting at a table across the room. "Well, this Belgian officer had a friend from the university named André Kaminker who had studied law in Brussels," Jean-Pierre explained. "So Georges introduced André to the two cousins . . . the scene of this introduction in the brasserie is part of our family lore, for the story is linked to my father's premature baldness, and to his intellectual prowess."[13] Georges mustered the courage to approach the women's table, introduced himself and then pointed in André's direction. André's bald head shone from across the room. "You see there the head of the most intelligent man I know." The women laughed, giving André his cue to join them at the table. Georges courted Rosa, and they eventually married. André and

Georgette married a few months after meeting, returning to Paris for their civil wedding on April 17, 1920.

Their families were not in favor of the marriage for a variety of reasons, the least of which was the couple's nine-year age difference. André was Jewish, and his mother was bitterly disappointed that her eldest son was not marrying a Jewish woman. Georgette's parents, both Catholics, were not pleased that their only child was marrying a Jew. However, since Georgette and André were not bound by any affiliation with religion, they were unfazed. She had distanced herself from Catholicism, and André simply did not consider himself a Jew. In his view, he was a fully assimilated Frenchman, and the fact that he was the son of Jewish immigrants was of little consequence.

André's father, Henry Kaminker, who was born in Poland in 1855, made his fortune in the diamond industry, where he was well known for his "ability to see the potential in raw stones and give direction to cutters for the best size and parity of the diamonds." André's mother, Ernestine Hirschler, was born in Austria in 1866. She and Henry met in Vienna and were married there before moving to Saint-Gratien in France, where André was born on July 20, 1887. His only sibling, Georges, was born three years later in 1890.[14]

Henry's reputation and success as a diamond cutter earned him a considerable income that provided a life of luxury, private schools, and university educations for his sons. André was a brilliant student with a prodigious memory and an interest in languages, which he learned easily. He took full advantage of the educational opportunities afforded him, and by the time he studied law in Brussels he had completely rejected his parent's Jewish religion and traditions. However, his financial security ended abruptly when his father's attempt to start his own business ended in bankruptcy. André was penniless when he joined the army in 1910 to fulfill mandatory service. After serving three years, he was forced to re-enlist when World War I was declared in 1914. His father died that year at the age of fifty-five.

Georgette Signoret was an only child, born into a family of modest means in Paris on January 14, 1896. Her father was Louis Eugène Charles Signoret, though he preferred to use Charles Signoret when he signed his paintings.[15] Charles was born on July 19, 1867 in Marseille, France, where his father was choirmaster of the Marseille Opera House, and his two brothers were both successful professionals: one a teacher, the other an engineer. Georgette's mother, Henriette Poncelet-Dubois, had such a sketchy family history that very little is known about her, other than that she was born in Valenciennes, France, and that she was the daughter of a butcher she claimed was a militant in the French Revolution and was executed by guillotine. Henriette had a cousin who moved to America, and she visited once, returning with stories that grew more extravagant each time she told them—particularly later on when she shared them with her grandchildren, who realized quickly enough that she had a penchant for the dramatic. Simone remembered her as a colorful figure, a tiny woman who was apt to sit down at the piano and burst into song with little ditties she had learned.

After their marriage, Henriette and Charles settled in Paris, where the couple maintained a unique love-hate relationship. Charles missed Marseille, a yearning he expressed by painting sunsets on the Mediterranean. Though a talented painter, he did not experiment with style enough to compete with the more popular Pablo Picasso. Charles's paintings occasionally sold to Greek shipping tycoons, and long after his death they were sold at Christie's. But during his lifetime, Charles, a man with dreams, yearning, and potential, never enjoyed success as an artist, and his family lived in a tiny apartment without benefit of electricity.[16]

At home, Henriette fiercely defended her husband against the more popular Picasso, whom she referred to as "the charlatan." In public, however, she tended to distance herself from her husband. When she visited the park, where she enjoyed chatting with strangers, she always introduced herself as the wife of the French stage actor Gabriel Signoret, though they were in no way related. She apparently subsidized her husband's income by working as a milliner, which accounts for her daughter's considerable skill with the needle and sewing machine.

The Signorets spent summers visiting Charles's family in Provence, where Georgette became an exceptional cook, favoring the cuisine of that region.[17] Growing up, she had been exposed to the arts and music, played piano skillfully, and was an avid reader. Though little is known about her formal education, Georgette was a cultured woman who enjoyed intellectual stimulation and conversation. She remained in Paris during the First World War, and it was most likely during that time that she gained experience as a typist, which qualified her for the job opportunity in Wiesbaden after the war.

André and Georgette were both penniless when they met and married. But they were nonetheless living in grand style in their requisitioned home, with secure jobs and the freedom to share their cultural interests during evenings spent at the theater, the opera, or art exhibitions, events hosted by the occupation army. Eleven months after their marriage, their first child, Simone Henriette Charlotte Kaminker, was born on March 25, 1921. Georgette left her secretarial post to care for her child, and apparently it was during this period that she began to view the French occupation of the Rhineland in a new light. The oppression she witnessed awakened her social conscience, a quality Simone was convinced she inherited.

Georgette could not ignore the suffering imposed on German families during the Occupation. The country's economy had plunged into recession after the war because the German mark no longer had purchasing power on the international market. As a result, the government was unable to pay reparations to the Allies, leading to severe reprisals for its citizens. German families were evicted from their homes and forced to wait in endless queues for a limited supply of food. Inflation was so high that some reported seeing mothers pushing baby carriages full of worthless money in order to pay for the most basic necessities. Children, many of them homeless, wandered the streets begging. The suffering weighed heavily on Georgette's mind even as she lived in comfort.

When André completed his tour of duty in 1923, he set his sights on the Paris suburb of Neuilly-sur-Seine, considered the bastion of the upper-middle class at that time. The couple settled into a tiny one-bedroom apartment on Rue de Sablonville, and André secured a job as a journalist for *Maison Damour*, an advertising agency that published *Vendre* (Sales), a trade journal. Advertising was a relatively new field at the time, and Andre's employer, Étienne Damour, was not only on the cutting edge, but had also assembled a creative team that was unrivaled in the business. Among others, he employed two men who became important figures in Simone's adult life: Marcel Carné and Jacques Prévert. Carné would become a renowned film director, and Prévert a celebrated poet, scriptwriter, and songwriter. Prévert and Simone would become close friends, and she would consider him a mentor. However, in 1923, when Prévert and Carné met Simone Kaminker for the first time, they knew her only as Kiki, a nickname Georgette had given her only child.

CHAPTER 2

"I Was an Only Child"

SIMONE LIKED TO BORROW HER MOTHER'S GOLD OR SILVER LAMÉ evening dress slippers, which Georgette had purchased on a whim at the outdoor marketplace on Avenue du Neuilly. Georgette had no intention of wearing them, because she never went out. But they were perfect for her daughter's dress up play, and she would stuff the toes with newspaper and produce an old drape to use as a cape when Simone played a great lady in her bedroom. This was one of Simone's only memories from early childhood; she had no recollection of life in Germany or their first home on Rue de Sablonville. The "vivid images" and fleeting impressions of early life began in their one-bedroom apartment with kitchen, dining room, and a living room that doubled as her parents' bedroom on the fourth floor of 7 Rue Jacques Dulard, where she played dress up and scared herself with illustrations from a Hans Christian Anderson fairy tale book.[1]

The early memories she shared did not include other children. "I was an only child," she explained, using the phrase five times in succession when she briefly describes her early years in her autobiography. "The Neuilly market looms large in my memories of an only child . . . . I was an only child and overprotected . . . . I was an only child, and only children especially, are included in the conversation."

Georgette was her constant companion, a diligent mother who cooked, cleaned, and sewed all of her child's clothing. Her marriage had not yet reached the point of irreconcilable differences, but André's charm had begun to wear off, and she no longer found his repetitive stories interesting or his jokes entertaining. She was also disillusioned with her husband's quest for material wealth, and she hated Neuilly-sur-Seine, where she felt out of place among the bourgeoisie. Yet she rarely left the confines of the suburb, because she rarely traveled much farther than she could walk. While her husband's tastes went to one extreme, Georgette was firmly entrenched in the opposite extreme. Taxis were excessive, she thought, and it wasn't necessary to spend money on a bus if one could walk. And, she walked a great deal, often with Simone in tow. She left Neuilly only to visit relatives and for a summer vacation on the Atlantic coast. They walked to visit Georgette's parents and took a third-class train for their vacation at the shore. She rarely visited the center of Paris other than for occasional lectures she thought worthwhile—and anything related to the author Marcel Proust was worthwhile in her opinion. While she despised the material elitism of the bourgeoisie, Georgette was a woman of many contradictions. She prided herself on her intellectual and cultural prowess, strong social conscience, and meticulous attention to hygiene, which clearly set her apart from the shallow members of the bourgeoisie who, while they dared talk about a book, probably had never read it.

Simone recalled accompanying her mother to a Proust lecture. While too young to remember the lecture itself or the bouts of fidgeting she must have endured, Simone apparently behaved well enough to be treated to a ride on the merry-go-round in the round-point of the Champs Élysées before she and her mother took a bus home. On the carousel, Simone tried frantically to catch the gold rings with her stick, something other children seemed to do with ease. When she missed, she looked for her mother's reaction, worried that Georgette would be disappointed in her daughter. However, Georgette's mind was clearly elsewhere, Simone recalled, though she smiled reassuringly at her daughter.

Georgette and André talked about Marcel Proust a great deal at home, and, as Simone was always included in their conversations, their words—which, like their subject matter, were often unintelligible to the young girl—set her imagination to work. She could not understand why her parents did not share her concern about Madame Albertine, who came to clean each week but who had apparently disappeared. Simone liked the woman and was worried about her. Later, she learned that Madame Albertine, who eventually returned to work unharmed, shared a name with a character in a Proust novel entitled *Albertine disparu*, the sixth in Proust's seven-volume novel, *Remembrance of Things Past*. Recently published, the book was a hot topic of conversation at the dinner table in 1926.

Her parents also talked about politics, art, and music. André told Simone the stories of Wagner operas and Greek myths, and she knew that the unintelligible word "SaccoVanzetti" signified an important event in America, though she didn't understand it. Georgette shared the growing worldwide concern that the pending executions of Sacco and Vanzetti in America were the result of intolerance towards immigrants and political dissidents. André's views were less clear, but Simone understood that he tended to favor the opinions of the right-wing conservative newspapers he read.

Simone's introduction to bourgeois society began when she entered school at the age of five in September 1926. The Cours Lafayette offered an exclusive two-year program, priding itself on employing the most modern techniques in early childhood education.[2] Ambassadors, members of parliament, and business leaders sent their children to the chic school. Some children arrived by limousine. Simone's vague memories of the place revolved around an aggravating little red-haired boy who sat next to her in class and liked to stick his hand up her dress, threatening that if she told, she'd be arrested because his father was a member of parliament.

Simone's own father lost his job in 1926. André's employer, Étienne Damour, suffered a massive heart attack and died; the advertising agency and the creative team he had built at Maison Damour did not survive without him. Damour had been a mentor to André, who at thirty-nine felt he was finally building the life he desired. He had been content with his job, and as advertising was a new field, there were many opportunities for growth. He was usually happy when he returned home at night and climbed the stairs to their apartment with a quick step, whistling Siegfried's motif from the Wagner opera *The Valkyrie*. However, the day Damour died, André returned home early, soundlessly climbing the stairs and then finally collapsing in tears on the landing outside the door to the apartment, shattered and inconsolable. Fortunately, he was not out of work long before he was offered a job as a journalist for the *Petit Parisian*, a daily national newspaper where he worked for several years before a new career emerged.

André was a dominant figure in Simone's life only on Sunday, a day when tensions at home tended to be more noticeable. Although he was not a walker like his wife, when the weather was pleasant enough, André liked to take Simone out on Sunday morning strolls, enjoying any opportunity to show off his beautiful daughter. Simone favored his Polish-Austrian good looks—particularly the startling blue-green eyes that would never be described the same way twice. To some they were the color of Wedgwood or sea mist; to others they were green or sky blue.

Later in Simone's life, a close friend, Betty Marvin, first wife the actor Lee Marvin, once described them as "the most beautiful blue eyes I have ever seen."[3] Simone had dark brown hair, which Georgette kept in a longish Joan of Arc style.

Simone would come to think of these father-daughter walks through the most elegant sections of Neuilly as "snobbish promenades," and a chance for her father to share his dreams unfettered by a disapproving wife. Father and daughter would walk down the posh Allée des Acacias and Avenue du Bois, and when they passed the pink marble palace, the *Palais Rose*, former home of Le Conte Boni de Castellane, André always tipped his hat as a sign of respect and shared the man's story. Simone thought the whole experience boring—certainly not as interesting or passionate as her mother's stories about Sacco and Vanzetti, who were executed on August 23, 1927, causing riots and demonstrations in Paris and throughout the world.

Nonetheless, the reason for her father's admiration of Boni was not completely lost on Simone, even at a tender age. Paul Ernest Boniface de Castellane, one of the last of the French aristocracy, was a man known for his style, intelligence, good looks, and sense of humor. He became a millionaire in 1856 when he married the American heiress Anna Gould, daughter of the infamous stockbroker Jay Gould, a man who had a reputation as a "robber." Boni took full advantage of his wife's fortune, spending millions on the purchase of castles, yachts, fine art, and lavish parties at the pink marble palace. But his luck changed in 1906, when Anna divorced him for infidelity and for "presenting her with kings and emperors one day, slaps the next."[4] Though she left him penniless, Boni was an optimist and resourceful. He had never worked a day in his life, but he found work as a journalist. Then, as an antiques dealer, he successfully brokered international deals. He wrote two popular books, *How I Discovered America* and *The Art of Being Poor*. While Boni never regained his fortune, he lived comfortably in Paris, and his reputation as an elegant member of high society remained intact. André admired the man's tenacity and style; Boni was indeed a man after his own heart.

Sometimes on Sunday afternoons, after their walk, André's mother, Ernestine Kaminker, came to visit, occasionally taking Simone out for a few hours. While the words "Catholic" and "Jew" had no significance to Simone, she was aware they were a source of friction between her mother and grandmother. Children often take their mother's side, and Simone decided she could not possibly like her grandmother, though Ernestine was always kind to her. Ernestine stressed Simone's need for fresh air (no doubt a jab at Georgette's somewhat reclusive child-rearing practices) and took her granddaughter out to the zoo or to the cinema. These were mostly unmemorable experiences in Simone's opinion, though she never forgot seeing *The Jazz Singer* in 1927. The first feature length "talkie" did not impress her at all. However, the story seemed to resonate with her grandmother. When the hero's non-Jewish wife grieved the death of his mother, Ernestine made a point of talking about how wonderful it was that a daughter-in-law and mother-in-law could love each other so much. Simone understood the nuances of her grandmother's observation.

Sundays usually ended with a visit to André's relatives. Around five o'clock in the afternoon, with his wife and child in tow, he paid a visit to his Uncle Marcel and Aunt Irène, wealthy relatives on his paternal side who lived in an opulent home on the Square Lamartine in Paris. Before they left for this ritual visit, Georgette and André always argued over his choice of transportation: He wanted to arrive in style, by taxi, which Georgette thought was excessive when they could just as easily ride the bus. They always arrived at 7 bis Square Lamartine by taxi.

Uncle Marcel and Aunt Irène were Catholic converts who liked to entertain the local bishop and other notable guests during teatime. André was in his element among the guests, the art, the antique furniture, the silver teapots, the tapestries, and the Persian carpets. He liked to be the center of attention there, becoming charming and animated when he told entertaining stories—which bored Simone and no doubt Uncle Marcel, who bounced her on his knees, quietly singing little ditties.

Simone paid careful attention to her mother through it all. Clearly her mind was elsewhere, as she tried to imagine what Georgette was thinking about, a habit she maintained in adulthood. Perhaps she was thinking about dinner, or Proust, or her parents who lived without utilities—the possibilities were endless. It's unclear if they were ever invited to stay for dinner, because the moment Georgette heard the clink of glasses and silverware as servants set the dining room table, she sprang to life with apologies about the late hour.

≈

Simone's first experiences with elementary school were a rude awakening for a child who had been so protected. The little red-haired boy at Cours Lafayette was mild in comparison to the boys at the Lycée Pasteur, where girls were in the minority in her class of more than twenty students. "I was not at all like the others. I was incorrigibly nice,"[5] she remembered. Simone was shy and timid, a perfect candidate for teasing. The boys stole her pencils, and worse still, as part of a game, rolled her in the gravel of the courtyard. Girls had to play spies when the boys played war games at recess. Once caught, the spies were rolled in gravel as punishment. Simone was particularly frustrated by one boy she called Malissard, whose sole mission in life, it seemed, was to plague her. He liked to play keep-away with her little hat, finally dipping it in a mud puddle before giving it back. Georgette caught him in the act and threatened him, which only fortified his resolve.

At home, Simone was very well protected. She was not allowed to have a cat, as it might scratch out her eyes. Roller skates were out of the question; she might fall and fracture her skull. She was not allowed to swim in a public pool, as it might cause sinusitis. Indeed, it seemed that Georgette always knew someone who suffered these tragedies. In the outside world, when they walked by Luna Park on their way to visit Georgette's parents, Simone understood that the amusement park was not suitable for children, though the sounds of laughter and the screams of joy she heard made it seem appealing. Crimes and gossip were not discussed in front of her. She was allowed to have canaries and goldfish. However, as death was not an acceptable subject, her pets lived forever—they simply changed color or size.

Until she entered school, it was never obvious to her that Georgette was not like other mothers. But once she became conscious of her mother's oddities, Simone was often embarrassed by Georgette—and then consumed with guilt because of it. The other mothers who picked their children up from school were always well dressed because they had servants to handle the shopping and cleaning at home. The Kaminker family no longer had a housekeeper. "Well my mother would come and fetch me carrying a heavy bag because she was coming back from the market and I would wish she would come properly dressed, but she wouldn't. That's very troubling for a child."[6] She never described her mother's clothing, but later in life Simone explained that on rare occasions when she picked her own daughter up from school, she liked to dress up a bit, "not overdone, just nice."

Religion had no significance in the family. At the age of seven, when most of her classmates began their formal religious education classes after school (particularly the Catholics), Simone was not part of it. She recalled feeling a little envious of the gifts her friends received after their first communions. Otherwise, she did not feel deprived of religious education. Her teacher and some of the parents were apparently concerned that Simone was being raised as an agnostic. While Simone was staying overnight at a friend's country home, the girl's mother tried to enlighten her on the importance of prayer, encouraging her to try it. She did, but felt nothing came of it.

Simone was quite certain that her teacher, Madame Hendrix, who also taught catechism classes after school, disliked her because she didn't attend. Madame Hendrix had ways of punishing Georgette through Simone, she thought, because her mother had a tendency to take over her geography homework. Georgette had a flair for art and drew exquisite maps of France, which she carefully shaded for accuracy. Madame Hendrix couldn't help but admire them and made a great ceremony of giving Simone two gold stars for the artwork. But then, as she walked by, the teacher stopped, reconsidered, and returned to Simone's desk to remove one of the gold stars.

Simone took piano lessons after school at the Cours Martenot, run by two sisters, Madeleine and Ginette Martenot, who shared an outstanding reputation in the music world. During her lessons, their brother Maurice, a cellist, was always at work on an invention, emitting strange sounds from the shed in the back of the house. Later, Simone learned what her brother was up to: He had invented the Martenot Waves, an early electronic musical instrument.

Life became far more interesting in 1930, when Simone was nine years old. Her parents had promised a sibling as a Christmas present, and that prospect was all she could think about. While most children hoped for toys, she wanted a brother or sister. Since she was not allowed to have skates or a bicycle, she planned to hold her parents to their promise that they would deliver the one thing that would ease the loneliness of an only child. Alain arrived a few days late, on December 28, 1930. During Georgette's maternity stay in the hospital, Simone stayed with her mother's second cousin, Rosa, who was now married to Georges. When Simone finally returned home and set eyes on Alain, she fell in love. Alain's birth was "the first really great event in my life." She would come to think it quite clever that her parents had used his birth as a Christmas gift to dispel any concern she might have about being displaced in the family. Nearly two years later, she was thrilled again when her youngest brother, Jean-Pierre, was born. However, his birth marked a turning point in her life.

❧

"When I was a girl I was given full responsibility for the whole family. It started when I was eleven." August 14, 1932, Georgette was eight and a half months pregnant with Jean-Pierre. André was away, and under the circumstances, she and Simone had decided to remain in Paris for the summer, rather than take their usual vacation at the shore. But, by the fourteenth of August, the eve of the Catholic Feast of the Assumption, a major holiday in France, Georgette had decided the city was too hot and uncomfortable. So, on the spur of the moment, she packed for a trip. Georgette always made an extensive inventory when they traveled, laying everything out and checking her list numerous times before she was satisfied that they had packed everything they might need—including winter clothing in case the weather changed. The next morning they planned to take a train to La Baule, a resort in the province of Brittany on France's Atlantic coast.

Georgette and Simone toted Alain, a large trunk, hand luggage for the family, and food for the trip. Georgette had strong opinions about train travel. Trains and dining cars were unsanitary. So, when traveling they had to wear old clothing so as not to ruin nice outfits, and they had to bring their own food. This perspective was confusing to Simone, who was old enough to notice the fashionably dressed women waiting on the platform. Though the Kaminkers could afford a porter and a comfortable first class carriage, after registering their trunk, they carried Alain, their luggage, assorted bags, and food onto a third class car. The trip was uneventful until they arrived in La Baule, where they faced a problem: "She hadn't booked a hotel or anything, and on the fifteenth of August in France you can't even find a closet, so when we got there she said, 'What are we going to do?' We found a room, I don't know how, in the kind of cheap little hotel where they put mimosa in a small vase on the table and you always have the same menu. Then my mother found a doctor and a clinic."

On the evening of September 6, 1932, Georgette woke Simone, declaring, "I think I'm going to have a baby." Simone got up, called a taxi, and, leaving Alain in the care of the concierge, she accompanied her mother to the clinic. Jean-Pierre Kaminker was born the next day, on September 7, 1932. The following week, on September 15, during Georgette's ten-day maternity stay, her father, Charles Signoret, passed away in Paris. She would not have the opportunity to deal with this loss until she returned home.

In the meantime, Simone had sole responsibility for her brother Alain. She ordered food from the menu, and fed, bathed, and played with her brother. They took a taxi to visit Georgette at the clinic, "and all that seemed perfectly natural to me." The eleven-year-old was on duty twenty-four hours a day, without adult supervision or time to play with other children, for ten days. She noticed the attention she and her brother received from others at the hotel. But she thought these strangers stared because they shared her admiration for her adorable little brother. "It never occurred to me this was madness."

CHAPTER 3

"The Peace Has Been Saved, Papa"

THE BIRTHS OF TWO SONS DID NOTHING TO REPAIR THE BREECH IN THE Kaminker marriage. In fact, she would always wonder why her parents, who had waited nine years to have their second child, had another two years later. If Jean-Pierre's birth represented an attempt to reconcile, it didn't work. André seemed more determined than ever to remain buried in his work, away from home. As a journalist, he had numerous opportunities to travel and had covered Hitler from the time he became chancellor of Germany on January 30, 1933. André's assignments put him in close contact with the diplomatic corps and inspired a new career as a conference interpreter. Though little training was available, his oratorical skills and fluency in German, English, and Spanish made him a natural. His total recall earned him a reputation as "the phenomenal André Kaminker."[1]

At the time, translation was consecutive; interpreters took notes while listening to a speech, and then took the podium to re-deliver it in their assigned language. This was time-consuming work, and accuracy was always an issue. However, André could listen to a ninety-minute speech without taking a single note and then re-deliver it, word for word, without missing even subtle nuances. His translations were flawless—as was twice verified many years later when he worked for the United Nations. But during the mid-1930s, he frequently worked for the League of Nations and the International Chamber of Commerce, work that also conveniently required extensive travel.

He was not the first to conceive the idea, but André Kaminker was the first to invent and use a system for simultaneous translation. His invention was primitive and cumbersome because the necessary technology had not yet been perfected. Years later, IBM successfully tested new equipment at the Nuremberg Trials, but until then, André had moderate success with his invention. In 1934, he simultaneously translated Hitler's Nuremberg Rally speech for French radio. Simone, thirteen years old at the time, recalled her father returning home that evening, exhausted from his efforts. She was not impressed.

But she could not ignore the significance of Hitler's speech, which marked the beginning of his program to purge Germany of Jews. The purge created an influx of refugees, who crossed the border into France in hope of securing passage to the United States or Palestine. In September 1935, after Hitler stripped Jews of their rights as German citizens, the number of refugees increased, and Georgette opened their home to refugee families. Though her father did not object to the idea that his home had become a sanctuary, he played no role in aiding Jews. But then, this was not really a surprise or cause for concern for Simone. She never thought of her father as Jewish and felt no personal connection to the refugees, other than concern for their plight—about which she heard bits and pieces when the refugees shared their experiences with Georgette, speaking German in hushed tones.

While she was proud of her mother for opening their home to people in need, this feeling was an exception. As a rule, the teenager was beginning to find her mother's social conscience embarrassing. Georgette was a Don Quixote fighting windmills, she thought. She made this comparison often during her lifetime. Later, her opinion was tempered by the realization that her mother was a woman of unshakeable conviction and courage. But the teenager found her mother's quixotic battles a source of endless embarrassment: "I can remember this so clearly—this was after the Axis Treaty between Tokyo, Berlin and Rome, probably in '36 or '37—and my mother bought a toothbrush in a shop and she came home and saw that the toothbrush was made in Japan, and so she put it back in the box and she said, 'Come on, we're going back to the shop.'"

Simone dreaded the trip and resisted as much as she dared, questioning her mother, "But why?" Georgette delivered a long lecture as they walked to the store, repeating it verbatim when the shopkeeper innocently asked, "Well, you're not happy with that toothbrush?" Georgette responded politely, "Well, it's probably a very good toothbrush." Simone felt her cheeks flush because she knew her mother couldn't stop there. "She couldn't just throw the toothbrush back, oh no. She had to explain."

On November 1, 1936, Hitler announced the Rome-Berlin Axis, a treaty of military cooperation with the Italian fascist leader Mussolini. Then on November 25, Hitler signed the Anti-Comintern Pact with Imperial Japan against the Soviet Union and the international communist movement; Italy signed shortly afterward. These Axis powers were all fascists plotting war, Georgette explained, and the money they raised from the sale of products—even something as seemingly insignificant as a toothbrush—would be used to make weapons for war. Georgette would not support those efforts under any circumstances.

"All right, you want another toothbrush," the shopkeeper responded sarcastically. But, this was not the reaction Georgette was seeking. "Yes, but I want you to understand I'm not a chauvinist." By now, Simone's flushed cheeks burned with shame as she watched the shopkeeper lose patience with her mother. Finally, he snapped, "Okay, here's a French toothbrush. Goodbye." Simone tried to ease her mother to the door as quickly as possible. "This for a kid is the most embarrassing thing that can happen. I would hate it. I would just die," she confessed. "But then I grew up and I thought, 'My God, she was right.'"[2]

≈

André Kaminker received several contracts for his new translation system after Hitler's historic Nuremberg speech. He had begun working with his brother Georges, who had joined him as a conference interpreter. The brothers had always maintained a good relationship, which endured throughout their lives. However, their wives and children spent little time together. Georges's wife, Cornelia, strongly disliked André. While André was at times very charming and amusing, with a "stock of fantastic jokes" and a penchant for playing practical jokes, he could also be haughty, sarcastic and "prompt to criticize what he did not like." He developed a similar reputation in his professional life as well. Cornelia could not tolerate his sarcasm and preferred not to be in his presence. For his part, André wasn't particularly fond of her. So, while his brother's family lived nearby, in Paris or the suburbs, the two families had little interaction.[3]

Simone's constants during adolescence were school and friends. She continued her education at the exclusive Lycée Pasteur on Boulevard d'Inkermann. During her high school years, although girls and boys shared many of the same teachers, female students were segregated and attended classes in a building across the street from the main campus. The rules of engagement between the sexes were so stringent that males and females were required to remain on their respective sides of the street when classes were dismissed for lunch and at the end of the day. But Simone and her friends worked around the rules, waiting until they were out of the authorities' sight before crossing over for a lunch rendezvous with their male friends at *Le Sabot Bleu*, a newsstand on the Avenue de Roule.

Flirting took the form of animated conversation and demonstrations of intellectual prowess. Simone contributed little to discussions about the latest films, because she rarely had opportunity to go to cinema and was hardly allowed out after school. During childhood she had to sneak out to see a movie. She managed to see Katharine Hepburn in *Little Women*, and had been horrified at age twelve when she saw Peter Lorre in Fritz Lang's *M*. Exposure to the theater came only through school, where she saw performances of *Hamlet* and of *Julius Caesar*, a production that inspired use of the Roman handshake as a greeting among her friends.

During lunchtime gatherings, the new jazz craze was the hot topic of conversation. Django Reinhardt was performing in Paris, and he was greatly admired for his ability to play the guitar even though he had lost several fingers in a fire. The French singer Charles Trenet was also popular, particularly with the young men, who tried to emulate his style of dress. But the most intriguing subject of discussion was the boys' new history and philosophy teacher, Jean-Paul Sartre. Simone would never have Sartre as a teacher because she did not attend her last year of high school at Lycée Pasteur. However, in the early years of secondary school, she always felt that she had learned from him by osmosis, because her male friends talked incessantly about him.

Sartre was an odd little man with protruding eyes that were slightly off-center. He dressed shabbily compared to other faculty. Sartre wore turtlenecks, instead of a shirt and tie, with a fake fur coat, an ensemble that sparked ridicule among his students. But after a few classes Sartre became a popular teacher, who had, as Simone observed, successfully engaged his students in learning about the world beyond Neuilly-sur-Seine. He introduced them to American authors, most notably Hemingway and Faulkner, whose fiction Simone also devoured. Sartre allowed students to borrow his books, and even met with some of them at a local café after classes, behavior that was simply unheard of at the time. He so inspired his students that they organized their own school magazine, the *Hyphen*, edited by Simone's friends Serge Dumartin and Chris Marker. She wanted to write for them, but Simone was assigned the task of taking proofs to the printer. Serge Dumartin and another friend, Jacques Besse, fought over who would escort Simone.[4] Simone was blossoming into a young woman, and male students no longer teased her. It wasn't just her beauty that made her so appealing, her lifelong friend Chris Marker[5] once noted. She had "a certain presence, a certain passion"[6] that was very appealing and attracted both male and female friends. She was talkative, engaging, and inquisitive, had a great sense of humor and an infectious laugh. Simone herself considered her penchant for energetic talk an aggressive behavior used to hide a deep shyness. Indeed, she believed that she suffered from shyness her entire life. However, she must have hidden it very well, because her youngest brother once remarked, "[I]f Simone was shy she was perhaps the only one who knew it."[7]

The big event in her life in 1935 occurred when her classmate, Rosita Luchaire (Zizi to her friends), announced that she was leaving school before the end of term to become an actress. It was scandalous, outrageous—Simone was stunned. The idea that a fourteen-year-old from a good bourgeois family would quit school to follow a fancy was simply ludicrous, and "like all the other little bourgeoisies, I laughed and shrugged and went back to my Virgil." But she was envious, particularly later on when Zizi, who had adopted the stage name Corinne Luchaire, had several bit parts in films. While no one else was impressed at first, opinions changed when their friend received laudatory reviews for her performance in *Prisons sans Barreaux*. Everyone made an effort to see the film and was impressed. Her classmate's success, however, was not enough of an inspiration for Simone, who felt it best to keep her own ambitions secret.

❧

Simone's first exposure to anti-Semitism occurred after Leon Blum was elected prime minister of France on May 3, 1936. The election of this left-wing Jewish leader from the socialist Popular Front prompted a bitter response from conservatives, who adopted the slogan "Rather Hitler than Blum." Simone was particularly horrified when she witnessed one of her classmates selling the conservative newspaper *Action Française* on the steps of a Christian church, hawking the headline "France under the Heel of the Jew."

Blum settled a national labor strike when he signed the Matignon Agreement a month later, on June 8, 1936. The new law, which went into effect immediately, guaranteed collective bargaining, paid holidays, a forty-hour workweek, and raises for the working class. These reforms did not have any particular impact on Simone. She was only vaguely aware of the handful of working class students from poor neighborhoods who were fortunate enough to attend her school as part-time students. They did not mingle with Simone's circle of friends or doodle on the portraits of famous people in their textbooks, which they had carefully covered for protection. These students could not even afford to purchase snacks or lunch on credit from the concierge. Simone couldn't relate to the working class. She was anxiously awaiting the end of the school, because she would spend three months during the summer and early fall as an exchange student in Sussex, England. She stayed with the family of a gentleman farmer. Their daughter, Audrey, was also sixteen, but Simone did not consider her a contemporary. Audrey was immature and spent much of her time talking to her pony, Pixie. A week after Simone's arrival, another female French student arrived, making it a full house. Simone, who was determined to become fluent in English, became the translator for the other, less than motivated student. After Simone returned home, Audrey came to stay with the Kaminker family but lasted no more than a week—which she spent crying because she missed Pixie, while Simone tried to comfort her in English.

In 1938 and 1939, the Kaminker family spent their summer vacations in Saint-Gildas-de-Rhuys, a resort town on the Atlantic coast of France in the province of Brittany. Her father visited once in a while but never stayed very long. He did not enjoy spending time at the shore and was distracted by his work. She had little appreciation for his work, but in truth, he had little time for relaxation. As a translator he was a member of the delegation from France, Germany, Great Britain, and Italy that crafted the Munich Agreement, a last-ditch effort to appease Hitler in the hopes of halting his progression through Europe. He had already taken Austria and was on the move toward Eastern Europe. Although Czechoslovakia was not invited to participate in the negotiations, the treaty, signed on September 29, 1938, forced that country to cede the Sudetenland—including key Czech military positions—to Germany. The agreement would turn out to be a grave diplomatic error. But at the time it appeared Hitler had been appeased, and this was cause for celebration. André sent a telegram to his family proudly announcing the achievement: "The peace has been saved, Papa." But not everyone was convinced of victory. The postman who delivered the telegram thought the members of the delegation were a bunch of idiots, Simone recalled.

In the end, the Munich Agreement did little more than play into Hitler's plans, opening the door to further demands and more aggression.

A year later, on September 3, 1939, the church bells of Saint Gildas tolled a solemn message: France and Great Britain had declared war on Germany. André convinced his family to remain in Saint-Gildas. "He explained to us that life in the city would be impossible, dangerous, even murderous, and my mother, who remembered the Big Bertha shellings, agreed not to go back."

CHAPTER 4

The Phony War

DURING THE EIGHT MONTHS THAT FOLLOWED THE DECLARATION OF war, there were so few military offenses launched against Hitler that the period of false hope would later be labeled the "phony war" by the British and *drôle de guerre*, the "laughable war," by the French. However, the declaration of war cleared out the vast majority of vacationers in Saint-Gildas. The men left first to report for duty to their respective military units, and their families returned home later.

Georgette took advantage of the off-season rates and rented an ocean-front villa for their unexpected stay in Saint-Gildas. The boys settled into the local elementary school, but the closest high school for girls was over thirty miles away, in Vannes, another resort town in Brittany. Simone spent the last year of high school there, missing her opportunity to have Jean-Paul Sartre as a teacher. Commuting by train, with its chug-along engine—obsolete even by 1939 standards—made daily commuting impossible. It was best that Simone find lodging in town.

In Vannes, Simone met a young man, Alain Resnais,[1] whose father ran a real estate agency from his pharmacy. Simone turned to Monsieur Resnais for help. When she approached him, he was taken aback by her unusually assertive and forthright manner, but he found a room for her in the home of the local surgeon, there during the school week and taking the train back to her family in Saint-Gildas for weekends. As it turned out, her mother's longtime friend, "Aunt Claire," was also staying in Vannes and offered to take Simone in, though she was raising a family of her own in tight living quarters. Simone felt more at home there, enjoying the lively family atmosphere and a newfound sense of independence away from her mother's watchful eye, though she continued her weekend visits home.

Simone never spoke about female friends in her small class of twelve students at the girl's lycée, but Alain Resnais remained a close friend. He had a crush on Simone, who was a year older than he but far more interesting than young women his age. She was never at a loss for conversation and was the first young woman he'd met who liked to talk about books, philosophy, and history. Simone introduced him to authors he'd never read and encouraged his interest in filmmaking. For this twelfth birthday, Alain was given an inexpensive 8mm camera, and by his teens, he was already filming short skits. He knew even then that Simone had camera presence and a talent for acting. But she was so fiercely independent that it wasn't easy to gauge how close one could get to her. And testing her limits was a risky business, because she had no difficulty shutting down unwanted attention. Once, when the two were meeting after school, Alain offered to help Simone with the heavy packages she was carrying. Her response to his offer was so unusual that Alain never forgot it. "The man does not carry the packages of a woman," the eighteen-year-old told him.[2]

Although Simone regretted that she could not have Sartre as her history and philosophy teacher, she admired Madame Lucie Samuel, who had a way of bringing subjects to life. And Madame Samuel was equally impressed with her new student: "Simone was my favorite. She had a very inquiring mind, a passionate girl. She was a student that you noticed right away, because of her distinguished beauty. She looked very Slavic, very Polish."

Much to Simone's dismay, Madame Samuel left unexpectedly in the middle of the school year. The two would meet up again years later, after Simone learned that her former teacher and her husband had changed their name to hide their Jewish roots. More importantly, she discovered, Lucie Aubrac (formerly Samuel) and her husband, Raymond, were prominent members of the French Resistance who began their opposition by writing anti-Nazi graffiti on walls before launching Liberation, an underground press. When the Gestapo arrested Raymond in June 1943, with Jean Moulin, a celebrated leader of the Resistance, Lucie arranged her husband's escape by appealing to Klaus Barbie, who was known as the "Butcher of Lyon." Lucie claimed that she was unmarried and made pregnant by Raymond. As French law allowed "marriage in extremis" for prisoners condemned to death, she convinced Barbie to allow a civil wedding on October 14, 1943. During Raymond's transport with other prisoners, Lucie and a band of resistors armed with machine guns attacked the truck and killed the Nazi guards, freeing the prisoners. Lucie and Raymond then went into hiding and waited for a coded message—"they will leave joyfully"—that would air on the BBC and signal their safe passage to London, where they joined Charles De Gaulle. Simone had no idea about any of these activities at the time.

The French military maintained a presence in Vannes, Simone noted with derision. Beyond the occasional reconnaissance missions, the soldiers spent most of their time on the terraces of cafes and crêperies, oblivious to danger. This causal attitude seemed to represent the general mood of the military as Hitler advanced. But on April 9, 1940, everything changed when Hitler invaded Denmark and Norway. Denmark quickly surrendered, while Norway tried to hold its ground, finally falling to the Nazis. "Then suddenly in May things happened very fast. It was the fall of France,"[3] Simone wrote later.

On May 10, 1940, Hitler attacked Western Europe, pushing into France and surrounding neutral countries. Luxemburg was occupied, the Netherlands surrendered on May 14, and Belgium surrendered on May 28. From the start, a steady stream of refugees packed the trains and roads leading into Saint-Gildas and the shore towns. Simone, trying to follow her mother's example, brought home several refugees, sure that they would be warmly welcomed. And Georgette was a gracious hostess until she discovered that many of her guests were anti-Semitic or fascists. The Kaminkers had not heard from André for several months. His last communication had come from somewhere near Bordeaux in early May, and though they had no proof, Georgette and Simone suspected that he was no longer in France, a fact that would be confirmed by the Nazis later on.

On June 14, 1940, the Nazis marched into Paris. The rumor in Vannes was that the Germans had bombed the city and destroyed the Eiffel Tower. Simone was so distraught when she heard this, Alain Resnais recalled, that she collapsed on the pavement outside the school. Later, when it was discovered the rumor was false, Simone's dramatic but sincere response would be the source of jokes between them.[4] But at the time, everyone was consumed with fear.

The first wave of German troops marched into town on horseback on June 15, the day after Paris fell, and troops began searching for housing. When Simone answered a knock at the door, she was greeted by a Nazi officer and soldier. Simone called to her mother. Georgette took charge, making all feel ill at ease for the few minutes she stood there, taking stock of the situation before asking them to identify themselves. The soldiers were taken off guard, then they regained their composure and explained politely that they were Germans seeking lodging. Though well mannered, their request was not open to discussion, and Georgette reluctantly agreed. Later, four more soldiers arrived. Three of them, according to Simone, were country bumpkins who had never seen the ocean and were terrified by the tides. The other soldier, an officer, was a gentleman farmer by trade, a well-educated man called Schroder, who asked too many questions about André. André had "disappeared," the family claimed, giving no hint of their suspicion that he had left the country.

The first German cavalry left a few weeks later and were replaced by a contingent of motorcyclists from Berlin who were far less polite and more demanding. The Kaminkers were forced to house twelve soldiers, including an officer named Link, who conducted investigations in the village seeking out "separatists" who were anxious to rid Brittany of Jews, Parisians, and British. Catching Simone alone in the kitchen one day, he explained that he knew her father was a Jew, and that he had left France. Simone and Georgette knew they were in a tenuous situation, but they didn't know what to expect next.[5]

They soon learned that their rented oceanfront villa was of utmost importance to the Nazis because it was well located for light sea-to-shore communications. The Kaminker family was given twenty-four hours to find other accommodations.[6] However, contrary to Simone's recollections of this period, which tend to be understandably scattered, they did not return to Paris right away. Her mother found another rental, a smaller house, inland, where they remained until the end of summer 1940. Simone had time to take her philosophy bac exam in Vannes before the move. Since the oral portion of the exam was suspended that year due to the war, students were only required to sit for the three-hour essay portion. Results were posted immediately, and Simone passed. "I had chosen a fine subject for my essay: 'Define the connections between passion and will.' It would not be long before I would find these connections in reality."

CHAPTER 5

"A Big Spot on My Life"

WHEN THE FAMILY RETURNED TO A DESERTED PARIS IN SEPTEMBER 1940, an eerie silence had fallen over the city. Thousands of Parisians had fled the city, leaving homes and shops shuttered against the invasion of Nazi soldiers, who dominated every space. Directional street signs were posted at every intersection for German military personnel—a change that had more of a psychological effect than anything else, because few civilians were able to drive their cars. Oil imports had been suspended, and petrol was rationed, leaving the streets open primarily to military vehicles. In the public gathering places, the *Décret concernant le commerce de vivres et d'objects d'usage dans le territoire occupe* was posted. The decree was meant to reassure Parisians that the Nazis would make food and other necessities available for the citizens of their newly occupied territory, and that life would continue as usual. However, these assurances would soon be revealed to be hollow gestures as food was rationed and suddenly in very short supply. And then, on September 27, 1940, the Nazis ordered the first census of Jews.

In Saint-Gildas, whenever Simone was asked about her father, her "Papa's disappeared" explanation usually had dramatic effect, shutting down the possibility of further questions about André. This tack, she learned, worked just as well in Paris, particularly with parents of friends who were concerned about Simone. But chances were good that they knew André was out of the country and might even have heard him on the BBC. No one knew the rules of the new order, and no one knew if listening to the BBC was permissible or even politically correct under the circumstances. The bourgeois was still enamored with Marshall Henri Philippe Pétain, a well-respected First World War hero and trusted leader who became prime minister of France in June 1940. He replaced Paul Reynaud, who had fled after making an impassioned appeal on the BBC, asking the world to come to the aid of France as the Nazis invaded the country. Simone recalled, "At the time Pétain was still a perfect symbol of reassurance . . . and the good people who had shared my adolescence had none of my reasons for terror and anguish."[1]

Simone would eventually learn the details of her father's disappearance, but even then, she tended to economize her explanations. He had fled the country on June 18, 1940,[2] to join Charles de Gaulle in London, she would explain later. She added that his departure coincided with a historic day marked by De Gaulle's speech from London on the BBC, in which the general encouraged the French people to resist. But as Jean-Pierre explained, their father actually left France much earlier, on or shortly after May 10, 1940, when the French government abandoned Paris, leaving it an "open city" weeks before the fall of France. André traveled to Bordeaux, then to an unknown destination before reaching London in mid-June and resuming work as a journalist and interpreter. He joined the Free French Army on August 1, 1940, and was commissioned as a second lieutenant on August 13. His first assignment brought him to the Gold Coast of Africa, where he was in charge of information services. Later, he was an envoy to Martinique and the French Antilles in charge of radio communications, and was often heard on Radio Brazzaville and the BBC. André returned to London periodically between assignments, but he did not return to France until the end of 1944. During his four-year absence, he left no forwarding address and made no effort to contact his family.

When he left Paris, abandoning their luxury apartment, the rent was unpaid, and he made no financial provisions for his family, perhaps believing Georgette would not return. So when the Kaminkers came home in September 1940, they learned that the rent was several months in arrears. Without a source of income, there was little chance they could catch up, let alone stay current on rent. They would have to make arrangements to pay, and Georgette took the risk of bringing her children with her to meet the landlady, a wealthy woman who lived nearby in Neuilly. But even with a reprieve, they had few options. It occurred to Simone that they had become displaced persons, a realization that increased her sense of isolation and fear.

Some speculated that André Kaminker felt he had to leave suddenly and secretly. Indeed, given his diplomatic work as an interpreter and his status as a Jew and a Gaullist, he wasn't safe in France, and his presence in the country might well have jeopardized the safety of his family. He told no one of his plan to leave—not even his brother Georges, who had fled with his own family to the Unoccupied Zone.[3] It is unclear if their mother, Ernestine Hirschler Kaminker, remained in Paris or left with Georges. However, she survived the Occupation, dying in Paris in 1949 at the age of eighty-three. Her story remains largely unknown, but in all likelihood Simone had no contact with her grandmother.

Even if André wanted to return home, he would have been prevented from entering the country. On July 23, 1940, the government enacted a law that stripped citizenship from anyone who left without a legitimate reason during the period May 10 through June 30, 1940. Fleeing Hitler was not deemed a legitimate reason. There was no evidence that André tried to return home, and laws and other circumstances aside, it appeared that he had taken advantage of an opportunity to make a clean break from his marriage and domestic obligations, believing that his wife's skill as a typist would sustain the family during his absence. If so, he was sadly mistaken. Georgette had not been employed in over twenty years, and while she managed the household, cooked, and budgeted what little money they raised from the sale of an oriental carpet, for reasons that remain unclear, she did not seek employment. The burden of supporting the family fell squarely on Simone's shoulders, and she was terrified by the prospect. But the nineteen-year-old accepted the responsibility without resentment or anger. Since the age of eleven, she felt that Georgette "needed protecting . . . and I gave"[4] willingly. Any resentment she harbored was directed at her father. She would never forgive him for leaving his family under the most terrifying circumstances. Though much later in life her opinion would soften, her relationship with her father would always remain distant.

Years later, it occurred to Simone that she had all the qualifications that forced some women into prostitution: She was young, pretty, and desperate to support a family. However, at the time the thought never crossed her mind. Although burdened by adult responsibilities, she was by her own admission a painfully naïve girl. Only the year before, she was so embarrassed by the sight of prostitutes making their mandatory weekly visits to the clinic next door to her school in Vannes, she crammed her beret down, nearly covering her eyes to avoid the sight of them. Until then she'd never heard off-color jokes and didn't get their significance unless her friends explained, in detail. The prospect of turning to prostitution was not on her horizon.

Instead, she turned to her former Latin and literature teacher at the Lycée Pasteur for help. Monsieur Phillippe Vantieghem had Melvyn Douglas good looks, she thought, and such a mesmerizing voice that he captivated his female students, who listened dreamily while he recited poetry or shared tales of his former wives—who had all apparently committed suicide. His male students thought he was an egotistical cad. In spite of his arrogance, however, Vantieghem provided Simone with a sympathetic ear and was quick to offer help, setting her up as a Latin and English tutor. "These lessons account for my false reputation as a 'language teacher,' a designation that still haunts me."[5] She did not enjoy this job, and she had neither the interest nor even the qualifications to become a teacher. Simone never even attended university. And while this temporary job was a lifesaver, it did not provide adequate support for a family. So she scanned the newspapers, having little luck until she saw a job that brought a glimmer of hope: Studio Harcourt was hiring sales associates with proficiency in German.

The advertisement awakened a long-forgotten fantasy; if she got the job, she might be "discovered." She felt guilty indulging herself this way, still burdened by bourgeois hang-ups. Yet, Harcourt was offering a tangible job, she reasoned, and a sales position was certainly a respectable way to earn a living. No one would argue with that, not even her mother. Getting the job was another story, but her old classmate Rosita "Zizi" Luchaire, now the actress Corinne Luchaire, came to mind. The two had not seen each other since they attended a school dance in 1938, and although Zizi had encouraged Simone to keep in touch, she never did. They were never close friends, but surely Zizi, an actress, would be willing to help an old classmate and had enough clout to influence a hiring decision at Harcourt. However, when Simone finally mustered the courage to call, her hopes were quickly dashed by Zizi's mother, Francoise Luchaire. Her daughter was no longer living in Paris; she had moved to the Unoccupied Zone and was unreachable at the time. Simone would learn that after a brief marriage, Corrine was enjoying an affair with Luftwaffe captain Wolrad Gelrach;[6] their child, Brigitte Luchaire, was born in 1944. Simone was not aware of these details at the time, but later, when she learned of Corinne's associations and of the price she paid as a collaborator, Simone was not sympathetic.

Madame Luchaire was curious about Simone's sudden interest in reconnecting with her daughter and pressed for more information. Simone explained reluctantly, only to have Francoise dismiss the Harcourt job.

An educated woman should have a more suitable position, she coun-seled, suggesting that Simone work for her husband, Jean Luchaire, who was leaving his job as editor-in-chief of *Petit Parisian* and starting his own newspaper. He would have opportunities available. Francoise would set everything up.

The job as a glorified clerk at *Les Nouveaux Temps* was "a big spot on my life," Simone once explained. But when she accepted it, she had no idea that Luchaire was a good friend of Otto Abetz, Hitler's ambassador to Occupied France, or that her employer would become known as the "Fuhrer" of the collaborationist press. He was not only founding director of the newspaper, but also served as director of the press corps for Paris's daily newspapers and for the national press corp. In short, Jean Luchaire controlled all of the press in the Occupied Zone.[7]

Simone was never convinced that her employer was truly a Nazi at heart. He was a weak man, she thought, an opportunist who espoused Nazi values while quietly intervening on behalf of Jews and others. Prior to the Occupation, he had enjoyed a distinguished career, which began when he worked with Aristide Briand, a pacifist who served as French foreign minister during the 1920s. Georgette Kaminker revered Briand so much that she hung his photograph over her bed. During his tenure, Briand forged a fruitful relationship with the German foreign minister Gustav Stresemann, and they created opportunities for collaboration be-tween their two countries. Together they were awarded the Nobel Peace Prize in 1926. Briand financially backed a pacifist newspaper and hired Jean Luchaire as editor, while Stresemann supported the efforts of an art teacher, Otto Abetz, who organized student exchange programs and a Franco-German magazine. Although Luchaire and Abetz quickly became disillusioned with their respective countries' failed attempts at peace-ful co-existence, they forged a close friendship through their work as-sociation, and it quickly became incestuous. Abetz moved to Paris and married Luchaire's first secretary, Suzanne de Bruycker. Before being expelled from France in 1938 for his Nazi associations, he also took Lu-chaire's daughter Zizi as his mistress. When Abetz finally returned to Paris in 1941, he did so as German high commissioner and ambassador to the Vichy government, and was one of the primary backers, on behalf of the Nazi Party, of Jean Luchaire's newspaper.

Jean was still in the process of setting the newspaper up when he met with Simone. Concerned about her welfare, he hired her on the spot and allowed her to start right away as an assistant to his personal secretary, Madame Baudouin, with a salary of 1,400 francs a month, a little less than one hundred dollars. Though the salary wasn't enough to pay rent on a luxury apartment, it seemed a gold mine at the time. Luchaire took Simone under his wing and even tried to console her, promising that she'd see her father again. She wasn't worried about that, but she played along.

The inaugural issue of the newspaper was published in November 1940 after its first issue was seized. Luchaire had chosen *Le Nouveaux Temps* as the first title of his newspaper, a play on words taken from a reputable financial journal, *Le Temps*, which had stopped publishing after the fall of France. The owners of the journal protested Luchaire's choice, and he was forced to change the name. In retrospect, Simone thought, the new title was far more appropriate to the new times they were experiencing, because every issue of *Les Nouveaux Temps* spewed out anti-Semitic and Anglo-phobic rhetoric with disgusting ferocity. Her presence among collaborators and exposure to their rhetoric was in complete contradiction to her upbringing and offensive to her, but Simone felt trapped. It was a job, she reasoned, one that helped put food on the table. The idea that she might make sacrifices by resisting never dawned on her. "I had no conscience then,"[8] she claimed. Survival was her only concern at this point. Luchaire gave her a desk in a corner of his outer office where, under the watchful eye of Madame Baudouin, Simone learned to type, screened messages, and ran errands as needed. She was in the thick of things, observing everything but remaining as unobtrusive as possible, minding her own affairs.

It was always dark, particularly after Hitler changed the time zone to Berlin time, two hours earlier than daylight saving time. Simone waited in the dark each morning for the bus that would take her from Neuilly to the newspaper on Rue du Louvre. And she returned home in darkness, especially when she worked late because Luchaire was hosting fundraising events for the Nazi Party and needed someone to answer phones. Her social life was limited to Sundays, when Simone was not working and could see her old schoolmates from the Lycée Pasteur. But it quickly became obvious to her that she no longer had anything in common with them. While she worked to support a family and worried about their safety, her friends were concerned with their university studies or wedding plans. "At nineteen, I would have wanted to go dancing. I didn't. I couldn't. It was all a matter of constant survival. It was learning day to day to face situations that were frightening."[9] She wouldn't discuss her personal business with anyone, but the situation at home was suffocating and getting worse every day. Their phone had been shut off, so when Simone had to work late she used the workplace pneumatic tube system to communicate with her mother. Her typed messages were sent by tube to the local post office in Neuilly, and then hand delivered by the postman.

In spite of the Nazi decree that promised adequate supplies to citizens and prohibited soldiers from pilfering, the military was provided for first, and after that, they often pilfered remaining stock, leaving little or nothing on store shelves for the queues that formed outside. Food rationing was so stringent the average intake was reduced to 1,300 calories a day for non-Jews and 1,200 calories for Jews. At first, bread, sugar, and noodles were rationed, and then, by October 1940, butter, eggs, and meat were added to the restriction list. Supplies were so scarce that ration tickets guaranteed nothing. Since coffee was non-existent, it had been replaced by *café national*, an appalling brew of acorns and chickpeas that had to be sweetened with saccharine to make it more palatable.

The Kaminker family's Jewish roots were not a cause for concern at that point. On September 25, 1940, the German high command issued an ordinance defining a Jew as an individual with more than two Jewish grandparents or two Jewish grandparents who were religious. The Kaminker children, who had only one surviving grandparent, were considered half-Jews and not required to participate in the census. The laws regarding Jews would change continually throughout the Occupation, as the Nazis and the Vichy government expanded the definition of Jewry, eventually including non-religious Jews and those married to Jews. But in 1940, while their half-Jew status was a touchy situation, the Kaminkers were not yet in danger.

Still, Georgette worried about the conditions, her daughter's job, and her safety, particularly when Simone had to work late. There was a stringent curfew, and according to Dominique Desanti, a French resistant and historian, the curfew changed frequently. "Generally it was from 11pm-5am, but if a Nazi soldier was killed, particularly an officer, we were punished up from 9pm."[10] Stringent curfews were imposed more often than not, as resistance efforts organized in spite of the warning they received through the public address systems each day: "The Nazi High Command will tolerate no act of hostility towards the occupation troops. Every aggression, every sabotage will be punished by death."[11] Desanti explained that many who knew Simone surmised that she must have received special dispensation from Luchaire on the evenings she worked late so that she could travel freely after curfew. Simone never commented on this issue.

✤

As the year 1940 came to a close, the weather became a formidable enemy. An unusually cool fall brought a brutal, bone-chilling, snow-filled winter. Many considered it the worst winter of the Occupation. The Kaminkers' luxury apartment had all the modern conveniences, including a coal-powered central heating furnace just off the kitchen, which delivered heat to radiators in each room. However, coal was so tightly rationed that Georgette was forced to close off radiators except in the kitchen and dining room, which had become a dormitory for the family.

Roles within the family unit became confused. As breadwinner, Simone viewed herself in a paternal role. "I was the father of the family," she often explained, sometimes defiantly, other times incredulously. But it was the only reasonable explanation for the position she found herself in: While she worked, her mother maintained the home and cared for the boys. They all awaited her return home each evening, anxious to share the events of the day, just as they did on those rare occasions earlier in life when André arrived home after work. Georgette cooked a dinner often restricted to the German sausages she could get with ration tickets, and with Simone as her partner and confidant, she discussed their financial woes. Once a month, Simone felt a sense of pride when she brought home her heavy, coin-filled pay envelope. Though she knew it wasn't enough to meet their needs, she also knew her mother was proud of her. In spite of her immense responsibility, Simone still needed her mother's approval.

On Christmas Day 1940, Simone stopped on the way home from work to pick up little gifts for the children, trinkets as cheap as the paper Christmas tree they would put up. The holiday had no religious significance for the family, but the tree and gifts added a bit of cheer. Later in life, Simone abhorred Christmas. "An old hurt?" her daughter Catherine wondered. Simone never explained.

CHAPTER 6

"The Grand Doors to a Splendid Dream"

THE DISCOMFORT OF COLD FEET ALWAYS COMPETED WITH GNAWING
hunger. Newspapers offered advice, encouraging people to maintain
their hygiene despite lack of fuel for hot water, and they encouraged
citizens to conserve their strength by remaining at home on Sunday,
their day off. The author Colette advised readers to make light of Sunday
chores and dinner so that the day could be spent in bed with a hot bottle
to warm the feet. However, staying at home in bed was not an option for
Simone, who on her day off spent hours tutoring students.

She wore her dark brown hair swept up in a chignon. The bun, popular at the time, was more a matter of practicality than a fashion statement. Her wardrobe was limited to the clothing she wore in high school,
because new clothing was unaffordable. And since fabric was rationed
and in short supply, even her mother's skill with the Singer sewing machine could do little to improve Simone's wardrobe. Fabric was so tightly
rationed that the allotment was never sufficient to make dresses proper
lengths, and short skirts became a fashion.

Leather was available only on the black market, and shoes were replaced with "les sabots," wooden clogs that created such a clip-clopping
racket against the cobblestone streets of Paris that they inspired little
songs and ditties, Jean-Pierre explained. "Les galoshes, especially for the
children . . . existed forever in the countryside. It's a variation of the
sabot, a high shoe mounted on wood." During the summer that he and
Alain would spend in the country later on in the Occupation, they had
wood-soled sandals. "My brother and I took them off . . . because the
harness broke the skin at the Achilles tendon."

For those with resources, cork-soled shoes were popular. Simone had her first glimpse of them when she worked late answering the phone during one of Luchaire's many fundraising events for the Nazi Party, held at the newspaper offices. Women arrived resplendent in their skunk-fur coats, elaborate hats, and fashionable cork shoes. Among the well dressed was Simone's old school chum, Luchaire's daughter Corrine, who never missed her father's events or the opportunity to stop at Simone's desk for a hug. Corrine did not gloat, but she no longer complimented her friend's handmade outfits as she once did at a school dance. Simone could only marvel at the girl's style. She always wore designer clothing, and Simone admired one lovely satin dress by Flath.[1]

Though self-conscious about her appearance, Simone, too, was stunning, with her Slavic good looks and curvaceous figure. Male co-workers at *Les Nouveaux Temps* flirted, though cautiously, no doubt warned off by their employer, who seemed to view himself as Simone's protector and father figure. However, when it came to flirting, Simone didn't need protection. She was too fearful that an indiscretion might lead to an unwanted pregnancy. She already had other mouths to feed, and she didn't encourage advances.

By March 1941, Simone faced the prospect of her twentieth birthday without enthusiasm. As far as she was concerned, she was already an adult, "as serious and full of conscience as a man of forty from responsibility,"[2] and there was no end in sight to the severe living conditions and feeling of hopelessness. However, that month, her introduction to the Left Bank and the intellectual life of Paris would mark a turning point in her life. The events were of such magnitude that she considered them far more important than her biological birth. "Actually, I could just as well have begun my story with these words: The person I am today was born one evening in March 1941 on a banquette in the Café Flore, Boulevard Saint Germain, Paris, sixth arrondissement . . . where at last I would find the world to which I belonged." Recognizing that this memory might sound a bit snobbish, she explained that her grand entrance was marred by her knack for clumsiness. As she sat down on the imitation leather seating, she tripped over her own feet, bumped into the table, and knocked the cover off a plate of faux macaroons.[3]

Her introduction to regulars of the Café de Flore began two nights earlier, when she attended the opening night performance of *La Main Passe* at the Théâtre des Mathurins.[4] Luchaire's secretary, Madame Baudouin, had given Simone a complimentary ticket, which Simone accepted though she felt uncomfortable going alone. Awkwardness turned to embarrassment during intermission, when a crush of sociable theatergoers filled the narrow lobby, forcing her into a corner. She buried her head in the playbill, reading it through at least five times by her count, before sensing that someone was watching her. When she looked up, she immediately recognized the actor Roger Blin, but she did not know his two companions, a young man and a woman. They observed her but made no attempt to approach her, and Simone returned to her playbill. Later, during the last act, Simone caught the young man's admiring glance.

After the show, as she squeezed through the crowd out onto the Rue des Mathurins, she saw the same three people standing outside talking in front of the theater. It soon became apparent that the young man was waiting for her. As soon as he spotted Simone, he broke away from his companions and caught up with her. He introduced himself as Claude Jaegar[5] and boldly invited her out for a drink (it would have to be an ersatz coffee or lemonade because Simone did not touch alcohol until she was twenty-three years old). Much to her surprise, she went with him without a moment's hesitation.

Jaegar was an attractive young man with a penetrating stare that unnerved her. But most attractive to Simone was his lack of pretentiousness. In fact, Claude had an open, friendly face and manner that engendered trust. This quality was necessary when Simone planned to share a confidence. She was sometimes more comfortable sharing personal information with a total stranger who had a trustworthy face than with close friends. But in March 1941, she had neither close friends nor a confidante and had kept her troubles bottled up for so long. Once she decided to share, a volcano erupted within. She admitted to being a half-Jew and talked about her father, who was no doubt in London working for Charles De Gaulle. She shared her disappointment in him and the despair she felt supporting a family on meager earnings. Jaegar let her talk uninterrupted, listening intently.

It wasn't until after he had accompanied her to the metro station that Simone realized she had made a grave error. She knew nothing about Claude, and yet she had just given him information that could easily be used against her with the Gestapo. The only glimmer of hope that she might be safe was that before leaving her at the station, Jaegar invited her out on a date. They would meet after work at a café on the Left Bank. Simone had never spent time on the Left Bank and was unfamiliar with the Café de Flore. Two nights later, dread and fear mingled with hopefulness as she walked briskly into the wind whipping off the

Seine, crossed the footbridge to the Left Bank, then walked up the Rue Bonaparte to the Boulevard Saint-Germain, where she found herself in front of the Café de Flore.

"At the time Saint-Germain-des-Prés was still a village and not what it became today, i.e. an excursion place for tourists."[6] Since the cafes had heat, they were popular gathering places for local artists, actors, writers, and intellectuals. Jean-Paul Sartre and his companion, Simone de Beauvoir, had taken up residence in the Café de Flore, where they wrote and then gathered with friends in the evenings. "No Germans came in; no cop came near it, because there were no prostitutes, no black-market alcohol, no music, only coffee with saccharin and talk, talk, talk,"[7] Simone explained.

After her clumsy grand entrance, she settled down, taking in the sights and sounds of the Café de Flore like a child in a toy store, intrigued because the clientele were not the sort one would see in the fashionable cafes of Neuilly. Men had longish hair and wore turtlenecks and corduroy jackets under grubby raincoats that had seen better days. The women wore no make-up, which surprised Simone almost as much as the fact that there were so few of them present. She felt "displaced" at first in the smoky, dimly lit café, with its wood paneling and mirrored walls and red imitation leather banquette seating. Still, she sensed it was a comfortable family environment and felt a desire to learn more and to belong.

As it turned out, her date was studying for the auditor's exam while dabbling with acting. It wasn't until after the war that Simone learned that his interest in accounting was only a cover. In reality, Claude Jaeger was a rising leader in the Francs Tireurs Partisans, the communist-organized branch of the Resistance. Now, he introduced her to his companions at the theater two nights earlier. She knew of Roger Blin, the thirty-four-year-old actor,[8] but as with Jaegar, she would not learn about Blin's resistance activity until after the war. Blin would eventually serve as a liaison between the French army and the Resistance. Their female companion was the twenty-three-year-old Sonia Mossé, a Jewish artist and stage actress associated with the surrealist movement. In 1938, she was the only woman among fifteen artists chosen to participate in Requiem of Mannequins at the International Exhibition of Surrealism in Paris. She was a close friend of Picasso and his lover, the photographer Dora Maar, as well as the American photographer, Man Ray. Her image was immortalized in the Man Ray photo *Nusch and Sonia Mossé*. Simone rarely mentioned a name unless the individual had significance in her life. Though her acquaintance with Sonia was brief, this woman would play an important role because she was one of the first people in Simone's life who became a victim of the Holocaust.

Simone paid tribute to Sonia in her autobiography: "She was terribly nice, and I never saw her without her smile during the months that followed—until the day I no longer saw her at all because the Gestapo came and took her and her sister to Drancy. They never came back." The women were not taken until February 11, 1943, when Sonia and her stepsister, Esther, were denounced as Jews and arrested. The sisters were deported to the Drancy deportation center, then to Beaune la Rolande, then back to Drancy, and finally on March 25, 1943—Simone's birthday—to Sobibor, a Nazis gassing center in eastern Poland.[9] In 1941, the mass deportation of French Jews had not yet begun in earnest.

Simone became so immersed in life at the Café de Flore that she spent one hour every evening there before curfew on workdays, and then every available hour on her day off. Among the new friends she was most impressed with were the actors—men for the most part. "They had no money, no houses, no work, no fame, but they were desperately serious and without complexes about being actors. For the first time, I felt that wanting to be an actress wasn't some frivolous schoolgirl wish," she explained. These aspiring actors had "opened before me all the grand doors of a splendid dream . . . whereas, I sought vainly to earn my bread by tiresome work," work she pursued six days a week at the newspaper, and then on Sundays tutoring students from the Lycée Pasteur. "But all that did not interest me,"[10] she added.

Simone was firmly entrenched in the Café de Flore family. However, in the months ahead, these new friends began to question Simone's continued employment at *Les Nouveaux Temps*. Even the tidbits of useful gossip[11] she brought back to them did not relieve the pressure exerted by people who had no tolerance for any form of collaboration, perceived or otherwise. Recognizing her youth, they challenged her, helping her to understand that she could not continue playing both sides, even though stopping might mean a loss of income and financial strain on her family. But she reasoned that it was sheer insanity to think that she could continue to spend her evenings with people wanted by the police and then return to work delivering messages from Luchaire to Otto Abetz.[12]

While leaving her job had repercussions, the others convinced her that the decision was as simple as choosing between good and evil. "In peace nothing is black and white, but during war, during occupation, things *are* black and white. It is horrible to say it, but then everything becomes so clear. There are good things and bad things, and you have a big line between the good and bad and you can make your choice." Those who were "bad" were easy to spot: "You could tell by the shoes. Somebody who had good shoes was somebody bad. It was as easy as that. Because good shoes, leather shoes, meant that this person was going to the black market; and if he could go to the black market he was making money; and he could not make money without working with the Germans. It was very simple. You could just look around and know who your friends were and who your enemies were because if they had good shoes and lots of cigarettes and ate in black-market restaurants where they had cream and butter and coffee and big steaks, they were your enemies."[13] The education she received observing others was invaluable.

In June 1941, three months after her introduction to the Café de Flore, Simone was ready to commit. She first discussed her decision with her mother, dreading the anticipated fireworks that would no doubt result when she brought up the subject of acting. She felt guilty, too, knowing that she was about to jeopardize her family's financial security. However, Georgette surprised her. She had seen changes in her daughter since she began frequenting the Café de Flore, a place Simone described for her mother's benefit as a gathering place for the working class, where interesting people gathered, people who mirrored her mother's values and social conscience—even though Simone knew her mother would never approve of the café crowd. But Georgette was not upset by Simone's desire to become an actress. She thought it worth a try and expressed heartfelt confidence in her daughter. Simone considered this a type of "rehabilitation" in her mother's eyes; she was no longer a child, and Georgette had confidence that Simone's upbringing would keep her daughter on the straight and narrow. Her mother worried about finances, too, but they would survive, she consoled Simone. And, in fact, the Kaminker family managed to remain in their apartment for nearly a year before their circumstances changed.

The day after her mother gave her blessing, Simone made an appointment with her employer and resigned. Luchaire was taken aback by the unexpected news. Simone was protected under his watchful eye and he thought she understood that. In the first months of her employment, he had learned of her father's whereabouts and called her in to share the news. Simone already knew André was in London but feigned surprise. Luchaire explained that under the circumstances, she was better off under his protective wing. Now, faced with her resignation, Luchaire inquired politely about her future plans. "The movies," she blurted out, surprising herself. Luchaire sensed her insecurity and smiled, knowing that it was a pipe dream, because Nazis censors would never allow a half-Jew into the film industry. But, he said nothing of this, and his smug reaction only served to fortify the resolve of the twenty-year-old, whose response would turn out to be prophetic: "In any case, I've got to leave. You see, monsieur, you're all going to end up in front of a firing squad."[14] Luchaire laughed, kissed Simone on the cheek, and wished her well, reminding her that she could come to him for help if need be.

With a newfound sense of freedom, Simone joined the ranks of the unemployed "artists" at the Café de Flore. During the early weeks of June, her relationship with Claude Jaegar developed into a comfortable friendship. He was four years her senior, and though there were hints of romance at first, Simone wasn't ready for an intimate relationship and was still very fearful of an unwanted pregnancy. Yet they remained close, with the Café de Flore serving as their home base. They ventured out, spending their time café-hopping in Saint-Germaine des-Prés. Simone reveled in new experiences. She and Claude were invited to lunch by Pablo Picasso and Dora Maar. During the meal, Simone thought about her grandmother's vigorous criticism of Picasso. "My God, I'm eating with the charlatan!" she thought, delighted by her circumstances. She ran errands for the painter Chaim Soutine, who asked her to pick up a tube of paint one day and then roared when she returned with the wrong color; getting bawled out by the artist was as much an honor as being asked to run an errand for him. Everyone around her spoke incessantly about the poet and screenwriter Jacques Prévert, though he had not yet returned to Paris. Simone's curiosity was piqued. She knew of Prévert because he had worked with her father. But she knew little about him and had never studied his work. By the time Jacques returned to Paris in 1942, Simone could recite his poetry by heart. When they met, he recalled meeting the young Kiki, who was now a beautiful young woman with potential but very conflicted. She was "a formidable girl," he explained, "who knew she wanted something, but didn't know what she wanted."[15]

Simone was living in a fairy tale world, and her new family was providing an education she couldn't possibly achieve in school. Simone knew instinctively that her experiences were important, not only on a personal level but from a historic perspective: "A memorable moment in your education comes the day you hear the 'charlatan' repeat for you the answer he gave the Germans the day they asked him about *Guernica*: 'Did you do this?' And he replied, 'No, you did!' You howl laughing because he's telling you himself; it's not something you will read years later in a solemn book about the occupation."[16]

However, by June 22, 1941, the inhabitants of this fantastic world were shocked back into reality when Hitler invaded Russia, breaking his peace treaty with the other country. Stalin immediately signed a mutual assistance treaty with Great Britain and launched an Eastern Front offensive. The United States offered aid to shore up Stalin's efforts. It was full-scale war, and the Nazis tightened security in their occupied territories. At the same time, in the Unoccupied Zone, the Vichy government began expanding its definition of Jews to include a broader segment of the population. All non-religious Jews, non-Jewish spouses, and half-Jews without baptismal certificates dated before June 25, 1940, were now classified as Jews. It was only a matter of time before the Nazis changed their laws in turn.

In the fall of 1941, Georgette filed for divorce, and the family began using her maiden name, Signoret. While the "Jewish question" was always a concern, at that particular point Georgette was more concerned that her husband's reputation as a Gaullist might have repercussions for her. Jean-Pierre surmised afterwards that by filing for divorce their mother had the "opportunity of saying, in case of necessity, that her lot was like that of France itself, and that her man had acted as much a failed father as a bad patriot." Georgette certainly had grounds for divorce, and her concern about the safety of the family was justified even though there was no immediate threat. It is unclear if the divorce was finalized, but after the war Georgette considered herself a widow.

Simone began using Signoret immediately, but quickly discovered that without an identify card bearing her new name she could not obtain the coveted professional identity card required for employment in the film industry. She had been baptized as an infant, but her baptismal certificate was lost. She could easily have arranged a baptism with one of the local pastors, who were willing to pre-date records to meet requirements. Simone also could have asked her former employer for help securing the needed identity card. Instead, she admitted later that she "went in for a little hypocrisy." When asked if she was related to the well-respected French stage actor, Gabriel Signoret, Simone followed her grandmother Signoret's example, claiming that the actor was an uncle.[17] She continued to carry her Kaminker identity card without fully appreciating the risks in doing so. If she were caught, she would have been arrested or killed. Her game put her in grave danger. But when she tried to explain her behavior, she was incapable of capturing the essence of her thoughts at the time. On the one hand, it was an act of resistance; on the other hand, her behavior didn't make sense to her.

Simone's dangerous game was put to the test right away in September 1941, when the first "call-sheet" arrived for Simone Signoret. She was offered a role as an extra in the film *Le Prince Charmant*, directed by Jean Boyer, for a salary of 120 francs per day. She was required to report to the Harispuru production office in Saint Maurice, a suburb 4.2 miles from Paris, at 8 a.m., dressed for her role in spring furs, an impossible requirement for a young woman still wearing clothing from high school. Much to the dismay of the production manager, she arrived at the studio on time, but wearing an old suit she'd pulled from her closet. To make matters worse, when asked, Simone claimed to have forgotten her identity card. It was too late to find a replacement for her, so she found herself being shuffled past the make-up room to a table in the back of a bar, where she would not be seen by the camera.

She was disappointed that she wouldn't be made up for role, and her mood darkened when the well-dressed male companion at her table commented on her dress, indicating that she'd never get anywhere in the business if she didn't have proper attire. To make matters worse, she thought it ridiculous that she had spent an entire day sitting around, applauding on cue though she had no clue what was happening. It infuriated her that during breaks extras were excused as though they were children, while the actors filmed scenes. The entire experience was stupid, she thought. She was bitterly disappointed and dreaded the questions her mother would ask about her first day as an actress, fearful that her mood would convey her true feelings: She hated acting and didn't want to do it. Instead, she avoided discussion, telling Georgette that she was tired and was turning in for the night because she had an early call the next day. And she did so knowing that this reaction gave the impression that she had an important enough role to be asked back.

Simone returned to the studio determined to learn. During breaks, she stayed and watched, and her efforts were noticed. The following day the extras were weeded out, and only she and a handful of others were chosen to remain. When filming was complete, the director, Jean Boyer, asked Simone to take an un-credited role as a speaking extra, a "silhouette," in his next film, *Boléro*, starring the French actress Arletty. Simone was scheduled to work two days per week, and Pathé Studio paid five hundred francs per day, an exceptional salary compared with the fourteen hundred francs per month she had earned at the newspaper.

Simone played the role of a milliner's apprentice and had one line in the movie: "Madame, the Countess d'Arménise awaits you in the salon." She delivered her line so quickly that it had comedic effect, and everyone laughed. The director thought she had potential as a comedienne and liked her well enough to recommend her to the Cours Pathé, a drama school designed to create a talent pool for the studio.[18]

CHAPTER 7

"There's No Law Against Dreaming"

THE COURS PATHÉ WAS RUN BY MADAME SOLANGE SICARD, A FORMER stage actress who had never enjoyed success in her trade. Simone nonetheless thought she was a wonderful teacher, one who focused her attention on what students should never to do in acting, like accentuating verbs. Students attended the Cours Pathé twice weekly and worked to perfect one scene that could be used for auditions. Simone focused on a scene from the second act of the play *La Femme en Blanc*, written by the French author Marcel Achard. Madame Sicard also thought Simone had potential as a comic actress, because she had a slight lisp that caused her to hiss on the *ch* and *j* sounds. But Simone took her work seriously, though she didn't yet feel fully engaged in her new career. Acting, at that point, was nothing more than learning lines and reeling them off as the teacher instructed, without emphasizing verbs.

Simone's missing identity card had escaped the attention of producers and the censors until she took on a small role in a film short, *Comment Vaincre sa Timidité*. After two days of filming, she was confronted by Pathé management, who expressed disappointment in her because she hadn't been honest about her situation regarding the identity card. She was fired on the spot. She was also prohibited from continuing at the Cours Pathé, though much to her relief, Madame Solange came to the rescue, offering free private lessons at her home.

Undaunted by her dismissal, the twenty-year-old tried again. In early 1942, Simone secured a screen test for a part in *Le Voyageur de la Toussaint*, directed by Louis Daquin. Six young women auditioned, but Simone was the only one retained, an outcome that gave her the impression this was her big break. "There's no law against dreaming."[1] But again, the identity card was an issue, and Daquin was unable to obtain the necessary authorization to hire her, though he could not openly say so. At that point, no one could come right out and say that they were discriminating against her because she was a half-Jew. But Simone read between the lines when the director, clearly embarrassed, took her aside and explained that she couldn't have the role because her hairdo wasn't right for the part. To compensate, he offered her a role as an extra. Simone accepted, but for the first time felt bitter disappointment. She had come so close to her big break; this would be "the saddest and most depressing failure I had during the period."

*&

In January 1942, the Nazis began to implement "the final solution to the Jewish question," with mass round-ups and killings at Auschwitz and other extermination camps. New laws aimed at Jewish persecution were enacted. On February 7, a new curfew for Jews was imposed, restricting them from being outdoors between 8 p.m. and 6 a.m. Jews were also prohibited from changing residences. The following month, on March 24, one day before Simone's twenty-first birthday, the definition of a Jew was expanded to include non-religious Jews, non-Jewish spouses of Jews, and half-Jews without baptismal certificates dated before June 1940. Then, on March 27, fifty-three Jewish members of the French Resistance were executed, and the Nazis began selective deportations of Jews, efforts that would intensify over the next few months.

At this point Georgette Signoret made arrangements to have her two sons baptized by Pastor Ebersolt, one of many Christian ministers willing to perform baptisms with pre-dated certificates. The certificates were not pre-dated to birth years, but to a time period before June 1940. After brief religious instruction, Alain and Jean-Pierre—now using the surname Signoret—were baptized on April 5, 1942 in the Reformed Church of France in Neuilly-sur-Seine, with their mother as witness.[2]

On May 20, the German high command issued another new law that would become effective on June 7, requiring all Jews to wear the yellow Star of David on their outer clothing. A month later, on July 8, another new law empowered the Gestapo to restrict the movement of Jews in public places. Shops were made available to them for only one hour per day—from 3 p.m. to 4 p.m.—rationing was restricted further, and a posted list of public places off limits to Jews was so extensive that the only places they were allowed were sidewalks and streets.

Simone was never required to wear the yellow star, a fact confirmed by her family. However, she was a half-Jew without the proper identity card, and her future as an actress was even more in doubt than before. Just as she was about to give up on film, a friend from the Café de Flore recommended her to the film director Marcel Carné, who was directing *Les Visiteurs du Soir* (*Night Visitors*). The screenplay was written by the poet and scriptwriter Jacques Prévert. She was of course familiar with Prévert and remembered that both he and Carné had worked with her father in the early years of their career.[3]

In *Les Visiteurs du Soir*, a film set in the fifteenth century, the marriage of young lovers is interrupted by a visit from two of the devil's envoys. Released in December 1942, the film was hailed as a cinematic achievement. The censors had completely missed the significance of the story's internal plot: the arrival of the devil and his failure to break down resilient young lovers. It was a story of resistance. Although Simone was cast as an extra, the film provided her with an unexpected break. The production traveled to the south of France, in the Unoccupied Zone, where the company would spend three months filming during the late spring and early summer of 1942. After every scene, Carné gathered all the extras together and chose those who would remain for the next scene. In the end, Simone was one of three extras retained for the entire production. She was one of the "dames du château," clearly visible at the wedding reception feast, in the dances, and riding horseback during the hunt. They were paid 170 francs a day, but extras could earn a little more—200 per day—if they rode horseback for the hunt. Simone had no such experience, but she embellished her qualifications a bit, telling the production crew that she could ride.

Simone reveled in the communal life of the actors and film crew, a luxury extras were never afforded in the Paris studios. She enjoyed socializing with the stars Arletty and Fernand Ledoux, and with her old classmates Alain Resnais and Jean Charmant, who also were extras. One Sunday afternoon, Simone was invited to take a bus ride to Saint Paul-de-Vence, where for the first time she saw the *Columbe d'Or* hotel. It would one day become a home away from home for Simone, and the location of many significant events in her life. But in 1942, it was far out of reach, and its reputation as a gathering place for artists and writers made it more intimidating. Since they were too intimidated to enter the famous hotel, they ate their lunch at an inexpensive café across the street where they could admire the hotel from a distance.

When filming for *Les Visiteurs du Soir* ended, Simone found work as an extra in *L'Ange de la Nuit*, directed by Andre Berthomieu. This film was not a memorable experience, and the film's release was delayed until December 1944—but it was work and an income.

❧

On July 16 and 17, the French police, in consort with the Nazis, conducted *"La Grande Rafle,"* the Big Sweep. Over thirteen thousand German and Austrian Jews living in Paris were arrested and detained either at the Vélodrome d'Hiver, an indoor bicycle racing track and stadium located on the rue Nélaton near the Eiffel Tower, or at the Drancy deportation center on the outskirts of the city. After five days of internment, without water, food, or bathroom facilities, nearly all the detainees—including eleven thousand children—were sent by railcar to the gas chambers of Auschwitz and other death camps. Deportations continued throughout the summer and became a way of life.

While the Kaminkers did not fear arrest, life soon changed dramatically and decidedly for the family. By late summer 1942, they were served with an order to pay down rent or face eviction. Simone sold off the last three oriental carpets they owned, along with several books they thought rare. Georgette found an attorney known for fencing property, who offered to buy two of her rings with a promise that he would hold on to them until better times—a promise she held him to in 1944.[4] However, their last ditch efforts to raise funds fell short, and by September 1942, the family was served with an eviction order.

Simone would remain in Paris, it was decided, but her mother planned to leave the city with her sons, though their final destination was not confirmed at the time. Eventually, they would travel to the Unoccupied Zone, first to the town of Sens, and then to Valcréas, where Georgette found employment at a Catholic hospital that offered a modest salary with room and board. She would begin employment as a secretary, and then later she was put in charge of linens. However, she and the boys did not arrive in Valcréas until January 1, 1943. Until then, their lives were "chaotic," Jean-Pierre recalled.

Anticipating eviction, they packed lightly, taking only the bare necessities. Georgette had one of her husband's old service revolvers, which she hid when the Nazis ordered citizens to turn in their arms. She sewed the gun into one of her son's old stuffed elephant toys for the journey.

Simone recalled having conflicting feelings during this painful period. On the one hand, she grieved her family's separation. On the other hand, she was relieved that she no longer had to invent stories for her mother's benefit about the importance of her role in films. She made no mention of the guilt and relief she must have felt knowing that the burden of supporting her family was alleviated. The exact date of the eviction is not known, and Simone's recollections of a painful parting were succinct: "We saved a few things that the Brazaines, friends of my parents, had put away for us before our things were seized and sold at auction; and following due legal procedures we were evicted from our apartment by the police commissioner of Neuilly."

Simone rented a room on the rue du Cherche-Midi in the sixth arrondisement of Paris, only a three-minute walk to Saint-Germain-des-Prés and the cafes. "I lived there like so many others, because it was for us the only 'livable' place in Paris," she later wrote. Rented rooms were affordable, and meals at the local cafés were not a strain on ration tickets. "When we were short on tickets, they did not refuse us and we were scrupulous enough to come the following day to repair our negligence." Women wore pants and men's shirts as a matter of necessity rather than fashion, because finances were tight. Simone found this new style both practical and infinitely comfortable, particularly during the winter months. The camaraderie among friends deepened as they helped each other through difficult times. "We did not fear loneliness . . . friendship was our only richness, the only comfort to our perpetual money worries," Simone explained. "We wandered day after day, on the boulevards, admiring without tiring, day after day, the old houses of the rue Saint-Benoit, which was for us the prettiest street in the world." But the historic Place Dauphine held a special attraction for Simone, who imagined living in the neat, well-kept historic square one day.

Her participation in *Les Visiteurs du Soir* led to a role as an extra, one of the women of Thebes in *Dieu est Innocent*, a stage adaptation of *Oedipus* at the Théâtre des Mathurins. The adaptation was poorly written, Simone thought, and though the pay was less than desirable at fifteen francs per day, the opportunity was appealing. However, the production quickly became a comedy of errors, and Simone's experience was short-lived. She was an extra, one of the citizens of the ancient Greek city of Thebes, who had to lament the death of their queen amidst the din of recorded crowd noise played just off stage. The script was so poorly written that the extras, standing on stage with their forearms covering their eyes, could not contain their laughter. On one occasion, a stagehand accidently played the wrong side of the record, and instead of crowd noises, they heard airplane noises, which caused uncontrollable laughter.[5] One evening, Simone was caught laughing and fired on the spot.

But far more memorable was the young actor she met during that period, Daniel Gélin.[6] Though their relationship began tentatively, it quickly evolved into Simone's first romance. He was infatuated. "I never met anyone so alive. Simone Signoret dominated everything with her culture, her intelligence, her brio and her love of laughter (ah! that wonderful clear laughter, so sensual and infectious,) her startling beauty and plain speaking."[7] Every evening after rehearsal, Daniel accompanied Simone on her walk home. Two weeks into rehearsals, he finally got the nerve to go a step further. "One night, very simply, I asked her if she wanted to come to my place. Very simply, she responded, 'yes.' The next day, I very simply asked if she wanted to move in with me. She said, 'yes.'"

However, she had no intention of giving up her rented room and brought only essentials packed in a hatbox for her move to his attic room in a hotel on the rue Monsieur-le-Prince, a cobblestone street that was so narrow, pedestrians had to walk single file on the sidewalk just off the Boulevard Saint-Michel in the Latin Quarter. The other residents of the hotel were local prostitutes. Gélin had befriended them all, and consequently they welcomed Simone and took such an interest in her career that they loaned her their shoes when she auditioned. As she would learn later on, this was a greater favor than she knew: "Shoes for a streetwalker are the most important thing, of course, and they'll invest any amount of money in them."[8]

Life with Daniel was idyllic at first. The two enjoyed many of the same interests—most of all, a comfortable sense of belonging. They passed the time playing Bing Crosby and Daphnis and Chloé records,[9] or took walks around the Boulevard Saint Michel. However, they no longer visited the Café de Flore because Daniel thought it was too far away, though it only a fifteen-minute walk. One night they stayed out too late and were walking home during curfew. If caught, they could be arrested or shot on the spot, so when they heard a patrol approaching, the couple hid in a subway stairwell until it was safe to move on. After that, Gélin didn't want to risk the trip to the café.While their friendship endured throughout their lives, their romance was short-lived. Though the same age, Simone was more mature, she explained. This realization became more obvious to her during Gélin's brief absence owing to a film opportunity. Unfettered, Simone resumed her visits to the Café de Flore, and it was there that she met another man, twenty years her senior, the actor Marcel Duhamel.[10]

This, too, would be a short-lived relationship, but Simone expected from the start that it would be, because Duhamel was married and made no bones about the fact that he still loved his wife, Germaine, who lived in the Unoccupied Zone. When his wife sent postcards, Duhamel unabashedly shared them with Simone—and he apparently also shared news of his extramarital affair with Germaine, who did not object. It was an odd affair, but not an uncommon situation during such transient times, when no one had a clear sense of the future. Simone was not jealous of Duhamel's love for Germaine, and she adored this man, who introduced her to the surrealist movement and to authors she hadn't read—most notably Henry Miller. He played records every morning and shared stories about his affiliation with the October Group; he was a founding member of the theatrical troupe, closely associated with the communist movement during the 1930s. More importantly, Duhamel was tender and loving, instilling such confidence that Simone felt secure in his arms.[11]

CHAPTER 8

"The End Was in the Air"

SIMONE MET YVES ALLÉGRET[1] IN JANUARY 1943, JUST THREE DAYS BE-
fore leaving for Dax in southwestern France for the film *Adieu Léonard*.
He was an older man, sixteen years her senior, but not any more settled
in life than she was at twenty-one years of age. His aspirations of becoming a film director were overshadowed by his older brother's career:
Marc was a well-established director who had received critical acclaim
for *Fanny* in 1932. Though Marc offered his younger brother work as
an assistant director, Yves could not break through on his own. His only
solo film accomplishment was a short, *Price and Profits, or the History of the
Potato*—and that had been destroyed in a fire.

Yet, Yves was highly regarded by the intellectuals of the Café de Flore,
where he and Simone first met. He was a founding member of the October Group and had traveled to Russia with the acting troupe. In the
mid-1930s he had also served as one of Leon Trotsky's secretaries during
the Russian leader's exile in Barbizon, France, and his political views
continued to lean more toward Trotskyism than Communism. Simone
was flattered that a well-respected older man would take an interest in
her, and the fact that he was also married and had a child was of little
consequence. Allégret had been separated from his wife for two years
and planned to divorce, though Simone never insisted he do so. After
they met, she dreaded leaving him behind for the three weeks she would
spend filming. She felt insecure about their relationship, and her concentration was broken by thoughts of him, as she worried he might not be
as interested in her as she was in him, and that their separation would
make a break much easier.

Adieu Léonard was a murder-for-hire comedy of errors written by Jacques Prévert and directed by his brother, Pierre. The cast was an odd conglomeration of established actors, singers, and comedians who were unable to secure work in their respective fields. The popular crooner Charles Trenet had a lead role, but his prominence did not make him happy because he couldn't get work as a singer. It was reported that his moods often contributed to tension on the set. Marcel Mouloudji, another popular but unemployed singer and actor, had a role as a chimney sweep, while Simone played a basket-weaving gypsy. During breaks, the cast would gather around Trenet, who performed some of the songs he had written that day. Mouloudji and other talents joined in. This band of gypsies was an endless source of entertainment. For Simone, this camaraderie was the most memorable experience of the filming.

On the journey back to Paris, Simone had her first frightening brush with the Nazis. She was sharing a compartment with the actor Julian Carette, his wife, and an assistant cameraman, a quiet man known only as Maréchal. Shortly after departure, the train suddenly stopped and Nazi soldiers boarded. They were checking passenger identity cards. Carette and his wife passed inspection without comment. When they checked Maréchal's card they discovered that he was a war hero, and the soldiers clicked their heels as a sign of respect when they returned his card. However, their examination of Simone's identity card caused confusion and took much longer. The soldiers examined the books of names they carried multiple times, searching for Kaminker. As they searched, the Carettes remained silent, staring out the window. But Maréchal made direct eye contact with Simone, who felt that he was offering comfort, in affect holding her hands with his steady gaze. Finally, the soldiers returned Simone's identity card and left. It was a close call.[2]

Allégret was waiting for her when the train pulled into the Gare d'Austerlitz, dispelling any doubts that she had about his feelings toward her. She gave up her rented room and moved into his at the Hotel Saint-Yves near the Boulevard Saint-Germain, and they spent their days haunting the cafes. As his sister and her family lived across the street from the Café de Flore, Yves visited now and again, leaving Simone sitting on the café terrace. His family did not welcome his visits because they were displeased with his lifestyle, political affiliations, and separation from his wife and son. Yves was undaunted by their opinion of him and often pilfered food from their generous stock.

The couple moved several times, finally settling into an apartment at 7 Rue du Dragon. Rent there was incredibly cheap, yet without ever explaining their reasoning, friends tried to dissuade them from taking the place. It was not until after the war, Simone claimed, that they learned the reasons for their friends' concern. The apartment was considered a "letter box" for the Resistance, so the rent was cheap because it was dangerous to live there. While Simone claimed innocence, the couple must have had some suspicions. The Gestapo raided the apartment on a number of occasions, looking for something they never found. One evening, their friend Claude Jaegar insisted that he was too tired to go home, though he lived nearby. He stayed the night and was gone before they awoke. At the time, the couple had no idea that Jaegar was in the Resistance and was unable to sleep in the same place every night.

Contrary to some legends, Simone and Allégret were never directly involved in resistance activity, something she would regret later in life. If she did anything useful for the cause, she claimed, it was done unknowingly. Earlier, in 1941, Aunt Claire, whom she stayed with while at school in Vannes, had asked a favor: Her son had been arrested and she wanted Simone to bring his belongings home. When Simone took the train to Vannes, she assumed the two suitcases she carried contained clothing and books. But when she arrived at Aunt Claire's, the two women discovered that one of the cases contained ammunition, which they quickly wrapped up and then dumped into the ocean. Simone contended that if she had known she was carrying ammunition, she might have been considered a heroine for risking her life. But she didn't know, and her ignorance reduced the significance of her action in her own mind.

According to Simone, the only act of defiance she and Yves knowingly engaged in occurred at a hotel restaurant run by a known collaborator. They ate well and then skipped out on the bill without the slightest guilt. That was it, as far she was concerned. But, there must have been a great deal more to the activity because at one point her former employer, Jean Luchaire, asked to meet. He was concerned about the people she was hanging around with. The Gestapo was watching, he warned, and he had seen a thick file (which has never been discovered) on her. There was also a report that Simone had helped the film archivist Henri Langlois in his efforts to hide forbidden films slated for destruction by the Nazis. Langlois was the founder of the *Cinémathèque Française* and was responsible for saving thousands of films slated for destruction by Hitler. He often recruited young women who transported films in a baby carriage to undisclosed locations. Simone was seen pushing one of those carriages.[3] If this story is true, she never thought it worth mentioning.

However, she had fond recollections of attending Langlois's clandestine film showings at his mother's apartment on Rue Troyan. Langlois would stop by the Café de Flore during the day, moving from table to table, quietly sharing the details of his next show. She saw all the classic films she missed in youth that way. During a film, Madame Langlois always served her son's guests. "It was a real feast, given rationing. We each got a bit of sweet wine and Turkish pastries from the family's monthly rationing. It was so festive."[4] And it was dangerous. Henri worked hard to stay a step ahead of the Nazis and often received tips about raids just in time to reschedule his shows.

Simone found work as an extra, un-credited, in a total of five films during 1943. She had been sending money to her mother whenever possible and visited the family once in Valcréas, staying overnight in the whitewashed room they shared. Allégret was also busy. Working under the name Yves Champlain, he directed *Two Shy Ones* with his brother Marc and Marcel Achard as co-directors. But by 1944, the couple stopped seeking work and tried to maintain a low profile. Like many men his age, Allégret was wanted by the authorities as an "insubordinate" for failing to report for *Service du Travail Obligatoire*, a forced labor and deportation program for men twenty-eight to fifty years of age. The men were shipped to Germany to work in the salt mines. There was such resistance to the program that by 1944, the police began conducting massive round-ups, sometimes cordoning off entire streets or neighborhoods to ferret out insubordinates living under assumed names. Everyone was maintaining a low profile to avoid notice because they were living in an "irregular" situation—including Simone, who was pregnant with her first child.[5] By June 1944, an atmosphere of nervous anticipation hung over Paris. The Nazis were losing the war. Air raids increased as the Allies bombed the outskirts of Paris, sending people indoors to shutter their windows. Determined to hold their ground and complete the Final Solution, the Nazis stepped up their raids and killing. It was so dangerous on the streets that people feared leaving their homes. "The end was in the air, and people suddenly felt panic that they might not live to see the end simply because they had gone out to fetch a loaf of bread," Simone explained.

On June 6, 1944, D-day, the couple decided to leave Paris for the Allégret family's country home in Sapinière Charmes-la-Grande in the Haute-Marne region of northeastern France. If they had been in the Resistance, the move to the country would have been considered "joining the Maquis," the guerilla bands of the French Resistance that operated in rural areas or in the mountains. But contrary to legend, Simone was not a member of a Resistance group. She used the term loosely, explaining that they had created their own Allégret Maquis that included their friends Serge Reggianni[6], an Italian actor who was wanted as a deserter, and his first wife, Janine Darcy. Later, they were joined by Daniel Gélin and the eighteen-year-old-actress Gabrielle Girard, who was living under the assumed name Danièle Delorme,[7] the stage name she had chosen after her parents were arrested and sent to Ravensbruck. Simone would become a mentor and mother figure to the young girl, though there was only a five-year difference in their ages. The young woman would become a well-established actress and film producer in France.

The sounds of gunfire drew closer each day, while the women focused on housework and the men went out into the village to find food. They scoured the garden for whatever overgrown vegetation they could find. Serge Reggianni had given the women short haircuts so that they appeared androgynous in their men's shirts, pants, and boots—though Simone's growing belly dispelled any doubts. Then, on August 25, 1944, after violent battles with the French Resistance, the Nazis surrendered Paris. The Allégret group listened intently to the radio as General De-Gaulle spoke: "We are here in Paris—Paris which stood erect and rose in order to free herself. Paris oppressed, downtrodden and martyred but still Paris—free now, freed by the hands of Frenchmen, the capital of Fighting France, France the great eternal."[8] They were furious that they had missed the action in Paris. They stay glued to the radio and took out an old atlas so they could keep track of countries that the Russians had re-captured from Hitler. But Charmes-la-Grande was still occupied by the Nazis, and while they listened to the bells of Notre Dame on the radio, they could still hear the sounds of gunfire in Chaumont, several miles away.

A few days later, they found American soldiers camping nearby and invited them inside. While the women listened to the soldiers' updates on the war and news about their favorite stars from the United States, the men went out to siphon gasoline from their vehicles. They all had their first taste of K-rations and enjoyed Lucky Strike cigarettes, and when it was time to leave the soldiers gave their hosts two motorcycles they had taken from the Germans and a five-ton Citroën truck, which the Frenchmen hid in the barn. But they would not have an opportunity to use the vehicles for their trip back to Paris. When the mayor of the town saw Allégret, Daniel, and Serge racing the motorcycles, he paid a visit and insisted that they return all the vehicles, including the truck. The group wound up hitchhiking back to Paris, using Simone as a decoy for unsuspecting motorists who stopped to aid a pregnant woman stranded on the roadside.

Shortly after their return to Paris in early September, 1944, Claude Jaegar commissioned Allégret to direct a documentary about the liberation of Le Mans by the FTP (Franc-Tireurs et Partisans), the resistance group controlled by the communists. Simone accompanied him to various campsites, where they interviewed members of the group. However, Allégret contracted diphtheria and was unable to complete the documentary. When they returned to Paris, Simone gave birth to their child, "and lost him due to monstrous negligence in a clinic that cost the earth."[9]

Patrick died nine days after his birth. Simone never shared the details, because in her view grief was a deeply personal matter, not something one shared with the public, and she could not really prove the cause of her baby's death. But with her family, she held the hospital responsible, because the sisters in charge had taken the infant without her permission to the chapel for baptism, something Simone would never have allowed. The infant caught a severe cold and could not recover. It is not known if there was a connection between the baptism and the infant's cold. However, in Simone's mind, the connection was clear and this lapse could not be forgiven. She chose to bury her grief by busying herself with attempts to launch her acting career. But grief could not be ignored forever. "Mama was proud of her Patrick," her second child, Catherine, explained years later.[10]

PART II

YVES MONTAND

CHAPTER 9

"This Was the End for Us"

THE INESCAPABLE FEELING THAT THEY HAD ENDURED SOMETHING FAR more horrifying than could be imagined tainted the joy of liberation for the French. Newsreels revealing the unspeakable horrors of the concentration camps played on even as trains arrived daily with survivors—many, Simone noted, still wearing striped prison uniforms. After watching the newsreel for the first time, the singer Yves Montand, whom Simone had not yet met, had a visceral reaction as he left the theater. "What about God now," he challenged his girlfriend, Edith Piaf, who prayed each night before bed. He could not understand how she could believe in a god that allowed such horrifying crimes against humanity.[1]

Simone rarely spoke of her feelings about this period, and when she did, she was always succinct, avoiding any hint of the internal turmoil felt at the time. "We were part of a different generation. It's impossible to speak of it," she once explained, and then generalized her feelings in her autobiography. "That was end of it for us." But Simone noted that it was only the beginning for the collaborators, victims and survivors. Among those missing from Simone's life was Aunt Claire, who had died at Ravensbruck. Maréchal, the cameraman who had held her with his eyes during her brush with the Nazis on the train back from Dax had been executed by the Nazis while helping a British parachutist. Sonia Mossé was murdered at Sobibor. These were but a few of the friends on an ever-growing list of the dead. Later in life, Simone provided a more personal glimpse into her internal turmoil and impressions during the Liberation through the eyes of Maurice Guttman, a character she created for her novel, *Adieu Volodia*:

Like some, he was astonished that people did so much dancing at
night, having done so much formal mourning of the dead during
the day. The known dead, that is. Everyone still waited to mourn
the others. Waited to know.

They were about to find out. The others began to return. By
groups and in convoys. In real passenger cars, but just as jumbled
together as they had been when they left in a cattle car. If Marcel's
friends were to see this, thought Maurice, he'd say it was still a
mess. To recognize them at the reception center, you had to do
more than simply look for a familiar face in the crowd. You had to
scrutinize all of them one by one; but what you really had to do
was show yourself so you could be recognized by people who had
become unrecognizable.[2]

The grief, celebrations, and joyful reunions were peppered by the
angry outbursts of the mobs that filled the streets, anxious to punish
collaborators in a legal purge directed particularly at women who were
accused of sleeping with the enemy, or "horizontal collaboration." The
accused were dragged into the streets, stripped to the waist, and their
heads shaved as they were forced to sit on public display so the crowds
could spit at them while hurling slurs and insults. Later it was believed
that many of the most vocal in the mob were themselves collaborators
hoping to distract attention from their own misdeeds.

Simone and Allégret settled into an inexpensive furnished apartment
at 54 Rue Vaneau, a quiet street close to the Café de Flore, yet removed
from the main action. And, continuing a theme in Simone's life, they
moved several times in the coming months. But they remained on the
same street, first moving to another furnished apartment at 52, and finally, when they had enough money to buy furniture of their own, to
number 56. When Georgette, Alain, and Jean-Pierre Kaminker returned
from Valcréas toward the end of 1944, Simone found them temporary
housing on the same street. From this point forward, she would do everything possible to keep her family close by and to support them in any
way she could.

Simone and Yves attempted to resume their careers in 1945, and she
played her last small and unmemorable role in Le Couple Idéal. Meanwhile, Allégret was working on a more substantial part for her in a film
he would direct, Les Démons de l'aube (Dawn Devils). It was a minor role,
but she had moved beyond the phase of serving as an extra. But then,

she became pregnant with her second child during filming that summer, and "the curtain went down temporarily on this small success."[3]

Simone's father returned after the liberation of Paris as a lieutenant in the Free French Army, and though Simone had little desire to see him, she made an exception when her former employer, Jean Luchaire, was arrested as a collaborator. The anger that had simmered for four years could not be contained when she saw André, so dignified and handsome in his uniform. When she wrote about the encounter thirty years later, she wrote in the third person, maintaining an emotional distance from the man she would describe as "the youngest old man I know, without a care in the world."[4] Simone was defiant when she caught up with him in the officers' mess. She knew he would not be pleased that the young girl he had abandoned had broken every taboo. She was unmarried, pregnant, and pursuing an acting career. And the defiant young woman had the audacity to demand that he write a letter of support for her former employer. After all, Luchaire had saved her family by providing a job and income.

André Kaminker complied with her demand, providing the only letter of reference. But it did nothing to aid her former employer. Jean Luchaire was found guilty of treason and executed by firing squad on February 22, 1946. His daughter, Corrine, was arrested with her father as they attempted to flee to Sigmaringen, Germany. She was pregnant at the time.[5] On June 17, 1946, *Time* reported on her trial: "Racked by fits of tuberculous coughing, her 25–year old face seared and drawn like a crone's, she heard herself accused of sleeping with a prize package of Axis agents," including Otto Abetz, who had served as German envoy to Paris. "Said the judge: 'While Frenchwomen suffered and fought, you led a gay life . . . ' Quavered Corinne: 'I was young and stupid . . . I did not realize . . . ' Cried her lawyer: 'What can you expect of a girl brought up in the depths of the elite.'" The jury was unmoved. After deliberating for one hour, they sentenced the actress to ten years of *dégradation nationale*, stripping her of all rights as a French citizen. She died on January 22, 1950, from tuberculosis.

Beyond her memories of Corinne as the teenager who had amazed her by quitting school to become an actress—and then succeeding—Simone had no interest in the young woman or sympathy for her fate. When the journalist Jean-François Josselin questioned her about Corinne, believing that Simone might have some residual feelings for an old chum, Simone stopped him, replying with agitation, "I know nothing about her."[6]

During her pregnancy, Simone was frequently reminded of her status as an unwed mother, a stigma in polite society. She had felt this stigma during her first pregnancy and certainly after the baby's birth. But she was not about to tolerate it during this second pregnancy. Simone steeled herself for the reaction she would receive when she arrived at the town hall on Place Saint-Sulpice, where well-dressed ladies from the upper class did their service to the community by distributing ration tickets to the less fortunate. The women demanded a "family card," and when Simone could not produce one, they asked her if she was an unwed mother, using a louder than normal tone of voice. Simone was defiant as she answered in an equally loud voice, "Yes. Unwed." Then, the ladies spoke even louder, so all could hear as they directed Simone to a section reserved for unwed mothers.[7] The women played this game every time Simone stopped to pick up more tickets; they could see her coming because she wore a plaid coat cut from a blanket that her old flame Marcel Duhamel had given her in 1942. The game continued later in the yarn shop, where a clerk tried to give her skeins of beige wool, the standard color for those in a family way. She refused them, explaining that she didn't want to dress her baby like a soldier and preferred other colors.

The stigma of unwed motherhood was passed on to Simone's child, because Allégret had not yet divorced, and French law at the time prevented a married man from giving his name to a child born out of wedlock. Catherine-Enda Kaminker was born of unknown father on April 16, 1946.

Les Démons l'aube was released shortly after Catherine's birth and received positive reviews. In her role as a barmaid in a sailor's haunt, Simone had few lines, but she demonstrated an uncanny ability to capitalize on body language. When her scene required her to kiss a sailor, those who watched were stunned by her performance. One observer noted: "A sensual little animal, a cat down to her claws and purr; she transformed that kiss into one of the most erotic moments of contemporary cinema."[8] This extraordinary talent was all the more startling because off screen, Simone gave the impression that she was a tomboy, not a female fatal. When relaxing off camera, she dressed in slacks and a men's shirt, a style held over from the Occupation years that was not yet fashionable.

After the success of the film, there was no question that Simone was on the move, though she didn't think so at the time. She had put aside career aspirations after Catherine's birth, focusing her attention on playing the role of mother and once again "closing the curtain." But twenty-one days after Catherine's birth, Simone was asked to audition for her first major role in *Macadam*, directed by Marcel Blistène. "It was as though Catherine's arrival had brought about the thing I had hoped for so long," she explained in *Nostalgia*—an instructive comment, because motherhood could not compete with what she truly desired: a role in a film. Motherhood would never be a focus in her life.

Ten women auditioned for the role of *Gisèle*, the sweet, comical yet sexy girlfriend of a gangster, who used her to con older man out of money and expensive jewelry. It was a solid role with adequate screen presence, and Simone was both shocked and exhilarated when she was chosen. However, this opportunity of a lifetime posed a new, unexpected dilemma: She could not be an actress and mother at the same time—at least not in the traditional sense of motherhood. She realized as much during the audition when she missed one of Catherine's feedings. Simone breast-fed and had enough foresight to express milk for two emergency bottles, though she was sure she'd be back in time for the next feeding. Her plans went astray. By the time she arrived home, hours later, the dress she had borrowed was stained with her milk, and she had missed a feeding. From that point forward, the twenty-one-day-old infant was bottle fed, often by caretakers. Catherine's life changed overnight.[9]

Simone found it completely impossible to balance the demands of a career with motherhood. She could do one or the other, but not both. Her choice was clear, but guilt had a way of creeping into her interactions with Catherine on Sundays, her day off when she felt distracted. To assuage the feeling, she convinced herself that all actresses shared her dilemma. It was easier to create emotional distance, speaking in the third person as though she were a casual observer when she wrote about her interactions with her infant in her autobiography. She explained that the actress returns home on Sundays to spend time with her child. She sees the child has grown and developed, but she really isn't paying close attention, as she should, because her mind is on her script. It wasn't fair to the child—she understood that—but she could not reconcile the conflicting demands she was juggling. Years later, during a 1960 interview with John Freeman for BBC, Simone became visibly nervous when asked about her daughter. She rubbed her nose and fidgeted in her chair as she explained, "I try to be a mother. I don't think I'm exactly what you may call a mother because if I was a real mother I wouldn't be an actress." Surprised, Freeman pressed: "Is there a conflict between the two ways of life?" Simone responded, "Yes, because a mother is a woman who is always there when the child goes to bed, when the child gets up in the

morning to go to school, and I certainly am not a mother in this sense
. . . . I'm trying to be a mother as much as I can, but I'm certainly not the
best example of being a mother."

She would never be as present as her own mother was for her. Indeed, she felt that she had been more of a mother to her younger brothers than she would ever be for her daughter. It was as though Simone
had expended all her caretaking energy when, at age eleven, she cared
for her brother Alain, and then during the Occupation when she supported the family and served as mother to her mother and a father figure
to her younger brothers. This energy was now spent, and nothing was
going to stand in the way of her dreams or desires.

Catherine was left in the care of others during her mother's long absences, which became increasingly frequent. But from the start, Simone
decided that her child should not have to suffer further by becoming a
subject for photographers, something she felt other actresses exposed
their children to in order to garner publicity. It begins with the pregnancy and then the birth, and then the family photos, always keeping the
actress in the public eye. The day Catherine was born, Simone made an
oath. "I swore unto myself she would never be photographed in a paper,
because I think it's terrible for a child and beside that, I, being an actress,
I don't think I can use any publicity of the fact that I am a mother too."[10]
A real mother would not be an actress.

However, when Catherine was six month old, Simone had a change
of heart. The press began to speculate: If Simone was refusing to allow
photographs, there must something wrong with the child. When she got
wind of the rumors Simone countered by setting up a photo session with
her child in a controlled setting. Photographers were allowed to capture
the healthy six-month old sitting on her mother's lap. Catherine bore a
striking resemblance to Simone. But this was the first and last time Simone subjected her child to publicity.[11]

❧

Though *Macadam* received mixed reviews, Simone's standing remained
intact. In 1947 she won the Suzanne Bianchetti Award as Most Promising Female Actor for both *Les Démons de l'aube* and *Macadam*. The recognition opened the door to a new opportunity for a supporting role in
Fantômas, a film based on a popular crime fiction character. Then, much
to her surprise, Simone was offered her first English-speaking role in
Against the Wind, filmed in London, England. As Michèle Denis, a Belgian

émigrée who is recruited as an operative by British Special Operations during WWII, Simone had a strong screen presence. But the film was not well received and did not garner attention.

During her absence for filming, Allégret and the producer Jacques Sicard began work on another film with her in mind. "*Dédée d'Anvers* was very important for me." She felt the film was a gift but she had no idea that it would generate so much publicity. Dédée was a "sympathetic character," one of the few that Simone would play in the early years of her career. Audiences could not help but feel compassion for the young prostitute, who dreams of a better life while working in a seedy nightclub on the Antwerp harbor. She lives with her pimp, who is also a porter at the nightclub. He loves only the sex and the money she brings in and mistreats her. Dédée feels trapped in a dismal life until she meets an Italian sailor. they fall in love and plot her escape. The film ends in tragedy, when the pimp finds out about her plan to leave and puts an end to it by killing her lover. Anguished, Dédée seeks revenge.

To prepare for the role, Simone shopped for her wardrobe in stores frequented by local prostitutes. She spent forty dollars on clothing and then another forty dollars on the all-important shoes. "I went to a place in Pigalle where the girls buy their shoes," she told *Herald-Tribune* reporter Art Buchwald in 1959. "At the time only prostitutes wore very thin, tall heels and it gave them a bouncy walk. Now everyone wears heels like that, and the bounce is no longer identified with the profession." *Dédée d'Anvers* was well received by the critics, who complimented Simone on the depth and breadth of her acting. She was a promising actress, well worth watching in the future.

In 1948, Simone had a starring role in *Impasse des Deux Anges* (Impasse of Two Angels) with the actor, Paul Meurisse.[12] She portrayed an actress, Marianne, who had fallen in love with a wealthy man and plans to give up her career for marriage. When he gives her a diamond necklace, Marianne becomes a mark for gangsters. The plot thickens when the man assigned to steal the necklace from her turns out to be someone she once loved. As far as Simone was concerned, the most noteworthy aspect of the film was that it provided a role for her young friend from the Occupation years, Danièle Delorme. Beyond that, she was not impressed with the film.

She made only the one other film that year, but she was far from inactive. In September 1948, when *Dédée d'Anvers* opened in France and then two months later in Sweden, she and Allégret began to enjoy the fruits of their long-fought battle for recognition. She was the new femme fatale of the cinema, and he was firmly established as a credible film director. They were both stars, and the future was promising. Allégret had finally divorced his wife, and as if to celebrate their success and freedom, which brought a sense of stability to their lives, they finally married. However, the marriage was more for her daughter's sake than any other reason, Simone stressed. Catherine was old enough to enter pre-school, and Simone did not want the child to suffer the stigma of being "born without father." After the marriage, her birth certificate reflected the change, and she became Catherine Enda Allégret. As an adult, Catherine expressed some regret at losing the hyphen in her very Polish first name.[13]

Simone's performance in *Dédée* earned her magazine covers and critical acclaim. "With *Dédée d'Anvers*, Simone Signoret has finally found the part she was looking for," one critic noted. "[It] immediately raises her up with the first rank of French screen actresses. The sobriety and the intensity of the performance astonishes in this very young artist who is almost a beginner. If she doesn't waste her talent, she will go far."[14] The publicity was flattering but invasive, and so unexpected that Simone was overwhelmed. She suffered from imposter syndrome, constantly questioning her ability and fearful that she couldn't live up to the expectations. She feared that one day someone would figure out that she had pulled the wool over everyone's eyes and was nothing more than an amateur.

Throughout her career, Simone suffered this onslaught of self-doubt at the start of every film, and though she came to expect it and knew such anxiety would pass, it was always unnerving. Adding to her concern was the realization that with the success of *Dédée d'Anvers*, she was firmly typecast as a prostitute, which meant, given her age, that her career might be limited to a few short years. What she failed to understand about the Dédée role was that audiences like a character they can sympathize and connect with, regardless of her role as prostitute, store clerk, or mother. Simone couldn't see that. She wanted diversity, and she found it in her next film. However, she was completely unprepared for the reaction she received.

In *Manèges*, again directed by her husband, Simone played Dora, a cruel and heartless woman who relentlessly uses and abuses her lover while her equally despicable mother eggs her on. Even Simone despised the character, "that monster, that bitch, that liar, that real whore without a sidewalk and without a pimp." Audiences felt the same way, and her performance was so credible that Simone experienced audience reaction on the street. Since audiences are often unable to separate the role from the actor, they simply hated her. Allégret was also heavily criticized for the film's negative portrayal of women.

Yet, offers continued to flow in. Immediately following *Manéges*, Simone left for Zurich to film *Swiss Tour*, later known as *Four Days Leave*. It was her second English language film and first comedy. Though the experience was as unmemorable as the movie, she was still enjoying the success of *Dédée d'Anvers*, which had been released in the United States on April 8, 1949. Hollywood began taking notice. Jenia Reissar, foreign production assistant in charge of the London office for Selznick Productions kept extensive files on talent to satisfy her employer, producer David O. Selznick, who was a detail man—excruciatingly so, much of the time. As there was no shortage of new talent after the European market re-opened to Hollywood after the war, Reissar maintained a system of profiles, typing in red ink to accentuate the name in the upper right corner of the page, before reverting to black for her notes. Later, she'd clip tear sheets and a photo to the page. After the release of *Dedee d'Anvers* in the United States, she started a new file:

Simone Signoret[15]
Married to Yves Allégret, the director
Very good in *"Les Demons de l'aube"* and *"Macadam"* her first
pictures.
The last one, *"Dedee d'Anvers"* is said to be an excellent one.

Later, Reissar added hand-written notes and pages as films were released:

1949 *"Manéges"*—Excellent
1950 *"Swiss Tour"*—takes full advantage of her rather inferior
role—*Variety*

Reissar clipped an informal photo of the actress relaxing on the set of *Against the Wind* to the profile. Simone, her face framed by a mass of curls dyed light brown for her role, smiled shyly at the camera. Yet, the shyness belied her casual manner as she leaned back in a director's chair with her legs stretched out in front of her. She looked at ease and comfortable in a short trench coat, belted at the waist, with cuffed trousers and ankle high shoes. She exhibited no glamour or attempt to pose for the camera, yet she seemed to glow with inner confidence.

Though she did not recall a contract offer from Selznick, she received offers from the Warner Bros., Paramount, and Twentieth Century-Fox studios. At first blush, the prospects were appealing to the twenty-eight-year-old. But Simone had begun to develop a strong business sense. Hollywood contracts were notorious for indenturing actors to seven years of endless films without right of refusal. Simone read English well enough to read the fine print in these contracts, and her lawyer concurred with her impressions. She decided to hold out for something more promising. It came in the spring of 1949, when Howard Hughes offered a lucrative four-year, four-film deal for movies of her choice. Simone accepted and planned to leave for the United States for preliminary discussions in the fall of 1949.

Hollywood would put the finishing touches on an adolescent fantasy. Yet, as was characteristic of a woman who always seemed to be on the verge of realizing her dreams, an obstacle stood in the way. But unlike her experiences during the Occupation, when circumstances were beyond her control, she had become the obstacle. Simone was feeling boxed in and restless. Time was passing too quickly, and much of it was spent working. It seemed just yesterday a loaf of bread was a luxury and fear was the only constant. Then, in a flash, it was 1949. Her daughter was three years old, and though Simone was only twenty-eight, she felt oppressed by the prospect of turning thirty. At this pace, she worried that one day she'd look back and reflect on a life lived through the eyes of a character in a movie. It was a disquieting thought, reminiscent of a quote from the French author Jean Giraudoux that she liked to recite: "If I'm not careful my life will develop without me."

There was no question that she loved every aspect of the cinema, from the camaraderie of the actors to costumes and make-up, and the hush that fell after the "all quiet" signal, when everyone waited anxiously for the sound of the clapper.[16] She tried her hand at impromptu filmmaking with a small 16mm camera she took on vacations and was always amazed by how different the world appeared in the lens and by what she captured of it, both purposely and inadvertently. However, she did not entertain thoughts of filmmaking. When push came to shove, she belonged in front of camera.

But, it was impossible to have balance in life while acting. She became so absorbed by the demands of her roles that she resented distractions in the real world. Though she could consume books with a passion when free, she couldn't concentrate on reading while working. Instead, she contented herself with flipping through a magazine, which didn't require much effort. She could knit and crochet while dragging on a perpetually burning cigarette because the activity kept her hands busy and mind free; if anything the repetitive motions enhanced her concentration. Beyond that, she had very little tolerance for diversions. "Let's not exaggerate. If a family member is ill, I'm very upset. But apart from that I get up in the morning to work, and I go to bed after work. And that's all I care about while I'm doing it."[17] When she was honest with herself, she didn't really like the person she became during those weeks of filming. "Oh, an actress can be a monster," she complained.

And it was that way with Allégret, too. He was a consummate professional and a demanding director, constantly working to perfect a scene, while at the same time scouting out prospects for his next project. To complicate matters, as a husband directing his wife in a film, he found it difficult to separate his professional and private lives. On the rare occasions when he and Simone weren't working, they tooled around Paris in Allégret's Morgan and enjoyed spending time at their old haunts on the Left Bank. They frequented the music halls and the new jazz clubs, or "caves," where many of their friends performed. But it wasn't the same, because their romance had slowly dissolved into a business arrangement. "I was in love with him," Simone explained, "flattered that an older man would pay me attention. But with him, I was the professional women first."[18] In retrospect, what began on the evening of August 19, 1949, at the Columbe d'Or hotel when she met the Italian-born French singer, Yves Montand, should not have come a surprise to either of them. Allégret was forty-four years old; Simone was twenty-eight. She explained it simply: "I was ready for a big passion."

CHAPTER 10

"Something Indiscreet and Irreversible"

"SHE WAS BAREFOOT AND DRESSED GYPSY STYLE, WITH A RUSTLING flowered skirt and a blouse knotted around her waist. She was outrageously made up, the way women made themselves up in those days, with far too much lipstick. I thought it a pity to paint such a mouth,"[1] Yves Montand later recalled his first impression of Simone as she entered the Columbe d'Or with Jacques Prévert. Montand was enjoying a rare night off from his summer concert tour of Provence, dining with two of his musicians, Bob Castella, a pianist, and guitarist Henri Crolla. Simone was vacationing with her daughter and stepson, Gilles, at the house she'd recently purchased in Saint-Paul de Vence, where Prévert was her next-door neighbor. Her husband was still in Paris at the time and planned to join his family in a few days.

They had never formally met, though each was well aware of the other. It was impossible to ignore Simone's photo in magazines and on movie posters. However, Yves Montand never had occasion to see any of her films, which he decided in retrospect was a good thing, because her performance as the malevolent Dora in *Manèges* was so credible that the film would have colored his overall impression of Simone. Beyond that, he recalled seeing her on a few occasions: once, after a performance, and then again at a benefit for war veterans.

She, on the other hand, was very familiar with the cabaret singer. Simone and Allégret enjoyed the music halls and were so impressed with Yves Montand that they attended his shows. Afterwards when they went backstage, however, they never attempted to greet the singer, because there was always a line outside his dressing room. Instead, they went to greet his guitarist, Henry Crolla, an old friend from the Café de Flore days.[2] She never mentioned whether she had seen any of his films. There were only three in his short-lived acting career. However, in 1946, in the film *Les Portes de la Nuit*, he was the first to introduce the song *Les Feuilles Mortes*, a poem by Jacques Prévert that had been adapted to music. At the time, the song was not well received, considered too nostalgic for a country still grieving from the losses of the Occupation years. But it gained popularity over time, and later, both the original song and a watered-down English translation, *Autumn Leaves*, would become popular and enduring hits.

While Montand's film career was short lived, he had been courted briefly by Hollywood studios. However, his first contract experience was a disaster. Unlike Simone, he did not speak English and apparently did not have the benefit of an astute lawyer, so he readily signed on with Warner Bros. before realizing that he had committed himself to an arduous seven-year stint. His attempt to break the contract resulted in a well-publicized lawsuit and earned him notoriety with other studios. At Selznick Productions in 1946, Jenna Reissar created a profile on the singer and actor, typing the entire document in red ink as though sounding an alarm:

Yves Montand (French)[3]
Broke a 7 year contract with Warners.
Had a law-suit settled out of court.
Cabaret Singer.
Credits: *"Doors of the Night"* (Les Portes De La Nuit)
 "The Way Without Stars" (Le Chemin Sans Etoiles)
 "The Idol" (L'Idole)

Clipped to the profile was a photo of a tall, lanky young man, with his thick dark hair cut short on the sides but kept longer and wavy on top, as was the style at the time. He was talking intently to his companion, leaning down towards her to compensate for his height, though even bent down, his 6'2" frame still towered over his petite lover, the singer Edith Piaf.

Anyone who followed Yves Montand knew that he had sung with Piaf before launching a solo act and that there had been a brief, but intense love affair between them. Some insisted that it was Piaf who launched his career, though in reality the talented artist had begun singing long before meeting her. While he would agree that Piaf helped him perfect his act, Montand would never credit her for launching his career. As was her style, when Piaf saw talent, she took the blossoming artist under her wing—and often into her bed. Yves, who was only twenty-three years old at the time, was impressionable and had fallen head-over-heels for the singer. As was also her style, after an intense fling, she cut him off without warning, refusing to see him or take phone calls. Rumor had it that Yves Montand had gone to her home and banged on her door in a fit of rage, demanding that she see him. Though he denied that rumor, the temperamental behavior was not out of the realm of possibility for the singer, who had a swift and ferocious temper that could generate shouting matches of Homeric proportions. Regardless, Edith Piaf did not respond to his attempts to reconcile, though in time they resumed a cordial professional friendship that endured throughout her lifetime.

Simone, who would become his greatest defender in all things, was convinced that Piaf had broken off with "Montand," (the name she used to avoid confusion with her husband Yves) because the singer felt threatened by the rising star who would soon become her equal. Regardless, their break-up provided the impetus Montand needed to step out on his own as a solo performer. It also prompted a steadfast resolve: He would never allow himself to get that deeply involved with a woman again. Five years later, in 1949, when he met Simone Signoret, he had not yet broken his resolve.

The realization that there was more than a casual interest between Simone and Montand occurred after dinner when guests retired to the hotel salon for drinks, and he treated them to an impromptu concert at the piano. "As I sang I stared—but not too obviously—at that woman and I saw that she was not indifferent to me, either."[4] They chatted briefly afterwards; it was casual and nervous banter. But everything changed the next day. He had gone to Nice on the morning of August 20 to rehearse for his evening performance at the Théâtre de Verdure, a popular open-air theater. When he returned to the Columbe d'Or, he and Henri Crolla joined Simone and Prévert on the hotel's garden terrace for lunch. The tension between Simone and Montand was palpable, and after lunch, Prévert and Crolla discreetly excused themselves, leaving the couple to their own devices. Catherine was sitting at another table having lunch during this famous meeting, but was too young to recall the events that followed.

When she spoke of it, Simone, in her characteristic style, skipped the details. "I'm not going to treat you to true confessions," she warned. However, Montand, who was not burdened with a need for privacy, provided the intimate details in his biography, *You See, I Haven't Forgot-ten*: "We drank white wine. Looked at one another. Picked up the non-conversation of the day before. I 'carelessly' took hold of her arm." "You have very slender wrists," he murmured. "I could have said anything to her, she would have taken it as a compliment, but it was true. We talked about it for years. She smiled and mumbled a few words I didn't catch. She drank her coffee, I lit a cigarette."

Then, the spell was momentarily broken when Montand checked his watch, explaining that he had to leave because he needed rest before his evening performance. "You can rest at my place, if you like," Simone offered without a moment's hesitation. She explained that she owned a house in the village nearby. He was taken aback by her response at first, as though completely unaware that his light touch and whispered compliment might be considered anything but a signal for his desire for something else. He maintained this sense of innocence with women in general, claiming, "As always, it was she, the woman, who took the ini-tiative, and as always I was surprised." But he accepted her invitation.

Simone provided a tour of her new vacation home, her first invest-ment, purchased entirely with her own income. Like the ancient, weath-er-worn village surrounding it, the house was built in the fourteenth century, and though small in comparison to other more elaborate dwell-ings, it boasted a grand stone terrace that pleased her nearly as much as the price she'd paid: ten thousand francs, her entire salary from *Four Days Leave*. The property was affordable and well worth the investment, con-sidering its close proximity to the Columbe d'Or and to Jacques Prévert.

After a tour and then a "siesta," Simone accompanied Yves Montand to his concert in Nice. "In those four days we had been struck by light-ning and something indiscreet and irreversible had happened."[5] Every-one had witnessed their comings and goings, noticing Simone leaving his annex room at the hotel. Even her stepson, Giles, who was fourteen at the time, was a witness to it all. Simone worried that she had put her friends and family in the untenable position of being accomplices to her indiscretion, and she envisioned the awkward silences with her husband when he finally arrived in Saint-Paul.

Fearful that he would learn of her affair through idle gossip over drinks, she had a moment of conscience and decided that she must be the first to break the news. So, she waited for her husband's arrival on the main road leading into Saint Paul. When he saw her standing on the side of the road, he pulled over. Simone unburdened herself, and the tears flowed more freely after Allégret, who was stunned by the betrayal, lashed out, slapping her twice with a vengeance before regaining his composure. There was a brief period of reconciliation after the family returned to Paris in the fall of 1949. However, this rapprochement was for appearances' sake on Simone's part because her heart wasn't in it. The separation from Montand was as insufferable as her guilty conscience. She didn't want to hurt Allégret, but it was clear to her that the marriage was over.

Meanwhile, Yves Montand miserably continued his tour. As he traveled to the towns of Dax and then Biarritz, he kept a photo of Simone clipped to the dashboard of his car and berated himself for breaking his vow to maintain emotional distance from women. He had fallen in love with a married woman, a mother with a young child. He felt helpless and wanted distance, but he couldn't resist responding to the letters she sent. When he returned to Paris in the late fall of 1949, he and Simone began meeting clandestinely.

"It was intense, violent, a joy, a celebration. And then, at seven, she would go 'home'—in other words, to someone else's home," he complained.[6] The emotional upheaval was affecting his concentration, a risk for a solo performer who had to be on top of his game every night. In an effort to regain some semblance of sanity, he scheduled another concert tour, this one out of the country in Casablanca, Algiers, and Tunis, as far away as possible. He wasn't quick to break off with Simone, but he felt that she was "dithering" and gave her an ultimatum: She had to leave her husband or break off their relationship. She couldn't have it both ways.[7]

The "dithering" on Simone's part was complicated. While her marriage had become more a business relationship than anything else, she cared about Allégret and had no desire to inflict pain on him. And she had developed a close relationship with his son, Giles, who reminded her of her younger brothers. She could see herself as an older sister, but never as the boy's stepmother. Simone was also torn by professional obligations. She was supposed to leave for the United States for discussions with Howard Hughes. But at this point, with life in an uproar, she couldn't bear the thought of leaving.

By the time Montand returned to Paris at the end of 1949, Simone's dithering was replaced by resolve. Her career would be put on hold for the foreseeable future, and she could no longer feign interest in saving the marriage. With bags packed, she moved into Montand's apartment, leaving her husband, young Catherine, and Giles behind. It was a bold move that made her the object of criticism and condemnation with some of her friends. Even the concierge weighed in, referring to Simone as a run-away mother. Simone endured the ridicule because it wasn't a permanent situation. She had every intention of filing for custody of her child when she filed for divorce. But at the moment, while details were being worked out, Montand's bachelor apartment on the Rue Longchamps in Neuilly-sur-Seine wasn't a suitable place to raise a child. And, in truth, a child had no place in the midst of a passionate love affair that was gaining intensity every day. Simone rationalized her decision to leave Catherine behind, contending that her daughter, who was three years old at the time, was already accustomed to her mother's absences and Sunday visits during film production.

Jacques Prévert explained the love affair between Simone and Montand this way: "Love for them was like discovering a new country; there was so much to learn, but they were never bored. Simone gave him culture, depth. He gave her an earthy sense of reality."[8] And, it was this earthiness that was so attractive to Simone, who was seven months older than Montand. They were contemporaries but had grown up in completely different worlds. Yves Montand, born Ivo Livi on October 13, 1921 in Monsummano Terne, Italy, was the youngest of three children in a poor, working-class family. In spite of attempts by some, including the Nazis, to find Jewish roots in the family's last name, both parents had Catholic roots. Giuseppina Simoni was a devout catholic who hid her religious practice from her husband, Giovanni Livi, who was raised a Catholic but rejected religion when he joined the Communist Party. However, his roots crept into his decision-making after the birth of his youngest child. He envisioned that this boy would grow up to be a fine lawyer, and named him after Saint Ivo, patron saint of the just.

Giovanni Livi was a broom maker, whose political affiliation with the communists made him a target of the fascist Benito Mussolini and his Black Shirts. When Giovanni refused to join the fascist party, he was accosted and beaten as a warning. Then, when the beating had little effect, they set his small backyard broom factory on fire, burning it to the ground. For the sake of his family's safety, Giovanni fled Italy, crossing the border into France in Marseille, where he worked a few months to prepare for his family's arrival. Ivo was two years old when his mother and his siblings, Lydia and Julian, left Italy clandestinely to join Giovanni in France.

While they were free of Mussolini's tyranny, the family's struggle to rise above poverty continued. At times, there was so little food that that the children had to share a single egg and slice of bread. Life improved when the eldest, Lydia, trained as a hairdresser and eventually opened up a salon in town. She earned enough to help support the family and her father's business.

Ivo had little interest in school and felt that he didn't fit in. He was unusually tall and lanky for his age and self-conscious about his looks—particularly of his prominent nose and wide mouth, which gave him a comical appearance. He left school at the age of twelve to work in factories before becoming an apprentice hairdresser in his sister's shop. He spent his free time in movie theaters, where he dreamed of becoming an actor. Indeed, he was so inspired by Fred Astaire that he took a few tap dancing lessons. Through the vigorous and unyielding urging of a mother—who, when necessary, would stand on a chair so she could she get close enough to her tall son to swat him with her broom—Ivo finished his elementary education, attended hairdressing school, and, after earning his diploma, found work in a salon.

All the while, Ivo dreamed of launching an acting career. Singing never entered his mind. But one evening, at the age of seventeen, while he and his brother hung out their apartment window to watch a local outdoor talent show, Ivo became critical of one of the singers. Annoyed by the smug audacity of his younger brother, Julien challenged him, suggesting that if Ivo could do better he should get out there and sing. Unable to walk away from a challenge, Ivo approached the manager and signed on to sing one song. He was moderately successful and the manager encouraged him to sign on for more.

The stage name he chose was a play on words familiar from childhood, when his mother shouted out the window of their apartment, calling her son home for dinner: "Ivo, monta!"(Ivo, upstairs): Yves Montand was born. With this new name came the responsibility of putting together an act. He liked to mimic his favorite stars and loved Hollywood musicals and westerns. Montand was most impressed by Gary Cooper and Fred Astaire, and he developed an act that combined both song and mimicry. His first appearances went well, and he was determined to take things to the next level. The first blow to his ego came when he attempted to take singing lessons and was told by the teacher that he not only sang off key, but he had such a thick accent that it was too difficult to understand him. Still, he persisted, and it paid off on stage before raucous and unforgiving audiences, who were not above booing or throwing rotten produce to get a performer off the stage. They liked the mimicry—particularly his imitation of a singing cowboy.

When France fell in 1940, Montand's singing career came to a temporary standstill, and he was forced to find other work. He worked as a dockworker and metalworker, hard physical labor that strengthened his muscles, filling out his bony frame. Although he lived in the Unoccupied Zone during the early years of the war, he was not immune to the Vichy government's requirement that all twenty-year-old males serve eight months in the work camps in France. He was assigned to the entertainment corps, but they were given few opportunities to sing. Once he served his time, Montand attempted to re-start his singing career. But as the war raged on, the Nazi and Vichy governments instituted a mandatory work program, and in September 1943, Montand was ordered to report for compulsory service in Germany's salt mines. Thanks to the efforts of his sister, Lidia, who used her influence with local authorities, Montand was given a temporary reprieve.

Early in 1944, the French and German police began house-to-house searches to round up dodgers. Montand was well hidden when the police kicked in the door of his family's apartment, and he was spared arrest. But his father worried, and he suggested that his son join the Maquis, a group of resisters hiding out in the mountains. Instead, Montand decided to take a chance on his career, and in February 1944, he moved to Paris and found work as a guest singer, introducing major acts, including Edith Piaf. When she was looking to replace a member of her act, Montand auditioned and was hired.

Montand knew the meaning of hard work and poverty. Simone, in contrast, had lived a life of relative luxury prior to the war. The differences between them were more a fascination than a concern for the couple during those early months together. Simone enjoyed Montand's humor and expressive body language, which gave him style and grace. She, on the other hand, was clumsy and likely to trip over her feet. Though she gave the appearance of confidence much of the time, Simone fell apart during emergencies, she claimed, while Montand remained calm. Yet, when it came to small issues, he lost his temper and screamed. While they complimented each other, it soon became clear that adjustments had to be made. Among the little things that Montand disliked was Simone's lipstick, which, as he said, he "lovingly" wiped off her face. He forbade her to wear it again. Simone acquiesced. She felt that the Occupation had robbed her of the years when a girl learns how to properly apply make-up and use it to advantage. And she was not really fond of the primping that absorbed most women's time. A natural look, accentuated by her seductive eyes and mouth, suited her well, and she maintained it for the rest of her life, regardless of the criticism she would endure as she aged.

For her part, Simone found Montand to be a bit jealous and possessive. He was apparently fearful that if she saw her husband again she might change her mind, and so she had to "sneak out to see my own husband and arrange the divorce." However, the threat that she might change her mind was unrealistic. Any attempt at reconciliation would have been motivated by guilt, not by a desire to resume her marriage.[9]

Simone found the differences between her film and Montand's live performances fascinating. A live performer had to get it right without the opportunity for multiple takes if the act wasn't perfect. If not well rehearsed, a performer risked failing in front of an audience. Still, Montand's rehearsals and need for intense concentration and solitude were no different than the demands of acting, when she became a "monster" unable to focus attention on anything but the role she was playing. Simone also learned quickly that Montand was a workaholic, constantly setting up performances, rehearsing and planning. If she wanted to see him, she had to immerse herself in his life and become a "groupie," a label she gave herself. She attended every rehearsal, watching quietly and going out for sandwiches or on errands when needed. One hour before a show, Montand wanted privacy, and she was forced to leave him alone in his dressing room. However, before a performance ended, Simone quickly made her way back to his dressing room, where she waited to hand him a towel when he finally walked through the door, sweating and exhausted. This was her new life, and she embraced it wholeheartedly without a single thought for her own career.

There were other reasons for making her presence known backstage. Yves Montand was a hit with women of all ages. His singing "acted on their nervous systems," Simone explained, and they played out their fantasies, shamelessly flirting backstage after a show. But backstage, Simone could aggressively defend her position: "Occasionally, when it gets too boring and a woman won't leave the dressing room, I put on my prostitute face and just tell her to scram."[10]

CHAPTER 11

"I Do Not Like to Speak of My Personal Life"

When I imagine them in the splendor of their love life, it is always this scene that I see: I was about four, alone with my mother in the living room waiting for Montand to come back from a trip. Suddenly, I hear the front door slam and I hide behind an armchair when he enters the room. He has one hand behind his back. Is he hiding a present for me? I was getting ready to surprise him, but I was too late. He already had his arms around my mother after having given her a little leather case. They kissed and the kiss lasted and lasted. It is still going on in my memory today.[1]

"Ma souris," my mouse, her mother called her, and it was an apt nickname, because Catherine, who remained hidden behind the armchair until she could escape without notice, was a quiet yet observant child who learned early on that she should not interrupt her mother and her new "Papa." This understanding was something she sensed without being told, and it left her with a pervasive feeling that she was easily forgotten and not important. She was an only child, as her mother had been for years. However, unlike Simone, she was not included in conversation or shielded by an over-protective mother who monitored her every move.

Her parents, who were married only one year during their six-year relationship, divorced in 1950. By then, Simone and Montand had found suitable living space for themselves and Catherine. It was also a suitable gathering place for Montand's musicians and those friends of Simone who were allowed back into her life—friends who approved of this new relationship. Simone had been anxious to leave Montand's bachelor apartment on Rue Longchamps in Neuilly-sur-Seine. Although it was not close to her childhood haunts, it was still in Neuilly and too close for comfort. Every evening when they returned home from one of his performances and had to stop at the traffic light on the Avenue du Roule, she couldn't help but relive painful memories, particularly about the eviction.

Montand also looked forward to making a clean break from familiar territory. His housekeeper ruled the roost and was so possessive that she went out of her way to make Simone feel an unwelcome intruder. She took notable pleasure in announcing messages from Montand's former girlfriends. Simone felt terrorized by the woman. The couple finally agreed that Neuilly-sur-Seine represented an old life better left behind. They wanted to make a fresh start elsewhere. However, housing was scarce and priced at a premium during the post-war reconstruction of Paris. Their search seemed endless until Henri Crolla told them about a rare bookshop that was vacating space on Place Dauphine on the western tip of Île de la Cité, one of two small islands in the Seine.

One had to have a keen eye to see potential in the narrow, cramped rooms spread out between the ground floor and a mezzanine level at 15 Place Dauphine. The six-story building had seventh-century charm and was one of sixteen connected buildings that lined a rectangular, sandy square. There were two front doors, one opened onto Place Dauphine and the other on the Quai des Orfèvres, running parallel with the Seine. Though a low wall and trees obstructed a ground level view of the river, they could see it from the balcony outside the bedroom on the mezzanine level, which also included a bathroom and storage closet. There was also an alcove area, so small that it held only a folding cot for Catherine. The ground floor level, formerly the bookshop, was a narrow, low space with storefront windows on the quai side facing the Seine. Montand barely had two inches to spare when clearing the low ceiling. His piano would dominate the space, leaving just enough room for a couch and a few chairs. The adjoining dining area was equally cramped, and the small kitchen on the Place Dauphine side, wasn't of particular interest to Simone who, by her own admission, could barely boil water.

It is unclear if Montand rented the apartment at first and then purchased the building later, or if he purchased it at the start, but 15 Place

Dauphine became the heart of the Signoret-Montand liaison, their Paris home for the next thirty-five years of their lives. Simone was thrilled. During the Occupation, when she and friends walked aimlessly about admiring architecture, she had fallen in love with Place Dauphine and had boldly and prophetically announced that she would live there one day. She set to work on the apartment right away, hunting through antique stores for tables, chests, and other pieces of furniture. She developed a passion for old oil lamps, which she cleaned and electrified. To compensate for the low ceiling in the living room, she purchased a low-backed couch and chair. She had the walls of the apartment painted white, but left them bare temporarily until she and Montand could afford artwork. Eventually, they purchased paintings from emerging artists. The floor-to-ceiling bookshelves that framed the fireplace were quickly filled with books and the mementos she was so fond of collecting. What pleased her most was that in spite of their cramped quarters, the apartment was a gathering place for their extended family of musicians, artists, writers and actors. She dubbed it "the trailer," because the atmosphere was similar to that of the trailers on film sets, where actors gathered for camaraderie during breaks.

They hired an acquaintance, Marcelle Mirtilon, to cook for the hungry group that congregated on a daily basis at Place Dauphine. And when Catherine moved in, they also hired a nanny—and then a series of nannies, nearly all of which became the bane of Simone's existence. The most famous among them Catherine called "Beelzebub Colette," an irresponsible and forgetful woman who on one occasion left the child standing out in the rain because she forgot to pick her up from school. She was known for feeding the child a steady diet of sardines and soup. Another nanny was apt to throw glasses of cold water in Catherine's face to stop tantrums. It was a disquieting life for a young child, particularly when Simone and Montand were on tour.

Reluctantly, Simone finally re-emerged from temporary retirement in 1950, appearing in four films, only one of which she found challenging. *Gunmen in the Streets* was classic film noir, directed by Frank Tuttle and Boris Lewin, and starring the American actor Dane Clark as a gangster on the run who turns to his former girlfriend Denise, a prostitute. She attempts to raise money for his escape. The film was released in France as *Le Traque*.

Simone then appeared briefly—again as a prostitute in the opening and final scenes—in Max Ophüls's classic *La Ronde*. *Sans laisser d'addresse*, directed by Jean-Paul Le Chanois, provided her with an un-credited supporting role she did not find worth mentioning. Three films back to back provided a jumpstart for her career. Yet, Simone was not satisfied. She was acting again, but she felt uninspired and distracted.[2] However, her next film, *Ombres et Lumières*, directed by Henri Calef, was both an expected surprise and change of pace.

Simone had found something she could sink her teeth into, playing Isabelle, a pianist in love, who had been traumatized while performing a Tchaikovsky concerto. Simone described the part as "a sort of 'Anti-Manèges'. . . . Tired of playing the lost girls, I wanted, finally, to play the dramatic role of a woman in love who was not suffering from a sexual pathology."[3] In preparation for the film's release, Simone was asked to write a series of articles, including one written from her character's point of view for a special promotional edition of *Cinémonde* magazine. She participated, but not without some irritation, because among the three articles she was expected to write, only one, "My Career and My Films," had any bearing on her profession. The other two articles, "Confidences" and "The Secrets of My Intimacy," were intrusions designed for publicity purposes. In "Confidences," the twenty-nine-year-old quickly got to the heart of her irritation: "I will be very frank: I do not like to speak of my personal life." She thought it was both "ostentatious and ridiculous" for an actress to tout the details of her life, a life that was not so different from those of the readers. Her personal life had nothing to do with her career, as she elaborated later, providing a unique perspective: "It goes without saying that the actress belongs to the people; but not the woman. Those are two separate zones that do not interpenetrate."

This conflict between her personal philosophy and the public's need to know would become an increasingly difficult challenge for Simone. She simply could not understand the need for fans to know private details; she was even surprised by the need for autographs. Though she gave them, the exercise baffled her. In spite of her own fascination with stars during adolescence, Simone had never wanted or asked for an autograph and couldn't imagine the benefit of having one.

In her articles, she spoke of her family, asking forgiveness because she had no intention of sharing details about her daughter. "What mother does not think that her child is the most beautiful?" Instead, she spoke of her brothers, who were both away at school. Alain, who was twenty years old at the time, was attending law school in Strasbourg. Simone suspected that he had interest in filmmaking, and in the future she would be instrumental in opening doors for him. Jean-Pierre, who was eighteen years old, was studying to become a professor of letters.

There was no mention of her parents, who never resumed their marriage after the Liberation, though André reunited with his wife long enough to visit the lawyer who held the rings she had hocked. Georgette remained in Paris and worked, or spent time in Provence with the Signoret family. But her visits with Simone were rare and strained, because Georgette was not fond of Yves Montand, who she described as a "clown." While Simone would always provide assistance to her mother, she did so from a distance. Their relationship remained distant for the rest of their lives. In the article, Simone did not elaborate about her father, whose career continued its ascent after the Liberation.

André Kaminker served as chief interpreter for the Council of Europe, then later, until his retirement, as chief interpreter at the United Nations. In 1953, he was a founding father and first organizational president of AIIC, the international association of conference interpreters. When he was asked to draft the first code of conduct for interpreters, he replied, "It is very simple, three articles suffice. Article 1: members are bound by the utmost secrecy. Article 2: members are bound by the utmost secrecy. Article 3: members are bound by the utmost secrecy."[4] He was accomplished and highly regarded in his field, but his relationship with family, particularly with his daughter, was strained.

Simone wrote in the past tense from her character's point of view in the article "Ombre et Lumière," describing at great length Isabelle's life, her breakdown, the young man she had fallen in love with, and the sister who tormented her. As Isabelle stares into a mirror examining her face, Simone wrote an inner dialogue that could have been a testament to her own life before meeting Yves Montand: "I had lived for twenty-eight years without love." Apparently, her creative attempt, which was spread over eight pages, was too serious for the magazine editors, who felt inclined to lighten the mood by interspersing the text with short quotes or facts with photographs: "Simone Signoret loves animals;" "If she did not live in such a small apartment, she would have dogs;" "I never wear hats." Simone would never understand the public's need to know such ridiculous tidbits of personal information.

CHAPTER 12

The Stockholm Appeal

HOLLYWOOD AGENT MINNA WALLIS ARRIVED IN FRANCE IN 1950 WITH the expectation that she would return with Simone Signoret, who was still under contract with Howard Hughes but had not responded to phone calls from the studio. Wallis found Simone and Montand vacationing in Saint-Paul de Vence and spent several days in town arguing her case with the couple. Simone was unmoved; she was not leaving Montand under any circumstances. Finally convinced, Wallis gave up the quest. Simone explained that Wallis confided that she understood Simone's reluctance to leave her lover.[1] Hollywood could kill a romance.

Wallis returned to the United States alone. However, unbeknownst to Simone, it was highly unlikely that she could have secured a visa. In spring 1950, Simone and Montand had signed a petition, unwittingly supporting what would be called "the most dangerous hoax ever devised by the international Communist conspiracy." Although it was not the only reason, her signature on the petition effectively closed the door on future opportunities in the United States. The Stockholm Appeal of 1950 was a pacifist petition released by the World Peace Council calling for a ban on the use of nuclear weapons and charging any country that used them with crimes against humanity. Over 270,000 people worldwide signed on, including, allegedly, the entire adult population of the Soviet Union. Simone and Montand, still relatively unknown outside France, joined such notable signatories as Duke Ellington, Thomas Mann, Pablo Picasso, Jacques Prévert, and Maurice Chevalier.

Up to this point, Simone and Montand had not as a couple taken active public positions on social issues. While married to Allégret, Simone was photographed in 1947 marching in an anti-American demonstration to protest the flood of Hollywood films that had saturated the market at the expense of French studios, a deal struck with the French government in order to access US economic assistance for reconstruction efforts after the war. Montand had signed a petition protesting the same issue. It had seemed to all involved at the time that this American invasion was hurting rather than helping the reconstruction efforts, as French studios suffered losses at the box office.

As a couple Simone and Montand attended meetings, "peace rallies" organized by the French Communist Party, and contributed financially to the cause when asked, particularly when peace efforts were involved. They were comfortable with their relationship with communists, who were not the enemy portrayed by the Americans. Indeed, the USSR had been an ally, fighting side- by-side with the French Resistance against the Nazis during the war. During the Occupation, many of Simone's friends were communists, though at the time she did not know or care. She liked and respected them and did not view them as the enemy.[2]

Closer to home, Montand's father and his brother, Julien, were ardent communists. Julien was a rising leader in the French communist trade union, Confédération Générale du Travail. While Montand no longer worked side-by-side with metalworkers and dockworkers, he understood the workingman's cause and supported it, often singing for protesters during strikes and rallies. For her part, Simone was pleased when her brothers joined the Communist Party, something their father was solidly against. "My father, in 1953, found out from a police informant that I was a Communist Party activist," Jean-Pierre recalled, "a fact I had tried assiduously to hide from him. He, having his whole life espoused rightist tendencies, was so upset by this piece of news that his first reaction was to consider cutting off the monthly stipend he gave me and which allowed me to carry on with my studies undisturbed. It was a threat without consequence, in particular thanks to Simone, who authorized me to tell him that if he cut off my livelihood, she would simply take over and support me herself."[3] Jean-Pierre continued his graduate studies, and Simone offered him and his wife an apartment at 15 Place Dauphine, where they remained for several years. Between Montand's family, who eventually moved into 15 Place Dauphine and Jean-Pierre, "the upstairs of this house was thus a hotbed of communists, which at the time was fine with her."

Simone and Montand were so passionate about the communist cause that they were known to accompany Pablo Picasso on missions to persuade potential party recruits. This was odd behavior, because Simone and Montand themselves never joined the Communist Party. "We didn't join the Party because we were often dismayed by its cultural positions," particularly what they viewed as suffocation of the arts. They were also in complete disagreement with communist censorship of Hollywood films. Their passion for the cause was confined to promoting workers' and women's rights and to world peace, which was a major concern in the decade that followed World War II. In 1950, France was engaged in military action in Vietnam, an aggression the Communist Party was sure had financial backing from the United States. At the same time, America had declared war on Korea and was pursuing a vigorous cold war against Russia in a race for dominance over nuclear weapons. "In France, you know, when we speak about war it's mostly the last one. Not the next one. There's nothing like anti-atomic clothes . . . or the shelter business—that doesn't exist in France. Merely because we think that if another war should come, there will be no use in having clothes or shelters," Simone explained.[4] Even her father, a conservative who was generally not inclined to take a stand on social issues, reportedly expressed his concern, telling Simone, "We have to leave Europe; there will be war between the Americans and Russia at any time."

When the Stockholm Appeal to stop the atomic bomb began circulating worldwide in March 1950, Simone and Montand felt they had no choice but to take a stand. They had seen photographs of Hiroshima and were certain that nuclear weapons would end the world. However, immediately after the petition was released, they learned that they had been duped. While the cause for peace was a just one, the Stockholm Appeal and the Peace Council were part of a successful campaign launched exclusively by the Soviet Union and backed solely by the Communist Party.

The United States had a delayed but decisive reaction. On July 5, 1950, John Foster Dulles, Republican adviser to the State Department, testified as follows before the Senate Foreign Relations Committee:"[I]t is my opinion that the leaders of communism are, before venturing an open war, trying to create a public opinion of the world to believe that they are the nations that stand for peace and that we are the Nation that stands for war, and they have made very good progress in doing that . . . . They know that everybody wants peace, and if they can pose as the lovers of peace, then, perhaps they can risk war." The House Un-American Activities Committee of Congress was asked to conduct a full investigation into the communist party and the peace movement and its activities in the United States and abroad. Nearly a year later, in 1951, the committee provided Congress with an extensive report titled "The Communist

Peace Offensive: A Campaign to Disarm and Defeat the United States." [5] In the report, the committee indicated that the peace movement had received the official endorsement of the Supreme Soviet:

> The Information Bureau of the Communist and Workers Parties (Cominform), successor to the Communist International, has given this campaign top priority. It has been designated as the major effort of every Communist Party on the face of the globe, including the Communist Party of the United States. Communists and their co-conspirators are spearheading this movement in cities and communities throughout the United States—at meetings, on street corners, in shops, homes, schools and colleges, in the press and on the radio—in fact, in every walk of life. Unless it is completely exposed, many may be deceived and ensnared.

Following the full report was a comprehensive list of Americans suspected of belonging to communist or peace organizations, many of whom had signed the Stockholm Appeal. Among those suspected of having communist ties were Paul Robeson and Langston Hughes, as well as members of the clergy, educators, and other US citizens. The list was categorized by state, by profession, and by the number of organizations the individuals were suspected to be members of. The committee expressed its willingness to publish a list of individuals whose names appeared on the lists erroneously owing to deception, as long they appeared before the committee and unequivocally assured Congress that they were not members of the Communist Party. Those who were not cleared were blacklisted or placed under investigation.

In France, the singer-actor Maurice Chevalier, who enjoyed a prosperous association with Hollywood, tried to retract his signature on the Stockholm Appeal, claiming that he had not really read the text and didn't realize what he had signed. While Simone and Montand never appeared on a published black list, they would learn soon enough that they were barred from entering the United States. Simone was convinced that the Stockholm Appeal was the reason. However, her signature on the petition was merely another item on a list of concerns. She and Montand had participated in communist peace rallies and anti-American demonstrations, and, more importantly, they were members of the peace movement, which in the United States was akin to being a card-carrying member of the Communist Party.

❧

In 1950, Montand was still serving as an opening act for other major performers and toyed with the idea of stepping out on his own, an idea Simone wholeheartedly supported. He booked the Etoile Theater in Paris and worked to perfect a formula for his show, one that would focus entirely on the act. His costume was kept simple: brown slacks and a brown shirt. He experimented with a light curtain that hid the orchestra; it was a new concept not yet popular with other performers in the music world. And, to insure that the audience would get their money's worth, he mixed song, dance, and short skits into a two-hour show without an intermission.

On Monday, March 5, 1951, Montand gave his first solo performance to a standing room only audience. The formula worked and became his trademark. Over one hundred performances later, Montand's success was unparalleled, and his popularity was cemented when his song, *Barbara*, hit the top of charts, earning him the *Grand Prix du Disque* gold record award. There is a photograph of Simone staring up at Montand, her face aglow with pride and adoration as he holds up a gold record for photographers and speaks to reporters. Montand had risen to a new level in his career. Simone was not yet ready to make a commitment with her own. Montand was her only interest.

PART III

THE IDEAL COUPLE

CHAPTER 13

"The Finest Film I Ever Made"

BOTH SIMONE AND MONTAND RETURNED TO THE CINEMA IN 1951. Neither of them was thrilled with the prospect, though for entirely different reasons. Any hope that Simone might find another "anti-Manèges" role as a women without "sexual pathologies" was quickly dashed when the director Jacques Becker[1] asked her to play the female lead, Marie, a prostitute, in *Casque d'Or*. Yet this prospect was not as discouraging as the mere thought that she would have to leave Montand's side for the filming. Her reaction was purely emotional, and an admittedly irrational reaction to an opportunity that would ultimately jumpstart her career, but the expectation of leaving Montand for the first time in two years caused such distress that Simone nearly quit before filming began.

Montand's reluctance to accept a lead role in *Wages of Fear* offered by the director, Henri-Georges Clouzot, was also emotional—but far from irrational. He was still haunted by memories of his earlier film endeavors in 1946, flops for the most part, which had shaken his confidence to the core. He had felt out of place and out of sync on the set of *Les Portes de la Nuit*, where he fumbled lines and missed his marks; any hope of launching a film career died there. Five years later, he was undoubtedly a rising performer in the music world, with no need to venture into a risky business. But his recent success was generating new interest, and he was flooded with offers from studios anxious to cash in on his popularity.

Montand finally accepted two film opportunities, both fun walk-on roles that were well within his comfort zone. In 1950, he was a street singer in *Paris Always Sings*, and then early in 1951 he portrayed himself in the low-budget Franco-Italian comedy, *Paris Is Always Paris*. But when

Clouzot insisted that he take the lead as Mario in *Wages of Fear*, Montand balked.

Clouzot, who was known both on and off the set as a quarrelsome and moody man, would not take no for an answer. He was convinced that Montand needed to work under a director willing to invest time developing the actor, and he was willing to coach Montand personally before the filming began. This arrangement left one more obstacle to overcome. The story takes place in South America, but for budget reasons Clouzot wanted to film closer to home, in Spain. Montand hesitated until Simone explained that as long as Franco remained the fascist leader of that country, they could not in good conscience set foot in Spain. Clouzot reluctantly moved the production to Camargue, on the Rhone River in southwestern France. Filming was set to begin August 27, 1951.

Simone accompanied Montand and was in seventh heaven on location, thoroughly enjoying being part of a company. From the camaraderie and practical jokes among actors, to the friendships that evolved, she had all the benefits without the responsibility of work. Clouzot's wife, Vera, had a lead role in the film, and though Simone found her irritating at times, the two struck up a friendship and spent time shopping. And when Montand had a break in the action, Simone was at his side, content to knit or crochet, always observing, unobtrusive but ever present.

A month into filming *Wages*, in September 1951 Simone was scheduled to catch a late afternoon train back to Paris for her film, *Casque d'Or*. Montand accompanied her to the train station, and during the journey she was unable to contain her emotion. "I was blubbering," she admitted. Her tears began when she said goodbye to the cast and crew of *Wages* and only intensified. For two full years, she and Montand had not been apart, and the separation imposed on them by her film was like a prison sentence. By the time the train pulled into the station, Simone was so distraught and irrational that on the spur of the moment she decided she simply wasn't going. Montand's coaxing had no effect, and the couple returned to their hotel in Nîmes.

When she returned to the hotel, Simone received a hero's welcome from the film crew, which was impressed that she had done the unthinkable. However, her agent, Paulette Dorisse, was outraged. She had never heard of such a stunt and wasn't looking forward to breaking the news to director Jacques Becker.[2] Simone remained defiant. The next day, however, her resolve weakened as she waited for the phone call notifying her that she would be sued for breach of contract. Hours dragged on without a call. Then, almost to her relief, Jacques Becker finally phoned and she steeled herself for an argument. However, much to her surprise, Becker was calm and collected. There was no cajoling or threats; he had another strategy. He completely understood her position. Love was infinitely more important than anything else, and she had no cause to worry because he already had two other actresses in mind for the role. Simone was stunned by the idea that she could be so easily replaced. She was back in Paris the next day and reported for work. Later, she was grateful she had changed mind. *Casque d'Or* was, in her opinion, "the finest film I ever made."

She had never worked for Becker and was unfamiliar with his style or methods. But she had met him several times, and she described their interactions as a three-act play—though from her account, they seemed more a comedy of errors. During the Occupation, a friend had put in a good word for her with Becker, and she then received an invitation to audition for his latest film, *Dernier Atout*. When she arrived Becker was incredulous, because he didn't recall inviting her. And, when he learned that Simone had no film credits to speak of, he rejected her before she had a chance to read lines, encouraging her to attend a drama school. As she walked out dejected, Becker stopped her and asked her to turn around, commenting that she was photogenic before he finally dismissed her. Yet, he still rejected her.

She met Becker again while filming *Les Visiteurs du Soir*. When he saw her, he thought she was someone else and expressed surprise that she hadn't bothered to tell him she was in town. Simone had no idea what he was talking about and questioned him. He thought she was someone else, Becker explained. Simone reminded him that she was the girl he had rejected before giving her the chance to audition, telling her to come back after she attended acting school. And Simone reminded him of this second encounter when they met again after the Occupation, and then again as he examined the roots of her newly bleached hair for *Casque d'Or*. Becker had personally picked her up at the train station and brought her directly to the hairdresser, where he insisted on a platinum-blonde dye job for her role.

Becker kept Simone on such a tight schedule, both in production and with publicity, she was sure he did it to keep her from grieving about her separation from Montand. In the November 17, 1951, edition of *Cinémonde*, a feature article with photos chronicled "24 hours in the life of Simone Signoret." The photographer, Michel Rivoire, captured Simone reading her mail first thing in the morning as the hotel's housekeeper made up the bed. On the wall next to her bed, Simone had pinned up six photographs of Montand. With the help of the article's author, F. G. Gohier, who provided commentary, Simone was captured drawing her bath and putting on shoes, (she wore tweed slacks, the caption explained). She then ate lunch with her co-stars Serge Reggiani and Claude Dauphin (she preferred steak frites), and later was photographed being besieged by cameras and recording equipment for a television and radio interview. Finally, Simone was photographed in bed with her back to the camera, so that she faced the wall in order to view Montand's photos as she fell asleep.

"Today we're going to have fun," Simone heard from Becker every day before work began on the set of *Casque d'Or* at Paris Cinema Studios. Though she missed Montand, the twenty-nine-year-old couldn't help but give in to the story—which she described as a labor of love—and to Becker's masterful direction and management of her activities. She loved the story of *Casque d'Or*, the "golden helmet," a reference to Marie's platinum hair, swept up in a tight, sculptured bun that sat atop her head like a golden helmet. Simone emerged in this film a golden goddess, an iconic image of the actress at the peak of beauty and perfection.

The story, filmed in black and white, was set in the underworld of the 1900s, where the mobster Félix Luca, played by Claude Dauphin, controls a gang of marauders, the local businesses, and the women he desires most. He keeps a watchful eye on Marie, who is involved in a loveless relationship with one of his patsies, "Pretty Boy" Roland, an obnoxious cad who orders her around with the snap of his fingers and who punishes her with slaps across the face. When Marie falls in love with a local carpenter, Georges Manda, played by Simone's close friend Serge Reggiani, the love affair becomes a dark story of jealousy, treachery, revenge, and death. It was a tragic and pessimistic story in the best tradition of the poetic realism of the 1930s, a genre that was beginning to define Simone's film career. She was nearly always cast as a woman who lives without love, but who finds it and then loses it, often through circumstances beyond her control.

The dialogue in *Casque d'Or* was so tight and so sparing, with emotion expressed almost entirely through body language, that it could easily have been a silent film. Several directors had toyed with the idea of making this film, including Simone's ex-husband, Yves Allégret. After his death on January 31, 1987, Catherine discovered that he had held on to the script, which she found in a trunk while sorting through his belongings. The story of how he lost out on the film is unknown, but it was obviously something he regretted.

Simone enjoyed making the film, but she had no regrets on days off when she took the train back to Montand, who was still filming *Wages of Fear*. Her quick retreat back to Montand during her free time was frustrating for her partner, Serge Reggiani, who had to waltz with Simone in the opening scene, which was already an awkward task, because prior to filming he had broken his leg while hiking and was in a cast. Simone couldn't dance and wasn't interested in spending free hours learning. So, Serge had to compensate by carrying Simone through the entire dance. "I'd decided on a certain posture: one arm hanging straight down and the other carrying Simone. Luckily, the dresses were long, so it wasn't too visible."[3] Indeed, Manda and Marie twirl around the dance floor as though they were both light on their feet, a passionate energy palatable between them.

Although she enjoyed the camaraderie and fun on the set, the most memorable experience was an unsettling incident that became a turning point in her career as an actress. She experienced "dissociation" for the first time. As she described it, the woman who normally helped with costume changes was out sick, and her replacement was unfamiliar with the continuity. After helping Simone struggle into a corset, dress, and accessories, she handed her a pair of shoes. But there was one incident that she thought most important, one that changed her opinion about acting. As she explained it, the character Marie had two pairs of shoes for the film, one brown pair for everyday use and the other black patent leather pair for dressier occasions. So, when the substitute dresser handed Simone the black patent leather shoes designated for the scene, Simone declined them, stating that she was going to wear the brown ones that evening. Since filming was not scheduled for the evening, the dresser was confused and questioned her.[4]

Simone had spoken in character when she referred to the shoes and was startled when she realized what she had done, but she decided to keep the experience to herself. Later, Serge Reggiani admitted that he had a similar experience with dissociation. There was a magical quality to the film that allowed the actors to become so deeply involved in the story that their characters took control. It was an instructive period for both of them, one that led Simone to toy with the idea that the character gets under the actor's skin and takes possession. This was such a firm belief that later in life, Simone bristled when others spoke of method acting as a process one undertakes to create the emotions or thoughts of a character—in essence getting under the character's skin: "What does that mean, the skin of a character? There is no skin because it is fiction.

Her skin . . . it's your skin. It's your hands, your head with its wrinkles that she takes. And, this woman—the character—she is your tenant. She moves in, and damn her, she often moves in a very cumbersome way."[5] But in *Casque d'Or*, this new experience with her "tenant" was a startling revelation, and she continued to pay close attention to signs that her character was taking control. She learned to allow the evolution without interference. "There are two schools of thought," she wrote reflectively twenty-five years later in *Nostalgia*. "There are those actors who explain to you that they know exactly how they're going to do the part . . . . And then there is the other method, which is to have no method at all. This is mine."

✣

Simone and Montand considered the institution of marriage rather bourgeois. But, Catherine had started school in 1951, and the couple felt that it was in her best interest that they legitimize their union. Simone always feared that her daughter would face undue criticism as a result of her public status. So after the filming of *Casque d'Or* and *Wages*, the couple planned a simple civil wedding, which was conducted by the mayor of Saint-Paul de Vence at 11:00 am on December 22, 1951. They kept things simple, avoiding any hint of ostentation. Simone wore a cream and black silk suit and fur coat. Her hair, still blonde from *Casque d'Or*, was covered by a simple black hat. Montand wore a blue suit. Neither the bride nor the groom had family members present. Jacques Prévert served as Simone's witness, while Montand's friend Paul Roux, owner of the Columbe d'Or Hotel, served as his best man. After the ceremony, the couple, surrounded by photographers and reporters, walked to their reception dinner at the hotel.

The dinner party was a small, tightknit group. The actress Deanna Durbin, who Simone had admired as a teenager, was there by default because she was staying at the Columbe d'Or at the time. The artist André Verdet and members of the Roux family were present, along with the filmmaker and author Marcel Pagnol and his family. Catherine, who was still considered too young to sit with adults, was present but out of sight. Pablo Picasso had sent regrets, but his chauffer delivered a flair pen drawing of a dove, which he dedicated to them with well wishes from both him and his mistress, Françoise Gilot. According to Simone, the gift arrived at exactly the same time that a dove flew into the dining room, nearly landing on her head. They considered the dove a sign of good things to come.[6]

They took two weeks off before Montand's engagement in Brussels, where *Casque d'Or* was also premiering in 1952. They watched the audience reaction, which was easy enough to read: People shifted in their seats and yawned throughout the film. *Casque d'Or* faired much the same in France, where there wasn't one aspect of it that the critics did not ravage, from the lighting and dialogue to the plot, which they regarded as an affront to the working class. Audiences shared the same feeling. In short, they hated it. They were expecting a thrilling gangster movie, not a romance. Serge Reggiani received the brunt of criticism, because he appeared too mild-mannered and tender. Indeed, the criticism was so severe that he was unable to find work for the next five years.

Yet, *Casque d'Or* enjoyed international acclaim, particularly in Germany, Britain, Italy, and the United States, where Simone and Reggiani were lauded as "an unforgettable couple." Although film critic Pauline Kael did not like the film, she applauded Simone's performance in her book, *Kiss, Kiss, Bang, Bang*: "Simone Signoret had her finest role (until *Room at the Top*) as the gigolette with the glorious helmet of golden hair . . . . Her performance [is] a triumph of sensuality and physical assurance." The film was so well received in Britain that Simone was nominated for and won an award as best foreign actress in a lead role from the British Academy of Film and Television Awards in 1952.

Montand did not fare quite as well with *Wages of Fear*,[7] but audiences were happy to see the man who sang to the hearts of the working class on the silver screen. Overall, this first major film endeavor had been a positive experience, and he had avoided the total damnation of critics, which bolstered his confidence and renewed his interest in pursuing acting as a career between concert appearances.

Married life suited Simone—so much so, that in early 1952 she announced her retirement from cinema so that she could settle down and devote all of her time to her husband. The decision was widely applauded in the press. How admirable that a wife could be so self-sacrificing, willing to give up a blossoming career for her husband. Simone and Montand were touted as the "ideal couple," an inspiration to all. While friends supported Simone's decision, they were skeptical. "Simone, give up making movies? I didn't believe that for a second," said Simone's friend, the actress Danielle Delorme. "She loved it too much, acting, but also all that went with it. Of course there was a time when Montand came before everything else, but she needed to show him who she was."[8]

Simone needed to show him that she was capable of being what she preferred to think of as a "Mediterranean wife," devout, dependent, obedient and faithful. However, this role would take some getting used to, because for all her bravado, Simone had begun to live in a way that completely contradicted her independent and strong-willed nature.

During 1952, the couple focused entirely on Montand's singing career. Simone observed all of his rehearsals and gave honest and reliable feedback, which Montand took seriously, making alterations to his act as needed. They went on tour, and she was present at every performance. During the second to last song, she quietly made her way backstage so she could be in the dressing room to hand him a towel. She reveled in serving as his "groupie," a term she enjoyed using to describe her devotion.

On the home front, Montand's brother Julian, his wife Elvire, and their son, Jean-Louis, were living in disastrous conditions without utilities and shower facilities. When Montand and Simone discovered these living conditions, they invited the Livi family to move into an apartment on the fifth floor of Place Dauphine. Once settled, the extended family unit gathered for meals, a completely new experience for Simone, who didn't cook, and more often than not, took meals on the run or in restaurants.[9]

During Simone's year of early retirement while she traveled with Montand on tour, she was torn by responsibilities at home and finally appealed to Elvire, suggesting an affable agreement: Elvire would quit her job, manage Simone's household, and care for Catherine. The impact of this decision was best described in 1994 by Catherine in her book, *Les Souvenirs et les regrets*: "I was nourished, dressed, shod, and loved with the greatest of care by a mother who did what she could, and whose greatest act of maternal love was to have enough humility to recognize that I would be better off raised and cared for by Tatie and Tonton on the 5th floor than in the little bedroom-office of the first floor that was to become their 'trailer.'" Catherine was packed up and moved out of her parent's apartment, then moved upstairs, where she shared an attic bedroom with her adoptive cousin, Jean-Louis. "Tatie and Tonton" were terms of endearment for Aunt Elvire and Uncle Julien. But Elvire become more than an adoptive aunt; Catherine considered her a second mother. "I loved this woman more than my mother for many years. I told her and she always said to me that a mother is a mother forever, and we only have one. . . . and she was right." With Catherine firmly entrenched in a family unit, Simone and Montand were free to travel without concern.

Montand's singing career took a decidedly left turn in 1952, when he sang at an anti-military rally protesting France's involvement in Vietnam. He introduced a controversial song, "Quand un Soldat" (When a Soldier), a pacifist anti-war ballad written by Francis Lemarque, a lyricist who had written several of Montand's top hits. The right-wing supporters of the war took offense and rallied support against Montand. The song was banned from the radio, and during a concert tour, in every town, Montand was greeted by angry mobs outside theaters and assaulted by passive-aggressive actions intended to distract the singer during shows. He kept his cool during these interruptions but was convinced that if protestors had jumped on stage, he would have throttled them. Stink bombs were thrown into a theater, his posters outside were tarred, and he received a series of death threats.

The message was loud and clear: Disagreement with the government was not acceptable. The similarity between the conservative mentality in France and the repression exercised in the United States under Senator Joseph McCarthy was unmistakable. However, Montand was not fazed by the attacks. He continued his tour, while "Quand un Soldat" quickly rose in popularity, eventually topping the charts.

CHAPTER 14

Thérèse Raquin

BY EARLY 1953, SIMONE HAD BEEN OUT OF WORK FOR EIGHTEEN months entirely by choice. There were offers after *Casque d'Or*, but she had no intention of breaking her retirement vow. She wanted to be free to follow her husband's concert tours and did so, until it became abundantly clear to her that her constant presence was getting on Montand's nerves. While he was by her definition a traditional "Mediterranean husband," both possessive and jealous, Montand held more liberal views on women working, and it irked him that Simone seemed to be throwing a promising career away without a care. She was by no means lazy, he knew, yet she seemed lackadaisical about her career, content to sit knitting, reading, or entertaining their extended family of friends. In contrast, Montand by his own admission was a workaholic, concerned about every opportunity and focused on perfection. He simply could not understand his wife's attitude. Later, her stop-and-start treatment of her career would be the source of vigorous arguments between them. However, in those early months of 1953 he bit his tongue until he could no longer bear it.

The breaking point—or "small household incident," as Simone called it—occurred while Montand and his musicians were rehearsing in the apartment. Simone was there, quietly knitting, when Montand realized that he was missing notes for lyrics, which he was sure he'd left on the piano. Someone must have moved them. Simone could laugh about the incident later, but she wasn't laughing when Montand flew into a rage of frustration, screaming at fever pitch, his arms flailing at his horrified musicians, who only watched, daring not to comment. Simone ignored the tantrum and continued knitting, oblivious to the fact that the clicking of knitting needles was as irritating as nails scratching a blackboard. Finally, Montand turned his anger on Simone. After watching her knit a few moments, he questioned why she was just sitting there. She explained that she was there because she wanted to be—if not, she'd be working. Montand reminded her, snidely, that she couldn't work unless someone offered her a role. His words cut to the quick, but she wasn't going to give in easily. She said that if she wanted, she could be Thérèse, referring to the most recent role she had categorically turned down: Marcel Carné's adaptation of the Emile Zola novel, *Thérèse Raquin*. Montand sneered, sharing a rumor he claimed was circulating: The producer didn't really want her for the role, and another actress was chosen over Simone. She was sure it wasn't true, but not wanting to take any chances, she made a quick phone call to producer Robert Hakim, who assured her that the part was hers. Marcel Carné agreed, and the script and contract would be put in the mail.

Simone wrote about this "household incident" with humor, yet at the time it was an instructive episode. The thirty-one-year-old was mature enough to understand that she was suffocating Montand, and that it was healthy for couples to have space and different interests. Yet, she feared separation, and this fear was deeper than the prospect of missing the man she loved. In truth, she dreaded the thought that she might lose him to another woman, and this was not an unrealistic fear. While Montand demanded fidelity from his wife, the rules against extra-marital affairs did not apply to him. He didn't cheat, in his view, because that would involve more than just casual sex, and he wasn't interested in a prolonged, complex affair. He loved Simone. However, when left on his own, he simply could not and would not resist the temptation of what he referred to as "adventures" with the ladies who lined up outside his dressing room to greet him. Simone knew that the movie set was also fertile ground for passionate affairs spawned by the heat of the moment. But backstage at the music hall, the sheer volume of prospective adventures was unnerving.

If she had to accept Montand's affairs, then they had to establish ground rules acceptable to both of them. He promised that he wouldn't engage in affairs that disrupted their marriage, and he agreed to leave her friends alone—particularly her two closest friends, the actresses Danièle Delorme and Jeanne Moreau.[1] This arrangement was not something Simone would discuss openly during those early years of marriage and oddly enough, turning a blind eye to her husband's indiscretions contributed to their image as an ideal couple. It was admirable that a loving wife was willing to give up her career for her husband and also understand the need for his indiscretions. But the image defied the turmoil Simone felt but could not express until much later, when she admitted, "The truth is I don't work much because I have a husband and a marriage to hold together."[2] And when she had doubts, she blamed herself entirely. She was simply a jealous wife, and jealousy was unhealthy in a relationship.

❧

Thérèse Raquin, originally released as *The Adulteress*, is a dark drama that departed from the Zola novel, adding a treacherous twist to the story of Thérèse, a young woman in a loveless marriage to her first cousin. Camille Raquin is a sickly, whimpering man who holds his overbearing mother and wife hostage to his fainting and spells. His mother dotes on his every need, and Thérèse, strained and depressed, is considered an ungrateful interloper in their relationship. When she falls in love with an Italian truck driver, Laurent, played by Raffaele "Raf" Vallone, the adulterous couple becomes embroiled in the accidental murder of her husband.

Carné's interpretation differed significantly from the original Zola novel, but it was still well received. Instead of the ghost of Camille, who haunts his wife and her lover, Carné added a witness to Camille's murder, and the lovers fall prey to blackmail. Filming, in black and white, began on March 2, 1953, with indoor footage shot in Neuilly-sur-Seine and exterior footage shot in Lyon. Simone did not share in the usual camaraderie on the set. She had to play a dark and challenging character with few lines; emotion was expressed continually in the strained body language she exhibited during constant screen presence. She spoke highly of her co-star, Raf Vallone. However, she drew the line on what could have become one of those movie set affairs she spoke of, making it clear to Vallone that she loved Montand and was not available. Vallone, an Italian, understood the perils of interfering with the wife of a jealous Italian hsuband.[3]

While she filmed in France, Montand was off to Rome with her close friend Danièle Delorme, filming *Tempi nostri*, a low budget film that was of little consequence to their careers. Although he admitted in his biography that "temptation gnawed at him," and he sensed, at least on his part, "an unsettling quality to their companionship," Montand respected the rules Simone had set out regarding affairs with her friends. Instead, he took time out to visit his birthplace.

Simone was pregnant during the filming of *Thérèse Raquin*. She barely showed and could easily hide the pregnancy with the sweaters or coat she nearly always wore on screen. But her condition added another dimension to the physical and psychological demands of her role, which took a tragic toll. When she returned home in August 1953, six months pregnant and exhausted, she suffered a miscarriage. She never shared the details of her miscarriage. It was Montand who discussed it publicly, both in the press and in his biography. There were, in fact, two miscarriages in the early years of their marriage, both occurring during the sixth month of pregnancy: one following *Thérèse Raquin*, the other much earlier. Montand was not clear about dates. During an interview in 1966, he suggested that he and Simone could have had two children, one who would be sixteen at the time, the other fourteen years of age.[4] For her part, Simone did not speak of miscarriages until much later in life, when she participated in a rally with the *Liberation de la Femme* (MLF), the women's movement in France, on behalf of abortion rights. Then, she said, "Let she who has never had a miscarriage shut up. I've had them, and the MLF protestors deserve everybody's support."[5] Until then, the miscarriages were private losses and immense disappointments, because Simone desperately wanted to give Montand children.

While she convalesced in a private clinic, Montand returned to Paris to prepare for another concert at the Etoile Theater, scheduled to open on October 5, 1953. He experimented with the program, choosing a song and dance formula that turned out to be a recipe for unprecedented success. His two-hour show was divided into four parts: one quarter popular themes; one quarter poetry—both spoken and sung—with a particular preference for the poems of Jacques Prévert; one quarter comedic sketches; and one quarter dedicated to political songs.[6] Rehearsals were intense, and Montand went on a strict diet and exercise regimen to improve his endurance. His sister-in-law Elvire cooked for him, but the family kept their distance, respecting his need to focus.

As a perfectionist, he always worried about minute details—a misstep or an off key note. These mistakes were intolerable during rehearsals, where he worked his orchestra until they achieved perfection. However, on stage, in the passion of the moment, anything could go wrong, and he was fearful of a mishap with his new show format. There was no need to worry. The show was flawless; the audience loved it, and he was treated to thunderous applause. After that, he retreated backstage. When the audience realized that he wasn't returning, they began whistling and booing; Montand could have performed all evening. Although he was booked at the Etoile for only three weeks, the engagement was extended, and he performed over two hundred concerts from October 1953 through early April 1954. He was no longer a lounge lizard. This was a turning point in the singer's career.

∗૮

The couple handled money cautiously, because if one is not careful, money corrupts the soul. Simone harped on this truism with friends throughout her life. Proof of it was evident in the excesses of the bourgeoisie, whom Simone and Montand despised, preferring to align themselves with the working class. While they had hired help to manage the household and business affairs, this was a matter of necessity, not an excess that set them apart and above others. And, they were careful to refer to hired help as employees, not servants. One dared not use the word servant in their household.

Simone also tried to distance herself from the bourgeoisie in issues of child rearing. Catherine was never allowed to feel that she was privileged in any way. She attended public school, and she did not have birthday parties, which were regarded as unnecessary extravagance, as were Christmas and summer camp. Children did not sit at the dining room table with adults until they were old enough to sit and eat properly, without assistance—at least that was the case for Catherine, who spent her early years in the kitchen dining alone or with the housekeeper. When Catherine was old enough, Simone insisted that her daughter learn to do housework, which Catherine hated as much as any child. However, Simone seemed to push her daughter to the limit with her expectations. Catherine was required to serve the housekeeper her parents hired to assist their cook, Marcelle. She was required to make the maid's bed and clean her bathroom. Before she lived upstairs with Montand's family at Place Dauphine, she was expected to make her own breakfast in the morning, as well as the housekeeper's. She then woke the housekeeper, before washing the dishes and leaving for school. Catherine said she felt that she was "the maid's maid." Simone would leave two notes in the morning: one for Catherine, encouraging her to do well in school and signed with hugs and kisses; the other note was for the housekeeper, with wake-up call instructions. Catherine would later be criticized for revealing these memories of her relationship with a well-respected icon. In the view of many, Simone could do no wrong. But Simone's child-rearing practices were arguably unusual and filled with contradictions. At times, Simone was much like her own father: rarely home, self-absorbed, and self-indulgent. Yet, unlike André, Simone did not see the value of offering a child piano lessons and private schools. Like Georgette, who was infinitely more attentive than she, and an ever-present authority figure, Simone shared her mother's disgust for the excesses of the bourgeois and was strict and unyielding on matters of proper behavior and etiquette, with a firmly held belief that children should not be waited on.

Regardless of the reasons for the behavior, the often stringent insistence that Catherine never be allowed to feel privileged was somehow viewed as the couple's most outward expression of their solidarity with the working class. But when the press saw a disparity between Simone and Montand's professed beliefs and their lifestyles, they were not focusing on childrearing philosophy. Simone liked fur coats and jewelry; Montand had his Bentley and tailored suits. They spared no expense on luxury and lived comfortably. It irked Simone when the press painted her as the mistress in her fur coat sending the servant out to buy a copy of *L'Humanité*, the French Communist Party daily newspaper. She resented the implication that her solidarity was anything less than sincere.

After Montand's successful concerts and record sales, he and Simone decided to purchase a second home, one far enough away from Paris to feel as though they had a getaway, but still close enough to the action in the city. In early 1954, they found the perfect home, Autheuil, a country estate in Normandy, only fifty-five miles from Paris. Simone rationalized the purchase: "The place symbolizes luxury for us, but not in the usual sense of the word as applied to a house. It symbolizes the luxury of being able to buy something with the fruit of one's labor, rather than to labor in order to buy something. That's what we mean by luxury; it's a very important notion to us."[7] Simone was the first to admit that their purchasing power really was the fruits of Montand's labor. While she earned a comfortable living from her own work, she didn't work enough to live in luxury. Owing to Montand's healthy income, she had the freedom to work when she pleased and to pick and choose roles. This freedom she also considered "an important notion." It was something she had learned from Prévert: Live a life in which you are free to choose and free to refuse. She had no need to chase after a role or worry if she wasn't offered one. She could afford to wait until a director envisioned her in a role, and she'd choose only those parts that she could put her heart and soul into, something with a good story. She was well aware that many of her closest friends were not in a position to choose, and that her luxuries created a stark contrast with her friends' lives. So, she was generous with Autheuil and with her money.

Autheuil was a magnificent yet simply designed twenty-four-room, two-level white house with a full attic and a terrace. It included a farm adjacent to the property, complete with barn, cows, and sheep. The rooms on the first floor were expansive and bright, with old, cracked ceramic floor tiles and plaster walls that showed signs of patching—this gave the house charm and a lived-in look. When they discovered the house, the couple rushed back to Paris to find Marcelle Mirtilon, their cook at Place Dauphine, and her husband Georges. The Mirtilons were both born and raised in Normandy and jumped at the chance when they were asked to become the caretakers of Autheuil. Marcelle handled cooking and light household matters, while Georges handled the farm and property. The Mirtilons were faithful employees, never servants—though at times during disagreements they felt they worked for bourgeois bosses. However, they stayed on at Autheuil, and their relationship with Simone and Montand would remain intact for more than thirty-five years.

Simone eagerly took on the task of decorating. She sewed window treatments and shopped the antique stores looking for furniture. She and Montand took over the bedroom on the first level. Catherine had a room on the second level, along with a housekeeper who helped Marcelle. The other bedrooms were constantly filled with guests. Simone envisioned this home as a more elaborate version of the "trailer" at Place Dauphine. Here, there was room to house simultaneously any number of artists, including directors and actors, writers and painters, and musicians. She envisioned Autheuil as a retreat, a place to write, rehearse, or simply rest, and the house was full to capacity whenever possible, particularly on weekends.

Serge Reggiani, who was unable to find work in the wake of the severe reviews of *Casque d'Or*, and the director Jacques Becker, who suffered his own career challenges after the film bombed in France, both lived at Autheuil for a time. However, Simone never wanted her extended family to feel that they were guests; they were family. The house was as much their home as hers, and her guests were free to enjoy life at Autheuil with no strings attached. It was communal living at its best, with unending laughs, well-played pranks, impromptu skits, and vigorous arguments that quickly blew over. Simone, who was often described as "tribal" in nature, was in her element as the central casting director of life at Autheuil. She carefully chose her guests, which included trusted friends—predominately male—and their lovers.

While Montand was affable, usually serving as the instigator of pranks and endless poker games, there were times when he felt out of sorts with the arrangement. It occurred to him that this close-knit group of friends was really Simone's from the start. And though their guests were now his friends, too, he sometimes felt disconnected, particularly when it came to their intellectual pursuits. He was always self-conscious about his lack of education. He'd heard criticisms in the past, such as "Simone is the brains, Montand the brawn." What worried him most was that he really did not share certain interests—books most of all—with his wife and friends, who read constantly, devouring a book in a sitting. Montand struggled through at a slower pace—sticking to it, though he lost interest. By the time he read through the last page of one book, the others were discussing another over glasses of cognac or wine. He couldn't keep up.

Montand honestly believed he felt no resentment towards Simone and fully appreciated the depth of her intellect. She was sensitive to his inferiority complexes and made efforts to include her husband in everything, bolstering his ego when needed. Although he had obvious difficulty expressing ideas, she sensed instinctively that the "brawn" criticism was unfair. Montand was instinctual, and his-down-to- earth, pragmatic views balanced her sometimes-lofty pretensions. Simone often joked that while she appeared competent in daily matters, when it came to a crisis, she completely fell apart and relied on Montand, who handled intense situations deftly and sensibly.

Yet, in contrast to her image as a supportive wife, Simone also had a habit of correcting her husband's word choices and pronunciation while he spoke, a tendency as irritating to those who witnessed it as it was to Montand. According to his biographers, Montand felt that Simone sometimes used their friends to make a point when she was critiquing his song or dance routines. She was his best critic, strongly invested in his performances and providing insightful suggestions for improvement, which he valued. But she could also be controlling and pushy, and it did not go without notice that their friends tended to endorse her suggestions when she was driving her point home. She was open to creative criticism from him, but somehow, this did not level the playing field between them, and he was becoming sensitive to other flaws in her nature, which led to bickering and sometimes to monumental screaming matches.

While he could not always articulate the irritations early on in the marriage, he was quick to produce a list years later, when the couple was interviewed for the June 4, 1963, issue of *Cinémonde* magazine:

She is intelligent, scatterbrained, disorganized, and undisciplined only in work. She is lazy except for in her work. She is easygoing, but perhaps, from time to time, disagreeable and aggressive. She is frank, honest, gossipy, a real chatterbox. She lacks perseverance. She is without ambition, never sets herself a precise goal. Incapable of playing a mean trick on anyone, but does hold a grudge. Loyal in friendship and in love. Absolutely not bossy, in spite of appearances. When she receives a bad blow, she sits down and cries. She smokes way too much. She has a habit of opening several packs of cigarettes at the same time and leaving them all over the house.

Still, overall, their differences were not such a major concern that they could not enjoy life at Autheuil with their extended family. Catherine joined them on weekends and school vacations, and though Simone was not one for extravagances, she had a swing set built for her daughter's benefit. Catherine hadn't asked for it; a swing set was something Simone had admired as a child when she visited her friend's country homes.

In an odd way, Simone hoped that she could make up for her lack of maternal attentiveness by exposing her daughter to their unique family of prominent artists, who doted on the child. Simone would have loved this opportunity when she was child. Unfortunately, it was not as impressive to the young Catherine as it would become later on during adulthood, when she fully understood the significance of her association with these famous people. These relationships with prominent adults did not really compensate for the loneliness she felt as one who seemed to stand on the outside looking in on the life of her parents. Yet, even from afar, one of her most prominent memories of life at Autheuil was that her parents were happy, and that the house was filled with the sound of her mother's laughter.

CHAPTER 15

Witches and Devils

DURING THE MONTHS THAT FOLLOWED HER TRAGIC SECOND MISCAR-riage, the only project that piqued Simone's interest was Arthur Miller's latest stage play, *The Crucible*, which had premiered in the United States in 1953 to mixed reviews. The obvious political overtones of the play were of great interest to John Berry and Jules Dassin, two American film directors who had taken refuge in France after they were blacklisted in Hollywood. But though they raved about it and promised Simone a copy of the translation, they were never able to make good on the promise. Then, months later, Simone and Montand were contacted by Elvire Popesco, a Romanian-born French actress and stage director who called with news that she planned to produce the play and wanted the couple in the lead roles of Elizabeth and John Procter. She also promised a translation, but that never materialized.

In early summer 1954, Simone and Montand received a call from A. M. Julien, director of the Théâtre Sarah-Bernhardt. He had procured the script from Popesco, and now he announced his desire to produce the play. They read it in bed after Montand's performance at the Etoile Theater and were so engrossed that they passed the pages back and forth, reading it through until they finished at five am the next morning, feeling exhausted but exhilarated. This was a play for them, its contemporary theme of false accusations and repression driving right to the heart of their growing discontent with American politics, where Senator Joseph McCarthy had taken center stage with his own brand of witch-hunts.

It was not difficult for them to see the connection between John and Elizabeth Proctor, the fictionalized Puritan victims of the Salem Witch trials, and Julius and Ethel Rosenberg, American Jews who had recently been executed for allegedly selling plans for the atomic bomb to Russia. Nerves were still raw from those executions, which had occurred a year earlier, on June 19, 1953. Their executions were considered politically motivated, even among those who believed that the Rosenbergs were guilty. There were far too many unanswered questions about the trial and about Ethel's brother, David Greenglass, who had indeed sold plans to the Russians and when caught, cut a deal with the government to save his wife, Ruth, from being charged as an accessory. In return for her freedom, David and Ruth accused Ethel and Julius of being accomplices in what would be called the great "atomic bomb conspiracy."

Regardless of political leanings and views about guilt or innocence, Simone and Montand shared a common French view that the death sentence was excessive; the punishment did not fit the crime. Many believed the Rosenbergs had been made into an example during the period of communist witch-hunts in America. This sentiment was particularly strong with regard to Ethel Rosenberg, who was arrested, tried, and convicted in the absence of convincing evidence that she was anything but a New York housewife bringing up two young children.[1] Ethel and Julius Rosenberg were executed by electrocution at Sing-Sing Prison in New York State on Friday, June 19, 1953, just before sundown, in observance of Jewish law. After Ethel's electrocution, the physician who examined her discovered that her heart was still beating, and a second shock was administered. *The Crucible* was in production that evening in the States, and Arthur Miller recalled that the moment John Proctor was hung during the performance, the audience stood up and bowed their heads in silence. "The Rosenbergs were at that moment being executed at Sing-Sing. Some of the cast had no idea what was happening as they faced rows of bowed and silent people and were informed in whispers by their fellows. The play then became an act of resistance for them."[2]

The play was now an act of resistance for Simone and Montand, who had supported the Rosenberg cause during fundraising events held on behalf of the Rosenberg children. Simone was always asked to read from the Rosenberg's death house letters at these events, but she couldn't do it. She refused to read the letters because they always evoked strong emotion, and she was fearful that the audience would focus more on her performance than on the content of the letters.[3] Instead, she chose to read Emile Zola's *Letter to Youth*, written on December 14, 1898, during the Dreyfus affair. She read the lengthy letter in its entirety, though any given passage conveys the central message that she felt would never lose its relevance:

Youth! Be always on the side of justice. If ever the idea of justice should grow dim within you, you would be a prey to every peril. I am not talking about the justice prescribed by our Codes of Law; that justice merely guarantees our social relationships. It must be respected, of course; but the justice I mean is a loftier notion. It lays down as a principle that all human judgment is fallible and deems it no insult to the judges to believe that a man found guilty may in fact be innocent.[4]

While it was not difficult to draw comparisons between the Procters and Rosenbergs, Arthur Miller insisted that he didn't write *The Crucible* to dramatize the Rosenberg case—or the issue of McCarthyism, for that matter. While researching the Salem witch-hunts of 1692–93, he became fascinated by the fact that after wild, unsubstantiated accusations were hurled at twenty farmers, they had been hanged by their neighbors. "The more I worked at this dilemma the less it had to do with Communists and McCarthy and the more it concerned something very fundamental in the human animal: the fear of the unknown, and particularly the dread of social isolation."[5] *The Crucible* was an expression of the human condition, because while Senator Joseph McCarthy was manufacturing accusations—often with nothing more than a suspicion—no one dared challenge him. Fear of communism in the United States was so palpable that college students turned in professors whose views were perceived as too liberal and therefore possibly communistic in nature, while others began to disassociate themselves from anyone accused of communist ties, real or imagined. They were fearful of guilt by association, a condition that had been running rampant in Hollywood since the end of World War II.

Ironically, while the House Un-American Activities Committee (HUAC) initiated blacklisting of suspected communists, the practice was widely supported by Hollywood producers, who agreed to enforce it. Countless artists were targeted, often because they gave a donation, attended a meeting, or purchased a newspaper that was deemed to have communist ties. Even former president Ronald Reagan, then president of the Screen Actors Guild, was called to testify before Congress. As an ardent anti-communist, he agreed to cooperate with HUAC and testified on October 23, 1947, providing specific information to Robert E. Stripling, HUAC's chief investigator—though much to his credit, he did not name names and cautioned the chairman about his vision of a "pure" America.[6]

However, Senator Joseph McCarthy believed in a "pure" America. As chair of the Senate Committee on Investigations, he believed the military had been infiltrated by communists and was hell-bent on proving it. With the assistance of J. Edgar Hoover, director of the FBI, all reports of suspected subversive activity, perceived or real, were investigated. Hoover encouraged American citizens to maintain vigilance, using the same doublespeak he accused communists of using.[7]

❧

In July 1954, with the French translation of *The Crucible* in hand and a production schedule developed, Simone and Montand were involved in securing a writer for the stage adaptation. Though they gave different accounts of what transpired—with Montand maintaining that he suggested the use of Jean-Paul Sartre and Simone indicating that doing so was Miller's idea—all agreed that Sartre seemed the obvious choice for a French adaptation. However, the philosopher and playwright's personal secretary declined on his behalf without ever asking his employer. In the end, they chose Marcel Aymé, another prominent novelist and playwright, to take on the task.

Simone was nervous about this new venture. While her husband was accustomed to performing on stage before a live audience, her only stage experience, at the Theatre des Mathurins during the Occupation, had been short-lived and disastrous (she was fired for laughing during a rehearsal). The stage was unfamiliar territory, but more importantly, Simone knew that her low, almost gravelly voice did not project well. This was never a concern in films. A soft, low voice was sensuous on tape, and she had mastered the use of body language so well that she had become a gifted communicator, capable of expressing more with a subtle raised eyebrow or smile than dialogue could possibly achieve. But Simone was so concerned she might not meet expectations that she insisted the director, Raymond Rouleau, avoid sparing her feelings if she did not measure up—even, she suggested, if it meant firing her. However, every effort was made to allay her fears. A low ceiling was installed on the set, and the technician constructed a voice resonance box, which would be carefully placed at her marks to help project her voice. Montand's concerns were far different, but nonetheless nerve wracking. While he was accustomed to appearing on stage, singing and dialogue were two entirely different things. He was so concerned about his diction that he leaned on actor friends for elocution lessons to help lessen the feeling he was speaking with a mouth full of gravel.

In the meantime, with rehearsals set for October 1954, Simone had three months on her hands. A break would normally be highly desirable, but she had not acted since her miscarriage and was ready to bury herself in work. When director Henri-Georges Clouzot called with an offer for his latest film project, *Les Diaboliques*, Simone thought there was enough time to squeeze in another production and readily accepted—then instantly regretted doing so.

Clouzot wasn't fond of Simone. He disliked her films and wasn't impressed with her talent. *Casque d'Or* was a travesty, he thought, and he did not spare her feelings, telling her that the film should be remade under his direction, with the actress Martine Carol in the central role. Although Simone was not one to speak harshly about another professional in public, she admitted that while Clouzot was a talented, first-rate director, he was nothing short of obnoxious, and so unreasonable and belligerent at times that during the months she spent with Montand on the set of *Wages of Fear*, she had told the director to go to hell on more than one occasion. Afterwards, they were forced to interact when Clouzot and his wife, Vera, began spending time at the Columbe d'Or.

In an effort to temper her criticism, she allowed herself to admire the insomniac who spent his sleepless nights conceiving new projects and learning new hobbies, ever vigilant in everything he touched. It was rumored that Clouzot had beat out Alfred Hitchcock in negotiations for the film rights to *Les Diaboliques*, based on the suspense novel *She Who Was No More*, by French authors Pierre Boileau and Thomas Narcejac. His adaptation was such a masterful formula, mixing base human emotion with psychological drama, that it set the standard for suspense films and did serve as a model for Hitchcock. However, on the film set, Clouzot's genius and attention to detail was a stress-producing formula, particularly for Simone. Simone was well aware that Clouzot wanted her for the part so that he could capitalize on her established name for his experiment in the suspense genre. He also wanted her because his wife Vera liked Simone. He had cast his wife in a lead role, though her only film credit was *Wages of Fear*. During that film, she and Simone struck up a friendship. Vera was so comfortable with Simone that she was the only actress Vera wanted to work with in this new venture.

While Clouzot was unendingly patient with his inexperienced wife, he completely lost patience with Simone. Beyond his obvious distaste for her professional abilities, Simone felt that he wasn't capable of separating their personal relationship at the Columbe d'Or from their professional life on the set. He judged Simone—unfairly she thought—based on weaknesses he perceived during their personal interactions. Clouzot couldn't distinguish between the personal and the professional Simone. Only later in her career was she able to see or understand that some of the director's concerns were legitimate. Simone's portrayal of Denise as a cold-hearted, scheming murderess was far too convincing. Denise was guilty, but Clouzot wanted that fact to be the twist at the end of the story; Simone was giving away the plot with her performance. But she couldn't see his point and found Clouzot's constant criticism unbearable. Finally, he erupted on the set, informing her that he regretted allowing her to read to the end of the script.[8]

Tensions intensified when delay after delay caused the production to drag on beyond the end of Simone's eight-week contract. Under normal circumstances, this extension would not have been a problem. But for the first time in her career, Simone hadn't paid attention to contract details, and when the production ran over, she discovered that Clouzot had a clause that obligated him to pay only for the eight weeks, with no provisions for delays or an extended schedule. By October 1954, sixteen weeks into the production, Simone was not only working for free, she had already missed the first week of rehearsals for *The Crucible*. After receiving a telegram ordering her to attend rehearsals, Simone had no choice but to keep pace with both productions. During the day, she played the murderess, and at night, she had to switch gears and became a strained, Puritan wife. During this period, Simone had stopped speaking to Clouzot and his wife.

While all agreed that they did not enjoy making *Diaboliques*, no one complained about the film's success at the box office in France and in the international market when the film was released the following year, in 1955. *Diaboliques* was considered a masterpiece, and while Clouzot was unhappy with Simone, her performance received positive reviews commending her for both depth and intelligence. Denise, with her short hair, tailored dress, and sturdy stride was far from the usual image Simone portrayed. But she was still a tart, far more evil and deceitful than usual, but with the same "sexual pathologies" that haunted her other characters.

The residuals earned from the film were generous enough to pay for an in-ground pool at Autheuil. The film, soon to be a classic in the suspense genre, would stand the test of time. *The Crucible* also turned out to be an unexpected and seemingly perpetual success.

CHAPTER 16

Disillusioned

ARTHUR MILLER DID NOT ATTEND THE OPENING NIGHT OF *THE CRUCIBLE*
in Paris. His passport was revoked after he refused to name names while
appearing before the House Un-American Activities Committee. Jean-
Paul Sartre attended the third performance and was so impressed that
he expressed disappointment he hadn't been asked to write the French
adaptation—only to be told that he had indeed been asked. His secretary
had screened the call and turned down the opportunity without consulting with his employer.

The play, billed as *Les Sourcières de Salem,* was such an unprecedented
success, its run was extended for 365 nights, split between two six-month
periods in 1954–55. In spite of their Puritan costumes, which constrained
movements and reminded Simone of figures in a Dutch painting, the cast
quivered with passion. Audiences were taken in, easily making connections to the Rosenberg trial and the dangers of political intolerance. Simone credited their impassioned performances to the director, Raymond
Rouleau, who had used the yellow star of the Occupation as a focal point
during rehearsals, speaking fervently of the Nazi tribunals, collaborators,
and the anonymous letters that had poured into Gestapo headquarters
from those willing to sell out their neighbors on a suspicion.

The cast was forced to take a break during the summer of 1955, because the Sarah Bernhardt Theater was booked for summer stock. Simone agreed to play Yvette, a French prostitute, in a film adaptation of
Bertolt Brecht's *Mother Courage.* Brecht's wife, Helen Weigel, who was
known as a first-rate stage actress, was scheduled to play Courage. Simone and the actor Bernard Blier considered it a great honor to be chosen as the only non-Germans to join Brecht's Berliner Ensemble for the

production. Filming was set in the east, in Babelsberg, the Hollywood of Germany before it was used to produce Hitler's propaganda films. Since the Berlin Wall had not yet been constructed, actors were given the choice of living in either East or West Berlin. Both Simone and Blier chose the East.

Her first indication that life in the East was not as idyllic as she expected under Russian rule occurred when she asked to use the phone to call home. She was politely informed that she could only make calls within East Berlin. However, the officials had a change of heart and finally arranged everything for her. Their lodgings in a traditional German gasthaus were located off the beaten path in a narrow alley. The accommodations were comfortable, and Simone enjoyed meeting and mingling with other guests. However, it was difficult to ignore the feeling of isolation created by the stockade fence that cordoned off the alley, its entrance guarded by a soldier with an aggressive German shepherd at his side.

One evening after a late dinner in the West, Simone and Blier returned to the alley only to have the guard refuse them entry. They explained their situation, but the guard would not budge. Blier lost his temper, and as Simone described it, screamed obscenities loudly in both French and German, and made references to the Nazi occupation, waking the residents along the alley. Lights were turned on by curious onlookers. Still, the guard refused to open the gate. Finally, a production assistant, known to them only as Fraulein Erika, came out to negotiate with the guard, and they were allowed to return to their gasthaus without further delay. The next day, the minister of culture apologized for the incident, promising that it wouldn't happen again. But Blier was so disgusted he packed up and moved to the West. Simone chose to remain in the alley, but the previous evening's incident raised concern. She did not realize that restrictions on movement between East and West Berlin were so stringent. It was clear now that the stockade fence was not a safety measure to protect people; it was a barrier, restricting free movement.

With only a few weeks left in the six-week schedule, filming was interrupted when Helen Weigel suddenly dropped out of the production without explanation. Only later did Simone learn about the political difficulties Weigel and Brecht suffered under Soviet rule. Simone assumed these problems caused Helene's sudden departure, as no other explanation was ever provided. In the meantime, the production could not secure a replacement for Weigel, and Simone was forced to finish her scenes with the script girl. The role of Courage was never filled, and the film was never completed.

The Crucible ended its run in December 1955, just in time for the Christmas holiday. The production was such a success that plans were underway for a film adaptation. This time Jean-Paul Sartre agreed to write the screenplay, and Simone and Montand were promised that the production schedule would be set around their schedules, as both had other commitments.

In early 1956, the couple traveled to Italy for Montand's latest film, *Uomini e lupi* (Men and Wolves). Simone remained with him, content to watch from the sidelines until March, when she was scheduled to leave for Mexico to film Luis Buñuel's *La Mort en ce Jardin* (*Death in the Garden*). She didn't want to go. She and Montand had never been separated by such distance for such a long time, three months. Simone knew about the time and the distance when she committed, yet when it was time to leave, it seemed to come as surprise. She considered breaking the contract, cried and fought the idea, before finally leaving, tearfully, for Mexico.

Death in the Garden was a French-Mexican co-production, based on a novel by Jose-Andre Lacour and directed by Luis Buñuel. Simone referred to him as "Don Luis," in recognition of his reputation as the father of cinematic surrealism. Although the film was not destined to be a great commercial success, it was classic Buñuel, with his themes of conflict between the classes, religious struggle, and the quest for salvation depicted through brutal surrealist imagery in brilliant Eastman color, the latest cinematic innovation.

Simone played yet another prostitute, Djin, who flees a South American mining post during a military coup with an unlikely band of evacuees that included a priest, a rogue adventurer, and a miner and his young daughter, who is a deaf-mute. The group flees into the unforgiving jungle without food or water and only the promise of reaching a safe haven to sustain them. It was a reunion of old friends for Simone. Castin, Djin's love interest, was played by French actor Georges Marchal. He and Simone had appeared together in her ex-husband's film, *Les Démons de l'Aube*. And, Charles Vanel, who played the old miner, had co-starred with Montand in *Wages of Fear*. In spite of her initial reluctance, Simone found filming a joyful experience. Buñuel gave free reign to his players, focusing primarily on their movements, while leaving the actors free to interpret their roles. He was also known to make quick work of filming, following the script and shooting in sequence; important changes were made in the editing room rather than through re-takes.

The jovial atmosphere among the actors, punctuated by water fights and practical jokes, was interrupted briefly by serious news from the Soviet Union. Reports of a speech attributed to but not officially made by Nikita Khrushchev in February had leaked out. Khrushchev had said Stalin was a tyrant, a "cult personality," and he renounced the former leader's reign of terror, giving details of Stalin's crimes against humanity. Though shocking, the news was not completely unexpected—particularly for Simone, who recalled her experiences in East Germany during the filming of *Mother Courage*. Montand heard the news in Italy, where he was still filming. He had not yet reached his wife's level of skepticism, and he listened intently to Italian communists who seemed quick to renounce Russia's "errors." When he returned to Paris, Communist Party members were still in a state of disbelief. His brother, Julien, an ardent communist, was so distraught that he wept. This reaction was shared by other comrades.

♣

Jean-Paul Sartre and Arthur Miller conferred by mail on the film adaptation of *The Crucible*, and by early summer 1956, the production was ready to begin filming on farmland in East Germany. The cast brought their children along. Catherine was allowed to accompany her parents on this trip. When Simone read the script, she thought the story was as close to the original as possible, though she agreed that Sartre had put a "Sartrian" spin on it. Miller concurred with that view: "Jean-Paul Sartre's screenplay . . . seemed to me to toss an arbitrary Marxist mesh over the story that led to a few absurdities. Sartre laid the witchcraft outbreak to a struggle between rich and poor peasants," a gloss that was inconsistent with the story. The Proctors were landowners, not poor peasants. "It amused me to see crucifixes on the farmhouse walls as they would be in French Catholic homes, but never of course, in a Puritan one." However, the film resonated with French audiences, and Miller was complimentary, particularly of Simone's performance. "Simone Signoret was immensely moving and the film had a noble quality,"[1] he explained.

For over a year Simone's interpretation of Elizabeth had been constrained to dialogue, and she struggled at first to reprise the role by "showing instead of telling." Montand had similar issues. At one point, the perfectionist director, Rouleau, insisted on a re-take of one scene so many times that Elizabeth's tears and John Procter's anger were no longer feigned for the camera. Those were but a few of the delays, which ranged from interruptions because farm animals walked into a scene unexpectedly, to lengthy discussions about how John Proctor looked during the hanging scene. Retakes were so excruciating that the summer season quickly passed, and October 1956 was upon them. Montand worried that they wouldn't finish in time for his next commitment; he had agreed to a four-month concert tour of Russia and the Eastern Bloc countries beginning November 6. He asked for a delay, and though the Russians agreed, they were not generous, giving him only until November 12. Under pressure, he finished his scenes for the day and then rushed off to meet his pianist, Bob Castella, for rehearsals. Both he and Simone, who planned to accompany her husband on this momentous tour, gave Rouleau daily reminders that he had to move things along. They were leaving whether the film was complete or not. The production finished in time, but as it turned out other events would delay Montand's plans.

In October 1956, a revolt against the communist government was brewing in Hungary, fueled by a successful worker revolt in Poland in June of that year. On October 23, discontentment finally erupted into a full-scale protest, as thousands of students marched through the streets of Budapest to the parliament building. They sent a contingent in to discuss their demands with government leaders, and the students were detained. When protestors demanded their release, the state security police were sent out to fire on the crowd. The offensive outraged citizens across the country, fueling violent protest in cities and towns, with demands for free elections and a withdrawal of Russian forces. Though the Politburo at first agreed to these demands, they suddenly reneged and called for military backup. On November 4, 1956, the Soviet army descended on Hungarian cities, using tanks to fire upon protestors. Over 2,500 Hungarian citizens were killed, and over 200,000 attempted to flee the country. A new Soviet-backed government was installed in January 1957.

Simone and Montand were glued to their television set whenever possible, horrified as they watched events unfold. This Russian suppression was the turning point for Simone. As her brother Jean-Pierre described it, her interest in communism—or "gauchism" as all left-wing philosophies were called—was "an affair of ideas and sentiments, and never involved belonging to an organization, or the acceptance of a discipline, or adherence to a theory." She was not a communist and felt no loyalty to the party. She had seen and ignored the signs of repression in East

Germany, and then heard Khrushchev's denunciation of Stalin and de-scriptions of the Russian despot's crimes. Now, with this latest aggression against human rights, Simone felt duped by an ideology that professed equality but did not deliver. But Montand had not yet reached the same point, and what concerned her most was his insistence on following through with his upcoming tour of the Eastern Bloc. She wanted him to break the contract, fearful that if he went, his tour might be perceived as support for the Russian aggression. Protests against the communist par-ty had already begun. Thousands had gathered at the Arc de Triomphe on November 7 to protest Russian aggression in Hungary. Then, nearly three thousand youths marched down the Champs-Elysées toward Com-munist Party headquarters, where violence erupted between protestors and party members.

Though it seems implausible that a singer and an actress could have so much influence, the Montands were the "ideal leftist couple," and up to this point, the best public relations strategy in the world could not compete with their daily presence in the public eye during the last two years. Though Montand's films did not enjoy the same commercial suc-cess as Simone's, audiences loved seeing him on screen and on stage. He was viewed as the workingman's idol, and Simone as his loyal and gifted wife. Their opinions in all matters were sought after, and they were highly regarded by intellectuals, artists, and especially by the work-ing class—and therefore, the Communist Party.

For Simone, this was a highly desirable position to be in, but one that carried immense responsibility. It was morally imperative that she and Montand take their public roles seriously—and just as imperative that they take a stand consistent with their professed values. But for the first time in their marriage, they were not on the same page, though she would never say so in public. Her experiences and doubts about the Communist Party were confirmed by others. She was especially moved when the author Jean Bruller, who wrote under the name Vercors, spoke at a meeting of the peace movement about feeling used as "an exhibition piece" by the communists. In other words, he had served as a public rela-tions tool to further the party's cause, particularly during the Rosenberg trial where he defended communist ideals against American aggression. This stance resonated with Simone, who had also sided with the com-munists in defense of the Rosenbergs, though she had no idea that the communists in Russia were committing similar atrocities by fabricating crimes, forcing confessions, and executing innocent people. Vercors was distancing himself from the party, and Simone was ready to do the same.

Montand was conflicted. He wasn't ready to completely write off communism—particularly now that Khrushchev was "de-Stalinizing" the party. And he was influenced by his brother Julien, who insisted on loyalty to the party regardless of its errors. Montand listened to both sides, but was tortured by indecision and fear.

Simone was the most vocal among those who tried to influence Montand to cancel his Soviet tour. While she never spoke of their conflict in public so as to preserve their image, in his biography Montand was open about his interactions with his wife. Simone was portrayed as a constant irritation. She wanted him to cancel the tour and harped on it every chance she had, often tearfully, as their discussions erupted into shouting matches. "If you go, you'll be finished. You'll never sing in France again,"[2] she warned.

Montand's family witnessed the arguments at Place Dauphine. "The pressure from his wife was terrible," his brother Julien explained. "I said to Simone, 'Aren't you ashamed? Can't you see what you're doing to your husband?'"[3] But when Montand was seized with doubt, seeing a glimmer of reason in his wife's angst, discussions between him and Julien also ended in shouting matches that rivaled those he had with Simone.

Montand did not find solace among his musicians, who under the circumstances were not thrilled with the prospect of going on tour. They left the decision up to him, but insisted that their fees should be doubled if he decided to go. To go or cancel; no one was letting him off the hook. Then, on November 11, when Hungarian workers called a general strike, Montand made use of the development and the recent conflict over control of the Suez Canal zone to postpone his trip. Exhibiting her flair for diplomacy, Simone helped him compose a statement: "My orchestra and I have jointly decided to postpone our tour of the USSR and the people's democracies. World events, and France's internal situation, make it impossible for us at this time to leave our wives and families and travel to any country whatsoever."[4] Montand had a reprieve. He hadn't canceled; he hadn't taken a stand against the Soviets or the Communist Party. But it was a temporary reprieve—there was no relief from his internal struggles.

In spite of Montand's dominant presence and genius on stage, he was not at all confident in personal interactions, particularly when he had to articulate his point of view in the face of opposition or criticism. Shortly after he announced the postponement of his tour, he and Simone were invited to lunch with the actor Gérard Philipe and his wife, Anne, and other friends. The conversation quickly turned to the Hungarian situation. Gérard spoke of his experiences in Poland, where he had witnessed abject poverty and suppression, and then spoke of his affiliation with the Communist Party, an affiliation he made because he had believed in the party's ideals. But ideals were not practice, and he regretted his involvement, openly admitting that he had made a mistake by supporting the party. This admission prompted a free- spirited discussion among the other guests. Simone remained silent throughout, as Montand's face grew dark with anger. Finally, he erupted. Shouting, he accused the gathering of ignorance about the Russian Revolution and the plight of the working class, something they couldn't possibly understand.

He admitted later that he knew they were right and knew that his defense of the party was hopeless, but at the time he felt attacked—and then remorseful, because his outburst had brought the conversation to an uncomfortable end. Worse, he felt that everyone looked on him with pity, as though he were a child incapable of reason. What others did not understand, he felt, was the turmoil he was experiencing. Though he was never a party member, he had grown up in a home where both his father and brother were ardent communists, and he had witnessed their struggles and the fervor of their convictions. Writing off everything he had learned, so deeply embedded since childhood, was not as easy as others wanted it to be.

Meanwhile, in the midst of this conflict, Simone was trying to find a way out of their tenuous situation. She had conceived the idea that if she asked the poet Louis Aragon, a member of the Central Committee of the French Communist Party, to intervene with the Russians, they might at least postpone Montand's tour, saving them all from further angst. Aragon declined, holding firm the Communist Party line that courage was necessary in the face of adversity. When she and Montand turned to Jean-Paul Sartre, he didn't give advice, but commented on their situation by summing up what she already knew: "If you go, you stand with the Russians; if you stay, you stand with the reactionaries." In the meantime, Montand was receiving a flood of letters, some threatening and others supportive. "Finally, we did leave. What made the decision was the famous drop of water that caused the pail to overflow," Simone explained. Montand had agreed to appear in Max Ophuls's film, *Modigliani*, scheduled to begin production after the tour. But when the producer called and informed him that if he went on the Soviet tour the film's backers would break the contract, the sheer audacity of the threat settled the issue for Montand. He was going on tour.[5] Simone spent the next weeks tearfully preparing for the trip, while Montand remained resolute. The final insult for Montand came days before their departure, when his rehearsal at the Olympia Theater was scheduled to be broadcast live on the radio show, *Musicorama*. When the radio station began promoting the live broadcast, management received threatening letters and warnings so numerous and detailed that the producers decided to cancel the event.

The night before their departure, Simone, still tearful, received a visit from her friend, actor Claude Roy, whose attempts to cheer her up fell flat. But he provided a bit of information about Louis Aragon that incensed her. While Aragon touted communist loyalty when Simone asked for his help in getting the Russians to postpone the tour, he conveyed a different message to their friends. Under the circumstances, he was against Montand's tour. Had he been honest when she asked his advice, it might have changed the final outcome. Simone was so infuriated that she tried calling Aragon every hour on the hour. He never answered. She would deal with Aragon later.

CHAPTER 17

"Sentimental People"

"I FEEL AS IF I'M IN A NEWSREEL,"[1] SIMONE WHISPERED, AS THEY ENTERED the backstage salon at the Tchaikovsky Concert Center in Moscow. A small reception line awaited them, a beaming Nikita Khrushchev at the forefront. It was the evening of December 24, 1956, and Montand had just finished his fourth evening performance before a sold-out audience of thirty-five hundred. Demand for tickets was so high that lines had formed outside the Tchaikovsky Center days in advance. The minister of culture had a public address system set up outside and in the Luzhnik Stadium nearby, so that between the two venues, another 16,500 could hear the performance. Twenty thousand people heard each of Montand's five performances. It was unheard of at the time.

Simone did not attend his show that evening. Instead, she had accepted an invitation to the Bolshoi Theater from Rutha Sudoul, wife of the French journalist Georges, and an old friend from the café days. Georges Sudoul was in Moscow at the time to receive an award. During a lengthy intermission, Simone was informed by the minister of culture and her driver that she must return to the Tchaikovsky Theater immediately. As no reason was provided, Simone worried that something must have happened either to Montand or back home in Paris.

She made it back to the Center just as Montand was giving final bows to a thunderous standing ovation and had enough time to notice that among the audience members was Nikita Khrushchev, who stood with other high-ranking leaders in box seats. She had barely finished helping Montand towel off when the couple was told that special guests, comrades of the Soviet Union, were waiting to meet them in another room. With Khrushchev's presence, they had expected a protocol visit,

and Montand was annoyed at first, questioning why they couldn't simply come to his dressing room like everyone else, without all the fanfare.
But the Montands were told that a special dinner had been prepared for
the occasion, and their presence was expected.

When they entered a small sitting room, which had been converted
into a dining room, they were stunned by the receiving line. After meeting Khrushchev, they were introduced to members of the Politburo: An-
astas Mikoyan, first deputy premier; Vyacheslay Molotov, first deputy
chairman of the ministry of the Soviet Union (who Simone thought
looked rather sinister); Nikolai Bulganin, minister of defense; and Geor-
gy Malenkov, former premier of the USSR. There were no photographers, television cameras, or tape recorders present, but the newsreel
atmosphere prevailed as the couple was seated at a long narrow table
for dinner opposite Khrushchev and the others. Montand and Simone
sat there in disbelief. Their interpreter, Nadia, who was shaken by this
unexpected gathering of heads of state, sat out of the way at one end of
table, providing simultaneous interpretation.

Khrushchev complimented Montand's performance, expressing a particular preference for the song "C'est à l'aube," and then Mikoyan toast-
ed the singer's family, naming each member individually. He had obviously done his homework for the occasion, and Montand was overcome
with emotion when the politician complimented his father. Montand's
and Simone's accounts of the story differ. When the conversation turned
to politics, Montand thought Mikoyan started it, while Simone thought
it was Khrushchev: "So, Monsieur Montand, the Fascists allowed you
to leave?" Montand was so stunned he could only stare, incredulous,
for a few minutes before finally finding his voice. It wasn't fascists who
prevented him from leaving, he explained, but rather the events in Budapest—deplorable, shocking events that had tested his opinion of the
party. He and Simone were not members, he reminded them, and they
were not bound by blind faith.

Indeed, they were also aligned with some of the ideals of capitalism.
To demonstrate the point, Simone displayed her diamond bracelet and
furs that she had purchased with the fruits of her labor. Montand spoke
of their grand house, Autheuil, and of his ability to sing what he chose
and when, without government interference. "He stressed that he alone
reigned over what he chose to choose," Simone explained. "By which
we meant to say that we personally had no reason to complain about a
capitalist regime, but that was no reason to think it was perfect for a lot
of others." They asked Khrushchev why Jews had to have that status

stamped on their identity cards, and why the Russians lied about their slave labor camps. Khrushchev accused them of being sentimentalists, and Simone agreed: "Look . . . I wear good clothes, good jewels; I work at what I want, when I want; I don't need to fight for a piece of bread. If I fight for causes, it's for sentimental reasons of the heart." And as sentimental people, she and Montand were shocked by pictures of the Red Army shooting protestors in the streets of Budapest. She accused Khrushchev of using her feelings as "push buttons."

Khrushchev was thoughtful and passionate when he responded, sharing in great detail the atrocities he discovered that occurred under Stalin's regime. He spoke about the liquidations, trials, and terrors, pounding his fist on the table every time he wanted to emphasize "sixteen million dead." Stalin had not propagated the socialist ideal, which Khrushchev was trying to reinstate and preserve. And, it was in the spirit of preserving socialist ideals that he had sent troops to Hungary to save it from fascism and imperialism. "Perhaps it was rather that the people believed they had a right to demand greater liberty, within the new socialism you had promised them . . . and this gesture was misunderstood?" Simone asked, skeptically. Khrushchev quickly responded, informing her that she and Montand were the ones who misunderstood. They countered by describing the turmoil in Paris after the assault: Communists were under siege, and even members of the peace movement had separated themselves from the party. If they misunderstood, as he suggested, they were not alone. Khrushchev and his Politburo listened so intently that Simone couldn't help but wonder if they were hearing about these events for the first time. Montand then took a risk, explaining that his arrival in the country did not in any way constitute approval for what happened in Hungary. Again, they were sentimental people and not bound by any loyalty to the Communist Party. An uncomfortable silence followed, which was quickly broken when someone asked Simone about her film career, a point of interest as she was relatively unknown in Russia at the point.

It was well after 4 a.m. when the couple returned to their hotel, exhausted yet exhilarated from an experience that was as historic as it was surreal. They were particularly proud of the idea that rather than just talking about it among themselves and with like-minded friends, they had actually communicated their concerns directly to the source of the problem—they couldn't go much higher than Nikita Khrushchev. Few would ever have the same opportunity and live to tell about it. "Now nobody likes us," Montand commented before turning out the lights. "But don't we feel good about ourselves!" But although Montand had heard about the atrocities perpetrated under communist rule directly from Khrushchev, adding to his disenchantment over events in Hungary, he was still not ready to write off the communist party. Simone was, and the tensions that began in Paris spilled over in Russia.

As rumors of the famous dinner circulated, Montand was bombarded with invitations to tour factories, schools, and clinics. He provided a concert at the Likhachov auto factory, where a flatbed truck was used as a stage before eight thousand workers. Mobs followed the couple through the streets and greeted them at every stop along the way. However, the Montands were always accompanied by officials who limited their visits, whisking them away from certain areas in order to focus their attention on what they considered noteworthy points of interest. Montand later commented:

> I was rather irritated by the little throng of people who stuck to us like glue, people who apparently lived very well. Simone and I weren't fooled; they were part of the *nomenklatura*, privileged members of the regime; they were a screen between the Russians and us. But the quarantine zone they established didn't prevent us from seeing women of all ages sweeping the streets in the snow, clearing snow at minus twenty-five degrees centigrade, or doing heavy work in the factories.

They accidentally wandered into a working-class neighborhood, where several families were housed together in wooden shacks. "Simone and I talked about it incessantly. I was shaken," Montand admitted. "I could see that it clearly wasn't paradise, and yet the old reflexes were still operating. Simone hammered away at things that depressed me—lines outside stores, different categories of restaurant—and I instantly bit her head off, because what she said sounded true and I didn't want to accept it . . . . 'Just wait, Simone, give them time. Khrushchev had the courage to tell us: they've made mistakes, okay, but give them time to recover. We can't junk it all now.'" But Simone had seen enough and continued to hammer away.

Montand recalled one particularly violent argument, when he felt pressured because Simone kept hammering away at him, hoping he could see her point of view. Finally, he was so frustrated and angry he took hold of her shoulders and shook her, while screaming that she would never understand. "I know today that my anger was a form of despair." Simone never commented on the incident.

Montand's run at the Tchaikovsky Concert Center ended after five performances. His next venue in Moscow was the Uljniki Stadium, an indoor sports arena that seated eighteen thousand. It was filled to capacity, holding the largest audience he had ever performed in front of in one location.

On New Year's Eve, Simone, Montand, and his musicians were invited to the palatial Kremlin, along with nearly three thousand other guests, the majority of them high-ranking members of the Communist Party. Included were ambassadors and a special guest, a Chinese dissident who had fled his country. At midnight, the lights went out, and Simone and Montand kissed. Just as the lights were turned on again, Simone felt a hand on her shoulder. Nikita Khruschev then pulled Simone out of her chair and kissed her on the mouth, a gesture, she noted, that was observed by the 2,990 guests that had gathered for the celebration.[3] He then shook both of Montand's hands vigorously, Russian style, before running off to greet other guests. They would never have an occasion to meet Nikita Khrushchev again, but would count these experiences among the most incredible and memorable of their lives.

Montand's final concert performances in Russia were held in Leningrad before the couple moved on to the Eastern Bloc countries. Between January 1957 and March 1957, Montand performed in Poland, East Germany, Czechoslovakia, Rumania, Bulgaria, Yugoslavia, and Hungary. It was a marathon tour with few breaks for time off. Simone maintained regular phone contact with family at home. Considering the controversy surrounding their departure, she had worried that her daughter might face taunting at school and had made special arrangements with the principal, who promised to ensure Catherine's well-being, even allowing her to remain at home if taunting became unbearable. Catherine, who was eleven years old at the time and in the care of Montand's family, had no memorable experiences during her parents' four-month absence.

Their reception in Warsaw, Poland, was chillier than the subzero temperatures. As the couple soon learned, while the communist government had acquiesced to worker demands during the national strike in June 1956, after the Hungarian Revolt, they had since cracked down with more rigid laws that removed the right to strike and imposed strict censorship. So when the couple arrived in a state plane used primarily to transport communist dignitaries, their reception was less than welcoming. In the minds of many Poles, Montand was clearly aligned with the Soviet rulers.

Soon after their arrival, Montand also learned that the price of tickets had been set so high that most couldn't afford them. When people complained, they were told that the price was high because Montand insisted upon being paid in American dollars. Outraged, Montand demanded a public retraction in the local newspapers. In it, Montand denied the claim that he wanted to be paid in dollars. He understood Poland's economic constraints and had arranged for his musicians to be paid in francs, while he was paid in zlotys. The tension eased, and at every turn, the couple was besieged with visitors who wanted to talk openly about socialist ideals and the spirit of the revolution that had begun in October 1956. There was so much talk, that at times Montand had to shoo visitors away from his dressing room so he could concentrate before a performance. The passionate talk affected him deeply, though he still held firm to the belief that although the communists had made errors, with time they would fulfill the promise of socialist ideals.

While the tour was an unprecedented success for Montand, one visit in particular would come to be viewed as a missed opportunity for Simone, one she would come to regret. She and Montand had just arrived in Prague when they learned that the next concert in Bratislava, Slovakia, had been canceled because it was inconvenient to make all the necessary arrangements there. This was an odd excuse that left the couple bewildered—but not ungrateful for the respite it offered. But negotiations were still under way the next day when Simone received a call from a relative she didn't know, Sophie Langer. Sophie spoke English fluently and explained their relationship on her paternal grandmother's side, which meant nothing to Simone. Then, Sophie expressed disappointment about reading in the press that Montand had canceled his concert in her area. Simone was instantly suspicious. "There was something so pressing about the way she said that she hoped *so much* that she would meet us, that when I hung up the phone I instantly classified her among those pains in the ass who work hard at it when they discover some family link with celebrities."

Although she did not yet attribute this period in her life to "monstrous egocentricity," she was indeed living the celebrity life, self-absorbed, at least in terms of her husband, and resplendent in a fur hat and coat, dripping in diamonds as she and Montand were whisked away in chauffeur-driven cars. They were special guests at embassy dinners and writers clubs. She had no time for obscure family members. But as she would learn later in life, Sophie Langer's interest in meeting her had nothing to do with establishing new family connections. Sophie's husband had been arrested for "deviations" against the communist government and was undergoing "rehabilitation" in prison. Sophie had hoped that Simone and Montand could use their influence to save her husband's life. However, she never had the opportunity to say this to Simone. The following day, Simone breezed past Sophie in the lobby of the Alkron Hotel where they were staying. Simone wouldn't recognize Sophie and was too self-absorbed to notice anyone—let alone the woman sitting in the lobby, hopeful that she might catch Simone's eye. Sophie dared not approach, fearful that the two men watching her in the lobby would stop her.

Two days after their arrival in Belgrade on March 6, the couple received an unexpected invitation from an unidentified caller who informed them that Marshal Tito, the president of Yugoslavia, had invited them to tea. This time when a car arrived to pick them up, it was not a state vehicle, but an old beat-up American Ford. Two burly men who never said a word or made an effort to greet them were sitting in the front seat. As Montand recounted, "The car left Belgrade and drove quite a distance. Suddenly, as we droved through a thick forest, everything about the ride seemed bizarre: the phone call, the car, these two rogues." Montand turned to Simone and whispered, "Where are we going? And who are these guys?" Simone had the same questions. "We had talked too much wherever we went and we knew too much," Montand decided, "so they were going to do away with us." He whispered to Simone, "Don't get scared. Watch the driver and I'll take care of the other one; if the car slows down, I'll jump him." In that case, he encouraged Simone to jump out and run. However, their fears were allayed when the forest road opened up to civilization, where they could clearly see fine houses and villas. Finally, the car stopped in front of a splendid villa. Marshal Broz, known as Tito, and his wife were waiting as the car pulled up. They were served champagne, and much to their surprise, they found the leader to be relaxed, open, and honest, speaking freely about his country's economic strife, his plans for the future, and his difficulties with the Russians. He distrusted Molotov. He spoke fervently about the liquidations under Stalin. A photographer was present to take group photos.

A few days after their "tea," Simone and Montand received two sets of photographs of the gathering: One set was signed by Tito, the other set was for their autograph, which they were asked to return.[4]

The final leg of their journey brought them to Hungary, a country still reeling from the Russian assault. Montand had received threats prior to their arrival. He was warned that tear gas bombs would be thrown in the theater if he sang in Budapest. A public relations campaign produced flyers encouraging a boycott of his shows. If Montand stood in solidarity with the Hungarians he would have refused to sing, it claimed. When Montand found out about the protest, he wrote a statement for the press with Simone's help, expressing his feelings and pointing out that the threats made against him only bolstered his resolve. He not only sang, as scheduled, but his performances were a success.

Montand was impressed by the Hungarian people, particularly the young women who waited to meet him backstage. "I saw the most sublime girls in Budapest, twenty-year olds, girls you could die for. And yet, not a single one . . . ." The ever-present Simone, who was tuned in to her husband's less than subtle interest, had put her foot down: There would be no indiscretions in Budapest.

PART IV

McCARTHYIST PURGATORY

CHAPTER 18

Me and the Colonel

SIMONE AND MONTAND FELT THE FALLOUT FROM THEIR CONTROVERSIAL tour immediately upon their return from the Eastern Bloc. "Nobody asked for me," Simone explained. She wasn't concerned at first, because they had maintained such a rigorous schedule for the prior two years that she was content with the prospect of uninterrupted rest, vacationing at the Columbe d'Or and at Autheuil. "But rest stops being rest when it goes on and on. Then it isn't called rest, it's called being out of work." And in acting circles, she explained, they call this "the trough of the wave." The trough would last nine months.

By August 1957, with no calls or prospects for future projects, Simone resigned herself to the idea that it was time to take stock of her career. She made a list of the roles she had played. It was not a lengthy list, but it left her feeling both accomplished and confident. Her list of obstacles was much shorter but none-the-less significant. Politics dominated that list. She would never apologize for her activism in what she considered "affairs of the heart," not politics. However, in the end, her involvement with the peace movement, the Stockholm Appeal, anti-atomic bomb demonstrations, and finally, the controversial tour of Russia and the Eastern Bloc had kept her in the public eye. She was controversial. And, if ever there was a reason for Americans to consider her persona non grata, the Soviet tour was it. French Studios felt the pressure and were distancing themselves from her, least they lose favor with the Americans, who were still dominant at the box office and provided financial support for the reconstruction of France.

She had long ago given up on the American market. The deal with Howard Hughes had quietly disappeared as McCarthy gained a stronghold. After that, she never applied for a US visa, because every time she had been approached with even the suggestion of a role in a Hollywood film—even one produced in Europe—the offers were always withdrawn with apologies before negotiations began. Simone had completely given up on the idea of breaking into Hollywood. That market was clearly closed to her.

Age was another seemingly insurmountable obstacle in an industry that marginalized women over forty. "I was about to be thirty-seven years old and the future belonged to the pretty young things and the attractive young women."[1] No one was looking for older actresses, particularly when new stars like the young, blonde bombshell, Brigitte Bardot—"BB," body beautiful—had emerged as a new box office sensation. Simone was not quick to criticize the competition, but clearly, Bardot would never play women of character and depth, as she had done. Still, she was always careful to give credit where credit was due, commenting with characteristic humor that Bardot "left everyone else standing."

The actress was popular in the "New Wave" of French cinema, where young, emerging directors were trying to infuse new life into film with Hollywood visual effects and themes in the tradition of Italian neo-realism. Simone was associated with the poetic-realism movement of the pre-war years and the New Wave directors despised those gloomy, fatalistic stories of social injustice and human fragility. Too old school. Again, Simone, who prided herself on selecting roles for "the totality of the story being told," made no apologies for her preference for this genre. She did not care for these new stream-of-consciousness films that left older actors out in the cold. Then again, no one was really asking her opinion or advice at the point; no one was asking for her at all. "I was at the bottom of the new wave," she explained—and she would remain there throughout the balance of 1957 and well into 1958.

In the meantime, the best thing she could do, she decided, was to retire quietly, with dignity and without regrets. She wasn't concerned about doing so—at least not financially—because Montand earned more than a comfortable income. And retirement would give her more time to focus her energies on family, particularly on Montand. She'd no longer have to feel guilty leaving him for a film. She accepted forced retirement without bitterness, she claimed. Although her status as an out of work actress was certainly a concern, friends could not imagine Simone accepting retirement quietly. And then, almost as if to test her resolve, in early September 1957, Simone received a call from the British stage and film director Peter Glenville. He was working on a Hollywood production to be filmed in Paris and the United States, and he offered her a role. Simone readily agreed to read the script.

Peter Glenville began his career as a stage actor, before making his directorial debut in 1944 at the Old Vic Theatre in London. He brought *The Browning Version* to Broadway in 1949, and directed a series of successful plays before branching off in 1954 with a film adaptation of *The Prisoner*, a play he had directed on stage. In 1957, he was nominated for a Tony Award for directing *Separate Tables*, by Terence Rattigan, and was currently working on a film for Columbia Pictures. Simone's account of this film, *Me and the Colonel*, was so confusing that the events surrounding it are often confounded with the film that followed.

The film, produced by William Goetz, was another adaptation of a stage production, *Jacobowsky and the Colonel*, a comedic drama about a middle-aged Polish Jew who was trapped in Paris as the Nazis advanced on the city. He purchases a car he can't drive for his escape, and then tries to convince an aristocratic German colonel to drive it for him. Although the colonel is anti-Semitic, he is so anxious to flee France that he finally agrees. In the meantime, the two men meet and fall in love with Marianne, a French restaurateur who joins them in their comedic adventure. This character would have several iterations and a name change before the film was produced, finally emerging as Suzanne Roualet, an entirely new and different character.

Columbia had originally tapped Rex Harrison for the role of Jacobowsky, but finally decided "that the role must be played unequivocally Polish."[2] Danny Kaye was selected. Kaye jumped at the opportunity, because his career was experiencing a downward spiral, and he had hopes that this film would spark a comeback. The popular German actor Curd Jürgens, known as Curt Jürgens in the United States, had signed on as Colonel Prokonzny. But in early September 1957, Glenville and Bill Goetz had not yet secured an actress to fill the role of Marianne.

Glenville took a risk and contacted Simone before running the idea by Goetz in a letter he wrote, dated September 6, 1957:[3]

An original and interesting idea was suggested to me the other day, namely Simone Signoret, and I think very serious consideration should be given to the idea. I think her performance could be as fresh and interesting as the performances we hope to get from our two stars. She looks about 30, is a very handsome woman-star and a fine actress and speaks absolutely perfect English. She made a great success last year in America in LES DIABOLIQUES but you cannot judge her personality by this performance as she was playing a monster and made herself unattractive for the part. Try to get a copy of CASQUE D'OR directed by Becker and you will see more the sort of woman she is. She would completely convince one of the bon-comrade-three musketeer element. One could certainly be convinced that she ran a restaurant and she has depth and charm rather than sprightly prettiness which would make one understand why she was important to both men and it would also make the ending extremely moving. She has a great sense of humor and is enormously professional rather than being a comedienne type which is I think what we need, and as a performer she would be equal in stature to the other two stars.

I have always found the part of Marianne a little lacking in character. . . . a woman with a strong personality like Signoret would give the whole part the real identity and particularity that is a little missing in the actual script.

The only other predictable suggestion among the accomplished French actresses who speak good English is Danielle Darrieux. She is of course a real comedienne and enormously expert. I am meeting her on Sunday and I do not know whether she would be interested and she certainly would be expensive. I would say around $75,000 as she gets the top price here. This is completely safe casting but lacks the originality and kick that Signoret will have. Darrieux is more feminine in a superficial way and Signoret has more depth and uniqueness.

Apparently Darrieux was not interested, and Simone was stunned by the offer. She was interested of course, but expressed concern that she did not have a visa or working papers for the United States. And considering the political atmosphere in the United States, she doubted she could obtain approval for one. Glenville was incredulous. "But McCarthy's dead," both literally and figuratively, he explained. Senator Joseph McCarthy had died that year, on May 2, 1957, but his reign of terror had ended years earlier when he was censured by the Senate. Things were easing up in the United States, Glenville assured her. Half convinced, Simone then agreed to read the script—but not as reluctantly as she suggested when reminiscing in her autobiography.

Apparently, Glenville was unaware of her status as an out of work actress, and Simone, a shrewd businesswoman, wasn't about to tell him. Glenville wrote innocently of his interaction with her in his letter to Bill Goetz: "She telephoned the office last night to say that she likes the script very much and would be prepared to do it, but she has to know within the week as she has another major French offer upon which she has to decide." By her own account, Simone wasn't impressed with the script or the character they were asking her to play. Though she prided herself on having a good memory for details, she marginalized the significance of the film so much in her autobiography that she couldn't remember it's title or the character, whom she referred to as "Fifi, Lulu or Madeline," the archetype of the sexy, shallow French women that Hollywood was so fond of portraying at the time. Yet she could easily recall what she ordered for dinner the night she met with Glenville and Goetz to discuss the film. Montand treated them to dinner, chez Allard, a popular bistro in the sixth arrondisement that specialized in traditional French cuisine. She ordered the pickled pork and lentils.

She had read the script, she explained to Glenville and Goetz, and she wasn't impressed with the character. Simone felt the character was shallow, and she decided she was too old to play the part. But as the two men had already discussed changes, they assured her that Marianne would emerge from editing as a woman of substance, "kind of a cross between Madame Curie and Simone de Beauvoir; tailor made for me." With that issue laid to rest, the conversation turned to politics, and she again expressed concern about getting a visa or work-permit for the production. She thought it ironic that Hollywood was asking for her, while in France the studios shunned her so as not to "get in bad" with America. Goetz had the same reaction as Glenville and assured her that McCarthyism was a thing of the past. Restrictions were easing up, producers were becoming more demanding, and he doubted they would have problems obtaining the necessary permissions for her work permit. They left the restaurant in high spirits and with a promise that a new script would be available shortly. It was a glimmer in a career that had for all intents and purposes ended.

Unfortunately, they would not settle her contract in one week, as she desired. Although the work permit was not yet an issue, there were other stumbling blocks in negotiations. On September 21, 1957, Claude Ganz, the film's Paris production manager, wrote to Bill Goetz, listing five issues that had to be resolved:

I would summarize Simone Signoret situation:

a) *Billing*—As she calls for the billing: Dany[4] Kaye-Simone Signo-
ret-Curd Jürgens, not only for English speaking territories, but also
for Europe, and as it will be very difficult for us to obtain the agreement from Curd Jürgens, Simone Signoret's agent will take care of
this and only asked for our help, which we agree to give her.

Of course, she asked that her name will be mentioned in the
same size that the ones of Dany Kaye and Curd Jürgens.

b) It was agreed that deal provides for ten weeks working plus
two weeks for travel or interruption of shooting. For these twelve
weeks, she wants to be paid in Francs 20,000,000 (twenty million),
of which part can be paid in Hollywood and in dollars. (It was a
question of 50% in francs and 50% in dollars.) The overtime, if
there should be any, would be calculated on the pro rata basis of
twelve weeks for twenty million.

c) The living allowance proposed to her was $300 per week. This
figure could eventually be revised later on.

d) Would you please have in mind that Simone Signoret has to give
an answer that she postponed, for another film.

e) If you decide to give the part to Simone Signoret, in the contract
which we will work out here, it will be, of course, mentioned, that
this contract has real effect, only after you have obtained a visa and
a working permit for U.S.A. for her.

She was not going to win on the billing issue, and the salary, twenty million francs—equivalent at the time to approximately $40,500—was far
from a deal breaker in negotiations. However, it remained a concern as
late as September 26, when Peter Glenville wrote to his assistant director, Jean Dewever, from the Columbia Paris office:

We sent a cable to Mr. Macnab from Columbia authorizing the re-
serving of the French personnel discussed by us when we were
both in Paris. We also sent a cable explaining why we could not
give an immediate answer on Simone Signoret. There has been a
little debate here as to the sum of money asked by MCA[5] in view
of the fact that Simone's box office here is as yet undeveloped; and

as regards the French market, we are already pretty strong with Jürgens and Kaye. However, I hope that the matter will be cleared up today or tomorrow and meanwhile, Bill Goetz is already making active inquiries about the working permit and the visa, which is really the crucial point.

Three days later, the "crucial point" came to a climax, and on October 1, 1957, Jean Dewever followed up with Glenville in a letter: "I spoke yesterday with Simone Signoret: I told her the production could not get her work-permit before the beginning of the picture. She understood very well and was very nice, especially about you. If you could find some time, I am sure she would like very much to receive a short letter from you." By then, Glenville both incredulous and apologetic, had already cabled Simone. He promised to find her another production. Simone responded with a brief cable expressing regrets, particularly for the impact the delays had on her other opportunity. But the battle was not over. That same day, October 1, Simone's agency, CIMURA MCA, sent a harsh Western Union telegram to both Glenville and Bill Goetz:

Surprised Goetz never gave personal answer independently visa question concerning conditions Signoret contract STOP American Embassy Paris denies completely information about workpermit and authorize us to tell you that answer her own tourist application will be given October sixteenth latest with 99% chances being granted STOP Embassy also says that once in States only two days necessary for transformation tourist visa in workpermit STOP we demand true explanation.

But the American embassy was either misinformed or maintaining a diplomatic position, because Bill Goetz responded with a long, multiple-page telegram to Simone, explaining that, indeed, "Washingtonian reasons" prevented them from obtaining her visa and work-permit.

Simone had no doubt that politics played in role in preventing her visa from being granted. McCarthyism may have been on the decline, but US immigration law prohibiting "communists and other subversives" from entering the country was still strictly enforced. Simone simply read between the lines. Her suspicion was confirmed later, when both she and Montand applied for US visas for another opportunity.

The character Simone was to play, Marianne, once an older restaurateur, emerged from editing as Suzanne Roualet, the charming daughter of a restaurateur, played by Nicole Maurey. Though Danny Kaye won a

Golden Globe as best actor in a musical/comedy, the film did little to re-vive his career. Peter Glenville received positive reviews for his direction and did not forget his promise to find Simone another role.

A week after the debacle with *Me and the Colonel*, he called her with an urgent request to meet. He was in Paris, about to fly back to the United States, and had something he wanted her to read. He didn't have a script in hand when he arrived at 15 Place Dauphine. It hadn't even been writ-ten yet, because they were in the very early stages of production. But he had a copy of a book he was sure needed no introduction: *Angry Young Men*, a best-selling novel by British author John Braine. Much to his disappointment, Simone had never heard of it, so he encouraged her to read it and to meet with the producers, two brothers who were his close friends, John and James Woolf, owners of Romulus and Remus Produc-tions. Simone was sorry to hear that Glenville was not available to di-rect. But, Jack Clayton, a thirty-six-year-old independent filmmaker, had agreed to direct. There was one major change to be made in the script from the original novel, Glenville explained: The British character, Alice Aisgill, would become a Frenchwoman married to a Brit, a change made especially with Simone Signoret in mind.

The film adaptation, *Room at the Top*, was an adventure in firsts. Jack Clayton, a cinematographer who would later become known for bring-ing novels to the screen, had never directed a feature film, and *Angry Young Men* was John Braine's first novel. The thirty-five-year-old former librarian was considered a member of Britain's "Angry Young Men," a group of writers and playwrights who were disgruntled with the conser-vative post-war social reform programs and class division that allowed the wealthy to prosper from the labor of the less fortunate working class. On this note, Braine joked that he wasn't really angry, "just a disagree-able young man,"[6] who had captured the gloom of post-war England in a novel with a twist. The central character, Joe Lampton, a POW during the Second World War, was not as concerned with social ills as he was with social climbing. After finding a job as an accountant in Bradford, England, he set his sights on the young daughter of a wealthy industrial-ist. If he could marry her, she would become his ticket to the top. But, his plans are waylaid when he meets and falls in love with an older, unhap-pily married woman, Alice Aisgill.

Simone loved the story and the role. "Alice was intelligent, generous, understanding, maternal, sexually liberated and socially without preju-dice. Alice was a character who had everything going for her, including her death before the end of the novel. Alice was a piece of cake to play. (I almost forgot: on top of it all, Alice was married to a complete cad.) Did I say a piece of cake? A wedding cake is more like it: a part whose like one seldom encounters in the course of a career."[7] And Alice wasn't a prostitute. She was "just an unhappy woman having her last love affair. She was in fact the same kind of woman who usually writes my husband."[8]

When Simone met with producer James Woolf, she cut to the chase. She wanted the role but didn't want to go further if there was even the slightest possibility that this would become another "Fifi, Lulu" situation, with McCarthy work-permit nightmares. She'd end the discussion right then and there, rather than invest herself in another emotional roller coaster ride only to wind up with nothing. Woolf assured her that Britain was unaffected by American politics, particularly since this was an independent project and not in any way affiliated with the standard British-American collaborative studio productions that were popular at the time. In any event, he assured her, she was a well-known and respected actress in England. She had won the British Academy Award as Best Foreign Actress for *Casque d'Or*, and more recently she received the same award for *The Crucible*. She was still revered for *Casque d'Or*. In fact, as both Glenville and Jack Clayton had intimated, she was selected for the role of Alice based on her performance in that film. Simone was, in their opinion, "the 'only' actress with combined maturity and sex appeal for Alice," Jack Clayton later explained to the press.

Simone had the opportunity to take a salary or a percent of earnings for the film. After taking a percent on *The Crucible* and then losing money with all the shooting delays, Simone chose a salary, a decision she would come to regret. Not only was the production on schedule throughout, with filming slated to begin in June 1958, this low budget black and white film would become an unexpected "watershed." Indeed, Simone Signoret and director, Jack Clayton, would be credited with creating the "New Wave" in British cinema. Simone was still in the trough of the wave as 1957 came to a close, but 1958 was shaping up to be an extraordinary and unexpected turning point in her life and career.

CHAPTER 19

Room at the Top

WHEN SHE TOLD FRIENDS THAT SHE HAD ACCEPTED A ROLE IN *ROOM*
at the Top they were far from impressed. It was well known that the British film industry was suffering a protracted death, which had begun at
the start of the decade. British-American co-productions still dominated
the film industry's output but were no longer generating box office, and
there were few successful independent ventures. Theaters were closing
their doors in record numbers, as audiences turned to television, the new
entertainment medium.

Since they couldn't envision a blockbuster, Simone's close friends worried that her involvement in this independent venture, a potential dud,
might jeopardize her already tenuous situation, and thus end her career.
She defended *Room at the Top* and was convinced that the film had potential. But there was no fanfare surrounding her departure. Only Montand
and Catherine were present to see her off when she boarded the luxury
Golden Arrow boat-train in Paris for England, where *Room at the Top*
was filmed at the Shepperton studios in London, with location scenes
filmed in the industrial town of Bradford, Yorkshire, the wool capital of
the world. After her mother's departure, Catherine, now twelve years
of age, returned to Autheuil for her summer vacation. Montand was off
to Italy to film *La Legg*, a Franco-Italian production. Though she called
home every evening to check on her daughter and spent a weekend with
Montand, Simone was so absorbed in Alice Aisgill that she never voiced
the regret she usually felt when separated from her husband. The Eastern Bloc tour had been an instructive period in their relationship, and
it was healthy to have time away, absorbed in her career. If there was

concern about possible indiscretions on their respective movie sets—particularly on Montand's part—they had apparently come to an agreement in advance. "We understood each other perfectly," she wrote without further explanation.

Jack Clayton and producer James Woolf had assembled a well-known cast for the film. The Lithuanian born British actor Laurence Harvey played Joe Lampton. Though she had heard rumors about his aggressive and disagreeable behavior both on and off screen, Simone reported no difficulties. Heather Sears, a friend of Clayton and relatively new to the screen, played Susan Brown, the young, virginal daughter of an industrial titan who would become Joe Lampton's ticket to the top. Hermione Baddeley, a popular British stage and screen character actress, was Elspeth, Alice Aisgill's British cousin. The cast clicked, becoming such a tight-knit family that they regretted ending the production in late July. Alice Aisgill had been so absorbing that it was difficult to lose her afterwards, and she remained with Simone longer than characters usually did. Simone continued to wear Alice's hairstyle and tailor-made blazer for a while, finally letting Alice leave her just in time for Simone to return to her role as Montand's "groupie" and confident in August 1958.

After filming *La Legg*, which was not as successful at the box office as he would have liked, Montand was anxious to resume his musical career and had set up a concert series at the Étoile Theater in Paris. He had not performed since the trip to the Eastern Bloc, and to ward off any perception that his music would have political overtones, he carefully worked out a new repertoire, adding sixteen new titles with light comedy and romance themes. Autheuil became a dormitory for his orchestra, which rehearsed throughout the month of August in the little theater he had created out back. When it was too hot indoors, they rehearsed outdoors on the lawn.

Simone was still without film offers and spent her time attending her husband's rehearsals, standing on the sidelines to toss him his top hat or to give feedback and support as needed. Montand was concerned not only about public response to his new show, but also about residual anger over his trip to the Eastern Bloc. So he arranged a full dress rehearsal before eight hundred invited guests to test his new repertoire. Simone remained vigilant throughout, watching the audience's reactions to every song and skit, while taking copious notes, which she shared with Montand and orchestra members. He was well received, and his opening night at the Étoile was so successful his concert series was extended from October 1958 through March of the following year.

In spite of her efforts to downplay excitement about the release of her latest film, Simone's star was rising. In November, she took a break from the concerts to attend the premiere of *Room at the Top* in London (the film would not be released to the public until January 1959). Immediately following the post-premiere celebration, Simone returned to Paris, anxious to read reviews; audience reaction had been positive, but she was not overly confident. Then, producer James Woolf began calling. He insisted upon reading the reviews aloud, and oddly enough, each review he read seemed to contain one sentence she hadn't read on her own: "There hasn't been the like since Greta Garbo." Simone was confused at first, but after a few such reviews, she realized Woolf was making the line up to please her. She played along, reading reviews she invented to him that included the phrase "the world's greatest producer since Irving Thalberg."

Jack Clayton followed a similar formula, calling Simone nearly every fifteen minutes. He used a different name and voice each time, asking for interviews for papers he allegedly worked for—usually trade magazines for chicken farmers or greenhouses. Simone compared their antics to those of high school students letting off steam after exams.

Though it received exceptional reviews, the film was also given an X rating, which caused a delay in finding a distributor. Still, Simone was euphoric as she returned to the theater in time to see Montand take his final bows. "He had no idea that it was Greta Garbo handing him his Turkish towel," when he returned to the dressing room where she waited. But "Greta Garbo" had to take a back seat for a little while longer.

Montand's crowning moment came in early December, when he received an unexpected visitor backstage after a performance. Norman Granz, an American agent, jazz impresario, and the owner of Verve Records, had watched the show and suggested that Montand come to the States—specifically to Broadway, where they would test the waters. If Montand was successful, Granz held out the offer of a tour. The journey was impossible, the couple explained. They would never get visas for the United States. It seemed a tired story, but Simone explained her experience with *Me and the Colonel*. Granz was unfazed and informed them that things had changed—another tired story. But Norman was so insistent that they agreed to let things take their course.

"Are you or have you ever been a member of the Communist Party or an organization affiliated with or having common activities with the Communist Party?" Simone recalled question number twenty in its entirety, because she would answer it many times in the years to come. It

Simone Signoret on the set of *Manèges*
(1950), directed by Yves Allégret. Credit:
Photographer, Sam Levin; Ministère de
l'Architecture et du Patrimoine, Dist.
RMN-Grand Palais Paris, France/Art
Resource, NY.

Simone Signoret and Yves Montand, ca. 1950, Paris. Credit: Photographer, Sam Levin;
Ministère de l'Architecture et du Patrimoine, Dist. RMN-Grand Palais Paris, France/Art
Resource, NY.

Simone Signoret and Yves Montand on the quais in Paris, 1950. Credit: Photographer, Sam Levin; Ministère de l'Architecture et du Patrimoine, Dist. RMN-Grand Palais Paris, France/Art Resource, NY.

Simone Signoret and Serge Reggiani in *Casque d'Or* (1952), directed by Jacques Becker. Credit: Kobal Collection/Art Resource, NY.

Simone Signoret and Vera Clouzot in *Les Diaboliques* (1955), directed by Henri-Georges Clouzot. Author's collection.

Simone Signoret, Yves Montand, and Arthur Miller on the set of *The Crucible* (1956). Credit: Ministère de l'Architecture et du Patrimoine/Roger Corbeau, Photographer/dist. RMN/Art Resource/NY.

Simone Signoret and Laurence Harvey in *Room at the Top* (1959), directed by Jack Clayton, 1959. Credit: Kobal Collection/Art Resource, NY.

Room at the Top (1959). Directed by Jack Clayton. Author's collection.

Arthur Miller, Simone Signoret, Yves Montand, Marilyn Monroe, Frankie Vaughan in Hollywood, 1960. Credit: Kobal Collection/Art Resource, NY.

Simone Signoret, Academy Award portrait, 1960. Author's collection.

Simone Signoret and Stuart Whitman in *The Day and the Hour* (*Le Jour et L'Heurer*) (1963), directed by René Clement. Credit: Kobal Collection/Art Resource, NY.

Simone Signoret and Stuart Whitman in *The Day and the Hour* (1963), directed by René Clement. Author's collection.

Portrait of Simone, ca. 1960s.
Author's collection.

Catherine Allégret (daughter of Simone Signoret and Yves Allégret) and Jacques
Perrin in *Sleeping Car Murders* (*Compartiment Tueurs*) (1965), directed by Costa-Gavras.
Author's collection.

Simone Signoret as Lisa in scene from the film *Games* (1967), directed by Curtis Harrington. Author's collection.

Simone Signoret, ca. 1968. Credit: Ministère de l'Architecture et du Patri-moine/Roger Corbeau, Photographer/dist. RMN/Art Resource/NY.

Simone Signoret as Clemence Bouin in scene from the film *Le Chat* (1971), directed by Pierre Granier-Deferre. Author's collection.

Simone Signoret as Madame Rosa in the film of the same name, directed by Moshe Mizrahi and released in 1977. Author's collection.

Madame Rosa, directed by Moshe Mizrahi (1977). Author's collection.

irritated her later on, and she would finally refuse to answer it. But in December 1958, on this first application for a visa, she and Montand took the question seriously and gave it their best efforts. They were not worried about the first half of the question: Simone and Montand had never been members of the Communist Party. The glitch was in the second half, and they could only be honest: Yes, they were members of organizations affiliated with communists, the peace movement and the communist trade union, Confédération Générale du Travail. Yes, they checked off on question number twenty-one, the previous question was abundantly clear. Then they signed their applications and sent them off, waiting with baited breath for the answer. It arrived a few days later in the form of a phone call from the embassy.

A young cultural attaché called to express great regret that their visa applications had been rejected. It was such a surprise and disappointment to the embassy that the consul wanted to meet them and discuss the decision in person. He wondered if they'd mind stopping by his office. They minded. Doing so was pointless, Simone thought, but she indicated that if he wanted to stop by the Place Dauphine, they would happily meet with him. Both the consul and a young attaché arrived the next day.

They were upset about the visa application rejections because the United States had just granted a visa to a mistress of Henri Lafont, the former head of the Gestapo in Paris during the Nazi Occupation. Lafont and his mistresses had hosted lavish parties at 93 Rue Lauriston, Gestapo headquarters, even as prisoners were tortured in other rooms. Neighbors of 93 Rue Lauriston woke each night to the screams of Lafont's victims. It was embarrassing to report that the United States would give a visa to a Nazi collaborator but not to Simone and Montand, and the embassy wanted to set the record straight, clearing its conscience. Simone and Montand had already heard about the situation with Lafont's mistress and explained that it was a big joke in Parisian circles. Simone tried to lighten the mood with another joke. She suggested that given the American interest in providing visas to Nazi collaborators, she should have emphasized the period she worked for the pro-Nazi newspaper *Nouveaux Temps*. The joke broke the tension and everyone laughed.

However, Norman Granz didn't laugh. Simone thought he took the rejection as a personal affront. He set to work on the problem, promising that their visas would be approved one way or another. They appreciated the effort but were not hopeful or even concerned. While a premiere on Broadway was certainly desirable, it wasn't an opportunity Montand had sought out, and he was not disappointed. If anything, the entire affair was a distraction, and he turned his attention back to his concert schedule.

In the meantime, Simone learned that *Room at the Top* would be distributed in January. Until then, with no other film opportunities in the offing, she was content to return to her place at Montand's side. Then, the couple received news that the United States would entertain another visa application in January, and chances were good that it would be approved. They were ecstatic, but there would be no time for celebration.

On December 10, 1958, Simone's twenty-eight-old brother, Alain, died tragically. He was filming a documentary on the fishermen of the island of Sein, off the Brittany coast in France. He and his crew were on a fishing vessel in waters that were turbulent on a good day and treacherous during a freak storm, when Alain fell overboard and drowned. Simone was devastated. Alain was her Christmas present when she was nine years old, and she had maintained a close relationship with him throughout his life. As an adult, Alain would often call his sister for moral support after their mother visited his apartment. Georgette was not fond of his girlfriend, Collette, because among other things, she bleached her hair at the kitchen sink. Her hostility resulted in numerous arguments between mother and son. Alain held his ground and then called Simone to share his frustration in conversations that usually ended with good humor.

Alain wanted to be a film director, and when their father insisted that he attend law school, Simone intervened by introducing him to her friend, the director Marcel Carné, who helped start the young man's film career. Alain began his directorial apprenticeship in 1955 on the film *Heroes and Sinners*, and then served as an assistant director on *Inspector Maigret* and *The Hunchback of Notre Dame*. His latest film, the documentary *La Mer et les Jours*, was his directorial debut; the twenty-eight year old had co-written the script with another friend of Simone's, Chris Marker.

This was a senseless death, a life lost too young. Simone and Georgette were so inconsolable that they did not attend his funeral (there was no account of André's whereabouts). Jean-Pierre was the only member of the family present in the Catholic cemetery, Île des Veuves, the Widows' Isle, where Alain was buried. While Simone never spoke of her grief, she spoke of Alain's death as a turning point. "Since then, without fail, I know whether a tale I'm about to tell, whether gravely sad or hilariously funny, took place before December 10, 1958—or after. It's a border."

The pendulum had swung from great joy to the deepest sorrow and then back again, as *Room at the Top* was released in the United Kingdom in January 1959. It was an instant box office hit. On January 31, the national British newspaper *Daily Express* published a review that summed up the film's success, mirroring other reviews:

NO ROOM
Standing room only for "Room at the Top."
    In seven days at a West End cinema, this British film has taken 10 per cent more cash at normal prices than any other film has taken in a similar period since the cinema was built 32 years ago. Once again quality of plot, direction, acting and presentation rings up a great success. And proves that good movie-making is good business.

What set *Room* apart from anything they had seen before in a general audience film was the steamy sex scenes, frank dialogue, and "savage" ending to the love story. Reviewers were ecstatic:

The sex is there, in torrents . . . magnificent . . . moving entertainment. *Sunday Express*

This week the British cinema grew up . . . a film that is startling, savage and unique. For the first time in a British film sex is given the status of an adult occupation. *Sunday Dispatch*

Sex was treated so carefully in films at that time, it was always inferred rather than depicted. There were rules: Couples were never seen in bed together, they were never naked, and there was certainly no dialogue about the couple's experience. *Room* broke some of these rules, while still maintaining decorum. The sexual act was never depicted, and there was no nudity. But the pillow talk afterwards was so over-the-top for the times that audiences were left feeling they were voyeurs in the bedroom of the people who lived next door. "It's so good for me, is it good for you, too?" Alice asks Joe after they make love. "I can't tell you how good," he whispers, as he pulls Alice on top of him. They are clothed—he in a tee shirt and pants; she in a camisole. When Alice gets up and puts on a robe, Joe comments, "I hate you to put your clothes on." She responds, "That's very sweet of you, Honey, but I'm far too old to walk about in my girdle." Later, when Joe tries to make moves on the young, virginal Susan and is rebuffed, he chastises her: "You lead me on so far and then you stop me. What do you think I'm made of?" Susan responds by asking what he wants of her, and he responds, "I want what every Joe wants." She then admits that she's scared and asks Joe to be gentle with her.

Joe is torn between two women, the older one he loves, and the younger one who represents his ticket to the top. But after an argument with Alice and a brief separation, Joe finally realizes that he can't live without her. He makes a choice: He asks her to leave her husband. Alice agrees: "I never realized it could be like this," she tells him. Then Joe learns that his brief liaison with Susan Brown made her "in a family way," and Susan's father offers him a job in the firm, if he will marry Susan. The only caveat is that Joe has to stop seeing Alice Aisgill. Lured by the promise of success, Joe agrees and cruelly breaks off with Alice. "We are only loving friends," he tells her. Yes, he loved her, but they had no future together and must never see each other again. Alice is devastated and goes to a local pub to drown her sorrows. Afterwards, wobbly on her feet from drink, she gets in her car and drives off.

The next morning, while friends at work are celebrating Joe's new job opportunity, he learns that Alice has driven her car off a road and been killed. It is a cruel death. The steering wheel severed her scalp from her skull, and as she crawled on the road, seeking help, she left a bloody trail. A farmer finally finds her mangled body the next morning. When Joe learns of her death, he plunges into drunken despair that leads to a brawl. His friends rescue him in time for his wedding day. He has lost the only woman he ever loved, but must pretend happiness for Susan's sake after their wedding, when he agrees with her, though teary-eyed, that he has finally received everything he wanted and deserved.

Simone's portrayal of the loving but unhappy wife of a man who cheated on her is so authentic and endearing that she easily won the hearts of audiences. She was an older woman, yes, but she exuded a sensuality that rivaled a younger woman's, thus inspiring other women. Every movement and expression—even the act of smoking a cigarette with a long, slow drag while gazing at Joe—communicated desire.

While Simone, Jack Clayton, and James Woolf were thrilled with the success, they considered it an "insular phenomenon,"[1] as the film had only been released in the United Kingdom at that point. Simone returned to Montand's side, as they set to work on new visa applications for the United States. Norman Granz was confident they would be approved for entry from July 15 to December 15, 1959.

When their passports arrived, Simone discovered a series of handwritten numbers that reminded her of a mathematical equation. Norman Granz explained that the formula indicated a waiver. While her English language skills were solid, the word confused Simone, and it became a running joke: "A waver . . . . To wave means to agitate a small flag or your hand, preferably with a handkerchief clutched in it." Simone imagined someone standing the shore waving a handkerchief to welcome her. Later, she learned that this waver was in fact a waiver; the United States government was waiving immigration restrictions by allowing their entry into the country for a limited period of time. The explanation didn't please Simone as much as her imagined story did.

With the issue of visas finally resolved, arrangements were made for *An Evening with Yves Montand* at the Henry Miller Theater on Broadway in mid-September 1959. Montand, who spoke not a word of English, was suddenly besieged by insecurity.

CHAPTER 20

From the Trough to the Crest of the Wave

ROOM AT THE TOP DOMINATED THE BRITISH ACADEMY OF FILM AND Television Arts awards in spring 1959. Simone won Best Foreign Actress, Laurence Harvey won Best British Actor, and *Room at the Top* took prizes as both Best British Film and Best Film from any source. Co-stars Donald Woflit and Hermione Baddeley were nominated for awards but did not win. *Room at the Top*, an unprecedented success, set the standard for "kitchen sink" realism in dramas and created a resurgence of the British film industry. Simone was now riding the crest of the British "new wave."

The film's American premiere, held on March 30, 1959, at the Fine Arts Theater in New York City, received overwhelmingly positive reviews:

It Never Quite Happened on The Screen This Way Before! One of The Best Pictures You Will See This Year! Archer Winston, *Post*

Extraordinarily Adult! A Whole New Chapter is About to Be Written in Motion Picture History! Arthur Knight, *Saturday Review*

The Fine Arts Theater scored a coup in booking Room at the Top for its New York Premiere, although the booking is costing a mint, as rentals go for houses that size . . . . Dorothy Kilgallen, *New York Journal American*

Continental Distributors, Inc. developed a campaign booklet for theaters that rivaled anything they had promoted in years: "Make Room for the

Top Box Office Record Breaker! Raves and Praise from all over the country . . . backed by one of the most comprehensive publicity campaigns in recent years."[1] To generate continued interest, they encouraged theaters to host essay contests based on the film's central themes: "A woman falls in love with a man ten years her junior. Can such a love story survive this age difference? What is an 'angry young man'?"

However, not all were pleased with the film's success. In route to the New York premiere, author John Braine expressed his disdain for the type of publicity the film adaptation was receiving, both in Britain and in America. During an interview, William Michelfeder of the *New York Telegram* quoted a viewer who said the film "is seething and simmering with sensuality." Braine protested, "There is nothing—absolutely nothing—in my book which can be called pure sexiness. My dear man, I challenge you to find a single detailed scene of sexuality in that book." When the reporter reminded him of the beach scene where Joe and Alice kiss, both of them naked beneath their trench coats, again Braine objected. "That is not detailed. It is pure suggestiveness. You cannot find anything clinical there. Nothing about this-and-that. Only the suggestion." Braine also had a change of heart about his association with Britain's Angry Young Men. "I renounce that buildup . . . these angry young men (authors John Osborne, Kingsley Amis, and John Wain) are not my dish. Theirs is a soft view of life. I am a man of strong beliefs . . . a practicing Christian, for example, who goes to church. I'm not angry—and it makes me angry that people say I am." His novel, *Angry Young Men*, would be a singular success in the author's career, and in spite of his objections—and much to the delight of audiences—*Room at the Top* continued to be billed as torrid, sensual, and shocking, a shoo-in for an Oscar nomination. Jack Clayton and James Woolf were on the phone again with Simone, sharing headline reviews they thought amusing: *Room Boffo, Room Whamm*, lingo she had never heard before, but she got the message. *Room at the Top* was a sensation in the United States.

Simone enjoyed a great sense of satisfaction in winning over an American audience, a satisfaction that surpassed even her pleasure over the film's success in Britain. In the past, her films played primarily in art houses for film aficionados, but never to general audiences. After the US government had rejected her visa for *Me and the Colonel*, Simone had lost hope of ever breaking through the barrier she'd call "McCarthyist Purgatory." But with *Room*, she had, in essence, stormed the back door to the country without Hollywood's help or the government's consent. Success was truly the best revenge.

She did not experience the same sense of satisfaction when *Room* was released in her own country in May 1959. Love scenes, pillow talk, and affairs with older woman were far from unusual in sexually liberated France. And French audiences simply couldn't relate to Britain's social inequity between the working class and the aristocracy. By and large, the critics were unimpressed, and Simone's international acclaim was ignored, even though she was nominated for a Golden Palm at the Cannes Film Festival. When she won the award, rather than photograph her reaction, the photographers took advantage of another unrelated and unexpected recognition at Cannes. Her brother Alain Kaminker was recognized with a posthumous award for his achievement as a young filmmaker. Simone was stunned by the unexpected honor and still raw from her brother's death. "I was taken completely unaware, and just as my heart was jolting with emotions at what had been said, the flashbulbs went off. And of course, it was these photos that appeared the next morning in most of the press, with captions saying: 'Ecstatically happy, she couldn't contain her feelings when her prize was announced.'"[2]

Arbitrary treatment by the press and the tepid audience reaction to *Room* in France were the exception, not the rule. Following the release in France and America, *Room at the Top* was released to international markets, from Eastern Europe to Hong Kong to South America. Overnight, Simone Signoret became an international sensation. Yet rather than luxuriate in the moment, she returned quietly to her husband's side, as he focused on his upcoming Broadway premiere. During this period, he had a sense that he was entering a dark tunnel of confused feelings, which ranged from euphoria at having this opportunity, to sheer terror at the thought he might fall flat on his face. His insecurities were not unfounded. Careers were made or broken in one night on a Broadway stage. He had never tested an American audience. His songs and skits were entirely in French, and he spoke not a word of English. The Broadway premiere was a risk, yet it was one he had to take.

Simone focused her attention on helping him practice English phrases so he could introduce his songs to the audience. But in spite of her best efforts to put her success in perspective, the phone, which had once been too quiet, sprung to life with unexpected offers. Among the callers was Elia Kazan, who offered her a role in his adaptation of Colette's *Cheri* on Broadway. Simone wouldn't take the call and rejected the idea without hesitation as a matter of principle. Kazan had named names during the HUAC hearings, an act that resulted in the blacklisting of other artists. She could not, in good conscience, give him or his offer a second thought. There was an offer to star in *The Lion* with William Holden, a film that would not be produced until much later, without Simone. And she was offered a role in an adaptation of Lawrence Durrell's novel *Justine*. Simone had read all of Durrell's novels but was not interested. A film deal with Bing Crosby was suggested, but she was in no rush to jump into Hollywood. Instead, she accepted a role in a low budget Italian film, *Adua e le compagne*, (Adua and friends), directed by Antonio Pietrangeli. Filming would begin in spring 1960. It was a safe bet, because by then Montand's anticipated US tour would have ended and the couple would be back in Europe.

The one offer she received from the U.S. that she was keen to accept was from the respected journalist Edward R. Murrow. He had called to invite her to participate as a guest on his show *Small World*, which aired Sunday nights on CBS. This particular segment, his first "all women symposium," would be taped at a later date, while she and Montand were still in the United States. Although Simone had never had an opportunity to meet Murrow, she was well aware of his reputation during World War II as a credible journalist of the highest caliber. Even more impressive to her was his successful attempt to expose and discredit Senator Joseph McCarthy on another of Murrow's show, *See It Now*. This attempt alone elevated Murrow's status in her eyes, and she readily accepted his offer.

During the summer of 1959, Simone's name was invoked in the international press so often she began to worry that the publicity might have a negative effect on her husband in America. She feared he might, as an unknown, be viewed as "Mr. Signoret," and not an artist in his own right. Simone contemplated the idea of delaying her arrival in New York by a week or two so Montand could have time to get his bearings without living in her shadow. In the end, they arrived together, but Simone was ever vigilant with the press, always on her guard, ready to set the record straight if a journalist strayed from focusing on Montand. However, as P. E. Schneider of the *Times* demonstrated in his feature article designed to introduce Montand to his American audience, it was impossible not to invoke Simone's name.

"Simone Signoret, whose mature, frank, warm womanliness in 'Room at the Top,' has endeared her to millions and brought her offers to star on Broadway and in Hollywood, has just left Paris for New York—but not to act there. 'I am going to New York to be with my husband, just as I would go with him to Toulouse or Montreux or Knokke-Zoute,'" he quoted. Schneider then turned his attention the singer, Yves—pronounced "Eve"

he explained (a name requiring explanation because it was common-
ly mispronounced in the United States as "Eves")—"the athlete of the
chanson," who treated audiences to over two hours of song, dance, pan-
tomimes, acrobatics, and juggling without an intermission. Montand put
aside his terror and was self-confident during this interview, claiming
that he was not at all worried about his performance on Broadway—at
least no more than he worried about every performance.

Simone translated the interview, and when the journalist turned the
discussion back to her, she again made her position clear: While her husband was on stage, she would be backstage watching, hidden from the
audience's view. Off the record, the couple lunched with the reporter,
who wanted to understand why the couple had not come to America
sooner. Simone explained that nothing had changed as far as they were
concerned. It was the American government that changed, allowing
visas.

When they arrived in New York on September 10, 1959, her concern about misplaced publicity was renewed, because she was recognized
as Alice Aisgill, or "Simonn," or "Miss Signor-rett" by nearly everyone
they met—from the officials at the airport immigration gate, to taxi driv-
ers, policemen, store clerks, and people on the street. Simone enjoyed
the recognition but worried about Montand, and with good reason. "He
didn't like it—he didn't like it at all," she explained to Peer Oppenheimer
of the *Sarasota Herald Tribune* later on. She worried that her recognition
was clouding recognition Montand should receive. And if by chance he
was not successful on Broadway, there was no way she could enjoy success. "I had a recurring nightmare that he would be forced to leave in
disgrace from this city where Alice continued to work for me while my
husband had missed his entrance.[3]

Her strategy of continually deflecting attention back to Montand and
her role as a supportive wife worked. The press became fascinated by this
"chic" international couple, and they were not only impressed with Simone's devotion to her husband, but to her willingness to speak frankly
about the dynamics of their relationship: "We have conflicts, more violent perhaps than in other households. We fight and then we get over it.
All that is very Latin. When I'm really mad, I sit in the back of the theater
and think, 'What a bastard! But my God, how good he is!'"

There was little time to explore New York City after their arrival. Norman Granz met them at the airport and whisked them off to the Algonquin Hotel at 59 West 44th Street, where they were introduced to the
Bodne family, Ben and Mary, owners of the famous hotel, which enjoyed

a reputation for catering to the needs of jazz musicians and writers. The Algonquin was Norman's second home, and it would become a favorite of Simone, who liked the family environment there, which reminded her of the atmosphere at the Columbe d'Or Hotel. She and Mary would become steadfast friends.

On that first evening, the Montands' only glimpse of the city was a quick but revealing walk to the Henry Miller Theater. Montand wanted to check it out, though it was closed at the time, and Norman led the way. They were surprised by their proximity to Times Square and overwhelmed by the sights, sounds, and bright lights.[4] They were so painfully aware of the fact that careers were made or broken by a single performance in one of these famous theaters that they had made tentative promises to Catherine. If Montand was successful on opening night, she could join them in New York for the balance of a six-week stint; if not, they planned to return to Paris immediately, and she'd see them there a few days later.

In spite of these fears, they easily lost themselves in the city the next morning, Friday, September 11, as they walked about on their own to see the sights and visit shops and museums. New York was experiencing Indian summer, and Simone was not accustomed to the high humidity and scorching heat that was so intense it softened the asphalt streets. The heels of her white stiletto shoes sank into the pavement and left track marks in her wake. The shoes were ruined and could never be worn again. But as Montand would discover twenty-six years later, Simone kept the shoes, storing them in the bottom of her closet as a memento of a time in their lives when they were in love and the future held endless opportunities.

For his part, Montand was miserable. He had two weeks to prepare for his opening night, and it seemed that every possible obstacle was presenting itself. A wisdom tooth was impacted, and as oral surgery had to be avoided at all costs, he made daily visits to a dentist—a frustrating experience because he couldn't communicate in English. Simone accompanied him to every appointment and translated, then waited for him until the procedure was complete. To combat the language barrier, Montand and his pianist, Bob Castella, attended a Berlitz course three times a week, which helped, but took precious time from rehearsals. Then, Montand learned that the musicians union would not allow some members of his orchestra to perform. Norman Granz took care of finding appropriate American replacements, but now Montand had a new group of musicians to acclimate to and get up to speed.

In the meantime, with Simone's help, he continued to rehearse twen-ty-second introductions to each of the songs he planned to perform. He learned these brief speeches phonetically. To aid the audience, an English translation of each song was prepared for the playbill. Granz took care of these important details, but all the activity had to be fit in between the interviews he arranged for the singer to promote his show. One inter-view followed after another, so that it seemed Montand had little time to catch his breath. There was certainly little time for sightseeing, though one evening Granz took the couple to the Apollo Theater to hear his cli-ent Ella Fitzgerald.

It was during this intense period, the "dark tunnel," that Montand felt the tug of an unsettling but all too familiar compulsion: He admired beautiful women. In retrospect, years later, he attributed this impulse to the start of a mid-life crisis. Like Simone, he was thirty-eight years of age, and forty was pressing in on him. When he attempted to describe these feelings to his biographers, Hamon and Rotman, they labeled the emotions "lyrical gusts." Montand felt "the frustrating, delectable, and unpredictable urge to love and be loved, to be the object of tenderness and to reciprocate without restraint"—but apparently not with his wife. He was caught up in a "lyrical gust" one morning while walking to a Ber-litz class. An attractive woman passed him on the street, and Montand was immediately taken with her. He turned "to race after the unknown woman who had excited him," but she had already disappeared into the throng of people on the street. This would be the first of several encoun-ters that unnerved him. However, Montand did not explain or provide insight into his reasons or share these experiences with his wife, who wasn't likely to be pleased or sympathetic.

The management of the Henry Miller Theater was so concerned about Montand's success that *An Evening with Yves Montand* was booked for only one week. This decision was recognized as a mistake on opening night, Monday, September 21, 1959, when Montand entertained a packed house, a scenario repeated each successive night for the entire booking. After a week, Montand moved to the Longacre Theater, where he con-tinued his successful run for the next five weeks. In all, Montand gave over forty sold-out performances. Reviews were consistently exceptional, and audiences were always regretful when the curtain closed on thun-derous ovations and calls for an encore. Talent surpassed the language barrier, and Montand was compared to Sinatra and described as "attrac-tive, sexy and exciting." These references to his looks were descriptions the singer had never heard before. He had always been sensitive about his appearance, painfully aware of his prominent nose and elastic but expressive mouth. Oddly, he never thought of himself as attractive— let alone sexy—despite the reaction he received from female audience members. Yet his charisma translated easily for American women, who flocked backstage in a gaggle to meet him. One of those women was Marilyn Monroe.

Marilyn attended his opening night performance with Montgomery Clift, who was her escort for the evening because her husband, Arthur Miller, was busy working on a final draft of *The Misfits*. She was so intrigued by Montand's performance she returned with her husband the following night. Arthur Miller had met both Simone and Montand when he visited the set of *The Crucible* in Europe, and he was delighted to meet them again backstage after the show. Reportedly, there was a joke about the performance, which the Millers shared with the Montands. Apparently, whenever Montand put his hands in his pockets on stage, the lighting hit the buttons on his fly. The glare made it appear that his fly was open, causing bursts of giggling during the show. Montand heard it, didn't understand it, and couldn't afford the distraction, so he had ignored it. The joke was received with good humor, which continued when the Millers invited Simone and Montand to dinner at their Manhattan apartment.

Montand's success meant that Simone could finally relax and enjoy the fruits of her success. She no longer resented the intrusion of Alice Aisgill: "It was pleasant when the three of us arrived at parties: Eaves, Simonn and Alice. She was no longer a nuisance." Catherine arrived three days after opening night, accompanied by Colette, the grieving fiancée of Alain Kaminker. The woman was still raw from her loss, and Simone had invited her, thinking the change of pace would be good for her. Simone then enrolled her daughter in the Lycée Français of New York. Catherine attended classes there for the rest of the term. The teenager adjusted to her new environment so well that when Simone and Montand left for the Canadian leg of his tour, she readily accepted the prospect of remaining in New York with Mary Bodne as her chaperone.

Montand was scheduled to spend one week in Canada, performing in both Montreal and Toronto before returning to America for a week in Los Angeles and another in San Francisco. After that, the entire family planned to reunite for the Christmas holiday in France.

❧

When they caught their first glimpse of the legendary Hollywood sign from their plane, Simone was surprised: "HOLLYWOOD, traced out in capital letters as though written by a child," so simplistic yet a symbol of dreams. She considered it the Mecca of their adolescent fantasies, and they couldn't help but reminisce. "I'm always sorry for the people who reject the gifts their adolescent memories may offer," she wrote in *Nostalgia*, expressing sorrow for those who dismissed their dreams as unrealistic fantasies. She and Montand were reliving their teen fantasies as the plane made its descent. They had finally arrived at Mecca—though Simone made a point of remarking that she and Montand got there without Hollywood's help.

The day after their arrival, on November 7, they were guests of honor at a party hosted by Kirk and Anne Douglas, a magnificent event that filled their hosts' living room and dining room, spilling out onto the patio. As they learned later, the party was held at the same time the Republican Party was hosting an event for Richard Nixon, the presidential candidate running against John F. Kennedy. Some guests visited both parties, but the vast majority remained at the Douglas party. While Judy Garland sang impromptu, Simone and Montand were introduced to an all-star group of guests that included Kim Novak, George Cukor, and Dean Martin, as well as Gary Cooper, Gene Kelly, Gregory Peck, and Henry Hathaway, all of them with their wives. Montand finally had an opportunity to meet Walt Disney. He had written to Disney as a thirteen-year-old and wondered why he had never responded. Simone was reunited with her agent, Minna Wallis, who enjoyed sharing the story of how she couldn't drag Simone away from Montand in 1949. Before he returned to the Nixon gala, Jack Warner stopped by for a quick visit, because he wanted to meet Montand, the "sonofabitch" who had broken his contract with the studio mogul. Warner had long ago overcome his anger about that event, but he was still defensive about his role in blacklisting artists during the McCarthy era. However, as Simone observed, "He bore no grudge against those he had wronged."

She was amused when the French actress and comedienne Capucine told her quietly that she had just attended a private screening of *Room at the Top*, which had been stopped after the first reel because the guests wanted to play cards. Yet, at the party, they gushed with praise and admiration for the film and her performance. Simone wasn't offended by this behavior, because insincerity was to be expected in a place called Tinsel Town. She had another favorite name for Hollywood: the "iridescent bubble," a plastic, shimmering world that hovered slightly above the earth, just out of reach of reality.

CHAPTER 21

Small World

MONTAND'S WEEKLONG ENGAGEMENT AT THE HUNTINGTON-HARTFORD
Theater in LA was such a resounding success that he was invited to make
his American television debut on the popular Sunday night program,
The Dinah Shore Show, on November 15, 1959, a live broadcast filmed in
"living color" on NBC. Montand sang two songs from his repertoire: "A
Paris" and "Un Garçon dansait" a song and dance skit about a waiter who
dreams of becoming Fred Astaire though he can't sing or dance. Then
Shore guided the singer through a carefully scripted chat about the difficulties of learning English. Montand had memorized his responses and
his ever-gracious hostess never deviated from their script. For the finale,
he and Shore sang a duet, "Ain't We Got Fun." The entire experience
went off without a hitch, and Montand was on top of the world when he
and Simone left LA for San Francisco the following morning.

They barely had enough time to unpack their bags before he opened
that evening for a week of performances at the Gary Theater. This was it,
the last leg of the American tour. By the end of November, they planned
to fly to New York to reunite with Catherine before their return to
France, just in time for Montand to reassemble his orchestra and begin
rehearsals for his next tour, in Japan, which was scheduled for January
1960. However, Arthur Miller and Marilyn Monroe had other plans for
the singer.

Earlier that month Marilyn had begun rehearsals for her next film,
The Billionaire, a musical comedy planned with Gregory Peck as a co-
star. The film was later renamed *Let's Make Love*. Marilyn hadn't read
the script when she signed and then realized later that she didn't like
the film. Her lightweight role was so marginalized that director George

Cukor and Twentieth Century Fox agreed to hire Miller to tackle revisions. In the meantime, Marilyn was already showing signs of the frustrating behaviors that haunted her productions. She was consistently late
on the set or a no show. The producers weren't too concerned by the
disruptions and delays at first, believing Marilyn would get back on track
after the script was revised.

The changes pleased her well enough; however, when her co-star,
Gregory Peck, read the revisions, he balked. Marilyn's role had been built
up so much that Peck wanted out and offered to return his hundred
thousand dollar advance. The studio reluctantly accepted and then fran-
tically turned to a list of likely substitute leading men: Charlton Heston,
James Stewart, Kirk Douglas, Yul Brenner, Cary Grant, Peter Lawford,
Tony Curtis, and Rock Hudson. All turned down the role. Miller, with
Marilyn's encouragement, recommended Montand as a possible solu-
tion, a decision that would provide fodder for the gutter press later on:
"MM herself, quivering all over in the most delightful way, had fought
like an untamed tigress to GET THE ROLE FOR HER NEW FRENCH
FRIEND."[1]

Everyone agreed that Montand was fresh, new, and on everyone's
mind after his successful appearances on stage and with Dinah Shore.
Miller thought Montand could handle the role owing to his credible
performance in both the stage and film adaptation of *The Crucible* in
France, giving credence to Marilyn's demand. There were obstacles, and
not minor ones, that had to be faced. Montand couldn't speak English
and was on a limited visa. However, given lost production time—delays that would affect scheduling of Marilyn's next film—Spyros Skouras, president of Twentieth Century Fox, agreed to accept Montand. The
Montands were no sooner settled into their room at the St. Francis Hotel
in San Francisco, when central casting called with the offer. Simone took
the call and agreed to read the script on her husband's behalf. Though
the story was weak, it was amusing at times, and she thought that a
musical comedy with Marilyn in a starring role and the popular Tony
Randall in a supporting role was a safe bet for a successful break into
Hollywood. Simone encouraged Montand to accept the film role.

The significance of starring with Marilyn was not lost on Montand,
and he needed no encouragement. As soon as he accepted, the Actors
Guild sent a representative to their hotel suite to handle negotiations
with the studio. Negotiations were conducted in a series of quick phone
conversations—three in all—that Simone translated for Montand's benefit. After Montand's agent turned down fifty thousand dollars, the studio

representative slammed his phone down in disgust. A few minutes later, the studio representative called back, this time offering seventy-five
thousand dollars. Again, the agent turned the offer down. Montand and
Simone were unnerved at that point, because he would have readily accepted the first offer. Clearly, this was a game, and they worried that this
agent's greed might compromise the opportunity of a lifetime. Montand's
hands shook as he lit a cigarette and turned to Simone: "These Americans
are crazy."[2] The agent reassured him, and within minutes, the phone
rang again. This time the offer was accepted. It was for one hundred
thousand dollars, more money than Montand could possibly imagine.
Euphoric, he and Simone hugged, opened a bottle of champagne, and
danced around the room like teenagers in joyful celebration. Then they
were struck by the complications of the situation.

Montand had to postpone his tour of Japan, and Simone had to make
arrangements for Catherine, who was finishing up a semester in New
York. Catherine was given two choices: After the semester ended, she
could either join her parents in, LA or return to France. She chose to
return to France.

Montand's issue was not easily solved. The promoters in Japan were
outraged by the news that they would have to postpone, when the theaters and stadiums booked for his performances were already sold out
and scalpers were taking advantage, inflating ticket prices daily. Montand
was accused of being irresponsible and heavily criticized in the press, but
the Japanese tour was finally postponed.

In the meantime, Simone prepared for her appearance on *Small World*,
nearly forgotten since arrangements had been made during the summer.
Small World was an innovative "four-way transatlantic conversation,"
created and moderated by Edward R. Murrow. Though Murrow was on
sabbatical from CBS at the time and in London, he had agreed to continue moderating the show, particularly this show, his first "all women
symposium."

Television was in its infancy and did not yet have satellite capabilities
for simulcasting a show from multiple locations. So, *Small World* was
pre-recorded using international telephone lines, while cameras pre-
recorded Murrow and his three guests in their separate locations. Later,
he and his producer, Fred Friendly, edited the program so that the audio
and visual components fit together seamlessly. The camera cut between
shots of the host and his guests as they talked, listened, or reacted. These
seemingly insignificant production details were important, because while
Murrow and his guests could hear each other, they could not see each

other, and it was easy to forget the camera in the heat of an argument, when un-checked body language communicated far more than dialogue could accomplish. And Murrow had assembled a controversial guest list: the choreographer, Agnes DeMille, a professed liberal; the gossip columnist, Hedda Hopper, a notorious right-wing conservative and McCarthy supporter; and Simone Signoret, an alleged communist apologist. The segment was pre-recorded on November 20, 1959, and aired on December 6. But the fall-out of this show would spill over into the next year.

Simone was well aware of the backgrounds of the other guests. Agnes DeMille, niece of Cecil B. DeMille, was a renowned choreographer and best-selling author. Murrow described her as "the gracious lady who revolutionized ballet in the United States" with her dance interpretations in *Oklahoma!, Carousel, Brigadoon,* and other Broadway hits. Agnes, a gracious and pragmatic woman who considered herself "the best known, not the best, the best known choreographer,"[3] was never blacklisted during the Red Scare as Simone was led to believe, but she was a professed liberal and an outspoken critic of Senator Joseph McCarthy. While she had never met Simone, DeMille was quite familiar with Hedda Hopper, the "pretty actress" she saw numerous times when she hung around her uncle's movie sets as a child. But then Agnes grew up and Hedda Hopper became a gossip columnist—and in DeMille's view, "a scourge . . . a tremendous reactionary."

Simone considered Hopper, "a dud actress who swapped the stage for journalism." But in Hollywood, Hedda Hopper was not so easily dismissed. She was a force to be reckoned with, and like her competitor, Louella Parsons, she was so successful with the poison pen, she had turned fear into a profitable business. Hopper and Parsons were self-appointed censors of Hollywood, and using their syndicated columns, they had the power to make or break deals, and ruin careers and marriages. Nothing about the lives of the stars—their politics, friends, family, health, or love affairs—was sacred. Arthur Miller described the two gossip columnists as "the guardian furies . . . the police matrons . . . the women's ferocity toward Communism was matched only by their duplication of some of its practices."[4]

The studios considered Parsons the lesser of two evils. If Louella had a story and they wanted it squashed, she was likely to comply with their request. She had good sources. Her husband "Docky," a studio physician, was the most productive of all. Chances were good that Louella knew about a pregnancy or illness even before the subject actress or actor was told. But her brand of gossip was mild compared to that purveyed by

Hopper, who hid a mind of her own beneath her famous hats. Even the most offensive and unscrupulous studio bosses feared her wrath. She took certain joy in describing herself as "the bitch of the world," and gloated over the stockpile of gifts she received from actors and studio bosses who wanted to remain on her good side. But if Hedda had a story, she was going to tell it, regardless of the impact.

The factor that contributed most to her menace was her influence beyond Hollywood. In her efforts to cleanse the industry of communists, she created a powerful alliance with J. Edgar Hoover, director of the Federal Bureau of Investigation, and she used that relationship shamelessly in the name of patriotism. She addressed Hoover as "My Dear Edgar," in her correspondence, and she was on the FBI's "Special Correspondents list" (it was noted in reports that she was to be addressed informally as "Dear Hedda").[5] She wrote to Hoover frequently to provide information during the Red Scare, and to compliment his efforts or task for his help. "I loved what you said about the Commies in the motion picture industry," Hopper wrote on April 7, 1947. "But I would like it even more if you could name names . . . . I'd like to run every one of those rats out of the country, starting with Charlie Chaplin." In her view, Chaplin had a lot of nerve coming to the United States to make movies and money, only to turn around and bite the hand that fed him by criticizing the government. Anyone who criticized or even appeared to criticize America was a subversive in her view, and when it came to Chaplin, she would stop at nothing to have him thrown out of the country. She aided that campaign, which succeeded.

In August 1947, she wrote to Director Hoover asking for help, because she had been asked to appear at a forum and was expected to defend the accusations she liked to hurl at victims she thought unworthy of breathing the same air she breathed. Because her accusations were often baseless, more suspicions than reality, she wanted to arm herself and needed help. "Naturally, I won't be able to accuse certain stars of being registered Communists," she wrote Hoover. "But you're so wise and have so many facts at your fingertips that I feel I can call upon your friendship. . . . Your information will be confidential. I won't use your name unless you give permission. In that case, I'd be very proud to say, Mr. J. Edgar Hoover, who is my choice for President, tells me so and so."

※

Murrow's guest list was controversial, and he wasted no time in setting up a contentious agenda with his first question. "Let's talk for a moment—the three of you—about this great American industry called gossip. It's now big business. How often does the writing of gossip invade the privacy of the life of the individual who is being written about?"

Hedda Hopper jumped right in: "I don't think it invades their private life very often. The people of the theatre and the people of motion pictures—everything they do is news, and I put gossip in the same category as news."

Surprisingly, Simone jumped in, questioning Hopper on rumors she'd heard that Hollywood actors and actresses actually asked for the type of publicity Hedda doled out in her syndicated column because it promoted their careers. Hopper educated her about the process: "A new romance, a new love affair would last about nine months . . . . Then the marriage . . ."

"And then the first baby," Simone added. The idea that some used their children to promote their careers always irked her, and she shared a little bit of herself with the others. "I have a child who is thirteen. . . . since the day she was born, I swore onto myself that she would never be photographed in a paper, because I think it's terrible for a child, and beside that, being an actress, I don't think I can use any publicity of the fact that I am a mother too, because if I was a real mother, I wouldn't be an actress, and I don't think I can use this quality of being a mother, for publicity."

The other guests hesitated a moment before chiming in with their own stories about children, but did not ask Simone to elaborate on her unique perspective on motherhood. Then Murrow picked up the thread: "Miss Signoret, is there anything in France to equal our gossip columns in the States?"

"Not exactly. There hasn't been for a very long time."

"Would you think that one reason there are so few gossip columnists in France is that the laws of libel and slander are more strict there than they are in the States?"

"I think it's not the reason," Simone answered confidently and without hesitation. "The reason is because we're freer toward the sexual relationship, if I may use the word, I don't know if it's allowed on the T.V. but . . . it's not important what other people do in their love life."

She said this as a statement of fact and not a criticism, without realizing that she had just revealed a weakness, one that Hedda Hopper would take advantage of in the near future. Indeed, as Simone would learn, gossip about celebrity love affairs was as newsworthy in France as it was in any other country.

"That would make it difficult for you to write in France, wouldn't it, Duchess?" Murrow asked, referring to Hopper, who had indicated in the introductions that she liked to be called Duchess.

"Yes, it would indeed. I wouldn't make a living there," Hopper answered wryly.

Murrow then cut to the chase with his next question, which provoked an electrifying debate that dominated the rest of the show. Later, Hopper complained she had been set up and outnumbered. Murrow was accused of creating an unfair advantage for liberals and of using tactics he had used to expose Senator Joseph McCarthy on national television.

"Well, I wonder if we could talk for a moment about entertainment and politics, or if you like, the arts and free speech. Is there any reason why a performer's political affiliations should either help or hurt his career?" Murrow reiterated the question: "Should a performing artist have either a penalty or a privilege as a result of his or her political belief?"

"Only if his political belief is doing harm to his country," Hopper jumped in. "They have a right to think as they like. They have a right to do as they like. But they have not a right to do or say anything that will harm their country."

Hopper felt there were subversives in the industry who were tampering with American values. As an example, she used the recently released film, *Blackboard Jungle*, with Sidney Poitier, which portrayed an inner-city school.

"Now that showed pupils of a high school—well, they were just all dreadful, dreadful people. Now, that picture went all over the world. It did a great deal of harm." Simone found her voice: "You're mistaken, Miss Hopper. It didn't do any harm to America; it proved that America was able to be free enough to tell things about itself . . . which is the best proof you can give to the whole world of freedom." But Hopper insisted that this single film had destroyed the world's positive opinion of America's educational system, and was convinced others concurred with her opinion. "Well, if they are idiots anyhow," Simone responded, "they won't . . . they will never think intelligently about anything."

Hopper's other concern was that infiltrators were changing the lyrics to old, time-honored songs like *Old Man River*. She thought it unconscionable that first Paul Robeson and then Frank Sinatra had systematically changed the song by eliminating references to "nigger" and "boss." "Our laws of subversion are not strong enough," Hopper summarized.

During this discussion, DeMille, Murrow, and Simone had all they could do to control their emotions. DeMille rolled her eyes or shook her head in dismay. At one point, Murrow snickered. Simone was shocked and could barely contain the overwhelming urge to laugh. Montand was there, sitting on a couch just off-camera, and she glanced at him several times during Hopper's tirade with the knowing look they often shared when they felt they were in the presence of a complete idiot.

But, amusement aside, the discussion offended her sensibilities. Hopper spoke about freedom without having a real sense of what the word meant. Simone took control of the discussion:

> I can very hardly interfere in this discussion, because I am not American, and I'm not aware enough of your problems. In fact, I think your problems are so different. . . . we had four years of Nazi occupation which has made us, whether we liked it or not, and especially people of my generation, we were twenty when it started, made us have to take conscious of certain problems, because it was a matter of life and death . . . certain problems toward freedom; toward peace; toward . . . how would I call it? I can't find the English word . . . I can't find the French word either.

Simone turned to Montand. "Comment qu'est-ce qu'on s'apelle?" "Intolerance," Montand replied.

> Yes, toward intolerance . . . because we have been so pressed; we have been kept prisoners for four years, that the thing we can't bear is intolerance. . . . England who has never been occupied, thanks God for them, they had a hard war. . . . they had the most terrible bombs destroying London, but they didn't have the Nazis; they don't know what the Gestapo is; they never heard someone knocking at the door at five o'clock in the morning; they never had their friends, who suddenly one morning disappeared. . . . they don't know where they are, and they never come back . . . and they never write because they are just standing [sic] in a camp somewhere, and they never saw their friends . . . some of their friends coming back in '45, looking like ghosts, in striped pajamas, and . . . and telling horrible stories, hardly telling anything because they could hardly speak. That's been the . . . the story of our generation; so, it's . . . it's formed us differently, I think, and thanks God, you didn't have that.

DeMille and Hopper listened in silence. Then Agnes agreed with Simone, but noted that while Americans had not experienced the Nazi occupation, they understood the need to preserve liberty and civil rights. "Whenever the real, creative freedoms are stifled for whatever reason, in the universities, in the newspapers, in art mediums . . . when that is curtailed, totalitarianism walks right into the country. It is the inevitable path."

"Could I get a word in edge wise here now?" Hopper asked, and then went on with a tirade of her own about subversive communists, who try to brainwash Americans. She and DeMille then continued a heated debate.

DeMille had high blood pressure and was so upset that during breaks in taping, she tended to a nosebleed and hives. Once she was composed again, DeMille continued talking about freedom.

"And our big freedom is what?" Hopper asked.

"The ability to protest freely among ourselves, not to subvert, not to betray, to protest and to criticize freely among ourselves, in whatever medium we choose to use. Don't you agree? I'm sure you agree to that."

"No . . . that shut me up completely. I'm dry."

And then Hopper said something that Simone could not believe: "I see where I'm in a nest of liberals."

It was the "last line," the only line Simone remembered. Clearly the use of the word "nest," often applied to communists, was intended to strike a nerve. In other words, the others didn't agree with Hopper and were therefore communists. Simone was so angered by the implication that after the show, she sent off a brief, terse, and challenging telegram to Hopper, thanking her for the "last line," and suggesting that she'd be waiting for the gossip columnist in France, where it had already been established that Hopper couldn't earn a living because the laws of libel and slander were so strict.[6]

Simone had responded in anger and then quickly forgot her reaction or wanted to forget it, because she never discussed the telegram in her accounts of the episode, which focused on the show's "last line." However, Hedda Hopper not only made a note of the telegram, she kept it in her file for future reference. She would deal with Simone Signoret later.

CHAPTER 22

"A Whacking Down to Size"

SIMONE WAS OBLIVIOUS TO THE FIRST SIGN OF TROUBLE WITH HEDDA
Hopper, who used her syndicated column to address the *Small World* episode immediately after it aired on December 6. While Simone received
many positive comments about her passionate description of experiences
during the Nazi occupation, Hopper merely gave her a cursory mention
before turning to the heated debate with Agnes DeMille. She took the
opportunity to thank those "loyal Americans" who had written in and
then, rather than comment further, she filled her column with quotes
from her correspondents, nineteen in all. All were positive, she claimed,
save one: "Your hat in the past has successfully hidden your main weakness, which is bigotry." Hopper only commented, "And all the time I was
misguided enough to think it was patriotism. To quote from some of the
wonderful letters":

"Your kind of old-fashioned Americanism is what the world needs."
"Wish more people thought as you do."
"You were a voice in the wilderness of brain washing liberals. Of
course this was a typical Murrow performance and his purpose was
quite clear."
"Your opposition reminded me of a watermelon, green outside
and red inside."[1]

Hopper was forced to mention Simone in her column on December 23, announcing that rumor had it the actress was slated to sign on
with Bing Crosby for *High Time*, "and it would appear that she and her

husband Montand would be working side by side at 20th Century Fox," she reported. It was rumor only; Simone never signed.

ψ

In early December, Simone and Montand returned to LA and settled into the Beverly Hills Hotel in bungalow number 20, directly across the hall from number 21, where Marilyn Monroe and Arthur Miller lived. The word "bungalow" was deceiving, Simone discovered. Bungalows on the sprawling grounds of the Beverly Hills Hotel were in fact large, two-story buildings, each with an executive suite on the first level and two smaller, but nonetheless spacious apartments on the second level. How-ard Hughes lived on the first level of the bungalow, and the Montands and Millers lived above him. The curtains to his apartment were always drawn, though Simone did have an opportunity to see him from afar on one occasion. But even at a distance, Simone felt a little embarrassed re-calling the contract she failed to fulfill with the mogul. As she explained in an interview, "I never showed up, or even replied to his request."[2]

The Montands and the Millers developed a comfortable, neighborly relationship during those first weeks of December. Although Montand and Simone were not completely unaware of tensions between Marilyn and Miller, they had no idea that the marriage was in trouble. Miller was devoted to Marilyn, and the only signs of real trouble had more to do with production issues than anything else. Montand had heard ru-mors that Marilyn had a reputation for being temperamental and tardy on the set. He was unaware of her emotional instability and far more focused on the task ahead. He had to learn his "English prayers," as Sim-one called them: learning lines in English by rote, without a clear sense of their meaning. He had written his lines on placards and colored scraps of paper, which he hung on the walls of their apartment. Simone helped at first, and then later, when time was of the essence, the studio hired a coach for him. While Montand struggled at the apartment, Marilyn continued to create problems on the set, where she was often late or a no show. On December 23, Miller was asked for a second re-write of the script to satisfy his wife's demands.

On New Year's Eve, the Montands attended at a party at Romanoff's. At midnight, after Simone kissed her husband, Gary Cooper asked Montand if he could dance with her. Since she was not a dancer, and Cooper had a limp, they danced a slow fox trot. In his arms, Simone began to enjoy the euphoria of living in the "iridescent bubble."[3]

In early January, Marilyn showed up at work once, for half an hour, and then left. Her agent called to say that she wouldn't return until January 18. The production was so far behind now that she would have no time to transition into her next film, *The Misfits*. On Saturday, January 16, Skouras hosted a party to welcome Montand to Twentieth Century Fox. Marilyn attended in high spirits, allegedly telling reporters that beyond her husband and Marlon Brando, she thought Yves Montand was the most attractive man she knew. Apparently, Montand reminded her of her former husband, Joe DiMaggio. She was in such high spirits that night that the studio hoped her mood would hold for her return to work on Monday, January 18. But on Sunday, Marilyn called in sick.

Frantic, director George Cukor[4] called Montand and asked him to be ready sooner than expected so they could at least film scenes that didn't include Marilyn. Montand was a nervous wreck. Though he had begun learning lines, he wasn't feeling confident. Now he felt crushed by the sudden urgency. But he reported to the studio on time. Marilyn finally showed up for work on January 25, and hope reigned on the set when she returned the following day for her first scene with Montand. However, hope was quickly dashed when she left unexpectedly several hours later. By now, Montand was feeling frustrated and angry. Beyond the obvious problems with Marilyn, he was having difficulty getting into his character, Jean-Marc Clément, spouting lines that made no sense to him. His role had been marginalized for Marilyn's benefit, yet she was nowhere to be found. On top of that, he was supposed to play a stiff, clumsy man who could not sing or dance, so Montand had to work at hiding his talent, making his moves awkward and unnatural.

At the time, he had mixed feelings about Marilyn. On one occasion, when the Millers and Montands went out to dinner, he was stunned by Marilyn's revealing dress. "I'd never, I'd never let my wife appear in public like that," he allegedly muttered. After work, the couples often gathered in the Montands' apartment for drinks and dinner. Montand was comfortable with Arthur Miller and felt that they understood each other in spite of the language barrier. The two men often took long walks while Marilyn bathed before dinner. He was not experiencing the "lyrical gusts" one might have expected with Marilyn, Montand claimed. "I was a million miles from thinking that anything whatsoever could happen between Marilyn and me. A million miles. If I was thinking of falling in love with anything, it was the English language. All around me people were eating, talking, living. All I could do was think of my script.

Because it wasn't sinking in, it wasn't becoming a part of me. It was the hardest time I've ever had in my acting career."[5]

During this period, Simone was enjoying life in the iridescent bubble, mesmerized by the pleasant weather, hummingbirds, garden lunches, shopping—and at night, by the silence, punctuated by the not so far off sound of coyotes howling as she drifted off to sleep. She had changed roles, from "groupie" to "Hollywood housewife." But she was without household or family worries, and she was in her element during luncheons. She impressed others with her intelligence, quick wit, charm, and seemingly carefree attitude about aging. She apparently felt no need to cover up signs of aging with make-up; she had begun to wear only a little bit of eye shadow to accent outfits. It appeared to all that she and Montand had an admirable and well-adjusted marriage, and that Simone had everything going for her. In retrospect, Simone was happy she had not come to Hollywood in her youth, when she might have fallen into a trap, believing the iridescent bubble was reality.

She and Marilyn spent time together on Saturday mornings with "the Bleacher," a retired hairdresser who dyed their hair at the kitchen sink. On one occasion, the couples were invited to visit the woman at her cottage on Hermosa Beach. Simone was impressed when Marilyn jumped up after lunch to wash the dishes. She seemed such a caring and indulgent friend.

Meanwhile, *Room at the Top* continued to play at theaters, and Alice was still working for Simone. "Both men and women find her candor and grown-up lack of artifice endearing," wrote Laura Bergquist, in a feature article for *Look* in January 1960. "She is a frank 38 and as offhand about her own ripe blonde looks as she is devoted to her husband. She is likely to comb her cropped hair with her fingers. In a simple belted trench coat, her working uniform for Room at the Top, she still generates more sex appeal than most women on lists of the best dressed." Simone surprised journalists with her pragmatic view when she spoke about her current status as a star. "I have no desire to be a truly big star," she claimed. "It is too big a job, and I am lazy about things that don't amuse me." On the role of Alice Aisgill: "It is wonderful to be loved—the public may be fed with little-girl dolls, so I am 'hot' this year. But next year, a new face will steal the picture."

After Marilyn and Montand left for the studio—when Marilyn was working—Miller would take a break from writing and knock on Simone's door to invite her for a coffee break. The relationship between them was a purely platonic, a comfortable friendship with Miller taking interest in her opinions and experiences in "the bubble." Afterwards, Simone was off to explore shops or to lunch with new friends. Yet, in spite of her desire to portray a housewife, seemingly at the expense of her career, Simone received an unending supply of film scripts to review. She turned all of them down. "They were almost always stupid stories with an admirable role for a no-longer-young actress." The worn, dog-eared corners of the pages gave a hint that these scripts had been circulating unsuccessfully for a long time. She envisioned the list of actresses that might have reviewed them and turned them down before her, from Anna Magnani and Bette Davis to Joan Crawford. None of these scripts, she noted wryly, was ever made into a film.

In January, CBS announced hopes of securing Simone and her former *Room* co-star, Laurence Harvey, for a *Playhouse 90* show, a dramatization of the Robert Shaw novel *The Hiding Place*, which they planned to film in London. These plans never materialized. However, Simone was fascinated by a short two-character psychodrama, *Don't You Remember*, written for the CBS Sunday night program *General Electric Theater*. Simone agreed to play the role of a vengeful woman hunting for the man who killed her husband and child in a hit-and-run drunk driving accident. When she finds the killer working as a hotel desk clerk, she checks in. Lee Marvin played the role of the drunk driver, who is enamored of the beautiful woman and surprised when she invites him to her room for a drink, only to discover that she has murder on her mind. While the thirty-minute drama did not receive laudatory reviews, it was billed as Simone's first dramatic acting role for American television and it paid well—ten thousand dollars for the episode. It was also the start of a new career opportunity for writer Alvin Sargent. "I had written this as an exercise for myself along with other small dialogues. I was a salesman at the time and many years later made a career as a writer of television,"[6] and then later, in film. Indeed, Alvin Sargent became an acclaimed screenwriter, earning two Academy Awards in his career.

⁂

When she finally showed up long enough to film a scene, Marilyn began to connect with Montand, and felt comfortable confiding in him, "You're going to see what it means to shoot with the worst actress in the world." He consoled her, in halting English: "So you're scared . . . think of me a little bit. I'm lost."[7] This confession seemed to give her confidence, and she survived the scene. On another occasion, Montand suggested that they rehearse together. Marilyn liked the idea, and rehearsals seemed to bolster their confidence. Still, she was constantly late, taking her time before leaving the dressing room to start a scene, while patience on the set grew thin. One of the reasons for her tardiness was the time she spent after work visiting with Simone and Montand. She enjoyed listening to stories. Simone was a great storyteller and did not need encouragement as she spoke of her experiences on film sets. Her narratives often went on long into the night. Marilyn never spoke about her career, which Simone thought curious. The only accomplishment she spoke of—and she did so repeatedly, testing even Simone's nerves—was the series of photographs taken by Richard Avedon, in which Marilyn impersonated other stars. Simone thought it odd that Marilyn only experienced satisfaction with her work when she was wearing disguises.[8]

Marilyn, on the other hand, was delighted with Simone's stories of the youthful complicity and camaraderie of actors on the set during and after filming. When Simone ran out of stories, she began telling Marilyn tales borrowed from some of her favorite scripts. Marilyn particularly enjoyed *They Shoot Horses, Don't They?*, a depression-era allegory about a young woman, Gloria, who is recovering after a suicide attempt. Gloria wants to be a movie star and meets Robert, a man who dreams of becoming a film director. They decide to enter a grueling dance contest. She is still depressed and weak from her suicide attempts and wants to quit. Her life is hopeless, and she believes she'd be better off dead. Gloria tries to talk Robert into shooting her. Simone was quite familiar with the script because she had read it on a radio show in 1946.[9] As she told these tales, Simone couldn't help but think of Marilyn as a young child trying to get another story to delay going to bed. Still, Simone, never at a loss for conversation, was happy to indulge Marilyn. She didn't mind the late hour, since she didn't have to go to work the next morning.

On February 10, Arthur Miller flew to Ireland to spend two weeks working with John Huston on revisions of *The Misfits*, Marilyn's next film. She was always suspicious of Miller's absences and so upset by this one that she did not show up for work the following day. When she arrived on the set on February 11, she was in a fragile state and in no condition to work, so she was sent home. She continued to call in sick or to leave the studio early for the next week. Finally, on February 18, she was a no-show. The studio called repeatedly, but she never picked up.

Montand tried calling, to no avail. Finally, enraged, he called Simone and asked her to knock on the Millers' door. Simone knocked and called out to no avail.

Montand was so angry that he returned to the hotel and worked with Simone on a letter to Marilyn, which would be slipped under her door:

> You can do whatever you like to Spyros Skouras and the Fox studio and all the producers in town, if that's what you want. But next time you decide to hang around too late listening to my wife tell you stories instead of going to bed, because you've already decided not to get up the next morning and go to the studio, please tell me! Don't leave me to work for hours on end on a scene you've already decided not to do the next day. I'm not the enemy, I'm your pal. And capricious little girls have never amused me.
>
> Best, Yves[10]

Simone slipped the note under Marilyn's door, leaving just enough of it showing so they could see if it disappeared inside while they waited quietly in their doorway. Finally, the note disappeared. When they received no response, Montand lost his temper and yelled in "Franglais" to Simone in the hallway so he could be heard loud and clear. There'd be no filming today because of absences, he cried, so they might just as well go out for lunch and enjoy the rest of the afternoon.

When they returned home, in time for dinner, they fully expected a note from Marilyn under their door, but there was none. Then, later that evening, they were awakened by a phone call from Arthur Miller in Dublin. Marilyn had called him because she was so embarrassed she couldn't face the Montands. Would he call them and apologize on her behalf, and ask them to knock on her door? When Simone knocked, she was greeted by a tearful Marilyn, who collapsed in her arms. "I'm bad, I'm bad, I'm bad," she cried, promising not to do it again. When Simone told this story to friends, it was like a punch line to a joke: Marilyn had asked her husband, who was in another country, to call their neighbors in America. Others laughed. However, Simone never found it amusing. For her Marilyn's behavior provided an instructive glimpse into the actress's emotional fragility.

On Monday, February 22, Academy Award nominations were made public. It was thought that Marilyn was a shoo-in for her performance in *Some Like It Hot*. Indeed, the film received several nominations: Billy

Wilder for Best Director; I. L. Diamond for Best Screenplay; and Jack Lemmon for Best Actor. Marilyn was excluded. Still, she showed none of the disappointment or malice she surely felt that day. She arrived at work as promised, and from that point forward continued rehearsals with Montand. She continued to arrive late—but she arrived, and remained on the set long enough to finish scenes and watch the rushes at the end of the day.

Marilyn was sincere and encouraging when she congratulated Simone Signoret on her Oscar nomination. Though her nomination was not completely a surprise, Simone was not overconfident. She had stiff competition in the most prominent leading ladies of Hollywood's inner circle: Katherine Hepburn and Elizabeth Taylor for *Suddenly Last Summer*, Audrey Hepburn for *The Nun's Story*, and Doris Day for *Pillow Talk*.

Hedda Hopper took the opportunity to slight Simone by omitting her name from her article on the Academy Award nominations. It wasn't an oversight, it was a strategy, one she used on other actors when she felt the need, she explained in her memoir, *The Whole Truth and Nothing But*. "Personally, like Louella, I've found that silence is the greatest blow you can deliver to a Hollywood ego when it needs whacking down to size. Not to mention the name of a star drives him half out his mind; they live and die by publicity."[11] Hopper was also accustomed to having her words or omissions taken seriously. Normally, if she panned an actor or omitted a name, she influenced decision-making. Instead, this time she was viewed as petty and underhanded, and much to her dismay, it was clear that no one had any intention of taking her seriously. Simone Signoret was a serious contender for the Oscar, with or without her support. And, since Hopper's kingdom was beginning to topple, she decided to find other means of accomplishing her goal. Simone Signoret would never know the lengths Hopper went to in order to prevent her from winning the Oscar.

❧

Filming for *Let's Make Love* came to a complete standstill on March 4, when the Screen Actors Guild announced a strike. Arthur Miller decided that it was best he and Marilyn return to New York for the duration. But they remained in Hollywood long enough to attend the Golden Globes on March 8. Marilyn had been nominated for Best Actress in a Leading Role-Musical or Comedy for *Some Like It Hot*. Simone was nominated in the film category for Best Performance by an Actress in a Motion Picture, along with Lee Remick in *Anatomy of a Murder*, Katharine Hepburn and Elizabeth Taylor in *Suddenly Last Summer*, and Audrey Hepburn in *The Nun's Story*.

That evening before the ceremony, Marilyn asked photographer Sam Shaw to come to her room. When he arrived, he found Simone, Montand, and Arthur, dressed for the evening, but waiting, silently, in the Millers' living room. Marilyn called out from the bedroom, but when Shaw entered the room, he found only Marilyn's make-up man, sitting alone waiting. Marilyn called out again; she was in the bathroom. Shaw found her in the tub, "encased in ice." "The ice cubs will keep my body up and firm," she explained. When she emerged from the tub, Simone was called in to help her with her bodice. Then the make-up artist went to work. Finally, Marilyn was ready and joined her husband and the Montands in the living room, completely oblivious to the inconvenience she had caused.[12]

That evening, Elizabeth Taylor won the Golden Globe for film, and Marilyn won for musical comedy. After that, the Millers prepared to leave for New York to wait out the Actors Guild strike. From their balcony, Simone and Montand, who had no choice but to remain in Hollywood, watched Marilyn and Miller walk to the car. Marilyn turned and waved to Simone and shouted out, "I know you're going to get it."[13] This was the last time Simone and Marilyn exchanged pleasantries.

As March 1960 progressed, the push was on to influence Academy Award voting, and *Room* producers hired a publicity firm to encourage a favorable outcome. This tactic was part of the game in Hollywood, based on the theory that one couldn't win without extensive publicity geared to the members of the academy. "It is not my money, I assure you," Simone told Murray Schumach, a reporter for the *New York Times*. "It is not that I am cheap. But it is so foolish I think." Scanning the trade newspapers, she picked out ads touting the merits of her performance and showed them to the reporter. "These advertisements about me . . . what can it mean? It is as sensible as if I write a letter to myself and say: 'Dear Simone you have given a great performance.' What I have done in *Room at the Top* is finished. Publicity will not make it better."[14] But she joked that Hollywood didn't corner the market on foolishness. "In our Cannes festival, there are all these young girls being photographed because they look interesting in bathing suits. But they do not win the award at the festival," she added with a twinkle in her eye.

Oscar fever—it was all part of the lifestyle in the iridescent bubble, she thought. Odd that an entire village would focus its attention on movies, to the exclusion of everything else going on in the world. "It is like living in a hospital, where what is important is that the patient in Room 4 has a broken leg and the man in Room 6 needs a bandage . . . . Myself, I am the one who has an extraordinary disease or a sudden auto accident and here I am, in what you call the accident ward." But while Simone was critical, she was not above playing the game. In February, when she was asked to support the film *Black Orpheus*,[15] the French entry for Best Foreign Film, she worked with Romain Gary, who was serving as counsel general of France at the time. They arranged a special screening of the film at the Screen Directors Guild Theater on Sunset Boulevard. Telegram invitations were sent out to reporters and other influential guests, including Hedda Hopper, who read it, wrote "NO" in the margin of the cable, and filed it away. Hopper had other plans.

In late March, with Simone very much on her mind, Hedda Hopper traveled to Washington, D.C. hoping to gain access to J. Edgar Hoover. However, when she arrived and called the FBI, she was informed that the director was away. The conversation she had with an agent was well documented in a series of memorandums reporting the event to higher ups. The identity of the subject she wanted to discuss was redacted from all documents, but is still easy to discern.

United States Government
MEMORANDUM

To: Mr. Mohr Date: March 23, 1960
From: C. D. DeLach
Subject: Hedda Hopper
    Inquiry Re ███████████████
    Star of ██████████████
    Yesterday, Miss Hopper called from the Statler Hotel (she will be in town until Tuesday, 3/24/60) and spoke with ████████ in my office.
    Miss Hopper said she was terribly concerned because ███████████████████ was being seriously considered as ████████████████ this year and, in fact, she has three full time publicity agents in Hollywood trying to get ████████████ . Miss Hopper said that ██████████████████████ background as a communist or a communist apologist had received some publicity. She added ████████████████ and ████████████████ had been entertained in Moscow by Stalin prior to his death. Hedda wanted to know if

the Bureau could help direct her to any information which would
help stop ██████████████ from receiving ██████████████ .
The film, ██████████████████ in which ████████ starred, is
described as adult film fare. Generally it received very laudatory
reviews in this country. This film portrayed several illicit love affairs and also reportedly a number of highly suggestive scenes.

Both ████████ and ██████████████ were permitted to enter
this country ████████ . They were granted temporary admission by
the Immigration Service in spite of their communist backgrounds
in Europe. This was based on a State Department report that both
████████ and ████████ had been associated with communist
groups but apparently recently their enthusiasm for communism
had lessened. We have not investigated either ██████████ or
██████████ and have no public source data to which we could refer
Hedda Hopper.

RECOMMENDATIONS:

It is recommended that we call Miss Hopper and explain that re-
grettably we cannot assist her but suggest that she might want to
consider the advisability of getting in touch with the State Department or some of her friends ████████████████████ to secure
the background data she is looking for. ████████

Further memos document FBI attempts to reach Hopper in order to convey this message, but she did not return their calls prior to her return to
LA. Simone was never aware of Hopper's attempt to stop her from winning the Oscar or the lie that Hopper told about Simone and Montand
meeting with Stalin. They were indeed entertained by Nikita Khrushchev, but never Stalin. However, as far as Hopper was concerned, there
was little distinction between the two Soviet leaders.

Regardless of Hopper's concern about Simone's rapid advancement
toward the Oscar, the way had already been paved for Simone. In late
1959, as though anticipating her nomination and any problems that
might arise because of her politics, the Academy of Motion Picture Arts
and Sciences had repealed a by-law in its constitution that barred communists from receiving awards. According to an FBI document in the
Hedda Hopper file that quotes "Daily Variety," the academy board of gov-
ernors issued a statement explaining that the by-law was "unworkable
and impractical to administer and enforce." Hopper was waging a losing
battle.

CHAPTER 23

"Sad, and Abysmally Stupid"

THE THIRTY-SECOND ACADEMY AWARDS CEREMONY WAS HELD ON April 4, 1960, at the historic Pantages Theater on Hollywood Boulevard. Organizers were under pressure to develop a new format for the show after the debacle of the previous year, when the program fell short of the allotted time. The comedian Jerry Lewis, who emceed the event, had to ad lib for twenty minutes. Arthur Freeman, a well-known director at MGM, was recruited to manage the show, with Vincente Minelli and John Houseman acting as his assistants. "The big problem with a show of this kind," Freeman explained, was finding "the fine line down the middle between dignity and entertainment. If we lean too heavily on the inherent dignity of the Academy, the show becomes stuffy and pretentious, not to mention, boring. On the other hand, we can't turn it into a vaudeville show." Bob Hope was recruited to emcee, and they chose two popular performers for entertainment: Ella Fitzgerald agreed to sing a medley of Gershwin tunes, and Yves Montand agreed to sing two songs, "À Paris" and "Un Garçon Dansait," the popular tunes he had sung on the *Dinah Shore Show*.

During the pre-event hours, Simone and Montand were at home in their bungalow nursing stage fright. She claimed they had four cases of it, as each worried about his or her own role in the event, and each had a case of stage fright on behalf of the other. Simone sat on the couch in their living room wearing a bathrobe with her hair up in curlers. She chain-smoked while carefully examining—for the umpteenth time—the packet they received from the academy with their gold embossed tickets. Directions indicated that all nominees were to be seated in the central isle of the Pantages Theater so they could have easy access to the stage in the event they won. There were specific directions about what to do if chosen, and an invitation for an after party at the Beverly Wilshire Hotel for all the Oscar nominees. Simone read and reread the directions, still checking to make sure she hadn't lost the tickets, while Montand tried to pass the time playing poker at the dining table with friends who had stopped by.

When they were finally settled into their limo, shortly before 8 p.m., both Simone and Montand were like schoolchildren, watching the spotlights sweeping the sky over the Pantages Theater. This was a moment they had only dreamed of in adolescence, and they felt giddy, alternating between fits of uncontrolled giggling and moments of sheer panic—particularly when Simone checked to make sure she hadn't lost the tickets.

At ten o'clock that evening Montand's mentor, Fred Astaire, introduced "Eaves" Montand. When Montand finished singing to uproarious applause, Vincente Minnelli directed him back to his seat. But Montand refused. He was sure that Simone would win Best Actress, he told Minnelli, and he wanted to remain on the sidelines to watch and greet her when she finally came backstage.

Simone was not as confident as her husband. The film *Ben Hur* had been nominated for twelve Oscars and was stealing the show, winning its ninth award when Charlton Heston won Best Actor. She had no reason to believe that *Room at the Top* could compete with the mega production and was sure it would take all the awards. She was also faced with the reality of having appeared in a non-Hollywood production. Even the press speculated. "No matter how highly Miss Signoret is regarded by fans and professionals, she stands an outside chance to grab an Oscar. . . . An Oscar is rarely awarded to a foreign film," Peer Oppenheimer wrote for the Sunday edition of the *Sarasota Herald Tribune*.

Then, Rock Hudson took center stage. "We had come to the moment for the best actress. I hunched down in my pretty black dress," Simone wrote later. Then, Rock Hudson opened the envelope and announced the winner. Simone would compare this moment to the exhilaration she felt when she learned of her first lead role in *Macadam*. A *Life* magazine photographer captured her reaction, as Hudson "literally yelled out 'Simauauaune Signoray.'" In the photograph, she is leaning forward in her seat. Her head is tipped back, her face aglow in sheer ecstasy as she grasps her chest with both hands as though to hold in a heart that is beating so hard she is sure it will explode. "Then, I heard a roaring noise which grew into the most frightening ovation I'd ever heard in my life! I felt as though I'd been bludgeoned like an ox! I got up—I rushed to the platform, in tears, running like a madwoman. Goodbye, cool head and self-control . . ."[1]

She was the second French actress to win in the history of the Academy Awards, following Claudette Colbert. However, Colbert had become an American citizen and won for a role in the Hollywood production *It Happened One Night*. Simone was the first French citizen to win Best Actress, and though neither Hollywood nor France had helped her reach this pinnacle of success, she felt a great sense of national pride that evening, which she expressed in her brief acceptance speech. She kissed Rock Hudson on both cheeks before breathlessly taking the microphone, stumbling with words at first: "Oh, I thank you . . . I thank you so much. I wanted to be very dignified. However, I can't. You can't imagine being French what it is for me. You can't imagine . . ." She then thanked her co-star and the film's director and producers before exiting hurriedly, anxious to get backstage. She saw Montand waiting in the wings, openly weeping as though he had recently buried his best friend.

She was no longer the Hollywood housewife or her husband's groupie at the celebration that followed at the Beverly Wilshire Hotel. Indeed, for the first time since their arrival in the United States, Montand was on the sidelines, as cameras flashed and well-wishers stopped at their table for a congratulatory kiss or hug. Still, Simone was ever sensitive to Montand's feelings, asking him on several occasions if he was okay. Montand claimed that he was not at all jealous of this attention or resentful of his back seat role.

Back at the Bungalow in the early hours of April 5, Simone placed the Oscar on the mantle of their fireplace, next to the framed photograph of Autheuil. She had brought along the photo for moments when she and Montand felt homesick. The living room was beginning to fill with flowers and telegrams. From the tone of some of the latter, Simone gathered that their new Hollywood friends thought her Oscar was more than just a victory for her, more than just recognition of her acting. She believed Hollywood had scored a victory by proving that McCarthyism and blacklisting were in the past. Simone didn't care and was not about to allow politics to color this moment.

The next day, however, with help from gossip columnists, the press turned its focus to politics, questioning her status in the country—no doubt egged on by Hedda Hopper. On April 6, the *New York Times* published a special report announcing, "Miss Signoret in U.S. on Waiver." According to the article, the State Department would not disclose information regarding the restriction, but indicated that the reasons behind it were more serious than her signature on the Stockholm Appeal. Simone fired back on April 7, according to another *New York Times* special report, indicating that she and Montand were not communists and had never joined the party. "Sure, I was refused a visa. . . . Someone said it was because I signed the Stockholm Appeal. . . . Maybe that was the reason—I do not know—but I know that when I applied again in 1959 I gave the same answers to all the questions—and I got the visa. Frankly, I don't believe it is anyone's business concerning my politics. But since the question has been asked I'm glad to answer. I am not a Communist."

Simone left Hollywood on April 9 to return to France for a short break before she was expected in Italy for her next film. This time, she felt none of the remorse usually experienced when leaving her husband behind. He was still inactive owing to the Screen Actors Guild strike. Marilyn had not yet returned. Anyway, when Marilyn finally did reappear, there would be little reason to be concerned about leaving her husband alone with the actress, because Simone was sure that Arthur Miller would be there. When a reporter asked if she were worried about leaving her husband behind with Marilyn, Simone was confident: "I like Marilyn very much. . . . Of course, I don't know what he does when we are separated. I have never read anything in the papers about him going out with other women or behaving in any way that might do me harm."[2] In any case, even if something happened between her husband and Marilyn, there was little she could do about it. Simone was anxious to return to work, even as the press seemed mystified by her decision to take on another low budget film when she could have her pick of Hollywood productions.

Marilyn Monroe and Arthur Miller returned to Hollywood on April 11 in anticipation of the end of the SAG strike, which settled on April 18. However, unbeknownst to Simone, Miller stayed only a few days before returning to New York. Marilyn was upset about his departure, and it was becoming clear that tension in their marriage was reaching a boiling point. Marilyn was paranoid, believing that Miller was using her, and she complained bitterly to Montand and anyone else who would listen. Unbeknownst to Montand, she would feel the need to test her husband's loyalty. But in the meantime, she and Montand resumed their private rehearsals, generally in his apartment. Once back at work, they continued this practice in the studio.

Montand later explained, "Every night after getting back from the studio we worked for an hour or two. When we got up after it was over, we were both still living in the tension of the rehearsal. I'd be smoking cigarette after cigarette, and then she'd smile and say: 'Okay, now we'll eat.' Then I looked at her, and I thought she was amazingly beautiful, healthy, desirable—but I didn't desire her, I was somewhere else entirely." Exactly where he was remains unknown. But he was certainly not thinking through potential mishaps with his co-star, who clung to him, becoming ever more dependent upon him.

They often dined out in the company of the ever-present Paula Strasberg, Marilyn's acting coach and confidante. It was Strasberg who encouraged Montand to visit Marilyn in her room one evening after the actress left the set early because she wasn't feeling well. "Go and say goodnight to Marilyn," she encouraged. "It'll make her feel better." If Montand had thought it through, a telephone call would have sufficed. Instead, he took Strasberg's advice.

ૐ

Simone was staying in a suite at the Excelsior Hotel in Rome, enjoying the pleasant spring weather and a spectacular view from her seventh-floor balcony. All the balconies were gilded and were gleaming as the sun set, and she enjoyed the old world ambiance of the city as she watched young lovers pass on their motor scooters. She was still living in the glow of her Oscar and enjoying every minute of it. Her new status as an Oscar winner had many benefits. She always had dinner invitations, enjoyed the company of new friends, and, for the first time in two years, she was working again.

Luxury and comfort ended at the hotel because they were filming *Adua E Le Compagne* on location in an old stone farmhouse outside Rome, near the Appian Way in southeast Italy. The farmhouse was in shambles, and the cast and crew worked twelve- to fourteen-hour days in the most austere conditions. "It's not Twentieth Century Fox," she joked, when asked about the small two-wheeled trailer she had to share with another actress. "Our director, Antonio Pietrangeli, likes to work in tight places," Simone explained. "He feels comfortable when he can take plenty of time. He does not enjoy working in a studio,"[3] particularly since studio space was at a premium in Rome at the time. An actress of her stature could have insisted on a lighter work schedule of ten hours a day and a trailer of her own. But, this was another low budget film, and Simone didn't ask for special consideration. The one luxury she enjoyed was that she could speak French for the production; they would dub her in Italian afterward.

She was Adua, an older, "fortyish" prostitute who dreamed of breaking free of her profession and starting a new life. After a police raid shut down the brothel Adua is working for, she convinces three other prostitutes, younger women who shared her dream of a new life, to join her in a venture. They would find a house, open a restaurant, and lead a respectable life. Unable to find suitable space in Rome, they venture out to the country, where they find a dilapidated villa. When they discover that their modest savings aren't enough to pay for rent and the licenses necessary for a restaurant, they turn to Dr. Ercoli, a wealthy businessman. He is willing to loan them money and the use of his name for licenses. However, he has one caveat: He wants the loan repaid and the villa turned into a brothel.

Adua has no intention of returning to her old profession. While the women clean and repair the old farmhouse, Adua meets a used car salesmen, a gigolo, played by Marcello Mastroianni. Adua, who had always been an object of desire, but not love, finds herself falling for the gigolo. He leads her on, letting her think that his interest in her is more than just the enjoyment of a few nights with an aging prostitute.

Once the restaurant is up and running, the doctor demands that the women make good on their promise. They refuse, and the doctor reports their past to the police. The restaurant is shut down. Adua turns to her lover for moral support, but finds him in bed with another woman. He turns Adua away.

In an act of revenge, Adua and her friends trash the old farmhouse in a violent rage and are then arrested. The film ends with the women back on the street turning tricks. A close up reveals Adua, drunk and tearful, begging potential clients who pass her. She is too old and no longer desirable. As it turns out, Simone would not have to dig deep to find the emotion necessary to play this spurned woman.

※

When Montand entered Marilyn's living room, he noticed that room service had delivered caviar and a bottle of pink champagne, her favorites. It did not occur to him that this was an odd combination for someone who didn't feel well. Marilyn called out to him; she was in her bedroom lying down. Montand approached, sat down on the edge of her bed and patted her hand, asking if she had a fever. She did, but assured him she would be okay. Then, he recalled, "I bent down to put a goodnight kiss on her cheek. And her head turned, and my lips went wild. It was a wonderful, tender kiss. I was half stunned, stammering, I straightened up, already flooded with guilt, wondering what was happening to me. I didn't wonder for long."

The next day, their connection spilled over onto the set, where Montand felt that they experienced "total symbiosis." Director George Cukor suspected that there was something else going on, but was pleased that they could get through scenes without Marilyn falling apart. Later, she spent the night in Montand's bungalow, making no effort to hide when the housekeeper arrived to clean the next morning. Another evening, allegedly, Marilyn was seen arriving at Montand's door dressed only in a fur coat. They were seen out dining together, usually with Paula Strasberg. With or without a chaperone, these frequent public appearances and late night rendezvous set the hotel's rumor mill on fire, as employees reported what they saw or heard to gossip columnists.

Arthur Miller paid an unexpected visit to Hollywood in early May and was aware without being told that something was wrong. Marilyn was distant and argumentative, repeatedly accusing him of using her to get ahead in his career. A rumor circulated that Miller found Montand and Marilyn in bed. The rumor was never substantiated, though Marilyn's behavior gave credence to such gossip. A few days later, as Miller was preparing to return to New York, he was allegedly heard muttering aloud, "What will happen, will happen"—and it did.

In June, the columnist, Dorothy Kilgareen was the first to report rumors of the affair. She didn't use names, but the suspects were obvious: "An Actress nominated for an Academy Award is sweating out a domestic crisis far more important than Oscar voting. Her husband—also famous—has fallen in love with a beautiful lady married to another Big Name . . . ." The gutter presses picked up the gauntlet and began churning out breathless gossip at a feverish pace.

Simone was shopping in Rome on a day off from filming when she passed a newsstand and noticed the headlines: *Schiaffi a Hollywood*; Slaps in Hollywood.[4] The headline amused her, and she approached the newsstand for a closer look, wondering what the article was about. But her smile froze when she discovered that she was the victim. According to the article, Montand had sent Simone a few vigorous slaps across the ocean to quell her jealousy over his affair with Marilyn Monroe.

She never spoke about her emotional state during this period. It was Montand who shared the details in his biography. As soon as the news was out, Montand sent Simone an apologetic cable. Knowing full well that eavesdroppers would monitor cables and phone calls, Simone did not respond. Instead, she sat alone in her hotel room clipping all the sleazy news articles out of the papers, then including them in a carefully written letter to her husband, "its tone deliberately neutral," Montand explained later. Rather than ask, "how could you do this . . . after ten years of marriage," Simone explained that she was trying hard to understand what had happened, how things could reach this point.

It was impossible to concentrate on her work and she tried to break her film contract. But the production was simply too far along to find a replacement, so Simone stayed. But her emotions got the better of her, and she lashed out. She was reportedly rude and difficult on the set and arrived late one morning, behaviors uncharacteristic of the consummate professional who considered co-workers an extension of her family. The Italian press called her the "angry tigress" when she renounced the "nonsense of the gossiping press," knowing full well that the affair was real.

Any attempt Montand may have made to stop rumors or end the affair were nullified by his public appearances with Marilyn at restaurants, film screenings, and cocktail parties. Yet Montand was besieged by conflicting feelings. "Not for a moment did I think of breaking with my wife, not for a moment," he claimed, "but if she had slammed the door on me, I would probably have made my life with Marilyn. Or tried to. That was the direction we were moving in." At the same time, he wanted to distance himself from Marilyn, realizing that their relationship was out of control, but he couldn't find a way out. He was fearful of her reaction if he broke it off with her. She was clearly unstable and unpredictable. He worried that she might make matters worse by reacting to a breakup in the press. Still, these concerns did not stop him from continuing his public appearances with Marilyn, even though he was beginning to take heat from others.

While he was viewed as a popular singer, it was Simone who was beloved and respected in Hollywood circles. She had not only earned respect as a dramatic actress of the highest caliber, but had endeared herself with her fresh perspective, friendly, relaxed manner, and great sense of humor. She had a seductive charisma, and people liked her. Many of her friends thought it unconscionable that Montand had betrayed and embarrassed her in such a public manner, sullying her name with scandal after she received the Oscar. Their unspoken question was: Did he do it on purpose to drag her down after her victory? Montand was beginning to receive the cold shoulder while out with Marilyn.

Marilyn suffered the same reaction when rumors circulated that she and Arthur Miller were having marital problems. Like Simone, Miller was highly respected and regarded as his spouse's protector, always there to prop her up, re-writing her scripts, catering to her whims, and apologizing for her disruptive behavior when depression and barbiturates took control. Marilyn was barely tolerable and had a reputation for having affairs. No one was going to make life easy for the woman who stole her friends' husbands.

One evening at a party at David Selznick's home, Montand and Marilyn received such a chilly reception that Montand decided to make a quick exit without Marilyn, who was already drunk and sloppy. When she realized he was leaving and had taken her car, she raced out, chasing the limo while yelling out to him.[5]

They filmed their last scenes together on June 16. Montand had to remain in Hollywood to dub scenes, but he was anxious to return home to rejoin Simone before he was expected back in LA for his next film, *Sanctuary*, with Lee Remick. Marilyn also had scenes to dub, but she developed laryngitis and called in sick or failed to show up. Finally, Arthur Miller stepped in on his wife's behalf, asking that she be allowed to return to New York to recuperate. He wanted her to dub scenes there, but the studio would not allow it.

Montand left LA on June 30. He would stopover in New York to catch his plane for France. When Marilyn got wind of his trip, she made plans to meet Montand at the airport. Oddly enough, as soon as his plane arrived, the airport received a bomb threat and had to be evacuated. His flight was delayed for several hours. Marilyn was waiting for him outside in her rented limo. She had booked a hotel room for them under an assumed name and begged Montand to join her there. He refused. Instead, they remained in the limo, drinking champagne and talking. Worried about her erratic behavior, Montand told her as gently as possible that it was over; he was returning to his wife. He had enjoyed their relationship, and—irrational as it seems—even as he voiced this sentiment, he hoped that the Montands and Millers could remain friends. He even invited them to Paris for a visit.

When he arrived at Orly airport on July 1, the press was out in full force, waiting. However, much to their disappointment, Simone wasn't there. She was still in Italy and had devised a strategy to deal with the situation, a plan she expected Montand to follow to the letter. He went to Autheuil, where he was instructed to remain until she returned a few days later. Montand had strict orders not to leave home for any reason, or to speak to the press under any circumstances. Montand complied.

"On my return, of course we had a fight, but just one, and we didn't mention it again for three months. At first our feelings were terrifying, violent; then things calmed down, peace returned—or so it seemed," Montand explained. Simone wanted him to tell her every detail of what had transpired so that she could understand how things had developed with Marilyn. He shared what he could, careful to edit out parts of the story that he felt would only inflict further pain. "There she was—beaten, sad, wounded at the thought that the fantastic ten years we had shared had been tarnished this way. I was sorry to have inflicted pain on her. That was what I was sorry for—only that." Montand would never apologize for his affair with Marilyn Monroe.

Simone's reaction surprised her husband. After their argument, she calmed down and was forgiving. Affairs happened; it was unfortunate that this one garnered so much publicity. But an affair wasn't unusual, particularly on a film set, she reasoned. From that moment on, Simone was Montand's fierce defender. "Do you know many men who would sit still with Marilyn Monroe in their arms," she asked reporters. She decided not to return to Hollywood for Montand's next film, believing that her presence there would reignite the rumor mill. Instead, she remained in France to deal with the torrent of press and the "sad . . . abysmally stupid" letters she was receiving from forlorn women who wanted to share their marital problems with her. Some offered advice: She should leave her husband; she should hang in there because it will pass. Others suggested she work on her sexual prowess if she hoped to hold on to her husband. As Simone had indicated during her appearance on *Small World*, when it came to affairs, there was little room for gossip columnists. The French were freer and more accepting of extramarital relationships. However, Simone quickly learned that Montand's affair was just as appealing to the French press as it was everywhere else. What made the affair more delicious was that Simone and Montand had portrayed themselves as the ideal couple, taking public stands against perceived injustice and doling out advice on moral dilemmas. Now, there was a chink in the armor, and a sensitive nerve was exposed. The ideal couple was not above scandal. The French press kept the fires burning with creative spins on the couple's relationship, which took gossip to a new level. There were rumors that the couple was still fighting, and that Montand wanted to escape so he could return to Hollywood. As Montand later reported, one newspaper went so far as to fabricate a story about him booking a flight to New York to get away from Simone. When she found out, so the story went, she booked the seat next to him. He then canceled his flight, and she canceled hers. It was all pure fantasy—and there seemed no end to it.

When Montand returned to LA, he discovered that the press was still churning out garbage there, made worse by Marilyn, who was in Reno filming *The Misfits*. She called or cabled Montand constantly and was pressuring him to divorce Simone. Eavesdroppers monitored her communications and fed information to the press. On July 25, Hedda Hopper wryly commented on the affair and the proposed divorce with a titillating piece: "Stories about M.M. Upsetting Montand." Montand, in turn, insisted that the rumors of divorce were untrue and proclaimed his love for his wife. Hopper claimed to have seen the entire affair coming. "During shooting I detected that something strange was happening to Mrs. Arthur Miller, who hadn't announced yet that she was going to get a divorce. She was falling hard for this Frenchman with the carefully polished charm. Between the end of that picture and the start of the next, *The Misfits*, the stories spread that he would divorce his wife, Simone Signoret. The gossip spread all over town, with some help from the Twentieth Century Fox promotion department and no hindrance from himself."[6]

Simone returned to Italy to complete the filming of *Adua*. Her next film, *Les Mauvais Coups* (Naked Autumn), was not scheduled to begin shooting until the New Year, so there was ample time to join her husband for the premiere of *Let's Make Love* and still have time afterwards for a much-needed rest. When Simone finally arrived in LA in late August, she was besieged by the press, which anxiously awaited the meeting between the lover and the woman scorned. Surely Marilyn was planning to attend. Simone maintained her stance that she didn't fault her husband for his affair, because no man could possibly resist Marilyn. Montand was finishing *Sanctuary* and had already signed on for another Hollywood production, *Goodbye Again*, with Ingrid Bergman. When asked if Simone planned to join her husband for his next movie, she continued to put on a good front and joked, "Do you think I'm crazy, leaving him first with Marilyn, then with Ingrid?"[7]

In the end, the press was never treated to a meeting between Simone and Marilyn. The premiere, planned for Reno, where Marilyn was filming, had to be postponed owing to brush fires that blackened the sky over Reno and cut off the city's power. However, the postponed premiere didn't stop Twentieth Century Fox from spreading reports about

Marilyn's Homeric arguments with her husband in Reno. Rumor had it that she was on the phone constantly, hoping to reach Montand. Any press the studio could garner from these tidbits would surely help with the promotion of the film, which was already regarded as a dud. The situation became more intense when Marilyn, angry, exhausted, and high on barbiturates was flown to Good Samaritan Hospital in LA to recuperate. There, she made repeated attempts to contact Montand from her hospital bed.

Simone was back in Paris on September 1, when Hedda Hopper unleashed a bombshell, taking the scandal to new heights. According to Hopper, when she learned that Montand was leaving to return to France for a visit, she stopped by the Beverly Hills Hotel to see him. Hopper had little hope of talking to him, she thought, but she took a chance and was shocked when Montand answered the door and then let her in. He knew Hopper was dangerous and that she despised their politics and held a certain grudge against his wife, though no one knew the lengths she had to gone to stop Simone from receiving an Oscar. But everyone understood that Hopper was dangerous and a formidable foe. Still, Montand let her into his hotel room. As soon as she entered, Hopper claimed, the phone began ringing incessantly. She went on to write:

"I won't talk to her," he told the switchboard operator.

"Why not," said I. "You'll probably never see her again. Go on. Speak to her." But he couldn't be persuaded. He suggested a drink, and I offered to mix them. I stirred up one hell of a martini to get him talking.

"You deliberately made love to this girl. You knew she wasn't sophisticated. Was that right?"

"Had Marilyn been sophisticated, none of this ever would have happened. I did everything I could for her when I realized that mine was a very small part. The only thing that could stand out in my performance were my loves scenes. So naturally, I did everything I could to make them good."

"I'm sure he knew what he was saying no more than half the time," Hopper explained. Marilyn was an "enchanting child" and a "simple girl without any guile." Montand said, "Perhaps she had a school-girl crush. If she did, I'm sorry. But nothing will break up my marriage."[8]

Hopper reported the conversation in her column on September 1, and the publicity mill started up all over again, working overtime.

The remark about the schoolgirl crush was widely commented on, and Montand was criticized for talking about his affair and his lover in such a cavalier manner—particularly since Marilyn was hospitalized and vulnerable. When the news reached Simone, she was immediately defensive, and for good reason. While she couldn't possibly fathom why her husband would speak to Hedda Hopper, or any press for that matter, she felt there was something strange about the reported conversation. Montand's command of the English language was minimal at best. A schoolgirl crush? "It can't be true," Simone insisted, "if for no other reason than by its grammatical form and its difficulties of pronunciation it would have cost Montand a week's hard work—if indeed he had ever pronounced those words to Hedda Hopper, as she claimed he did the day she decided to take her revenge."[9]

Indeed, Montand was still practicing his lines phonetically. His dialogue was so unintelligible at times that many of his scenes had to be dubbed. But despite Simone's defense, there was no accounting for Montand's repeated conversations with the press, or his references to his affair as an "adventure." And his meeting with Hopper had stirred up the embers of a perpetually smoldering fire. Now Marilyn, humiliated by Montand's cavalier brush off, stepped up her attempts to make contact. She called and cabled repeatedly. Montand would not answer. The gutter press worked hard to unravel all the details of the affair, revisiting the period the couples lived next door to each other at the Beverly Hills, Simone's Oscar, Miller's script re-writes, and the affair. *Hush-Hush Magazine* ran an exclusive: How Marilyn Monroe's Marriage Almost Went PFFT—When She Got a Real-life Crush on her Current Reel-life Hero!!!"

Back in Paris, Simone had barely absorbed the impact of Hopper's article or even had time to unpack, when she was faced with another demand. A friend, Claude Lanzmann, a filmmaker and journalist, came to visit on behalf of Jean-Paul Sartre. They had developed a petition to take a stand against the French war in Algeria, and they wanted Simone to sign. Simone was knocked off balance at first. She had been so caught up in the "iridescent bubble" and her personal troubles that she had lost touch with world events. Algeria was a French colony, and the government in Paris had launched a military offensive to squelch Algerian demands for liberation. French citizens who had aided the Algerians in their offensive were being tried by a military court. The petition was controversial and direct: "We respect and find justified the refusal to take up arms against the Algerian people. . . . We respect and find justified the conduct of those Frenchmen who believe it their duty to give aid and protection to the oppression of the Algerians in the name of the French people . . . ." The petition called for the end to colonialism. More negative publicity to face, Simone thought, reading the document again in hopes of finding some word that she could object to. Then, she felt guilty. It's okay to talk about injustice, but when faced with taking a stand against it, she wavered—and despised herself for her hesitation.

Simone made two quick decisions: She signed and then refused to sign on Montand's behalf. She insisted that this was not a passive-aggressive move intended to punish her husband. They had never signed each other's names to any document sight unseen and without discussion. And, with the distance between Paris and LA and the urgency for publication of this petition, there was no time to contact Montand and explain the situation. She claimed the phone wasn't working well. She alone signed.

When the petition was published in the newspapers, the press picked up on the exclusion immediately. This was the first time Simone's and Montand's names did not appear together on a petition, and Simone's act of signing alone was viewed as a "moral divorce." Simone regarded this conclusion as "mixed up thinking." But she had made a statement loud and clear. For the first time, Simone had stepped out and taken a stand without offering the shelter of her name to Montand. When he returned to Paris he was angry and resentful that he had been excluded. He felt she didn't need his permission to sign such an important document. Of course he was against the Algerian War. His name should have been on that petition. But the damage was already done.

By then the petition, known as the Manifesto of the 121—reflecting the number of people who had signed—was already generating repercussions. The petition was regarded as an act of disloyalty against the government; signers were considered dissidents. Those who signed the petition were immediately banned from working in television, radio, stage, and film, and were threatened with prosecution. Employers who did not heed the ban were threatened with loss of government subsidies.

In protest, artists, writers, and actors who hadn't signed refused to appear on television and radio unless the blacklisting ended. "And that's why, naturally, Montand refused to participate in any of the end-of–year programs to which he was invited," Simone explained. However, this refusal backfired on him. The popular opinion was that he had taken the easy way out. He could afford to remain out of show business, because he was making money in Hollywood. "All this was going on while those letters, those sad, abysmally stupid and anonymous letters, still poured in," keeping the Marilyn affair front and center, Simone explained. But she continued to maintain her dignity under fire, and the tide began to turn slowly in her favor. She was admired as a woman of great courage and respected for her self-control.

But the emotional upheaval was beginning to show. When Simone visited Italy for the premiere of *Adua*, she was photographed lunching with Shirley MacLaine. Simone appeared tired and worn. Back in Paris, the news reported that the French government was considering prosecution of signers of the 121 Manifesto and that jail time was a possibility. Meanwhile, Marilyn continued to call and cable Montand in hopes of reaching him. And by November 1960, news broke that she and Arthur Miller were divorcing, news that unleashed yet another round of publicity. Montand was blamed for causing the divorce; clearly Marilyn was in love with him. And, the French press was reporting that all was not well with the Montands. For once, the rumor was true. Simone and Montand fought constantly, while Marilyn continued to call. At one point, Montand locked himself in the theater he had built for rehearsals at Autheuil. Catherine recalled her mother fiercely banging on the door, calling out to him.

Other, never substantiated rumors circulated. Allegedly, Montand was due to arrive in New York. Marilyn got wind of this plan and threatened to track Montand down when he arrived. During this period, Marilyn's press aide and confidante, Pat Newcomb, reportedly heard a phone conversation between Marilyn and Simone. Simone allegedly called Marilyn in New York. Marilyn took the call, but not before asking Newcomb to pick up the extension phone so he could listen in. "Simone begged Marilyn not to see Montand, to please leave him alone," Newcomb reported. "I felt so awful. Here was this wonderful woman, such a fine person, pleading with Marilyn." Newcomb never described Marilyn's reaction to Simone's request. According to rumor, Montand then canceled his trip, and Marilyn was devastated.[10]

In January 1961, Montand flew to Japan to film *My Geisha* with Shirley MacLaine. Simone was in Burgundy, filming *Les Mauvais Coups*, and when Montand saw her in a televised interview promoting the film, he wanted to return home to comfort her. She looked tired and stressed. Her role in the film couldn't possibly improve her condition. As Roberta, Simone portrayed a forlorn woman, fortyish, who is married to Milan (Reginald Kernan), a moody man who no longer desires her and shows little interest in anything else. He has given up his career as a race driver and wants to spend time writing his memoirs. The two can't seem to get out of each other's way, and they fight constantly. Roberta drinks too much and is sarcastic. He doesn't care about her. And is interested in a younger woman.

Simone helped director Francois Leterrier with casting for this, his first feature film. He wanted an unknown to play opposite her in the role of Milan, so he and Simone parked at a table on the terrace of the Café de Flore and watched people on the street until they found the perfect prospect. They chose a tall, lanky man with graying hair: Reginald Kernan, an American doctor. He agreed to accept the role.

Of all her mother's films, Catherine Allégret hated *Le Mauvais Coups* most of all. It was too realistic and reminiscent of what was going on at home during that period, when Marilyn was calling constantly and her parents were fighting. Simone drank a great deal and was apt to lash out with cruel sarcasm. At the time, it seemed that her attempts to hold on to her marriage were as futile as her character's. While away on their respective locations, Montand and Simone wrote to each on a daily basis, but he was distracted, and she felt it. Marilyn was still trying to reach him and had threatened to come to Tokyo to see him. She never arrived. But the tension left Montand feeling out of sorts and "completely adrift" at the time: "I did a lot of stupid things all over again." Indeed, Montand's distraction was a one-night stand.

When Shirley MacLaine met Montand, she found him to be a charming man and, in retrospect, a man of many contradictions. On the one hand, he reported to the press that his affair with Marilyn was an "adventure" and not serious. She questioned him about it when they met, and he concurred that it was only that, an adventure. He was in love with Simone. Yet, years later, when she read his biography, MacLaine was surprised to learn that Montand thought he and Marilyn could have made a life together, and that their romance was serious. MacLaine and Montand spent a great deal of time rehearsing lines and dining out together, usually with the cast. He was always charming and worked hard. "But soon I realized that there was a subtext in his personal approach. He seemed to have a need to experience intimacy in complicated circumstances." Montand talked often about the relationships that develop between actors on the set. He explained that he was lonely and "a man in transition." Yet he spent most nights in his room alone. Then one evening, after a long day of filming, the cast had dinner before returning to their respective hotel rooms. MacLaine reports, "Soon there was a knock on my door. I opened it to find him standing in the hallway, his arms dangling by his sides, looking lost and forlorn. I pulled him into my room and folded him gently into my arms. We melted together. Then, at long last, fell into bed. It was sweet—a relief more than anything."

Shirley MacLaine's husband, Steve Parker, was away on business at the time. When he returned, his wife felt guilty about her tryst with Montand and confessed. However, her husband's reaction wasn't quite what she expected. As she explained in her autobiography, *My Lucky Stars*, Parker told her that Montand had flaunted his relationship with Marilyn in front of Arthur Miller. Then, Parker told her that Montand had made a bet with him at the start of the film that he could make Shirley fall for him.

The next day, she confronted Montand: "He looked stunned, hurt, frightened, and trapped all at the same time. He knew he had placed Simone Signoret in an untenable position in France. Her pride was hurt, yet she still loved him. His conduct had exposed her to a lot of gossip, even regarding her own sexual preference. Because of the women who seemed to continually inhabit Montand's life, people questioned why Simone never objected enough to take a strong stand." Now, confronted by MacLaine, Montand realized for the first time that anything he did or said would only cause the situation to spiral out of control. So he remained silent, and this extra-marital affair came to an end. It is unknown if Simone was aware of the dalliance.

In October 1961, Montand was back on Broadway for another six weeks of *An Evening with Yves Montand*. Simone accompanied him this time. Although she felt that everything they had accomplished in America had been tarnished by the Monroe affair, this trip was a chance to relive fonder memories. They took the bridal suite at the Algonquin Hotel, and Montand sang to sold-out audiences. On his fortieth birthday, Simone gave him a watch with a simple message engraved in the wristband: "For another October 13-1961."[11]

PART V

MONSTROUS EGOCENTRICITY

CHAPTER 24

The Little Foxes

SIMONE WAS ON LOCATION IN TOULOUSE, FRANCE, FILMING *THE DAY and the Hour*, when Marilyn Monroe died on August 5, 1962. Caught up in her role, Simone, oblivious to the outside world, had not heard the news and was enjoying dinner with assistant directors Costa-Gavras and Claude Pinoteau, when Montand called to tell her. The couple never shared the details of their brief conversation, but it was clear from their immediate reactions that they understood the ramifications: The press would seek them out for comment and there was little to lose.

When Simone returned to her hotel, the manager informed her that reporters had already converged on the site. He had the foresight to refuse their requests for rooms and had cleared out the lobby. Simone was grateful for his discretion, because she had no intention of weighing in on Marilyn's tragic life or death, or of reopening old wounds—certainly not with the press. "That same press . . . had latched on to the four of us—Marilyn, Montand, Miller and myself—in order to make us play parts we had never learned in a play we hadn't read," about a blonde heartbreaker, a moody dark man, a book worm, and an admirable wife standing on her dignity—these were the labels the press had given them for the drama.

Simone was both saddened and magnanimous while reliving her emotions that evening. She claimed she had forgiven Marilyn, and understood why the actress had fallen for her husband. She easily explained away his behavior: "He is first of all a man, in every sense of the word. What happened to them, to the poor woman Marilyn Monroe and him, can happen to anyone of us,"[1] and did happen in countless marriages. However, these stories would never be told, because such lovers and victims could live out their stories in privacy instead of on the front page of newspapers. And so, while she resented the intrusion and the embarrassment the affair had caused, she didn't blame Marilyn and was saddened by her death. "She never knew to what degree I never detested her," Simone wrote in *Nostalgia*, "and how thoroughly I had understood the story that was no one's business but ours, the four of us. Too many people were concerned with it during troubled times when many more important things were happening. She's gone without ever knowing that I never stopped wearing the champagne colored scarf she'd lent me one day when I was being photographed. It went so well with what I was wearing; so well that she made me a present of it."

Simone and Montand both claimed to have picked up the pieces of their marriage, though they agreed that their relationship had changed. "Passion does not always burn like an inextinguishable volcano," Simone explained. Montand described their new beginnings as "a bond that was calmer but just as strong." They had taken stock of their marriage and their careers and had faced the reality of turning forty together.

The prospects of mid-life were terrifying, and the loss of two close friends in 1960 brought mortality into focus. On February 21, 1960, Jacques Becker passed away at the age of fifty-four. Simone could not contain her tears whenever she spoke of him, especially after *Casque d'Or* was re-released in 1963. He had endured undue criticism for his film during his lifetime, and it was ironic that it would be lauded as a masterpiece and he as a genius only after his death. During low points in his career, he had often been a guest of the Montands at Autheuil. Becker was part of their extended family, and his loss weighed heavily on their hearts. The loss of Henri Crolla, Simone's friend during the Occupation and Montand's guitarist during the post-war years, was a loss that especially unnerved them because Crolla was so close to them in age. Montand was so distraught that he wept openly at the funeral and was inconsolable. Henri Crolla died on October 17. He was forty years old.

As their respective fortieth birthdays approached in 1961, they celebrated tentatively. For Montand, the changes he felt were internal; physically, he was showing signs of a graceful entry into mid-life. He was no longer the skinny and lanky kid who felt awkward. Dance had given him grace and style, and he was svelte and elegant. Montand was maturing while Simone aged. She was self-conscious about the little bit of weight that had begun to fill out her waistline, though the added pounds were not visible in the nineteenth-century costume she wore in *Les Amours Célèbres* (*Famous Love Affairs*), a Franco-Italian compilation of vignettes directed by Michel Boisrond.

She was sultry as Jenny de Lacour, an older woman conflicted about both aging and the lover who wants to leave her. Jenny stands in front of the mirror examining her face critically, her fingers working nimbly at the sagging skin under her chin and around her eyes. She pulls back the skin to tighten it, imagining a youthful face and neckline. Simone had created a similar scene in front of the mirror in *Room at the Top*. The mirror would become an important prop and aging a dominant theme in her films from this point forward. *Les Amours Célèbres* was Simone's only film production in 1961, when she seemed to be easing back into her professional career after a tumultuous year.

On October 3, 1961, her father, André Kaminker, succumbed to cancer in a Paris hospital. He was seventy-four years old. It is unclear if Simone visited him before his death. She never spoke of his death or expressed her feelings at the time. However, between the deaths of Becker, Crolla, and then her father, Simone was besieged with fear of a protracted death from cancer, a fear she would one day be forced to face head on.

She tried balancing marriage and career with a new perspective and zeal in 1962. During the first months of the year, she traveled with Montand on his tour of Japan and England, and then remained in London to reunite with Peter Glenville in the British film *Term of Trial*. Simone played a supporting role in this film. Laurence Olivier played the lead as Graham Weir, an alcoholic schoolteacher whose career is at a standstill because he was arrested as a conscientious objector during WWII. He is a quiet, shy, and unassuming man, despised by his colleagues for his cowardice during the war and by his wife, Anna, played by Simone. She bullies and berates her husband for his inability to earn more, for his lack of fight, and for their less than amorous marriage. She wanted children. He wasn't able to provide them. He could not afford a family, and she despises him. Their lives take a decided turn when he offers to tutor one of his pupils, Shirley Taylor, a young teenager who immediately falls in love with him. When he refuses her advances, she accuses him of sexual assault, and he is arrested and tried. The plot focuses primarily on the love interest of Graham and Shirley Taylor, played by Sarah Miles, giving Simone a backseat role. Off the set, Olivier and Miles took their roles to another level with an affair. Simone had no stories to share about the camaraderie she normally enjoyed in filmmaking. The role of a disgruntled, bullying wife did not resonate with her, and though her performance was authentic to a fault, it was not critically acclaimed. Laurence Olivier was nominated and won the British Lion as Best Actor, and Sarah Miles won as Most Promising Newcomer to Leading Film Roles.

In May 1962, Simone and Montand took time out to help their friend Chris Marker with *Le Joli Mai*, a documentary that mixed voice-over commentary with man-on-the-street interviews about every aspect of life, from post-war culture, to the latest fads, the quest for happiness, politics, and world events. Montand provided the French commentary, and Simone the English language version. Marker, unseen throughout, filmed the interviews. The documentary essay won Best First Work at the Venice Film Festival in 1963. With that short assignment completed, Simone was on to her next film, *The Day and the Hour*, directed by René Clément.

Simone admired Clement. Though she found his direction ambiguous at times, there seemed always a method to his off-the-cuff remarks. Shortly before filming, Clément met her at the Café Flore. "René sat looking at me. And then, out of the blue, he said, "Just an idea . . . I'm not sure, mind you, but maybe ages ago, when she was in her teens, Thérèse had to bear some enormous grief; perhaps she had an illegitimate child, or perhaps she loved her father more than her mother, or maybe she wasn't allowed to marry someone she really loved. . . . Who knows? Whatever it is, forget everything I've just said." Simone was incredulous. How could she forget?

She was far more engaged with her new character, Thérèse, than she had been with Anna in *Term of Trial*. Thérèse, a wealthy Parisian living alone with two young children during the last days of the Nazi occupation in 1944, must make life-changing choices. Simone described her character as a woman in transition who was living without a sense of purpose. When an opportunity for adventure arises, she must decide if she will follow her heart or continue living in her current circumstances. While visiting family in a country village bordering Belgium, Thérèse is accosted by the police, who seek information about British and American pilots who have been shot down in the area. Dissatisfied with her answers (she knows nothing), they slap her for her seeming impertinence. She is finally released. Once outside, she stops at an outdoor trough to splash water on her burning cheek, as she glances in a metallic mirror that slightly distorts her face.

The trains are not running, and she accepts a ride from a friend who is transporting goats. She discovers that the British and American pilots are also hiding in the back of the truck. In Paris, she offers them assistance because the pilots can't speak French. She allows them to follow her to their safe house. When they arrive at the safe house, she learns that there isn't room to house all the men, and she reluctantly agrees to take an American pilot to her apartment. In spite of her reluctance, she falls in love. When he must leave on a perilous journey through the mountains to find a Resistance camp and safe passage to Spain, Thérèse leaves her children in the care of a sister-in-law and follows him. When they reach the Resistance encampment, he is given a motorcycle and speeds off toward the border and freedom, without saying goodbye.

ৎ৩

When Simone took stock of her life and career after the events of 1960, she decided that it was time to step out, refining her repertoire by combining two interests she'd never thoroughly pursued: translation and theater. Like her father, she enjoyed translating text, an interest she had had since childhood. Unlike André, she didn't learn languages easily. Still, she was fluent in English and spoke Spanish, Italian, and German well enough to communicate comfortably. She was confident that she could translate a play she could also star in, an exercise that would satisfy an itch to try the stage again. She had enjoyed great success in *The Crucible* and was confident she could take that experience to another level.

Why she chose Lillian Hellman's *The Little Foxes* is the subject of conjecture. She knew Hellman. They had met when she and Montand were in New York, and Simone had visited the playwright at her apartment, where everyone spoke in hushed voices and the mood was somber so as not to disturb the sleeping Dashiell Hammett, the author, who was dying. She respected Hellman's liberal views and admired her spunk for refusing to name names during the Red Scare. Simone also respected Hellman's work and had read her plays. But beyond the idea that *The Little Foxes* spoke to the injustices and inequity of social conditions in America, Simone never really explained why she chose a play that she could only describe as "kind of *Gone with the Wind* in reverse." It was a play, she would learn later, that held absolutely no appeal for French audiences.

When Hellman agreed to the production, she insisted upon getting other opinions about the quality of the translation and chose Professor Jacques Guicharnaud, an authority on French theater at Yale University, to review Simone's work. Guicharnaud was complimentary, and Simone began assembling cast and crew. Rehearsals were difficult, and she would blame herself for that. She realized only later that she should not have played the part of Regina. She couldn't engage in the role because she was too concerned about her translation text and didn't want anyone to ruin it with his own interpretation.

During rehearsals, Simone contacted Hellman on numerous occasions and invited her to Paris so she could weigh in on the production. Hellman always refused, claiming that she had faith. In December 1962, when Hellman finally flew to Paris to watch rehearsals she was horrified by what she discovered. "Bad, bad, bad," Simone recalled hearing from the playwright time and again that afternoon. As Hellman described it in her memoir *Pentimento*, "I had never seen so much bad so early." She ticked off the offenses with ferocity. She hated the translation, believing that it was too literal. The Sarah Bernhardt Theater was the wrong venue; it was "a theater meant for a pageant or an ice show," not for a play. The set was too cluttered, the props too large. And she was appalled by the "Texan sombreros" the men wore; they were supposed to be bankers from Alabama, not Texans.

After Hellman had berated the cast and argued with Simone, the drama continued at dinner, where the cast, Simone included, played out their frustration through childish behavior. Hellman did not speak French, and Simone had to translate conversation. Whether it was Simone's translation or the mood of the group, just about everything Lillian said caused laughter. Hellman knew the laughter was at her expense, and this factor made the situation more uncomfortable. The dark mood prevailed during performances for the next six weeks. French audiences were unimpressed with the play and critical of Simone.

When Hellman wrote about this experience nearly ten years later, in 1973, she went right for Simone's jugular, describing the actress as "an intelligent, charming woman, as remarkable in front of a camera as she is bewildered by a stage. Not knowing much makes many people in theater turn natural sense and humility into nonsense and pretense." When Simone read this assessment, she couldn't argue with Hellman. "All right, I can take that," she said. But she was outraged by Lillian's description of events, particularly her claim that she had arrived two weeks in advance of opening night, time enough to make appropriate changes in the production if anyone had listened to her. Simone fumed and fought back in *Nostalgia*: "Lillian, you know perfectly well that you arrived only the day before the opening." If she had responded to Simone requests to arrive earlier, they might have been able to make some changes. But dress rehearsal is not the time to for changes. "Does one really forget? Or does one arrange? Or does one contrive?" she asked Hellman.[2]

CHAPTER 25

Zorba the Greek

WHEN SIMONE WAS ASKED TO WRITE AN ARTICLE, "THE PRIVATE LIFE of Simone Signoret," published on February 15, 1963, in the Mexican magazine *Cine Universal*, she did not waste time belaboring the point that her personal life should remain private. Instead, she dived right in, providing a startling but insightful commentary on her marriage with the first sentence: "When Yves and I have an argument, a more or less harsh one, I decide that I never want to see him again in my life. I go to the theater where he's singing to tell him that I want to leave him." And then, she quickly changes her mind: "I have seen his performances thousands of times, but when I watch him, it only takes two minutes to forget my grievances. He is a great artist, a superb artist without parallel. And I realize that an artist of his stature deserves my consideration." At that moment, her selfish grievances seem frivolous, and she returns home with "humility" to wait for him. Their marriage was not as passionate as in earlier years, she explained. "Montand and I have lived together for thirteen years. In thirteen years things happen that mark a life. Love does not conserve the same intensity over the passage of time." They had to work to keep a balance between "heart and mind," but when they were able to find it, the marriage became a safe haven of love and friendship.

Surprisingly, she spoke with honesty about her husband's career as an actor. While he was unequaled in the field of music, she couldn't disagree with the criticism that in acting, "the art, dramatic, pure and simple is not his forte"—at least not at that point. But he was tenacious and talented, and she was confident that he would improve. This subject brought her to the heart of something that bothered her most. There was "a legend" that she was the brains of the marriage and he the brawn. The myth developed when they first met, and it gained currency with Montand's critics, particularly after the Monroe affair. The only reason he had made it in show business, some asserted, was because of her approval and advice. Without her, he would not be as successful. Still worse, she thought, this legend perpetuated the idea Montand had little to offer her in return. "Nothing could be farther from the truth," she countered. Yves Montand was a self-made man, successful because of his talent, instinct and hard work. Yes, she helped him in any way she could, but she was not responsible for his success. As for the give-and-take in a marriage, she waxed philosophical: "Love is an interchange, the base of true and lasting happiness. If I have given something to Yves Montand, he has also given to me. Thanks to him I have known new worlds whose existence I had previously ignored. Thanks to him I have a place to return to, to find order and peace."

The image of the ideal couple had reemerged. While the trust and passion of youth had waned, the relationship was now more mature and grounded in love and friendship. Simone would continue to perpetuate this image, though trust was lost and the order and peace she spoke of in their marriage was punctuated by violent rows. They spent as much time together as possible, but not nearly as much as they had in past. While Montand focused on reviving his singing career in France after his movie making hiatus, she appeared to have a renewed interest in her career. During time spent apart, they sent each other love notes. However, when they were together, they argued with ferocity over anything and then repeated the pattern: arguments, separation, and love notes from a far. When Montand was asked to sing at President Kennedy's inaugural anniversary celebration on January 17, 1963, Simone was not present.

She dived into work with ferocity the following year, and from this point forward, began a long process of redefining or attempting to redefine herself as an actress. Simone was quick to tell others at that point that she embraced aging and would use it to her advantage by taking more challenging roles. She had no appetite for spending hours in front of the mirror primping, like actresses who wanted to make themselves look younger. She would not use plastic surgery to tighten her face or erase signs of aging.

But when Anthony Quinn and director Michael Cacoyannis offered her a role in *Zorba the Greek*, Simone was anxious. "I was already forty–three years old. But I was only forty-three years old," too young to play Madame Hortense, an aging French hotel owner fifteen years her senior who lived on the Island of Crete. "I don't think I can do it. I don't think it's me," she told them honestly.[1] Quinn pressed. Madame Hortense was certainly an older, wizened woman, he reasoned, but Simone's interpretation could be one of the great roles of her career. It took some persuading before Simone finally acquiesced to the pressure, half-heartedly. Sensing her continued discomfort, Quinn tried to bolster her confidence by suggesting that they rehearse together until she felt more comfortable. Doing so did not appeal to her: "Oh, I don't like to rehearse. I like to play spontaneously."

This bit of news did not please Cacoyannis, who liked his actors to rehearse. And as if to drive home that point, Quinn thought, Cacoyannis pushed Simone too far during the first days of filming. Instead of easing her in when she was clearly uncomfortable, the director started with her most difficult scene. Madame Hortense had not aged gracefully, and Simone was outfitted with a plump derriere, sagging breasts, a gold front tooth, and a wart. Her cheeks were stuffed with cotton to fill out her face and her hair was frizzed out—ridiculously so, she thought. Simone was horrified when she looked in the mirror. To make matters worse, they had photographed her as a younger Madame Hortense for a portrait that would hang on the wall. The image of a beautiful young woman with a coif reminiscent of *Casque d'Or* was a painful reminder of Simone's former glory days. With this portrait in full view, Madame Hortense was expected to dance around, making a fool of herself in front of Zorba and his companion Basil, a British journalist played by Anthony Bates. Simone struggled with the scene.

"She was not ridiculous enough, not pathetic enough in her portrayal," Quinn remembered. So Cacoyannis kept at Simone, pressing her for a better performance in take after take. The mood grew ominous, as they worked late into the night without success. Then things reached a crisis. During a break in the action, Quinn found Simone sitting on the floor, completely undone, "She was weeping deadly, deadly tears." He tried to console her, explaining things would improve if she gave it a chance. "No, Tony," she sobbed, "I think it's wonderful. But Hortense is an old woman, and I've got a young husband. I can't let him see me like this." The next day, Simone made plans to break her contract and return home.

Although she was released from her contract without repercussions, she was ashamed of herself for giving in to the worst case of vanity she had ever exhibited. It was safe to use her husband as an excuse, because Montand certainly kept an eye on younger women. Fidelity did not have a place in the "order and peace" of their marriage. But, in truth, it was she who couldn't bear looking at herself as old and undesirable. And it embarrassed her that she had been so sure of herself in public after she accepted the role. During an interview, a young Greek journalist dared ask if she had any concern about playing an older woman. She brushed him off impatiently, as though he had asked a stupid question: "[N]o, not at all." She wasn't proud, but there was no time for reflection, because she had signed on for three more films, back to back.

Simone did not have difficulty embracing the role of a deposed Spanish Condesa in *Ship of Fools*. On May 7, 1964, while still in Crete, she sent a letter to Bill Thomas, costume designer for Stanley Kramer productions, to provide specific feedback on the designs he had sent her and to discuss her measurements. As she was still waiting to have those measurements translated into inches, the best she could offer him at that point was a self-portrait of her physical attributes. This was necessary, she explained, because she was sure that Thomas would be dumbfounded when he finally received what appeared to be more a study in haphazard construction than the dimensions of a star. Any weight she had gained found its way directly to her thighs, which were infinite, she explained. Somewhere between large breasts—very large breasts—and the thighs, she thought she had been shorted in the hip department, not to mention the fact that her neck was almost non-existent, and her arms were skinny and clearly out of proportion to the rest of her body. In the end, she thought her feet were her best asset. This attribute was unfortunate, she joked, as her feet would not get the attention they surely deserved. She had suggestions on tailoring her gowns to create a more curvaceous figure. "V" necks were more complimentary, and it was best to start the bias line beneath her breasts. After that, they could use any lines they desired, as long as they didn't appear to add inches to her waist. Full-length sleeves were best to fill out her arms.

She was far more serious about the costume designs, though careful not to be too critical because the gowns were lovely, she reassured Thomas. But the more she examined them, the more she thought they were a little too rich and a bit too stylish for a deposed Spanish Condesa, a drug addict who had lived a harsh life as a political dissident and was on her way to prison. The gowns, carefully tended while traveling from place to place should be a testament to the glory days of the past—nice but no longer stylish. After the humor and insightful feedback, she added an instructive, clearly egotistical postscript to her letter: Given her stature as an actress, she hoped it was understood that she couldn't possibly wear fake furs.

Like Madame Hortense in *Zorba*, La Condesa was older, more than ten years older than Simone, yet the two characters represented the extremes of an aging woman: one wizened and foolish in love, the other attractive, stately, and sensuous. La Condesa is older, wiser, and still desirable. Even in her worst moments of struggle with her morphine addiction, she is never a fool. The role resonated with Simone. The story, which evolves through vignettes set during the birth of the Nazi era on a cruise ship, portrays anti-Semitism, intolerance, discrimination, and the scars left by lost dreams—themes that were appealing to Simone.

Lee Marvin played Bill Tenny, a former baseball player who drinks to forget his disappointment over an unsuccessful career. He meets Mary Treadwell, played by Vivian Leigh, a divorcée ravaged by age and disappointed in love. An anti-Semitic businessman, played by José Ferrer, offends with his pro-Nazi rants and rages. A dwarf known only as Glocken, and a Jew, Lowenthal, form a friendship when they are excluded from the dinner tables of other guests. An American couple, David and Jenny, bicker constantly because he is unhappy with his career as an artist. "Everything is staccato, loud, crude," wrote critic Pauline Kael in *Kiss, Kiss, Bang, Bang*. "But audiences will 'buy' the doomed lover right out of *One Way Passage*: Oskar Werner's Dr. Schumann compassionately giving injections and adoring love to La Condesa, Simone—sexy, sad, never-met-the-right-man-until-too-late—Signoret":

DOCTOR: You're so strange, sometimes you're so bitter. Then you're a child, soft and warm.
LA CONDESA: I'm just a woman.[2]

Simone and Werner earned Academy Award nominations as Best Actors for their performances.

When she arrived in Hollywood for *Ship of Fools* during the summer of 1964, Simone discovered that the "iridescent bubble" was no longer shimmering with the intensity of the past.[3] The country still grieved the assassination of President John F. Kennedy, a loss Simone grieved as well. She had been tearful when she invited Jane Fonda, who was living in Paris at the time, to Place Dauphine to watch the news because she didn't want the young actress to be alone.[4] Jane took her up on the offer. Nearly a year later, a cloud still hung in the air, and it seemed that every restaurant in Hollywood continued to pay tribute with photos and busts of JFK.

There were still lavish dinner parties, especially those hosted by costar Vivian Leigh, who continued to live the fantasy of *Gone with the Wind*; its theme song always played in the background. Although Leigh and Sir Laurence Olivier had divorced, she still referred to herself as Lady Olivier and lived in the past. Simone had little patience for Vivian. The two women were not fond of each other.

On weekends, the cast of *Ship of Fools* spent a great deal of time at the summer beach house Lee and Betty Marvin rented in Malibu. Simone and Lee had co-starred in *Don't You Remember* in 1960, and a comfortable friendship had developed between them. Simone and Betty were particularly close, and Simone was invited to stay in the Marvins' two-bedroom guesthouse, which she shared with Larry Hagman, another close friend of the Marvins. At that point, Lee's drinking problem was spiraling out of control. He drank far more than other guests and was so unsteady that his wife had him seen him crawling along the beach. He was also flaunting an extra-marital affair. Betty was devastated, and Simone was concerned. As Betty wrote, "Simone had become very fond of Lee and was saddened by his obvious spiral downward. She also saw the trouble I was in with my marriage. One day she had a driver take her into town and returned with a book for me, leaving it on my bed. It was a copy of Malcolm Lowry's *Under the Volcano*, the story of a hopeless alcoholic."[5] Betty began reading and was overcome by despair. When she didn't attend their cocktail hour, Simone came looking for her and found Betty curled up on her bed in tears. As Betty remembers, "She came over, and gave me a tender embrace, and sat down next to me. 'I'm sorry my gift has upset you. As a friend, I wanted to give you a message, but I'm afraid I've just made things worse. Please forgive me.'"

They talked about the failing marriage and Lee's alcoholism, and surprisingly, Simone encouraged her to leave Lee and start a new life. Betty felt that her husband needed her, particularly in his current condition. But, Simone insisted that Lee would survive. It was more important that Betty sever the tie. Simone offered that if given a choice, "[I]t's better to lose an arm than to lose a life,"[6] ironic advice from a woman who had chosen to turn a blind eye to her husband's affairs and who was herself well on her way to becoming an alcoholic. Simone didn't see the connection.

According to Betty, Simone had adopted a different strategy for handling Montand, which she demonstrated one day when he called her at the Marvin's home, an incident that shed a light on just how much their relationship had changed. In the past, Simone would drop whatever she was doing to talk to Montand. Now, she let him leave a message; she was busy and she'd get back to him when it was convenient to do so.

❧

Simone returned to Hollywood for the film opening in summer 1965. She expected to remain only long enough to attend the premier and the parties, and to visit old friends. But her stay was extended when she was asked to read a script, *A Small Rebellion*, a one-hour television drama for *Bob Hope Presents the Chrysler Theater*. She thought that "It was beautiful, very intelligent, and very Pirandellian."[7] Simone accepted and called Montand to tell him that she was staying longer than expected. She played the character Sarah Lescault and George Maharis, the popular star of *Route 66*, played Michael Kolinas. Appearing on an empty stage, they portrayed actors debating the dynamic of the roles they would play in a stage production.. Filming took place over a six-day period without rehearsals. The program was fast-paced and effective, earning Simone an Emmy Award.

But during those six days of filming, Hollywood's iridescent bubble finally burst, when the Watts neighborhood of LA erupted in violence on August 11, 1965. The riots began with a single incident: Marquette Fry, a young African American, was pulled over by a highway patrol officer on suspicion of driving while intoxicated. His arrest and the arrests and treatment of his mother and brother, who arrived at the scene to help him, drew a crowd of local residents and fueled a riot that lasted from August 11 to 15. Watts was aflame, as rioters burnt down buildings and looted businesses.

During the filming of *A Small Rebellion*, the crew listened to the latest reports. Everyone was frightened and talking about the news. Simone was stunned when a grip suggested they send atomic bombs to the area, and then disgusted when another warned her to lock her doors at night because "bands of niggers" were roaming around. But in spite of her aversion to these suggestions, she allowed fear to get the best of her: "Disdaining and insulting myself profusely, I never-the-less double locked the door that evening." She remained glued to her television set, watching the events on Saturday, her day off. By Sunday, she learned, the police had apparently restored order. Simone noticed that as rioters were pushed into paddy wagons, they all turned to the television camera and waved. Their behavior clearly suggested that this was not the end of their struggle against profiling and discrimination.

❧

The year ended in France with a family affair, *Compartiment Tuers*, (The Sleeping Car Murders), directed by Costa-Gavras. The film revolves around six passengers on a train from Marseille to Paris. During the overnight trip, a girl is killed in her berth, setting off a murder spree that continues after the passengers arrive in Paris. The central character, Inspector Grazzi, is under pressure to solve the crime, as all but two passengers are murdered. According to the director, he showed the script to Simone in hopes that she would find it worthy of production as his directorial debut. She liked to encourage new talent and would often open doors for new directors. Simone not only liked the film, but agreed to take the role of Éliane Darrès, an older woman with a young lover who is murdered after she is interrogated by Inspector Grazzi.

When Montand joined the discussions, he too expressed interest. "I was dreaming: Yves and Simone for your first movie!" Costa-Gavras recalled. "'Read the script,' I stammered, 'If a part appeals to you, take it.'" Montand was tempted by the character Cabaud, a sexually disturbed introvert wrongly suspected of murder . . . but I had other ideas,"[8] Costa-Gavras explained. He wanted Montand to play the role of Inspector Grazzi. Montand could credibly pull off a Marseille accent—along with a perpetual cold— throughout the murder investigation.

Montand remembered an entirely different and less fanciful version of the story. Costa-Gavras could not find financial backing for this first film and had turned to both Simone and Montand for help. They agreed to play roles and take a percentage of earnings. According to Montand, the decision for him to play Inspector Grazzi was made at the start, and the idea of his character's accent came later on. For Montand, these were important details, because this role, which he was allowed to interpret freely, was the long-awaited breakthrough in his acting career.[9]

The film also launched Catherine's career as an actress. When Costa-Gavras approached Simone about the possibility of her daughter's participation, she insisted that Catherine, now eighteen, first pass her "bac" exam, Catherine had failed on the first try. Simone was adamant that Catherine retake it and had hired a tutor to help. When Catherine passed, Simone insisted that her daughter be treated like anyone else. She had to audition for the role of Bambi, one of the two surviving passengers Inspector Grazzi must try to save.

Simone maintained a professional distance from her daughter during filming, though she helped on the first day of filming by showing Catherine her marks. They jokingly referred to each other as madame and mademoiselle, with Simone breaking ranks only once after a day of filming, when she gave her daughter feedback about her behavior because Catherine had not responded well to feedback from the director.

This advice was delivered in private, during a phone call. Beyond that, Simone maintained her professional distance.

She did not want others to think that Catherine had preferential treatment because of her status. Later, she took this idea to another level by refusing to exert her influence to help Catherine secure roles, though Simone was well known for helping to launch new careers. Catherine had to earn her roles. In the end, the young woman noted with frustration that her mother might just as well have helped her, because whenever she landed a role, she was criticized for getting it simply because she was Simone's daughter. It was an untenable situation and a barrier that was difficult to overcome. Even in her new profession, Catherine lived in the shadow of her mother's life and career.

CHAPTER 26

"Sorry, William Shakespeare"

SIMONE WAS CONVINCED THAT WOMEN ONLY PRETEND TO TAKE AGING in their stride, something she discovered about herself while watching daily rushes for *The Deadly Affair*, an adaptation of John Le Carré's spy novel, *Call for the Dead*. She portrayed Elsa Fennan, a fifty-five-year-old survivor of a death camp whose husband, Samuel, has allegedly committed suicide. Elsa's facial expressions are strained, and her attire is as dowdy and colorless as her home, which has been decorated with great care on her husband's foreign service wages. Charles Dobbs, a British secret agent, played by James Mason, believes Samuel's death resulted from foul play and suspects Elsa of knowing more than she is willing to admit.

Little make-up was used in the creation of the matronly Elsa, only enough to blot out Simone's skin's shine under lights, mascara to accentuate her eyes, and a pale lipstick to give more definition to her lips. The puffy face, the deep creases in her forehead, and the tiny wrinkles around her eyes were not the work of a make-up artist. They were Simone's, and they haunted her throughout the eight weeks of filming. Although she and Mason were nominated as Best Actors by BAFTA, she never gave this film more than a passing comment.

It was egotism that prompted her to return to the stage in October 1966 as Lady Macbeth at London's Royal Court Theater. While in retrospect she could be honest about her motivation, she was always a little defensive about it. It wasn't her "stunt," she claimed. The entire idea had been conceived when her friend Sir Alec Guinness decided to return to the stage in a "modernist" version of *Macbeth*. And regardless of the heavy criticism the director, William Gaskill, received from traditionalists who were offended by the thought that anyone had to shake the dust off the Bard, there was no question that an appearance by Guinness would result in sold out shows months in advance of opening night. As for Simone, there seemed no rhyme or reason for casting her as Lady Macbeth, except that she still had strong box-office appeal in Britain—even though *The Deadly Affair* was not the most popular of her British films. A Guinness-Signoret team appearing in a contemporary Shakespearean production was unusual, but still considered a worthwhile risk.

She still dreamed of making a transition to the stage. *The Little Foxes* had been a mistake because she was more concerned about her translation than her performance. *Macbeth* was her redemption, she thought, and she prepared for this new opportunity with gusto at Autheuil, where she settled down to study six different versions of the play. However, this approach only added to her confusion, because each one had a different take on her character. In every version she'd read, she understood that Lady Macbeth was childless. Yet in act 1, scene 7, Lady Macbeth spoke of a baby.

Confused, Simone focused entirely on learning her lines. When friends stopped by, she asked them to listen to her recitations and was particularly grateful to Françoise Arnoul, who helped her with one troubling line: "Nor place, nor time." The word "time" kept eluding her, until she finally used an interpretation provided by Françoise, who prompted her by pointing at her watch. She kept this image in her mind when she recited her lines and was quite satisfied with herself when she finally memorized them all. Later, she would look back on her preparations and compare them to that of an amateur trying to learn to walk the tightrope without instruction. By the time she arrived for rehearsals, her mistakes were firmly entrenched in her confused interpretation of her role. It was only in retrospect that she realized how much her pride had clouded her instincts as an actress. Her timing was off, her low, gravelly voice didn't carry on stage. Worse, her Shakespearean diction, delivered with a French accent, created an unintelligible jumble of words. She joked that English and Shakespeare were two different languages. The production offered to hire a coach to help her, but she refused. Instead, she had a portable blackboard delivered to her hotel room and spent hours writing out her lines, practicing pronunciation and timing. Alec Guinness, William Gaskill, and members of the cast also tried to help. But she complained that it would have been helpful if someone had been honest enough to tell her that she wasn't working out in the role.

The illusive "someone" that hadn't come forward soon enough to help out on *The Little Foxes* had once again failed to appear in time for a rescue. In truth, only a total stranger observing rehearsals would dare risk giving strong enough feedback to make the necessary changes before opening night, because Simone was not at all open to criticism. She was a professional and could overcome obstacles. Unlike her tentative approach to films, where she was apt to worry about her performance and offer to quit if it wasn't up the to the director's liking, now Simone had no intention of letting go of her role. When it became obvious that only a casting change could save the production, Simone dug in deeper.

Montand tried to give her advice during a two-day visit. He had recently performed with great success in France on stage in *A Thousand Clowns*, a play about a successful children's filmmaker who decides to give up his career and riches to spend time with his twelve-year-old nephew. He had enjoyed the experience and was warmly received. But then, Montand was a master on stage. While she thought his criticisms were "pertinent," she chose to ignore them.

In spite of the appearance of self-assuredness Simone maintained in the face of looming disaster, there was always a shadow of doubt lurking around her subconscious, and it finally revealed itself to her on opening night. She was supposed to read a letter during the first act, and while waiting backstage she noticed that the paper she was holding was quivering. Indeed, both hands were shaking uncontrollably. She felt lightheaded as she spoke her lines, realizing that her diction was horrible. As her anxiety built in those few moments, she was sure she was going to faint, Simone remembered. And then she completely forgot her lines and stood, horrified, for ten seconds.

Alec Guinness immediately took control, taking Simone in his arms to steady her while he jumped ahead with a line that actually came later: "If we should fail . . . ." Simone regained her composure, nodded acknowledgment, gently pushed Guinness away, and stepped forward to face the audience. Though they barely understand a word she said, the audience knew she had scored a victory by overcoming fear and gave her warm applause. But the reviews were not as kind: she was miscast and unintelligible; she was cone-shaped and matronly. After reading one gruesome review, Simone folded up the newspaper and refused to read another.

To her horror, the unfavorable reviews didn't convince audiences to stay away, and Simone struggled through every performance in a sold-out theater. They came to watch her fail, she thought. They came to see how much weight she had gained or how much she had aged since her role as Alice Aisgill in *Room at the Top*. Admittedly, her feelings were hurt by the criticisms, but she persevered, making a few changes, improving timing as best she could, and experimenting with a hairstyle that had been compared to a Medusa's head in the initial reviews. She also changed her diet. Simone was sure she needed an infusion of protein before performances and ordered an early dinner of steak tartare, which she chased down with quick sips of Scotch whiskey. She despised the meal but was afraid to deviate from it. The one time she dared eat something more enjoyable, her performance had not gone well. It was psychological, she was sure, but she wasn't going to take chances. She had to preserve until the day came when she could wake in the morning without fearing what was to come that evening. And that thought sustained her as she relived the nightmare every evening through thirty performances. Her memories of October 1966 were dominated by bone-chilling fear.[2]

During the last of week of *Macbeth*, Bernard Weinraub of the *Saturday Evening Post* arrived at her hotel room for an interview. He would spend the next few days with her intermittently in London and then in Paris. The reporter was awed by her pleasant and engaging manner. "But she is restless," he noted. Her hands moved energetically while she talked and smoked, hands that were surprisingly not delicate but worn, as though she had toiled at hard labor. The words "amusing" and "clever" were favorites, and when she was amused by a clever joke Weinraub told, she'd embrace it wholeheartedly, throwing her head back and clapping in delight. The journalist found her laughter infectious. During an otherwise pleasant interchange about film and theater that continued into the next morning, the reporter had the opportunity to see another side of Simone, when their visit was interrupted by a representative of Universal Studios. She had signed on for *Games*, a suspense mystery with James Caan and Katharine Ross, but the production had hit a snag because she refused to fill out the form for a US visa. The studio rep brought it along in the hopes of gaining her compliance.

Weinraub reported the incident. "'No. This is a form I will not fill out again. Listen:' (she holds it up) 'Do you take dope,' they ask. 'Are you a member of the Communist Party?' Not the Nazi Party, mind you. That's very funny, no?'" She complained that she had recently filled out the form for *Ship of Fools*. Wasn't that enough? Why did she have to fill it out every time she visited the country? They knew her and nothing changed since her last visit, yet they insisted on a restricted visa reserved for potential threats; the same restricted visa she and Montand were given when they were first allowed in country. "Look, if they don't want to give me a visa, well . . . . With what's going on now in the world, I won't do it. . . . Now it's a question of pride. It's insulting. After going there as often as I have, I have to fill this out? Enough, right? Enough is enough." This speech was delivered while she paced the room, periodically running a hand through her hair in frustration. The other hand held a perpetually burning cigarette. The unnamed studio representative tried to calm her, switching from English to French in hopes of changing her mind. Simone responded in English: "Look my love, I don't need the money. I don't need the fame. There's one thing I have. My name. I've answered all those questions already." When he left empty-handed, Simone turned her attention to Weinraub. It's morning, and he notes that she is still rubbing sleep from her eyes, yet she mixes a drink while explaining her point of view: "I've been very lucky. I've never had to do things I didn't like for money. I can do this because we are both working, and we are both making enough money to be completely free to choose and free to refuse, which is an even bigger luxury. . . . If you're old enough not to take any nonsense, you can have a clever life."

Universal managed to secure paperwork for Simone, but it was apparently more time-limited than usual, and *Games* had to be filmed at breakneck speed. Simone knew she would not be nominated for an Oscar. She played Lisa, a fiftyish Frenchwoman with apparent psychic abilities who barely earns her living selling cosmetics door to door in Manhattan. At least that is the story she tells her prospective client, Jennifer, played by Katharine Ross. Jennifer isn't interested in her products and is about to send her packing, when Lisa has a fainting spell. Feeling sorry for the worn-out saleswoman, she convinces her husband, Paul, played by James Caan, that they should put Lisa up in their spare bedroom for a few days so she can rest and recover. Unbeknownst to Jennifer, the entire scenario is a ruse: Paul and Lisa are conspirators in a plot to steal her money.

While *Games* was not award-worthy and Simone's performance not her best, she liked the story and enjoyed the fast-paced filming. Although she was playing an older woman, Lisa had depth: She was mysterious, diabolical, and charming. Lisa was still a desirable woman, and Simone liked the role. "Too bad if when I play an evil femme fatale some of my real me seeps through,"[3] because, she claimed, she grew tired sometimes of playing nice women, just as she had tired of playing prostitutes. Katharine Ross and James Caan, who were both newcomers to the business, so impressed Simone that she arranged a screening of the daily rushes for director Mike Nichols. As a result, Ross was offered a role in *The Graduate*. Simone held her in high esteem because the young actress never forgot to mention the favor when talking about her career.

Simone's visa allowed her to remain in Hollywood through Christmas 1966, and she was invited to spend the holiday with the Fonda family. A restful period was needed after a whirlwind year, and she was quite content to immerse herself in what was left of the old "iridescent bubble," with its warm pleasant weather and delightful hummingbirds. She took morning strolls on the beach with Katharine Hepburn, lunched with friends at the Polo Club, and shopped for the Christmas presents she would bring to the Fondas. But the change in Hollywood was unmistakable. The lavish parties of the past had been replaced by intimate dinner parties, where conversation quickly turned from chatter about the superficial concerns of a fairy tale world to heated debate about the Vietnam War and the civil rights movement. Simone recalled one dinner party at the home of Gregory and Veronique Peck that took an uncomfortable turn. Someone referred to the Vietnamese as the enemy. Peck took offense to the comment, because he did not believe the Vietnamese were enemies of the United States. Simone was impressed and thought that this new and emerging social conscience among fellow actors in America far surpassed that of her colleagues in France.

CHAPTER 27

The Seagull

TRANSLATING HELLMAN'S *THE LITTLE FOXES* HAD NOT BEEN AS SUC-
cessful a venture as Simone had hoped, and she still blushed whenever
she thought about the *Macbeth* debacle. Simone would never agree to act
on stage again, yet she was still drawn to the theater and to the art of
translation, two fields of endeavor she was determined to conquer.

It was an impulsive decision, she admitted, to take a year off in 1967
to tackle a translation of *Fever*, a short story written by the American
author, Peter Feibleman, and published in France by Gallimard in their
Du monde entier collection. Simone was convinced that only a handful
of people ever read her translation. The piece was longer than usual for
the short-story format and a challenge to translate. Ever conscious of
criticism that her translation of Hellman's play was too literal, Simone
worked to discover and convey the writer's intent, rather than her interpretation of it.

In the end, the fact that she had now translated two American texts
counted as a personal victory. She tackled a third text, title unknown,
which was tucked away in a drawer and never saw the light of day.
Again, these experiences were a validation. "There is no doubt that I
have a taste for translation," she confessed. She would savor this accomplishment for a while, before putting it to good use again on a project
that would have great significance in the future. Until then, Simone re-
emerged as an actress.

In early 1968, she was asked to participate in a television series of
selected screenplays. While most of her fellow actors were reluctant to
transition to television, Simone had positive experiences in American
television and welcomed the idea of premiering on French TV, though

finding the right story was a daunting task. She toyed with several ideas before selecting a play with a theme that she had begun to explore while making *The Day and The Hour*: the decision an individual makes when faced with choosing safety and comfort over love and personal conviction.

She chose *La Femme Juive* (The Jewish Wife), a one-act play from Bertolt Brecht's *Fear and Misery of the Third Reich*. Set in Berlin in 1935, it is the story of Judith Keith, a Jewish woman who is packing for a trip to Amsterdam, ostensibly for a few weeks, though she knows she will never return. She is leaving to protect her husband, Fritz, a non-Jewish doctor whose career at a local clinic is in jeopardy because of their marriage. To protect himself, Fritz has become a Nazi sympathizer. *La Femme Juive* was pre-recorded and broadcast on April 28, 1968. By then, events that would alter the fabric of French society were well under way.

It began in March, when André Malraux, France's cultural minister, cut funding to the Cinématèque in an effort to remove Henri Langlois from his post as director, ostensibly for mismanagement. While Langlois was a master film archivist, an artist highly regarded in the film industry, he was so wrapped up in his vision and projects that he lacked the financial management skills necessary to run the Cinématèque. But the move to terminate his involvement with the museum he had founded caused an unexpected uproar. Simone joined fellow actors and directors in demonstrations, while prominent international directors—Alfred Hitchcock and Federico Fellini among them— flooded the ministry office with telegrams. The government backed off. Langlois was allowed to remain, and funding was reinstated—but at a much-reduced level, causing continued financial difficulties.

Outrage over the Langlois affair was only an indication of public dissatisfaction with the French government. Simone was not in Paris in May 1968 to witness the rioting and demonstrations sparked by police reaction to student occupation of college campuses after France's first wild cat general strike and citizen occupation of factories, offices, and transportation. She was staying at the Columbe d'Or in Saint Paul-de-Vence when the protests began and had planned to attend the Cannes Film Festival. However, after initial entries were previewed, the event was canceled as an expression of solidarity with the students and workers. A mass transit strike would have made it difficult to return to Paris, yet oddly, Simone had no immediate desire to return home. Montand, who was in Paris at the time, was also removed from the action. Rather than join in the demonstrations, he watched the turbulent clashes between the police and protestors from the fifth floor of Place Dauphine, where he had a clear view of the center of activity across the Seine on the Boulevard Saint Michel. Even from his vantage point, the spray of tear gas stung his eyes.[2]

Under any other circumstance, Simone would have been first to take a stand in the protests, and she was disturbed by her ambivalence. The initial student occupations of college campuses and high schools had begun over demands she could certainly support: greater equity and opportunity for all social classes. At the same time, the riots also represented a protest against her generation. For the first time, Simone was faced with the realization that aging had created a divide, a realization so unsettling that she felt the need to write about it. On June 2, 1968, while sitting in her room overlooking the pool in the relative comfort of the Columbe d'Or, she composed a letter to herself that focused on two conflicts: the desire to go back and the desire not to go back, "desires that alternated at high speed, like spasms or gusts of wind."[3]

On the one hand, she wanted to be a witness to the events unfolding in Paris, events so turbulent that President DeGaulle had fled to Germany, where he could set up a military operation in the event the government fell. It was an ironic move for the leader who fled to England to set up a military offensive against Germany during the war. When Simone finally returned to Paris, she knew friends would ask why she wasn't in Paris taking a stand, a question she had asked others after the Nazi occupation. She felt ashamed of her ambivalence as she sunbathed by the pool at the Columbe d'Or while Paris was under siege.

But if she went back, what would she do? She had no place at the Sorbonne University with the young people. Since she was part of the generation they were protesting against, the students would not welcome her. She could have joined some of her fellow actors in their demonstrations, but she thought their participation was insincere. In the past, these actors had been absent during protests against political assassination and colonialism. They had always maintained the position that they were actors, not politicians. Now they grew their hair long to look like the young people, and took up a place in a demonstration against the virtues of their own generation. It didn't make sense, and she wanted no part of it—not only because she was fearful of criticism, but also because she was fearful that she might get caught up in something she couldn't defend later on. In the end, Simone could understand the plight of the younger generation and felt they had every right to discount hers, the generation that spoke of "faith, honesty and courage." These were the virtues of survivors of a period in history that had passed and wasn't part of the future. What she couldn't understand was why President DeGaulle did not recognize the plight of this younger generation, the true "National Genius," who wanted to stake their claim in the country's future. De Gaulle's actions, or lack of action, had burst the bubble of her secret admiration for the general who had marched victorious into a liberated Paris many years earlier.

Simone did not return to Paris until the demonstrations ended and only the remnants of the upheaval were still visible: the Lion of Belfort had been painted red; there was graffiti on walls and holes in the streets where cobblestones had been torn out—all physical signs that would be cleaned up and repaired. "But people had changed. Some of them irreversibly," she recognized.

※

In August 1968, Simone was in Stockholm, participating in a film adaptation of Anton Chekov's *The Seagull*. It all began when Simone, James Mason, David Warner, and Harry Andrews were filming *Deadly Affair* in London for Sidney Lumet. The cast was so connected that they thought it would be fun to reunite for a Chekov play. Sidney Lumet made the dream possible. Vanessa Redgrave also joined the cast, and the two women developed a steadfast friendship. Indeed, the entire cast considered the production such a labor of love that Simone compared it to the filming of *Casque d'Or*. It was a summer vacation with a family. They spent all of their work and free time together.[4] Simone was convinced that the euphoria they felt must be akin to taking an LSD trip: emotions were heightened and colors vibrant.

She played the role of Arkadina, an actress who refuses to age—"a real bitch," Simone explained—in a plot she summarized as a story about unhappy people who desire more out of life but never seem to find what they seek, as the world passes by without notice. Ironically, Simone was so caught up in her role, the friendships, and the euphoria, she was allowing the world to pass by without her notice. She heard news about the Soviet invasion and occupation of Czechoslovakia on August 21, 1968, and watched news reports on television, but she and other cast members had only passing interest. They were anxious to return to the Chekov world they were creating. This sense of complacency was a new experience for the woman who was likely to insist that "something must be done" in the face of injustice.

While in Algiers filming *Z*, directed by Costa-Gavras, Montand had a visceral reaction to the Soviet invasion of Czechoslovakia: "I was knocked flat on my back. Since 1956, Hungary, and my visit to Eastern Europe, I had kept my distance, but I stayed within the family circle." Never a member, but still a friend of the Communist Party, he had hoped that the party could be reformed. But that hope died in August. He was so upset and angry about the invasion that it became the turning point. He could no longer defend the party and wanted nothing more to do with it. However, he kept his own counsel at that point until September, when he appeared on a Radio-Luxembourg program and minced no words, publicly criticizing Soviet actions in Czechoslovakia: "When people go on lying and killing and—what is even more disgusting—informing, then that damns a whole political system."[5]

His break with the communist "family" reached the inner core of his own family, prompting a horrific argument with his brother Julien, who remained an ardent member of the party and a high-level union boss in the food industry. The two men stood toe to toe, screaming at each other with such intensity that their argument nearly ended with blows before Julien stormed out of the apartment. Montand had screamed so loudly that he lost his voice and had to cancel two evening performances at the Olympia Theater. After their argument, Julien avoided Montand, and then finally moved his family from Place Dauphine, a move that was upsetting for Catherine.

Two weeks after the fateful argument, their father, Giovanni Livi, died on October 17, 1968. Montand dared not cancel another performance and did not attend the funeral, sparing himself another confrontation with his brother. Montand buried his grief in work and in preparations for his next film, *On a Clear Day You Can See Forever*, with Barbra Streisand. He was expected in Hollywood in November. Leaving nothing to chance, Simone planned to accompany her husband.

She returned to Paris with Vanessa Redgrave in October 1968, in time to catch one of Montand's performances at the Olympia Theater. Catherine was working for Montand at the time, and she had taken on her mother's supportive role during his rehearsals and backstage. Simone was now free to enjoy the show as an audience member.

Redgrave remained at Place Dauphine as a guest, and she and Simone slowly returned to the reality they avoided while in Sweden. The fire of passion was stoked when they learned that five Soviet intellectuals were on trial for protesting against the Czech invasion. Simone, Montand, and Redgrave composed a telegram of protest to the Soviet ambassador.

Redgrave was so inspired by their activism that she considered it a turning point: "Perhaps my short stay in Paris with Simone and Yves and the sense of political hope I now found gave me the courage to work again in the theater."[6]

Vanessa admired Simone immensely. She was "the most beautiful woman I had ever met, warmhearted, loving and amusing. She was everything I had imagined her to be since I first saw her as a girl in *Casque d'Or*." This was the woman that friends knew best. But something had changed; Simone had an edge. The warm and amusing impression she had left on Redgrave was not the impression Simone chose to allow others to see five months later, when she visited New York in January 1969 to promote the United States release of *The Seagull* and was interviewed by columnist Rex Reed from the *New York Times*. Simone's drinking had taken a strong hold, and her darker side was emerging.

"There she is. I don't know what people expect her to be like from the roles she plays, but she's no fading Colette heroine. Nowhere is there a trace of the ripened older woman from *Room at the Top* inspiring passions in younger men," Reed wrote, describing his first impression of the actress. "She's no femme fatale, either." Instead, he saw a woman with tousled hair, masculine hands, broad shoulders, and a hard, forced smile. She used four-letter words liberally and purposely flicked the ashes from her perpetually burning cigarette on the floor. Simone had been drinking and made no effort to hide it.

When faced with the prospect of filling out another US visa, Simone had refused and instead of the H-1 work permit, they had given her a B-1 "visitor's visa." She could not appear on television talk shows. In essence, she was unable to promote the film, and this trip was a waste of time. The visa issue irritated her, and she was insulted. But the good news, she explained, was that now she didn't have to appear on the "Mr. Merv-What's-His-Name" show, which was fine with her, because she truly hated these publicity trips. The only reason she had agreed to this one was that it was an opportunity to reunite with the cast from *The Seagull*. And, since she couldn't work, she announced that she might just as well spend the time "boozing it up"—a realization that prompted a call to room service.

She spoke to Reed of her career, covering the same scripted stories she always shared, though she was honest when she admitted that she worked as little as possible in order to hold together her marriage. She thought they must be doing something right since she and Montand had been married eighteen years at the point. Then, the interview with Reed was interrupted by another reporter, a minister from a Baptist college in Texas. Simone was always impatient with the superficial questions asked by star-struck novices, but this particular reporter apparently irritated her more than others, and she wanted to get rid of him as quickly as possible. Reed observed, "The interview with the preacher continues for half an hour, then Signoret rolls up her sleeves as though she is about to tackle a hard day's wash, and says: 'Look, I have no problems with religion. I'm a complete agnostic and I don't believe in God. Life after death is bull and the principle that we should live a certain kind of life in one place because it will prepare us for another life somewhere else is ridiculous! There's no mystery, no heaven, no life hereafter. For others maybe, but not for me." When the stunned reporter left, Simone got up, announced that she was going to wash her hair, and left Rex Reed, "Mr. New York Times," as she called him, in the sitting room of her hotel suite. He was welcome to stay, she told him, but it was clear that the interview over.

The Seagull's run in the States was short-lived, and it wasn't popular on the international market. Critics complained that Sidney Lumet had treated the film as a play rather than an adaptation, and the actors were criticized for exaggerated performances—particularly from Simone.

CHAPTER 28

Army of Shadows

WHEN HE AND SIMONE WERE IN HOLLYWOOD IN 1959, MONTAND noted—during a conversation with Americans about the Nazi occupation—"You know, really, we're survivors." The realization had shocked both Montand and Simone. They never thought of themselves as survivors and tried not to dwell on the "common disaster" that had defined their late teens and early adulthood. Yet Simone felt a "certain kind of nostalgia"[1] for that time, which she felt compelled to explain, because "it's an awful thing to admit." However, during those nightmare years, as treacherous and uncertain as life was, they had a predictable existence. The divide between friends and enemies was obvious, and the sense of camaraderie in the extended family—which saw no future and focused only on surviving the moment—gave one an odd sense of belonging and security. Simone had begun to explore themes from the occupation period in her films, themes of personal choices made when individuals were tested by extreme circumstances. However, up to this point, she had never portrayed a resistance fighter. So when Jean-Pierre Melville asked her to portray Mathilde in his film *Army of Shadows*, an adaptation of Joseph Kessel's book of the same title, Simone accepted. She was both intrigued by the opportunity and concerned.

Though Kessel had fictionalized his experiences as a member of the French Resistance, he realistically portrayed the often-gruesome life of resistance fighters, men and women who willingly made personal choices that went well beyond choosing safety over conviction. "You had to renounce your personal safety, and also your family, renounce everything in life, everything that makes life worth living,"[3] he explained. The life of a resistance fighter was lonely and frightening, the antithesis of the glorified Hollywood version of heroism in *Is Paris Burning?*

Simone had never been the type of person Kessel described, and the prospect of portraying a composite of prominent female resistance fighters was all the more daunting an endeavor, because the primary model for Mathilde was Lucie Aubrac, formerly known as Madame Samuels, Simone's history teacher in Vannes during the first year of the war. "It was very troubling for me to portray that woman whom I'd known as a girl," Simone said. "But what made it even more ambiguous for me, what made me feel a bit indecent, was that my makeup artist, a woman named Maude Begon, was another Lucie Aubrac." Begon, a resistance fighter who was later awarded France's Legion of Honor, had been arrested and imprisoned before she was sent to a concentration camp, where she remained for nineteen months, until liberation.

Every time Simone sat in front of the makeup mirror, she carefully watched Maude "fix me up so I wouldn't be too ugly, because a female resistance fighter in a movie can't be ugly, after all," and wondered what the makeup artist was thinking about, given her background. Simone admitted to feeling ashamed. Finally, while Maude applied false eyelashes, Simone couldn't help but break the awkward silence by asking a question she already knew the answer to: "Did you wear false eyelashes in Clermont-Ferrand when you went to meet people in your network?" Maude laughed, and the tension of the moment was broken, as Simone explained her discomfort. "It really bothered me that I was that age and I was playing that role, when I knew I hadn't been that type of woman in real life." While they were risking their lives, Simone was working for a collaborationist press, fighting not a common cause against evil, but a battle of conscience that was easily lost owing to concern about her family's financial security. Her lack of "conscience" during that period—a dark spot on her life—always weighed heavily on her heart and mind. Worse, now she found herself making a living portraying the heroism she had never demonstrated.

The discomfort she felt in the makeup room continued on the set of *Army of Shadows.* It was one thing to portray a historic figure from the past when there were no witnesses alive to critique the authenticity of her performance. But it was quite another thing to portray someone from her own past, someone who knew her and could judge her performance. This was such an unsettling thought that Simone lost confidence, requiring affirmation from Melville, who generally preferred to give his actors freer rein with their interpretation of their roles. He had only a few hard and fast rules: a character must be created; actors must never play themselves; never wear a false nose or show bare skin.

Simone often required more encouragement than direction. And, when Melville gave direction, it was often as ambiguous as that of René Clément, who hinted but never gave direct suggestions. However, unlike Clement, Melville was not an affable man. Indeed, he and Simone could be adversarial and had only recently reconciled after a falling out five years earlier. In 1965, Melville had been planning to make a film. Simone explained that she had completed a screen test, and all had gone well until they quarreled about some matter, which she preferred not to mention. It is unclear if the film in question—title unknown—was made with another actress, or if it was completely abandoned. Neither Simone nor Melville would speak of it. In any event, Simone preferred to focus her attention on Melville as a "craftsman," not a man that could be feared and sometimes despised by those who worked for him.

Everything Melville did was carefully planned and executed; everything had purpose. When no one thought it possible, he succeeded in obtaining permission to shut down traffic on Place Charles de Gaulle for a re-enactment of a Nazi military parade marching past the Arc de Triomphe. Filmed in black and white, it appeared as realistic as news footage. He had an argument at the start of the film with Lino Ventura, who portrayed Phillipe Gerbier, the leader of a Resistance network. Rather than smooth over hard feelings for the sake of the film, Melville purposely pushed Ventura to the limit, refusing to speak to the actor except through an assistant. The director also criticized the actor publicly. If it was possible to make Lino work harder than necessary, Melville found a way, leaving the actor feeling abused, angry, and ostracized. But, the isolation Lino felt was exactly the mood Melville wanted to achieve for the lonely Gerbier, who planned reconnaissance missions, arranged executions of members who had talked, and had to spend weeks hiding in complete solitude.

Army of Shadows was devoid of the summer vacation environment Simone relished on other film sets. Filming for Melville was hard work, and she was often so nervous that she was apt to ask him if they could have a short cocktail hour before shooting her scene. This meant that if filming were scheduled to begin at 1:00 p.m., they would be delayed until at least 4:00 p.m., when Simone was fortified and ready to tackle her scene. Yet Melville acquiesced to her requests for cocktail hours and was sensitive to her insecurities. She was, "no skim milk actress," and once in front of the camera, she commanded a scene, leaving no doubt that Mathilde was a bastion of secrecy and courage. Simone had few lines to learn for this film. More often than not, she was seen rather than heard, mapping out and executing elaborate strategies to free captured resistance members, often putting her own life at risk.

In the one lengthy conversation she has with Phillipe Gerbier, Mathilde reveals a weakness: She is married and has a teenage daughter. They do not know of her involvement in the Resistance, she explains. She keeps a photo of her beautiful daughter in her wallet and proudly shows it off. Gerbier advises her to remove the photo. If Mathilde is captured, the Gestapo will find it and use her daughter as a tool to break her silence. Mathilde agrees to remove it, but never complies.

Simone's most difficult scene comes at the end after Mathilde is questioned by the Gestapo. Her comrades have reason to believe that the Gestapo has threatened to send her daughter into prostitution if Mathilde doesn't talk. Unbeknownst to Mathilde, she has been labeled a risk, and her compatriots wait for her in a car outside Gestapo headquarters. Although they have no evidence that she revealed secrets, they can't take chances. Gerbier wants her gunned down in the street. Simone was already unglued about the apparatus she had to wear for this scene, with all its complex tubes wound around her body that contained stage blood. She was hypersensitive to the onlookers and embarrassed by the thought they could see too much while technicians wound the tubes around her body. But this public display was not as worrisome as not knowing how to play her final scene. "I was to come out of Gestapo headquarters and walk up the avenue. We rehearsed. I exited, walked with eyes glued firmly to the ground," she wrote later. She looked to Melville for affirmation; he told her the walk was fine, continue. But Simone had doubts and hesitated: "And I, who never want to explain anything, somehow felt compelled to add: 'Well, maybe . . . still, she's just betrayed her pals.'" Melville was incredulous. "Who told you she's betrayed them?" he asked. She explained that she had read the script: Mathilde's friends were going to kill her. "So what," Melville responded. He wasn't present when she was questioned by the Gestapo, Melvile explained. Just because her friends think that she talked too much doesn't mean she did. They had to kill her because she was a risk.

Simone felt this was entirely ambiguous and unhelpful direction. But in the end, it was perfect for the actress, who was a master of non-verbal communication. When Mathilde walks out of Gestapo headquarters and sees the car waiting, her expression changes rapidly, expressing an array of emotions: her eyebrows raise in surprise; her eyes widen in terror; and then her face takes on the pall of complete understanding as she realizes that she must die. In the same instant, she is shot multiple times and falls to the ground.

Army of Shadows was not well received when it was released in France in 1970. Melville made one tactical error in the film: He portrayed General Charles de Gaulle as a hero. Although the general is seen only in silhouette as he hands commendation medals to members of the Resistance, in the wake of the events of May 1968 the French had no appetite for recollecting his heroism. Gaullist values were no longer respected, and as had happened with *Casque d'Or*, the film was panned by both critics and audience alike, then forgotten. Only in 2006 was it re-discovered, restored, and released on the international market as a cinematic masterpiece.

&

There was never time to dither in Montand's world. He was either performing on stage or in front of the camera, always with an eye toward the next project. While filming *On a Clear Day You Can See Forever* with Barbra Streisand, and with Simone playing the role of vigilant Hollywood wife in the background, he received a phone call from director Costa-Gavras. Gavras and their friend Jorge Semprum had just read a new book, *L'Aveu* (The Confession), the autobiography of Artur London, which recounts his experience as a co-defendant in the trial of Rudolf Slánsky, a former leader of the Communist Party in Czechoslovakia. In 1951, he and thirteen lower-level leaders were accused of affiliation with Trotsky and Zionism, and on November 22, 1952, they were tried and convicted of conspiring against the government. All fourteen men admitted guilt and signed confessions. Eleven were executed, and three—including Artur London—were given life sentences.

At the time, the trial did not capture the attention it deserved. The world was focused on the Rosenberg trials in the United States. Simone and Montand were involved in protesting the Rosenberg case and had turned their attention to *The Crucible*. The couple was still enamored of the Communist Party and fond of quoting French author Paul Éluard, who mirrored their own sentiments: "I have too much to do with the innocent proclaiming their innocence to spend time on the guilty proclaiming their guilt." They had in fact signed Éluard's petition, expressing that sentiment. Opinions changed after the Hungarian Revolution, and for Simone and Montand, their visit to the Eastern Bloc was a turning point.

But London's book was an eye-opening account of a forced confession and years of physical and psychological torture endured during "rehabilitation" under the Communist Party. Simone and Montand devoured the book. He agreed to participate in the film adaptation, but Simone was reluctant to accept at first. The couple wanted to make it clear that their participation in a film exposing Stalinism in no way indicated that they had moved to the other side, or were in agreement with the imperialism they saw at the heart of US involvement in Vietnam. Yet at the same time, they were aghast about the events that followed the publication of London's book. After the Czech government allowed its publication and sale in 1969, the authorities suddenly turned on Artur London. His citizenship was revoked, and the Communist Party waged a propaganda campaign against him. "It was too much," Simone admitted. The film adaptation was an important counterpoint.

Portraying Lise London was another matter. Lise had not seen or heard from her husband after his arrest in 1951. Her first indication that he was alive and well came a year later during the trial, when his confession was broadcast on the radio. After hearing it, she went home and wrote a letter denouncing her husband to party leadership. Simone was horrified: "I would be incapable of lending my face, my eyes, my voice—in other words, myself—to an enterprise that's contrary to my most profound convictions." Lise London commented on Simone's reaction, "For her, it was unthinkable for a wife to act toward her husband in that way. Whatever he had done, you remained loyal to him. To persuade her, Chris Marker organized a showing of an Italian documentary about The Confession, which explained why I had written that letter. After that, she accepted,"[4] but with reservations. Lise London had renounced her husband because of her devout allegiance to the party. If the government said her husband was guilty, then he must be guilty. And Artur London was not disturbed or upset with his wife's reaction, as he, too, was convinced that he must be guilty—even though he suffered doubts. Still, Simone had difficulty with her lines. "I can't use those words, they aren't me," she complained often, wanting re-writes.

"It was painful for her to embody a character that she despised ethically, and we crossed swords several times during shooting," Costa Gavras explained. Montand, on the other hand, embraced his role to such a degree that he wanted complete authenticity. He lost twenty-five pounds in six weeks and was emaciated, as one would expect of a man imprisoned and tortured. Rather than stay in the hotel suite with Simone, he took a small room and turned it into cell, with its windows covered to block out light. More often than not, he chose to sleep on the floor and allowed himself no comfort or even the companionship of the other actors after a day of filming. Montand was so obsessed with his role and with self-imposed depravation, he had nightmares so horrific he often woke other cast members with his screams. His physical decline was profound, and Costa-Gavras became concerned, insisting that they take a break in the filming. Their friend, Jorge Semprum, who had written the screenplay and witnessed Montand's decline, believed the actor was purging himself of the past: "He paid obstinately and heavily for his past ignorance, for his blind faith, for his smart-ass remarks. . . . but he paid too, for all of us. He paid our debts and set us free."[5]

Montand's performance was so passionate and authentic that he crossed the divide that separated him from Simone as a credible actor. Critics hailed the couple's performances, but focused primarily on Montand and the impact of the film on audiences. After the film's release, the Communist Party expressed outrage, believing that it was more than simply an anti-Stalinist statement. It was in their view anti-Communist, and both Simone and Montand were severely judged for their participation in the project. Montand's brother, Julien, was so angered by the film that he wrote Costa-Gavras—not his brother—a three-page letter of criticism. Montand was hurt and frustrated, but chose not to respond.

PART VI

MONSTRA SACRÉ

CHAPTER 29

A Dark Chapter

IT'S IMPOSSIBLE TO CONTINUE A STORY ABOUT SIMONE WITHOUT looking behind the scenes at a dark chapter in her life. Spanning the mid-1960s and stretching through the next decade, it was a period when—with the aid of alcohol and other indulgences— she aged so profoundly that Catherine described the period as her mother's "slow descent into hell." In her quest to keep her private life from intermingling with her career as the actress, Simone left only surfaces accessible. As a result, it was easier to assume, as many continue to do, that her lost beauty and alcoholism were misplaced reactions to her husband's affair with Marilyn Monroe, rather than reflections of far more serious pain. "Signoret didn't just flaunt the scratches she had sustained from life's minor tussles," the French actress Catherine Deneuvue remarked. "She bore Marilyn etched on her face like a permanent scar. It was too much—at once too big and too petty."[1]

Montand, as it turned out, was well aware of the deep-seated reasons behind his wife's descent. But he, too, avoided addressing the truth and spoke as though insulted and mystified by Simone's behavior: "It wasn't seeing her get old that I couldn't stand. It was her tendency to self-destruct, the methodical nature of that self-destruction. I told her so. I asked her what had happened to our so called great love now that she was letting herself go. She smiled and said: 'Yes, I'm letting myself go, yes, I find myself ugly, so what? Might as well accelerate as step on the brakes, no?'"[2] If she had to age, she wanted to accept the inevitable and move on. She did not want to become a Greta Garbo, whom she liked to cite as an example of an old woman who spent her time trying to re-capture her past as a glamorous star. Simone had no intention of being snared by that trap. She refused the idea of a face-lift or dye to soften her salt-and-pepper hair, and she used no make-up. She would age naturally, she insisted, just like everyone else.

But, Simone did not age like everyone else. And it appeared that she saw little or no connection between a face that would become bloated and scarred by deep wrinkles, and her need to consume a bottle of alcohol a day—preferably scotch whiskey. "I'm not a big drinker," she declared in an instructive interview with journalist Pierre Démeron for the September 1979 issue of *Marie Claire*. Simone implied that people do not usually become alcoholics unless "they are wired that way." As far as she was concerned, she was just like everyone else in her trade, where "alcoholism begins with the need for something, to communicate, to give fire in the belly to begin work, to begin a task."

While she drank only a little, in her opinion, she never took drugs:

I do not even take sleeping pills. I never have. I've always had a moment of really good sleep. At the worst moments of my existence and at the most beautiful, there is always a moment when I fall asleep. Even if I have lived through some horrible moments the evening before, when I wake up and think I've had a nightmare. I can't give a better example than that of the death of my young brother about which I really, really don't like to talk about and which marked a boundary in my life. Well, the night following his death—he died in the afternoon—I fell asleep, and it's only in the morning that I began to live with this death, but I had slept! You can find it monstrous, but that's the way it is. In these cases, in complete grief, I can't manage, but I compensate by sleeping. Each one of us compensates as he wants, as he can!

She compensated with sleep and spoke of alcohol as though it served as a restorative, rather than an anesthetic. Yet her physical decline suggested that she was compensating for some untold sorrow and deep-seated anger. She agreed that she was a jealous wife, though she never gave Marilyn Monroe more power than she deserved. It was the public humiliation surrounding the affair that had taken a toll. In the meantime, Simone endured harsh criticism about her looks, criticism that continued long after her death. The critic David Thompson wrote: "Gallantry cannot conceal the thought that few women so dazzling at thirty faded so much by fifty . . . . In *Thérèse Raquin* she was moody, sensual and glowing like a greengage. But those features became lost in overweight, and her brooding face went sour with dismay. It was a great loss."[3]

It wasn't until 2004, nearly twenty-five years after Simone's death, that her grandson, Benjamin Castaldi, shed light on the darker side of her life in his book, *Now Everything Must Be Told*. In it, he reveals confidences his mother, Catherine, shared with him, secrets that shattered the image of the ideal couple Simone had worked so hard to preserve. The revelations were so startling and scandalous that the French reacted by criticizing both Benjamin and Catherine—particularly since Simone and Montand could not weigh in to confirm or denying what Benjamin wrote. Criticism of Catherine was so severe that she was forced to respond with a book of her own, *World Upside Down*, which affirmed her son's account of a tumultuous life and a mother who "swept it under the carpet," turning a blind eye for the sake of her marriage. In retrospect, the cover of Catherine's first book, *Memories and Regrets, Also*, provided a hint that there were secrets: The front cover features a photograph of Catherine as a young child with her forefinger pressed against her lips as though to signal quiet or a secret. Her choice of photos was not a coincidence.

The trouble began when she was four or five years old, while the family vacationed at the house Simone owned in Saint-Paul-de-Vence. Montand was helping with her bath, and Catherine recalled the unmistakable feeling of violation when he touched her inappropriately. She never spoke of it, and it never happened again. However, there were periods in her life, particularly during adolescence, when Montand made her uncomfortable by teasing her with aggressive and suggestive behaviors or remarks. The aggression came to a head when Catherine was a young woman during a violent scene at Place Dauphine while Simone was away. Catherine was on the first floor of Place Dauphine; Montand was in her parents' bedroom on the mezzanine level. He called to her, and she went upstairs to see what he wanted. "I was not wary," she explained. It was not unusual to be called to her parents' bedroom for one reason or another, particularly if Montand was performing and wanted her to get a shirt for him or run an errand. But this time, Catherine explained, when she entered the bedroom he threw himself on her and forced her to the bed while trying to slip his hand up her skirt. She fought him off in a struggle so violent the heel of her shoe caught in the threads of the bedspread Simone had crocheted, and it was torn. She was able to stop Montand's aggression by reasoning with him, but she was terrified by what had happened and then fearful of Montand's anger when he got up and looked in the mirror to examine the scratch she had given him under one eye. He was upset about the wound because he had to perform at the Olympia Theater that evening.[4]

Although the chronology of events is unclear, at one point Catherine complained to her mother about Montand's behavior. According to Catherine, Simone responded, "But that is not serious, my darling . . . in a way it's kind of nice . . . it is a little way of prolonging our history," as though to reassure her daughter. Catherine received a similar reaction from members of Montand's family, who reminded her that she was not his biological daughter. These were shocking, unconscionable, and unforgivable reactions. Yet, as disturbing as it was, there appeared to be a rationale behind Simone's thinking. In effect, Simone was acquiescing to Montand's expressed desire to have a relationship with her daughter. According to Catherine, he had on numerous occasions indicated that he'd asked Simone's consent to date her and that he had even written Simone a letter. In effect, Catherine, with her startling resemblance to her mother, could be Simone's replacement, continuing their "history"— perhaps even giving Montand the child he wanted but Simone could not provide. Based on Simone's reaction, Catherine could only surmise that her mother had given Montand permission, reacting to the situation as she did to his numerous affairs: "I don't want to know."

Catherine's reasoning is understandable, but the assumption that her mother was not shocked or devastated by Montand's request is supposition. Simone was anguished enough to share a confidence with at least one person, the author Bernice Rubens. During filming of the adaptation of Rubens's novel, *I Sent a Letter to My Love*, Simone confessed that she was mortified by Montand's behavior and expressed profound sadness—if not for the untenable position Catherine was in, then because she could not understand why her husband would want to hurt her that way.[5]

There were rumors that Catherine and Montand did have an affair, rumors that were never substantiated and which Catherine denied. However, the gossip took on a life of its own when Catherine became pregnant in 1969. Although she was dating Jean-Pierre Castaldi at the time, many speculated that the child was Montand's. Indeed, Simone must have had some doubts, doubts that might explain why she tried to dissuade her daughter from marrying. Marriage wasn't necessary, she told Catherine. Benjamin Castaldi was born on March 28, 1970, three days after Simone's forty-ninth birthday. His resemblance to the Castaldi family is undeniable, putting all doubt to rest.

Benjamin described the relationship between his mother and grandmother as that of a "cat and dog" at times. However, the two women still sought each other out. Catherine and Benjamin were frequent visitors at Autheuil. While he had pleasant memories of time spent with his grandmother, "Mamie," and Montand—whom he referred to as his grandfather—he revealed darker memories of the couple's relationship, the part Simone often referred to but never explained when she said they fought "Italian style," or spoke of "violence." Benjamin described one incident that occurred when he was very young, a scene at Autheuil that became for him the hallmark of his grandparents' battles. As with all the Simone and Montand's disputes, the trouble began with a quarrel over a trifle, then accelerated to fever pitch as they exchanged insults. "Suddenly, Montand rose, red with anger, grabbed Mamie by the hair and dragged her into the hallway about fifteen meters, past the dining room to the television room. I was petrified hearing Mamie's howls. Their slanging matches [verbal insults] were famous and dreaded in the small circle that visited Autheuil."[6]

Simone was not a sloppy drunk. Indeed, much of the time it was difficult to tell she had been drinking, because she remained lucid and articulate. But alcohol did loosen her tongue, and the bitter, sarcastic lashing it was capable of giving was unrelenting, even as Montand's face grew red with rage. However, Montand, sober, was no better. His violent rages were tantrums, and he dove right in with conviction, desiring a win. "They acted out *Who's Afraid of Virginia Woolf*, twenty-four hours a day," Catherine explained.[7]

Although he was criticized for the comparison, Benjamin described Montand as having a Dr. Jekyll and Mr. Hyde personality. One moment Montand was affable, humorous, and fun to be around, and the next, he was angry, jealous, petty, and explosive. Mr. Hyde was feared. Montand was a man experiencing a mid-life crisis with the ferocity of teenager, a fact duly noted by Simone, who referred to him as her "oldest one," as though he were a child. According to Montand's biographers, "He no longer fought temptation: he looked for or grabbed every opportunity with something like a glutton's delight." Later in their marriage, he rarely stayed home, making his affairs easier for Simone to ignore, though her unhappiness was evident to others. When he was home, they fought, and as they no longer shared a bedroom, after perilous arguments they often retreated to their own rooms, where they wrote notes slipped under each other's door. One such note Montand kept and re-read often, because Simone's brutal honesty cut to the quick: "You like to make me feel guilty because you are not happy. You are not happy because you're built that way." She described him as selfish, jealous, and wounding, a man who was nice to people he didn't know, but hurtful to those who loved him. And then, she offered him the most obvious solution: "You loathe yourself for being yoked to this too old, too fat 'contemporary.' Shake off the yoke. I won't love you any the less."[8]

Montand never took her up on the offer, and though she certainly had grounds for divorce, she never asked for one, though she threatened. When they had been married fifteen years, Simone told him that she was not "in love" with him anymore but she still loved him. And, Montand would joke that it was easier to wake up with *Casque d'Or* than the *Madame Rosa* she had become. Though they had long since stopped waking up next to each other, he still professed his love for Simone. But he also loved other women, and the lessons about indiscreet behavior from the Monroe affair had not sunk in. Montand the playboy was not immune to scrutiny, and when his indiscretions reached scandal stage, Simone was invariably dragged into the mire.

On May 5, 1971, *France-Dimanche* published a contrived interview with Montand about his alleged affair with German actress Karin Shubert. The phony interview was titled "My Wife Allows Me To Be Unfaithful Sometimes" and included a photo of Simone, who appeared to be biting her nails. Simone and Montand sued for libel and won. *France-Dimanche* was forced to publish a retraction and paid a fine. But once again, Simone had become a target of unwanted publicity.

The following year, Montand became involved with the actress Anne Drossart Fleurange while they filmed *Vincent, Francois, Paul and the Others*. Though intermittent, the affair lasted two years. But the ramifications of this affair would haunt Montand for years to come. After Simone's death, Fleurange insisted on a paternity test for her daughter Aurore Drossart. Montand refused. However, in 1998, seven years after his death, Drossart finally won a court injunction to have Montand's body exhumed for DNA testing, and the gravesite he shared with his wife at Père Lachaise cemetery was violated. The test proved that Montand was not the father.

Within the context of this turbulent life, Simone aged profoundly, burying herself in work from the mid-to-late 1960s with a battery of films, the tragedy of *Macbeth*, and her attempts to gain credibility as a translator. She was trying to redefine herself in the midst of personal conflict. And then, during the 1970s, in the throes of alcoholism, Simone slowed her pace significantly. Her selection of films, television series, personal projects, and social activism become far more focused, and her popularity soared once again, earning her the title, *Monstra Sacré* of French cinema. It was a title she shared with her male counterpart, the actor Jean Gabin.

CHAPTER 30

Garden of Dreams

ONE AFTERNOON DURING THE EARLY 1970S, WHILE THE COLUMNIST Liz Smith was dining with the writer Mario Puzo at the Carleton Hotel Beach Club in Cannes, he became distracted by a woman sitting at another table, a middle aged woman who was "more than plump, casually dressed, wearing no make-up." Puzo turned to Liz Smith, stunned: "That's Simone Signoret . . . I was madly in love with her after *Room at the Top*. She was my idol for years, my fantasy. But look at her now. She looks just awful, terrible."[1] Smith reacted:

> I looked at Mario. He was fat and slovenly. His short hairy legs hung out of crumpled shorts. He was wearing a red Lacoste polo shirt that emphasized his rather pendulous breasts. Not becoming. He had a stubble of beard with a cigar stuck in it and resembled an old bulldog. I said, "Mario, look who's talking. No doubt back in 1959 when *Room at the Top* was released, you looked a lot better yourself than you do today. She doesn't have to keep looking like the movie image of your dreams. You can be kinder than Rex Reed was recently; he wrote that her skin now resembles an orange rind. It's not fair."

After taking this in, Puzo laughed and then agreed—before deciding to introduce himself to Simone so he could apologize for his remarks. Since Simone hadn't heard the conversation, Smith warned him off: "Well, don't do that. Just grant women the right to be as unattractive as men sometimes are. Although, you might stop by her table and say who you are and express your admiration." Puzo did just that.

But, it wouldn't have surprised Simone if he had remarked on her lost beauty. She was used to it. The one incident she liked to share occurred while she was filming *Le Chat* with Jean Gabin in 1970. During a break, two men who had been watching the action on the sidelines approached and greeted her. They had seen *Diabolique* on television the night before, they told her, and then one of them ruefully remarked on the fact that she had aged so much.

She was tempted to make a sarcastic remark about their own ages and appearances, but she refrained.[2] Their reaction annoyed her until she realized that they had, in a sense, paid her a backhanded compliment. She wasn't the young star of *Diabolique* anymore, but she was still holding firm, when many of her contemporaries had faded away before "their expulsion from the garden: the garden of dreams. They have to go, for fear they will erase those dreams that they inspired for a few years." It was different for her, she thought, because they were stars and she did not consider herself a star—at least not as she defined the word: "Hordes of young girls never copied my hairdos or the way I talk or the way I dress. I have, therefore, never had to go through the stress of perpetuating an image that's often the equivalent of one particular song that forever freezes a precise moment of one's youth."

It was rather ironic that lost beauty, the very reason stars were expelled from the garden, was exactly the attribute that was allowing her to stay, though she confessed how startled she was when she realized that she was the first choice when directors were looking for old, tired woman.[3] In the early 70s they had to make her look older for those "worn" women she was asked to portray. Later, the task would not be as arduous. By then, she had already perfected an attitude for public consumption: she was a woman who accepted aging and used it to her advantage: "I've lived, I've aged, I've grown fat, and basically I've tried to make an asset of it,"[4] she insisted. Her daughter, Catherine, saw through this front: "Despite her grand declarations about age, I am not sure that deep down inside Mama didn't suffer very badly through it all. It was truly the sin of pride: I am Simone Signoret, and I will work with wrinkles, my years, and so on."[5] Simone would also call it pride, not courage. But, once she moved from the shock of changing from glamorous to "worn," she opened the door to the stories that might not otherwise be told through unique characters who allowed her to explore more mature and interesting themes—themes with roots in her own life. One dominant theme was that of loneliness in the life of middle-aged women who dream of knowing love one more time.

In *Le Chat* (*The Cat*), a 1970 adaptation of a Georges Simenon novel, Simone is Clemence Bouin, a former circus acrobat whose career ended after a perilous fall. She walks with a limp and drinks to dull the pain of frustration as she tries and fails to recapture the love in her marriage to Julien, a retiree who pays more attention to his cat, "Le Greffier," than to his wife. They are an old couple in a seemingly loveless relationship. They cannot recapture the burning passion of their past and have no future together. Even the house they lived in for twenty-five years is slated for demolition. They continue to receive and ignore eviction notices. Their house will be demolished to make way for new high-rise buildings.

The cat takes center stage as the source of bitter battles in their relationship. Clemence is determined to get rid of Le Greffier. First, she tries to turn her husband against his pet by purposefully tearing important newspapers he has stored in the basement and then blaming it on the cat. When that tactic doesn't work, she becomes more creative. In the film's only humorous scene, she tries to leave the cat in the seafood section of the local supermarket. After placing it on a display of fish, she hides in the aisle and watches to see what will happen, but then decides it's a bad idea and reluctantly returns home with the cat.

During one of the vicious arguments between husband and wife, while they are standing on steps to the basement, they hurl insults at each other, and Clemence mimics the cat, viciously exaggerating as its meow "Mi-yoo . . . mi-yoo . . . mi-yoo," she screams, her face distorted with hurt and anger. If she were a cat, would he love her? Why won't he pay attention to her? She asks what he wants: a new life, a mistress—what? What about her? "Oh you, you, you, you," he screams back. In the meantime, the cat brushes past Clemence, causing her to stumble and fall down the stairs.

The journalist Jean de Baroncelli revisited this tumultuous scene in his review for the May 5, 1971, issue of *Le Monde*: "There they are, the two of them, face to face, he with his blue eyes, his thin lips, his shoulders like those of a tired fighter, with a dragging gait, he grunts and roars; she with heavy eyelids, her features swollen, her sensual mouth, and the sharp gaze where we see alternating lights of hardness and tenderness . . . . Having loved each other passionately and now hating each other, or believing that they hate each other, no longer able to stand each other and yet tied together by memories, habit and the fear of old age." The description could have been a page taken from Simone's marriage.

In desperation one day, Clemence finds the cat in the basement, and after arguing with it and threatening it, she takes her husband's handgun and shoots the cat. When Julien finds out, he refuses to speak to her and communicates by writing only two words on scraps of paper he flicks in her direction: "the cat." Unbeknownst to him, Clemence keeps all the notes in a box she hides under the bed. Finally, Julien walks out and doesn't return for a few days. Clemence suspects he is seeing another woman. One morning, she sits on her bed and goes through all of her husband's notes, reading "the cat," over and over, until she becomes so distraught. Not knowing how to fix the mistake or save her marriage, she suffers a massive heart attack. When Julien arrives home and discovers her body, he collapses on the floor next to her. Grieving inconsolably, he commits suicide.

Gabin and Signoret were a formidable team, and the film was well received. Still, in spite of the recognition, Simone did not consider herself a star, a denial that became the source of an inside joke: "Between two takes of Le Chat, Gabin and I used to joke around. Gabin used to say, 'Come here sweetie, are you an idol or what?'"[6]

Simone returned in 1971 with another adaptation of another Simenon novel, La Veuve Couderc (The Widow Couderc). Set in 1934, the film features Simone as a hardworking, still attractive middle-aged woman, who works on her late husband's family farm while battling in-laws, who are trying to strip her of potential ownership rights. Her elderly father-in-law owns the farm, and to remain in his favor, she sleeps with him and then endures the ridicule of other women who regard her as a gold digger. The widow Couderc believes she is entitled to the farm. She has worked to keep it going since youth, suffering through a loveless marriage. Since her husband's death, she has been lonely and unsettled. Then she meets and hires a younger man, Jean Lavigne, played by Alain Delon. Unbeknownst to her, he is a criminal wanted by the police. She falls in love with him and sets out to prove that she is still capable of seducing a man—even as her young niece by marriage, whom she refers to as a "slut," tries to seduce Jean. In fact, her niece's interest in him only fortifies the widow's resolve. She has allowed Jean to live in her home while he helps with farm chores, and she takes advantage of the opportunity to seduce him. She does so gradually, until one evening she comes right to the point and suggests that he join her in her bedroom.

The women in town wash clothing on the river's edge. When they see that the widow, who should be grieving her husband's death, is washing men's clothing, she endures harsh stares and sniggering, which she confronts with ferocity. While neighbors criticize her for failing to grieve properly, her in-laws are aghast because she has given her dead husband's clothing to the hired man. But she doesn't care what others think of her. She is in love for the first time and has lived happily for a few weeks, the best weeks of her life.

Happiness ends when her in-laws discover Jean is a criminal, and they alert the police. He tries to flee without the widow, but then quickly returns when he discovers that the police have surrounded the house, leaving no way to escape without a confrontation. He encourages her to leave; the police will let her go. But when she realizes that without Jean she has no life to return to, she chooses to stay and defend her lover until the bitter end. Unable to dissuade her from staying, he tries to save her by running outdoors to meet his fate. He is killed in a spray of bullets that hit the house. One stray bullet hits and kills the widow.

ა

In 1970, Simone starred in two lesser-known films in addition to *Le Chat*, and she had supporting roles in *Compte à rebours* and a made-for-television drama, *Un Otage*. But after *Le Chat*, Simone's productivity slowed considerably to one film per year. In each of them, her physical decline was dramatic and startling but fit well with the worn, tired characters she portrayed.

In 1972, she appeared once again with Alain Delon, in a suspense movie, *Les Granges Brûlées* (The Burned Barns). She played Rose, a woman who was forced to give up her dream of being a teacher when her mother became ill, and who had to remain on the family dairy farm to help her father. Oddly, with the exception of one small piece of land she will one day inherit, the farm has always been leased and brings in only a little income for the family. After World War II, Rose marries Pierre, played by Paul Crauchet, a former resistance fighter whom she admires, and they take over the farm and start a family. They have two sons and a daughter. Catherine Allégret played the role of her daughter, a teacher, the only child who has fulfilled her mother's dreams.

The film opens with a murder during a cruel, snowy winter in eastern France. A woman's body is found just outside the entrance to the farm; a sum of money has been taken from the victim. Judge Larcher, played by Alain Delon, is sent to investigate. He has interviewed Rose's two sons, Louis and Paul. Both were out the evening of the murder, and as they do not have good alibis, Larcher suspects that the family is hiding something. He begins visiting the farm regularly in search of the truth. He is curious about Rose. She is the matriarch of the family, and he admires and respects her, but he is confused by her efforts to keep the farm going when it barely sustains them.

Her husband has lost interest in the farm and family. He is lethargic and prefers repairing old clocks to spending time with the family or alone with his wife. Rose's sons have no interest in the farm, resent working there, and feel that they don't earn enough money. Her eldest son, Louis, wants her to sell the portion of the property she owns so he can have money to start a new business. He feels burdened by his wife and two young children, who live at the farm, and he dreams of being set free. The youngest son, Paul, drinks too much. His wife has left the farm and lives in town. In the meantime, Rose's daughter is pregnant and has decided to leave to join her lover.

Paul and Louis behave so suspiciously that Larcher brings them into police headquarters for questioning, and the family begins to unravel under the pressure. Louis's alibi is weak because he is trying to hide the affair he's having with his brother's wife. However, Larcher can't get to the bottom of Paul's strangeness: He drinks excessively and exhibits bizarre behavior. It is Rose, not Larcher, who accidentally discovers the cause when she finds the stolen money in Paul's closet. She confronts him, and he admits to stealing the money, but insists that he did not murder the woman. As he confesses, Rose is taken aback by Paul's demeanor; he quakes in her presence and is fearful of her attempts to console him. She has been both domineering and unwavering in her demand for loyalty to the farm. She has been tight-fisted with money and denied her children living wages. They resent and fear her. This realization is a crushing blow for Rose.

Her marriage is a disappointment. Her children care less about the farm and have more fear of her than respect for her. Rose realizes that she has sacrificed her life for nothing. She decides to sell her land and give the money to her children, as they desire. Paul is so grateful that he tries to thank her with a kiss, but she is disgusted and pushes him away.

When Larcher learns that two girls on the run were responsible for the murder, he returns to the farm to share the news with Rose. At that point, she can no longer protect her son and returns the money he stole. Larcher will not prosecute them. She has suffered enough and he leaves her to pick up the pieces of her life.

❧

When Simone was a child, her parents told her that tramps left signs on the front doors of farmhouses. The signs were actually little symbols cut into the wood, barely perceptible to anyone else. But other tramps knew what to look for when they approached to find out if the owners were generous with food, or if they required work. Simone was sure that the thick wooden door facing Place Dauphine contained some of these symbols, because she was inundated with visitors—not tramps but representatives of one cause or another who needed help. They came to ask for financial support or for her signature on petitions. The need was at times overwhelming, and Simone wanted to become more focused with both her energy and financial resources. She had not, for the most part, stepped out on her own without Montand on any particular issue since signing the 121 Manifesto against the Algerian War, when her solo signature was regarded as a form of "moral divorce," a reaction to the Monroe affair. But that behavior changed in 1971 when she signed the Manifesto of the 343.

Simone de Beauvoir had crafted the text for the pro-choice declaration demanding the legalization of abortion and birth control. Even though doing so might subject them to prosecution, 343 women who admitted to having illegal abortions signed the statement, and it was published by *Le Nouvel Observateur* on April 5, 1971. Critics of the text referred to it as the "Manifesto of the Sluts." Simone Signoret signed because she considered her miscarriages a form of abortion and spoke of them for the first time when she addressed critics of the manifesto: "Let she who has never had a miscarriage shut up, I've had them and the MLF protestors deserve everybody's thanks." In her opinion, the militants of the *Laissez-les-Vivre* (Right to Life) movement were also pro-capital punishment.

But, beyond agreeing with the abortion issue and with the demand for equal pay for women, she insisted that she was not a feminist. First of all, she had been liberated long ago when, as an unwed mother, she argued with the women who distributed ration tickets for wool. However, she was not comfortable with what she perceived as feminist bigotry towards men. Men were not the enemy, she said, and for that reason, Simone shied away from association with militants in the feminist movement, even as they applauded her for her independence and willingness to portray older women without artifice. She insisted that she was a Mediterranean wife, a loyal woman who stood by and submitted to her husband. This was not the point of view of a woman trapped between two generations. Simone had no point of reference for this concept of the Mediterranean wife; her mother had not played that role and the women Simone admired most were not submissive to men. The role of Mediterranean wife was self-prescribed, based on some unfulfilled need she could never describe. Simone was not a victim of the past or of a generational divide; she was a victim of her own desires.

In 1971, a group of protestors at the Sorbonne were engaged in a hunger strike to protest deplorable prison conditions. One Sunday morning during breakfast, Montand read a brief article about the strike in the press. He and Simone were curious and decided to visit the group in the Sorbonne library. When they learned more about prison conditions, they considered the issue a civil liberties matter and were disturbed that the severity of the conditions and of the hunger strikers protesting them had not garnered more than a few lines in the press. Simone decided to use her influence with Pierre Lazareff, the editor-in-chief of *France Soir* and *France-Dimanche*, to gain more public attention for the cause. Lazareff was a friend of her father's and obliged her by sending in a photographer. While Simone had always believed that actors had a responsibility to use their celebrity status to bring attention to worthy causes, this was the first time she saw the real power of her position. From this point forward, she would use her influence to step out on her own, earning for herself a reputation as an advocate for social change and justice.

CHAPTER 31

Nostalgia

THE EXTENDED FAMILY AT AUTHEUIL HAD SHRUNK CONSIDERABLY OVER
the years, making it all the more difficult to ward off the loneliness Simone felt. The death of Jacques Becker had left a permanent void, and
other friends who had filled the house on weekends or lived there as
permanent guests had for the most part moved on with their own lives.
When Serge Reggianni remarried and wanted to build a country house
for his young family, Simone was disappointed. "But this is your home,"
she protested.

While friends still gathered and were loyal to Simone, by the 1970s
this closeness was more difficult to achieve because she was not always
easy to be around. The light, infectious laughter that had once filled
Autheuil had been replaced by the bitter sarcasm of alcohol and behavior that most people were unaccustomed to witnessing. The journalist
Catherine David noted, "This was the dreadful period when her face
was all swollen with drink, of evenings with friends when she would
start to belch like an old tramp or drunkard, not like a woman who has
just had one too many."[1] When Montand was present, the conversation
invariably turned sour, as the couple quickly rose to the challenge of any
argument that presented itself—even a trifle—and matters always accelerated, making everyone ill at ease.

Simone's inner circle, which had always been dominated by male
friends, was even more so now. As a rule, Simone always felt she had
little in common with most women. Now her distance from other wom-
en was a matter of survival in her marriage. "I detest women who come
too close to him," she admitted, as though they were wholly responsible for Montand's interest. "Our friends are very carefully selected."

However, Montand was no longer a constant in the circle that gathered around Simone. In fact, he stayed home as little as possible, focusing his attention on films, concerts, poker games, and extramarital interests. Simone's interests were not his, and he despised her drinking and her behavior. Adding to the discomfort of their friends was the knowledge that Montand made no effort to hide his affairs. Though Simone looked the other way, she knew, and she was feeling an isolation and loneliness that only alcohol could dull.

Simone did not play a part in Montand's complete break with the Communist Party and renewed interest in politics, though they still made public appearances as a couple to protest global issues. Instead, his time was spent with the author Jorge Semprum, an acquaintance of Simone's from the Occupation years. Montand resented the fact that nearly all of their friends had come to him through his wife. In reality, Montand did not attract friends. While he was charismatic on stage, he was not a magnetic personality off stage and had difficulty developing the close interpersonal bonds his wife was capable of creating and maintaining with ease.

In his biography, *You See, I Haven't Forgotten,* Montand shared the story of his first meeting with Semprum. Jorge and his wife, Colette, were sitting at a table on the terrace of the Columbe d'Or Hotel with Simone, when Montand arrived. Much to his irritation, Jorge was sitting in the chair Montand usually took at the table. Montand was so annoyed, he gave Semprum a disgusted look before Simone had a chance to introduce the two men. Then, Montand was curt to the other man. However, after talking to Semprum, Montand realized that they shared many of the same interests, and a friendship developed, which Montand described as a platonic love story.[2] Semprum was assuredly a "soul-mate," Montand thought, and their brotherly connection far surpassed anything he'd ever experienced with Julien Livi. Semprum was also a sympathetic ear, quick to take the singer's side when Montand criticized Simone, particularly when he thought she was disrespectful to her spouse by demeaning him with curt remarks. Few were willing to challenge Simone for fear that she would cut them off from her inner circle or hold a grudge, as she was quite capable of doing. But Semprum was not afraid of her, or afraid to call her out when she referred to her husband as a "playboy," or as her "oldest one."

Montand was happy to leave Simone behind to her own devices—alone more often than not—or with her friends, engaged in the constant "uninterrupted" conversation she was fond of generating about books, politics, and other intellectual pursuits. He couldn't understand why she preferred this activity to her career, which had practically come to a standstill. Simone "floated through life," he often said, and her inertia both concerned and infuriated him. Yet, in spite of appearances, Simone was rethinking her position and her work, testing her limits and new interests—though not always willingly.

With the exception of the 121 Manifesto against the Algerian war, the couple always appeared as a team when taking a stand against injustice in the world. That association would not change. However, in 1972 Simone discovered for the first time that she was not only capable of stepping out on her own with causes that appealed to her, but that the issues did not have to be global in nature. She could affect change much closer to home.

Working conditions at the Renault factory had not improved since the strike in 1968, and tensions were high in late January 1972, when three workers were fired for roughing up management during a dispute. In protest, on February 1, the men began a hunger strike, staged in a small chapel near the factory in Billancourt. The event received little more than passing comment in the press, though Jean-Paul Sartre had taken an interest. Since Simone had been influential in generating press during the hunger strike at the Sorbonne, the Renault strikers asked Sartre if he could get her involved in their cause. Sartre always seemed to send an emissary when he wanted Simone's help, and this time he sent the author and architect Jean-Pierre Le Dantec to Place Dauphine. Simone was reluctant at first, explaining that she didn't feel qualified to weigh in on the plight of workers at Renault. Le Dantec explained that the strikers were not interested in her involvement; they wanted her influence with the press to attract attention to their cause.

She agreed to accompany Le Dantec to a chapel on rue Billancourt. When they arrived, there were banners advertising the strike and messages encouraging visitors, Simone recalled. When she entered the chapel, three men installed on camp beds immediately perked up. They were thrilled that she had actually come to see them, and they expressed hope that she could rally the press. Simone promised to try, but she warned them that things might not work out as they hoped. When she left, she was determined to make a few phone calls on their behalf, but she had no intention of visiting the strikers again or getting involved. Then curiosity got the better of her.

She couldn't stop thinking about the hunger strikers, especially at meal times. So Simone returned to visit them—always with bad news, because the press was not interested in the story. As the strike progressed and fewer people visited, Simone remained the constant. She was as intrigued by their tenacity as they were by hers. She felt foolish about this new ritual she had established but couldn't explain it. It seemed ridiculous that she, a woman of means, was visiting the working class to observe something she couldn't possibly relate to. The endeavor felt insincere. She began to compare herself to wealthy ladies in novels who made ritual visits to the less fortunate.

Feeling helpless, foolish, and uncertain about her role, she used her discomfort to entertain the strikers by poking fun at herself through little skits she performed for their benefit. The entertainments made the strikers laugh and seemed to ease the tension. She brought friends along, and on one occasion even enticed her taxi driver to stop in. But as the days passed and the strikers grew weaker, it was clear to her that something serious had to be done to generate interest. Without realizing that her words were prophetic, she had joked with the strikers about the lack of interest from the press, suggesting that something as dramatic as a death would have to happen.

The strike ended nineteen days later, and Simone was there to watch them pack up their belongings. A pall hung over the chapel. The strikers were so weak they required medical attention. It seemed their protest had been for naught. But the next day, February 20, 1972, the working conditions at Renault captured the attention of everyone when Pierrot Overney, a twenty-year-old factory worker, was shot and killed by the company's abusive security force while he was distributing flyers for a rally. Simone was stunned: It was true, the press would not budge unless someone was killed. She found the concept frightening.

Simone did not as a rule attend funerals, including those of her family members. She would attend the funerals of friends only if her presence was important to the family of the deceased. However, she decided to attend Overney's funeral because her presence was a form of protest against his killing, and against the working conditions that had caused it. She was amazed by the number of people in attendance, particularly women, who like her, attended without their spouses, a phenomenon she had never witnessed. The cruel fate of a young man who had died so violently and needlessly spoke to the hearts of mothers, and they filled the streets, joining Simone on the long walk to Pere Lachaise cemetery. If Montand had been in Paris at the time, he assuredly would have joined his wife. But his mother had passed away, and he was in Marseille for her funeral.

Simone refused to acknowledge that her presence at the funeral was important or helpful to the cause, because doing so would have been, in her opinion, an egotistical notion. She still felt the outsider, a ridiculous rich lady satisfying her curiosity by observing from afar. But her solidarity with the working class was duly noted. Her involvement had brought about a new realization, one that would influence her decisions in the future. She realized that she didn't have to share someone's circumstances or live the same life they did in order to help and support their cause.

In 1973 Simone explored the plight of the working class in *Rude Journée Pour La Reine* (Rough day for the Queen) as Jeanne, a cleaning woman with a dismal life, made more unbearable by an abusive employer and by Jean's husband Albert, an ungrateful bully. But Jeanne has a secret weapon to combat the drudgery of her existence: her imagination. When things became too bleak or ordinary, Jeanne, dowdy and unadorned in a housecoat, imagines scenes in which she plays a variety of characters from soap operas, history, or the news: a queen, a butcher, a criminal, the wife of the president of the Republic, and a ruffian, among others. Eleven such fantasies in all allow her to explore new and exciting lives while working through her frustration with her own.

The "queen's rough day" begins when Jeanne's stepson, Julien, asks her to get involved in a perilous plot. He is a troubled young man who spent a year in prison. His girlfriend, Annie, gave birth to their child during his incarceration. He wants to reunite with his girlfriend and their child, but her parents won't allow him to see her. His father has disowned him and won't help, so he turns to Jeanne, who has always been fond of him. He asks her to deliver a letter to Annie that outlines a plan for her escape with the baby. Jeanne is troubled by this plan and considers it nothing short of abduction, a thought that inspires her imagination: She becomes a criminal sought after by police. In the end, she agrees to help reunite the young lovers, even as she imagines herself as a queen planning their elaborate wedding.

Like so many of Simone's films, *Rough Day for the Queen*, directed by Rene Allio, was not as well received when it was released in 1974 as it would be when it was re-discovered years later, in 2009. Critics praised the imaginative twists and turns of parallel worlds masterfully navigated by Simone, who injects both humor and authenticity into Jeanne and the various characters that people her fantasy world. When the film was first released, Simone was already engaged as Lady Vamos, another role she took on to help the new director Patrice Chéreau[3] launch his first feature length film, *La Chair de l'orchideé* (Flesh of the Orchid), a psychological thriller.

ঽ৲

Simone had toyed with writing for years, often jotting down ideas or short stories on scraps of paper, which Montand inevitably found stuffed in a drawer. He often liked what he read and encouraged his wife to continue. She was in part responsible for a skit they filmed and used during his concerts. In the skit, a man calls the telegraph office to send a cable to the woman he loves. The camera focuses on Montand throughout, and the audience can hear the telegraph operator (played by Simone), a fast-talking gossip who puts him through his paces on the content of the cable. The skit served as an intermission during concerts, allowing Montand time to change from his tuxedo to his standard brown shirt and slacks; it was humorous and always well received by audiences.

The only other writing venture Simone had taken on for public consumption dated from much earlier, just after the Liberation. Jean-Pierre Kaminker recalled that his sister had written a program for radio, an audience participation program where various characters from well-known stories were brought together in a drama. The audience had to guess how the story ended. Unfortunately, the recorded program has not yet been discovered in archives.

Beyond that, Simone's interest in creative writing remained limited to her skills with dialogue revision for her roles. This desire to write was one of her best-kept secrets, because she did not believe her dream could ever be taken to another level. "If like me, you started your acting career in the role of a pretty little tart in *Macadam*, it was better not to tell people that you had been good at essay writing," she explained. "It was even better to pretend to be illiterate."[4] Actors could not be writers too. One had to choose.

The seeds of inspiration for writing an autobiography were planted in the spring of 1975 during a drive to Saint Paul-de-Vence with Régis and Élisabeth Debray,[5] a young couple Simone had recently befriended.

My memory having been jogged by I don't know what, I told one of those anecdotes that I usually save for dessert when you bring it to places where my husband, my daughter, my old friends are not in attendance. When people have been in your life for a long time, even if they are young, you have little chance to astonish them. Regis and Élisabeth are young, and young in my life; young people are not difficult to astonish even when they have seen a lot, which is the case with them, if one just tells them old stories from the time before they were born, and especially for the first time. It was the first time, and it must have been one of my best ones, I don't remember which, but in any case, after I was done, they said, 'You should write all that down!'[6]

With the support of Simone's friend Chris Marker, they pushed the point, contacting Jean and Simone Lacouture, who were looking to publish a series of testimonials or biographical sketches for Editions du Seuil.

Simone was not a willing subject. She had been asked on numerous occasions in the past to participate in writing an autobiography and had always refused. She was not a fan of biographers, sociologists, "slices of life" or the idea that someone might enjoy financial gain by telling her story. But Jean and Simone Lacouture persisted, suggesting that she at least test the waters by allowing publication of a taped interview with the author Maurice Pons. She recalled: "Of course, finally I said yes. Well, I said 'Yes, maybe,' without a contractual obligation." She would participate, answer his questions, and then if looked good, she'd think about the next steps.

The interview took place at Autheuil over the course of six days. Maurice Pons brought along Dominique Roussillon, the daughter of Simone Lacourture, as an assistant to man the tape recorder so they would not be distracted by mechanical issues. Simone nonetheless found the recorder more intimidating then a camera. Accustomed to seeing herself on screen, she found listening to her disembodied voice disconcerting.

They began with an "awkward, over respectful attitude" towards each other, before loosening up over the course of those six days. Simone, who had stopped drinking for a while at that point, rather enjoyed the opportunity to revisit the past. When they finished, Pons promised to send the transcript for her review, and the project ended on a positive note. However, her mood changed considerably while waiting for the "tapuscrit," as she called it. She discovered an advertisement announcing her commitment to a biography published in collaboration with Maurice Pons. When questioned, Jean and Simone Lacouture denied responsibility, but the publisher, Editions de Seuil, had sent along a contract and an advance of ten thousand francs. Simone was insulted but pragmatic. She returned the unsigned contract and the check, explaining that this was all very premature. She would make no decisions until she read the transcript. But she was now suspicious of the entire project, and her mood did not change when she finally received the transcript in the fall of 1974.

She was at Autheuil then, and from the moment she settled down to read the six-hundred-page transcript, she knew the project was doomed. She didn't like it. If one listened to the tape—or better yet, saw the interview on film—her conversation flowed. However, on paper, without the benefit of seeing her hand gestures, thoughtful expressions, or hesitations, it was "unreadable." Sometimes using street language, she had spoken so informally, without careful presentation, that she complained it sounded more like a life story of *Dedee D'Anvers* than the actress who portrayed her. The manuscript was shoved in a closet out of sight for the next year.[7]

❧

In 1975, Simone and Montand made their last film appearance together in *Police Python 357*, a suspense drama directed by Alain Corneau. This was Corneau's second film, and he worked with the Montands extensively before filming began, explaining what he wanted for the characters and the plot while gaining their perspectives on their roles. It was during their developmental work together that Corneau discovered Simone's talent for writing authentic dialogue. And once filming began, it was also evident to all involved that Simone and Montand were struggling with their relationship. This conflict would play out in an emotional scene at the end of the film.

Simone played the role of Thérèse, an invalid confined to a wheelchair. While weak of body, she is still a strong-willed woman who controls her husband, Ganay, a high-ranking police officer, played by Francois Périer. No longer sexually active, Thérèse allows her husband to have an extra-marital affair with an ex-prostitute. When Ganay finds out that his mistress is also having an affair with one of his officers, Marc Ferrot, played by Montand, he kills her in a fit of rage. But it is Ferrot who becomes the most likely suspect in this murder, thanks to the efforts of Thérèse, who tried to protect her husband at all costs. In the end, Ferrot kills Ganay in a shootout and clears his own name. Devastated by the death, Thérèse believes that she no longer has a reason to live and wants to commit suicide.

During the suicide scene, Thérèse, sitting in a Mercedes with a gun in her hand, is supposed to ask Ferrot (Montand) to help her pull the trigger. But at that moment, Simone froze and words completely failed her. It was as though she were facing the real possibility of asking Montand to help her end it all. Finally, she got the courage to go on and quickly adlibbed to get through the scene.[8]

CHAPTER 32

"The Next Day, She Smiled"

ALTHOUGH THE SIX-HUNDRED-PAGE TRANSCRIPT OF SIMONE'S INTERVIEW was tucked away out of sight, it nagged her, demanding attention until 1975, when she finally decided to do something about it. One afternoon, she began writing out some of her childhood memories, just to see how they played out on the page. Once she got started, she couldn't stop.

Simone purchased an inexpensive portable typewriter, which she carried with her everywhere she went, and began writing in earnest without consulting the Pons transcript, which she considered "his" book, not hers. She began with little stories at first, without connecting them as chapters. She was frustrated at times, because she discovered that delving into her memory and writing were not as easy as she thought—particularly when she was interrupted by her work. While filming, the best she could hope to accomplish was a flip through the pages of a magazine, something that didn't involve any effort, especially if she only looked at the pictures. But when she had the energy, she wrote in earnest. Simone likened the experience of exploring her past to that of deep-sea diving. "At first I felt my way timidly, as does any beginner who is learning alone. I did my underwater diving slowly, to bring to the surface the corals and flotsam that lie at the bottom of one's memory." This analogy was an important one, and she would use it again much later in writing her novel. For now, writing stories about her own life was beginning to take precedence over everything else. She discovered that the one thing she feared most and never wanted was the only thing she needed while writing: solitude.

At Autheuil, she set up the typewriter in the family room, where she tried to write. She couldn't concentrate there, and both her presence and

her need for solitude became problematic when Montand was entertaining guests or when her grandson, Benjamin, was visiting. Whenever
Simone returned to the page she had left in the typewriter, hoping to
pick up where she left off, she discovered that Benjamin, then a toddler,
had taken interest in the keys and plinked letters across her work, forcing her to re-type the entire page. Montand finally addressed the problem by creating a writing space for his wife, a pleasant room on the attic
level of Autheuil, complete with long skylights that brought in natural
light. She outfitted the room with a full-sized bed for those moments
when exhaustion or frustration created the need for rest, and set up a
work table rather than a desk, which she turned to face a blank wall,
keeping the skylights at her back so she would not be tempted to stare
out the windows. When words failed her or she wanted to work out a
problem, she stared dreamily at the wall in a haze of cigarette smoke.
The cigarette dangling between her fingers was poised for that one puff
required after the spark of inspiration pushed her forward.

The only time she pulled the Pons transcript out of its closet was to
address specific questions he had asked, which would eventually make
their way into her story—though in a different format, with more precise answers than she had originally given. Beyond that, she avoided the
transcript completely.

She visited old neighborhoods and haunts to refresh her memory,
and consulted the French historian and author, Dominique Desanti, to
check dates, facts, and names of people she had long since forgotten.
While considering the various people in her life, Simone was vigilant.
She wrote about family members and friends with great care, hinting at
the anger she felt towards her father but never taking it to another level.
And it was during the writing of her early life that Simone realized she
really loved her parents, and that she missed them. Her father had passed
away, but her mother was still living in Paris. For reasons she never explained, Simone did not maintain a good relationship with Georgette,
who suffered memory loss in her later years.

The "book," Simone decided, was not a vehicle to "settle old scores."
Beyond the Nazis, there were no "bad guys" in her story. She was careful
with her descriptions of others, honest in her appraisals but never cruel.
When she finally finished, Simone was taken aback by the sheer volume
of pages she had typed and spread out over the bed in her office.[1] The
text, all three hundred ninety-two pages, would become *Nostalgia Isn't
What It Used To Be*, a title inspired by graffiti seen sprawled across a wall in

New York City. However, she was quite certain that her interpretation of this title was not the same as that of the writer of that Yogi Berra-esque statement. "I have a good memory. What I don't have is nostalgia," she claimed.

Since Simone had begun with Maurice Pons, the publisher insisted that he write the introduction to the French version, originally published in 1976 by Éditions du Seuil. Later, for international publication, Simone dropped Pons and wrote her own introduction. *Nostalgia* was an instantaneous success, with over five hundred thousand copies sold, far surpassing anyone's expectations—particularly Simone's. The book earned more money than she had ever received for an acting role, Simone claimed, and its publication on the international market two years later in 1978 would cement her writing success.

The book is entertaining and written with a flair that could only be Simone's. As was her style in everything she did, she broke all the rules by refusing to stick to any form of chronology. It was the story that mattered, and as one story always lead to another, the narrative is impossible to follow at times because she jumps around, often moving back and forth in time. And it is not surprising that the book isn't really about Simone Signoret. Instead, it is about Montand and the experiences they had shared because of her devotion to him and his commitments and career. She makes it clear that her own career commitments were often interruptions. Indeed, Simone was in such a hurry to get to her first meeting with Montand that she covers childhood, teen years, the four long years of the Occupation, the death of her first child, the birth of Catherine, and her brief marriage to Yves Allégret in four chapters.

By the end of chapter four, she has already met Montand, and by chapter five, she is packing her "goods and chattels" to join him. She pays homage to him for the rest of the book, even through the turbulent period with Marilyn Monroe, giving only hints of her personal feelings, but never details. *Nostalgia* is a perfect example of her earlier proclamation, "It goes without saying that the actress belongs to the people. But not the woman." The public life of a passionate love affair between two celebrities was the public story; the private life and turmoil of the woman would not be shared in great depth.

Montand was taken aback by Simone's book. Without his input, she had assumed the role of family historian and keeper of his legend.[2] By his own admission, he was also conflicted about his wife's unprecedented success. While he was proud of her accomplishment, he felt "dispossessed" and a bit jealous. There were few things Simone could do that he couldn't do, in his opinion, but this was one of them. He could not write; someone else would always have to tell his story.

In 1977, Simone was still riding the wave of success, not only because of *Nostalgia*, but also for her role in a popular six-part television series, *Madame Le Juge*. It was an unusual role for the actress, whose skepticism about the French judicial system often bordered on contempt.

But the role that would effectively cement Simone's popularity was one she had to give careful consideration to because her husband and friends were all against it. For *Madame Rosa*, an adaptation of the best-selling novel *The Life Before Us*, by Émile Ajar, Simone would have to transform into an ancient retired prostitute, a survivor of Auschwitz who earns a meager income by caring for the children of other prostitutes. Technicians would make her look grotesque for this role with padding that increased her girth, hair that frizzled, and a face aged beyond her years. For Montand and others close to her, this was a role reminiscent of Bouboulina in *Zorba the Greek*, and they were concerned that she was setting herself up for another failure.

In truth, Simone was also worried at first, but for entirely different reasons. She worried about the credibility of Ajar's book because it was too close, in her opinion, to Peter Feibleman's *Fever*, which she had translated years earlier. But the director, Moshe Mizrahi, finally talked her into it, and once engaged in the role, she decided that this was a good decision after all. Like the role of Alice Aisgill, Madame Rosa was a gift. "A role like that comes every twenty years. It is a cake. She is everything—liar, sincere, gourmand, poor, stupid, intelligent, warm, nasty. And she dies on top of that. If I had said 'no' and another woman had played it, I would have been sick."

Simone had to limp for the role of this former prostitute who had once been beautiful and useful—and had even been in love—but now struggled with her weight, a heart condition, and hardening of the arteries which pushed her unexpectedly into catatonic states, or caused erratic and irrational behavior. They permed her hair into a kinky bob of curls, covered her legs with padding carefully wrapped in Ace bandages, and stuffed cotton in her cheeks to fill them out. She wore outrageous housedresses with large floral patterns that accentuated her weight, particularly since the dresses didn't fit properly. She chose the dresses for this role, and she bore the burden of sheer ugliness without complaint, as though it was doing penance for her failure with *Zorba*. And, as the journalist Catherine David suggested, there was little doubt that Simone was also consciously putting finishing touches on an anti-*Casque d'Or* image.

What fascinated Simone most was the blue numbers she had to wear on her arm to represent the tattooed identification numbers Jews were forced to wear in concentration camps during the war. With great reverence, she watched as Maude Begon, her make-up artist from *Army of Shadows* and a survivor of the camps, carefully drew on her arm with one of her blue pencils a special number: 17 329. Maud was "the only one of us to know that Madame Rosa, deported in 1942, was perforce one of that little band of people whose only identification mark from then on was a number in which the two first figures could only be sixteen or seventeen thousand." Madame Rosa was one of the first to be rounded up in Paris. Simone treated her number carefully, not wanting it to fade while washing.

On May 10, 1977, the second day of filming, Simone was made up and in costume, with twenty minutes to spare before her first scene. She decided to pass the time listening to the radio and had tuned in to a program in progress, held at a book fair, where the journalist and radio commentator Anne Gaillard was interviewing two guests, Marie Cardinal and Jean-Edern Hallier, both writers and critics. Since *Nostalgia* was soon to be released in the United States, Italy and Britain, the book became a topic of conversation. Gaillard implied that since Maurice Pons had written the introduction, and then Simone used some of his interview questions at the end of the book, she probably didn't write the autobiography. Her guests agreed. It was impossible for an actress to rise to that level of literary accomplishment. Simone must have used Maurice Pons as her ghostwriter and then "signed her name to a work written by another."

Alex, a make-up artist present at the time reacted: "[S]hit, no!" And then Maude: "It's not possible; it's not possible what they're saying." She had witnessed Simone working away at the little typewriter she brought everywhere. Simone was stunned and hurt by the critics' dismissal, which affected her ability to perform that day. We would know little about this event or what happened next if Simone had not written a sequel to her autobiography, *The Next Day, She Smiled*, another bestseller that would never be translated into English. Critics insisted that she shouldn't have written this second book: "She protests too much," some said. Others noted that Simone must have been drinking when she wrote it, because her sarcasm has a ferocious, lingering bite, as if she was settling a score. But the sarcasm is in fact quite humorous, and the account Simone gives of her experience when she sued Gaillard for libel and of the other important projects she had been involved in during this period—while seemingly "floating" through life under the influence of alcohol—is an invaluable source of information and insight, even if the story can only be told as she told it, without chronology.

After the program aired, Maurice Pons wrote a curt letter to Anne Gaillard, chastising her for the libelous remarks she made on her program. He confirmed that Simone was the only author of *Nostalgia*; beyond the introduction, his role ended when she began writing. He demanded that his letter be read on air, or that Gaillard publicly retract her statement. Three days later, when Gaillard did not respond, it was "Rosa," Simone explained—giving credit to her character, because she had been completely inhabited by this "tenant"—who called her attorney. But it was Simone who appeared in court and found herself in an untenable and unexpected position. First, she was stunned that the courtroom was filled to capacity with curiosity seekers. And then, the young defense lawyer turned the tables on her, putting her on trial in front of all those people: "No, Madam, you do not know the joys, the anguish, the fevers and the sorrow. . . . in front of the blank page, you do not know the solitude of the Writer in front of his table." Simone summed up her reaction this way: "The very young man was handsome, nice, respectful. He still is, I suppose. I'm sure of it. But if I had listened to my impulses at that moment, I would have risen from my bench, (very polished and nevertheless aged), and I would have shouted, 'Shut up, you little idiot, you don't know what you're talking about.' I would have certainly yelled very loudly. Tears loading my vocal cords. . . ." But Simone did not act on her emotions.

When the lawyer talked about the writer's need for solitude, Simone's immediate fears were dispelled, as she recalled her struggle to capture moments of solitude while writing, painting a picture of a woman sitting at makeshift tables, writing a few sentences here and there between takes on a movie set. From that point on, she told the story of her need for solitude and of those bleak moments when she did not know how to proceed, but then found the germ of inspiration which carried her forward and filled the blank pages. She understood the writer's relationship with the blank page because she was the author of *Nostalgia*.

Simone won the lawsuit, and the radio station was forced to pay damages. But, Simone was not finished. Perhaps she felt that Maurice Pons wasn't convincing enough in court, or that he could have taken a stronger stand. Regardless, she doubted his sincerity, and when they left the courtroom, she turned on him as they descended the stairs, shook her finger at him, and accused him of agreeing with her critics. There was nothing he could do or say to change her mind, and the friendship that had developed during his interview sessions with her abruptly ended. He was no longer welcome in her inner circle.

Simone began writing *The Next Day, She Smiled* immediately after the trial. The book's title was taken from a song she heard on the radio that fit her mood. She started with an account of her involvement in *Madame Rosa* and moved naturally into the accusation on the radio and then the trial. But when she finished, she found herself at a crossroads. Simone had no idea how to transition to another topic. In desperation, she came up with a creative solution, an "intermission," and used it to describe her experience recording Jean Cocteau's *La Voix Humaine* (The Human Voice), a one-act play about a woman who speaks to her lover on the telephone for the last time. He has left her and will marry another woman the following day. Simone's intermission became "Recipe: How to Record Jean Cocteau's La Voix Humaine, cheaply and without having at your fingertips slices of life stained with the blood of yesterday's tears."

As only the actress's voice is heard, Simone's "recipe," more a long list than a true recipe, provides insight on her creative processes for this role—and in such depth that it becomes a story of its own. In order to keep costs low, she recommended recording at home. She taped the piece in her bedroom at Place Dauphine, which she had stocked with an adequate supply of Kleenex for the tearful, anguished phone conversation she would have while lying across the bed with the lover who has left her for another woman. The phone conversation is interrupted, and then resumes. The audience only hears the actress: "I was about to tell you that if you lied to me for kindness's sake, and that if I realized it, I would only have even more tender feelings for you. Of course! But you are crazy. My love. My dear love . . . ." She advised actresses not to listen to other recordings of the famous conversation before taking on this role, and cautioned that they pay close attention to the clever dots Cocteau had inserted in the script after the woman's lines to represent the phantom replies of the unheard lover. This technique allowed the actress to "imagine the replies that will cause her the most pain . . . a little memory doesn't hurt."

Simone chose a Saturday evening for the recording session, because after a long workweek, her nerves were taunt enough from weariness to allow emotions to easily bubble to the surface. Then, she followed her own advice that the actress should prepare herself at least two hours in advance of the recording session, so there was ample time to "Condition yourself to Solitude." She unplugged the phone, put a note on the door to let friends know that she should not be disturbed, and began walking around the apartment, "touching various objects with no apparent value, except for you and your memory. Take out from the closet two plaid bathrobes bought in London long ago and which you no longer know which belongs to whom, and put on the one that has the odors of his cologne and his cigarettes stored in its fibers." Dressed in Montand's bathrobe, she made a simple meal of two hard-boiled eggs, which she ate in silence while standing in the kitchen leaning against the stove. Fortified, she entered the bedroom and emerged an hour later, her face stained with tears. "I say THE bedroom, because if all has gone well, YOUR bedroom has become HER bedroom, THEIR bedroom! And as for what went on in THE bedroom, during this hour, you will forever keep to yourself."

While waiting for the crew to rewind the tape, Simone shared a bit of the absurd behavior she used to leave her character behind and return to the present: "Laugh out loud, which will really shock the producer surprised by your tearful face and now by your laughter. Laugh and laugh, don't explain—he will think about the artists and their caprices—he has certainly known his share." Once in the present, the actress is serious again, listening to the recording with the same attention a hostess gives to the food she will serve when guests arrive. If the food isn't appetizing, she must discard it without regret. Apparently, the performance met with the approval of both Simone and the producer.

At that point in her "recipe," the husband returns home. Montand was returning from one of his performances. "He's coming home to his house. It was just after 6pm when he left the conjugal home to go to the theater, where his friends will give him real replies and the crowd, the audience will laugh a lot, cry a little and applaud enormously." He had spent "healthy hours, while you, because of pride, challenge or vanity, have given yourself the luxury to cook up, in an organized solitude, the only dish you would have never chosen from a menu for own life. End of Intermission."

Simone, now ready to continue with her story, devoted the last section of *The Next Day, She Smiled*, to the trial of Pierre Goldman, another case of injustice that she took on with the same persistence she had demonstrated with the Renault workers and their hunger strike. Her involvement in this trial occurred while she writing *Nostalgia*. As with everything else, the story jumps back and forth in time.

PART VII

AUTUMN LEAVES

CHAPTER 33

"My Guilty Conscience"

IN 1969, WHEN TWO PHARMACISTS WERE MURDERED DURING A ROBBERY in Paris, a young man, Pierre Goldman, was considered the perfect suspect. His sordid background included a year spent in Venezuela, where he trained as a revolutionary with Régis Debray, who had recently become an acquaintance of Simone. After leaving South America, Goldman was a suspect in the high profile robbery of the Royal Bank of Canada in 1969, but he was never caught. In France, he was implicated in several robberies, to which he would later confess. So, in the minds of the police, his background made him the prime suspect, though they didn't have a shred of evidence linking him to the murders. Goldman was arrested and pleaded not guilty. When his case was brought to trial, he was so sure that his innocence would speak for itself that he refused to have character witnesses testify on his behalf. But his innocence was not evident to the prosecution, which was determined to close the case at any cost.

Simone learned about the trial and the potential for a miscarriage of justice from friends and began attending the proceedings. She was so appalled by the lack of evidence against Goldman, she continued to attend the trial until the guilty verdict was announced on December 14, 1974. From that moment on, Simone explained, her association with the Goldman case became "impassioned, not for the condemned man, but against the jury of my peers, who in my name, and the name of all the French, without asking a single question, and therefore without questioning themselves, swallowed falsehoods, unbelievable tales, flagrant lies rattled on by the gang of witnesses that were paraded in front of them."[1]

Her concerns were confirmed when Goldman, who was given a life sentence, wrote and published *Obscure Memories of a Polish Jew born in France*, which recounted the details of the trial and the false allegations made against him. In it, he explained that what helped him through his ordeal as he sat in the courtroom listening to charges, was the constant presence of Simone Signoret, whose deliberate eye contact with him for the entire trial, both moved and comforted him. He recalled memories of seeing *Casque d'Or* and *The Day and the Hour* with his mother. Simone's presence at his trial made it seem as though his mother were there, lending support through the actress's unspoken concern. After his book's publication, Simone, Jean-Paul Sartre, Régis Debray, and the writer Françoise Sagan were among those credited with criticizing the trial so fervently that the evidence was re-examined and Goldman was re-tried and acquitted in 1976. Simone attended that trial, too, seeing it through to its conclusion while trying to finish up her autobiography during evening hours in her hotel room.

❧

Madame Rosa earned the Oscar as Best Foreign Film for 1977, and the César for Best Actress went to Simone in 1978. With the recognition and continued success of her autobiography and its anticipated publication in America, Simone was fascinated by this unexpected peak in her career. "When I was young and beautiful I never appeared on the cover of a magazine. And now at 57 I am on the cover. Suddenly there is this infatuation with a not-so-young woman. It is ironic."[2] But it pleased her that she was still appearing on screen in major roles at a time when her contemporaries struggled.

She had no shortage of film opportunities, and in 1978 made two movies back to back, *Judith Therpauve* and *The Adolescent*, before taking on another film with director Moshe Mizrahi in 1979. *Chère Inconnue*, based on the novel, *I Sent a Letter to My Love*, by Bernice Rubens, is a story about Louise Martin, a spinster who has given up her life to care for her middle-aged brother, Giles, an invalid wheelchair bound since childhood. They both are lonely and overwhelmed with boredom and irritation with each other, when Louise discovers Giles's ad in the lonely-hearts column in their local newspaper. As he waits for responses, which never arrive, Louise feels sorry for her brother and decides to perk up his spirits by creating a fictitious woman who will correspond with him. When he receives his first letter, Giles is happy and continues to write letters to the post office box Louise has set up. She puts her heart and soul into her letters, communicating the loneliness and desires she feels. This game begins to have an effect on both of them. Giles becomes cheerful and shamelessly flirts with their neighbor, who stops by regularly to deliver bread from her family's bakery. Louise suddenly feels more attractive. She buys new slimming black slacks and visits the hairdresser for a new coif.

But her plan to keep the fires of this fictitious romance burning goes astray when Giles decides that letters no longer suffice; he wants to meet the woman. Louise gives her character excuses: She can't come because she can't leave her sick mother, who is close to death. Giles loses patience and tells her that there is no sense continuing the correspondence if they can't meet. The thought that this game might end upsets Louise, who decides to hire an actress to play her brother's correspondent. She then arranges a meeting between them. Much to her surprise and to the actress's irritation, Giles's illness hasn't affected his sexual prowess. He gets too frisky during this staged meeting with the actress, who storms out. Louise's plan has failed. The letters stop, and life returns to its former drudgery for her—but not for Giles. He now realizes that he is capable of enjoying a sexual relationship and asks his neighbor to marry him. In the last scene, Louise sits in a church pew watching the wedding ceremony. Although no words are spoken, it is clear from the mixed expression of sadness and feigned joy on Louise's face that she has come to realize her brother was always capable of leading a normal life. She gave up her own life for his sake and must now return home, alone, to an empty house.

The film was well received in France when it was released in 1980 and then took on a life of its own during the next five years on the international market. It was released twice in the United States, in 1980 at the Chicago Film Festival, and then again, in 1981, in New York City. It was also released in Finland, Austria, Japan, and both East and West Germany.

⳺

Simone's international appeal as a social activist continued to blossom in 1978, when both she and Montand took public stands against the "Dirty War" in Argentina, calling for a boycott of the World Cup games, which were to be hosted in that country. Simone's expressed solidarity with Mothers of the Plaza de Mayo, an association of Argentine mothers whose children had "disappeared" through abduction during the military coup, elevated her popularity in that country. But in 1980, Simone took a year off to work on a project much closer to home, a translation of *Convictions: Memories of a Life Shared with a Good Communist*, a recently published best seller written in English by her cousin, Sophie "Jo" Langer, the woman she had ignored in Prague and in London during her period of "monstrous egocentricity." Langer's story was "at the origin of one of the worst moments of my guilty conscience," Simone confessed, as the past came back to haunt her.

It wasn't until 1969, when she read Artur London's book and starred with Montand in the film adaptation, that Simone was awakened to the reality of Stalin's purges in the Eastern Bloc. Anxious for more information, Simone read other books on the subject written by survivors or witnesses. She was reading the autobiography of Josefa Slanska, when she was surprised by an account of the trial and incarceration of her cousin's husband, Oskar Langer. He was a well-respected economist, one of fourteen leaders of the Czech Communist Party, including party leader Rudolf Slánsky who were accused of being Trotskyists, Titoists, and Zionists. Their trial, the famous Slánsky trial, was staged, the testimony falsified. Years after Stalin's death, it became clear that the torture, forced confessions, and convictions of the defendants were part of Stalin's efforts to purge the communist party of Jews.

Reading the story, Simone recalled the times she had been rude and disinterested when Sophie tried to make contact with her. "I was deeply ashamed," she admitted. She remembered a letter she had received from her cousin after she returned from filming *The Seagull*. "I felt ill at ease as I read the letter." The words had stung. "I had decided never to get in touch with you again since it was so obvious that you did not like us," Sophie had written. "I hope that today you can understand . . . . I crossed the border forty-eight hours ago between Russian tanks and guns. It was a nightmare. We got out with two suitcases, thanks to the little car bought with the price of my husband's blood."[3] Simone was upset but not inclined, at that point, to respond, and had tucked the letter away, unsure what to do about it. After reading the account of Oskar's case in the Slanska book, she scrambled to find her cousin's letter and sent a response off, hoping it would reach Sophie after so many months of delay. Simone wrote asking for "forgiveness for my egotism and my sins of ignorance." Sophie forgave. However, the ramifications of Simone's failure to meet her cousin were clear. Oskar's life might have been spared if only she and Simone had met in Prague; Simone might have put in a good word for him. It was too late now. Although he had been "rehabilitated," his physical condition had been so compromised by his years in the labor camp that he died shortly after his release in 1966, in Bratislava, Slovakia.

Sophie (known as Jo to family and friends) wrote about her efforts to rescue Oskar in *Convictions: My Life with a Good Communist*, an emotional account of her life. After her husband's arrest, the Communist Party disowned her; she lost her job and was evicted from their home. Without means of support and fearful, she took refuge in the country, where she tried to rebuild her life with her daughters, while also seeking ways to save her husband from the torture of the labor camps. Simone was part of her plan to rescue Oskar. "In the beginning of 1957 I heard that a second cousin of mine was coming to Czechoslovakia," Langer wrote. "I heard the news because she is famous, not because she is my second cousin. I had heard about her when I was much younger because she was the favorite granddaughter of one of my grandmother's sisters. The little cousin was called Kiki. She grew up to become Simone Signoret." She then described the details of her two contacts with her cousin, the first in 1957 when Simone and Montand were in Prague on his tour of the Eastern Bloc, and then later, in 1966 when Simone was in London for *Macbeth*. "I didn't know anything about her politics," Jo explained of that first contact, "but I was sure that if I spent a few minutes with her, and told the story about Oskar, that she would believe me and try to help me. I didn't want to ask her to do much, just to ask a little question of someone at an official dinner, and because the officials would panic, Oskar would probably be discretely released."

When Simone politely declined to meet with her second cousin, Jo went to the Akron hotel in the hopes of catching her in the lobby. But Jo became distracted by two men who were watching her closely and worried that they were agents of the government. Before she had a chance to react, "there was Simone, next to her very tall, handsome husband, surrounded by an entourage. She passed in front of me in a split second, elegant, royal, hurried, head high . . . . I glimpsed that she was annoyed, nervous and bored." Simone never glanced in her direction.

Then, in 1967, after Oskar had died, Jo made arrangements to visit Simone at the Savoy Hotel in London, where she was staying while performing *Macbeth*. When she called, Simone was receptive and invited her to stop by for tea with her daughter, Tania, at 4 p.m. Jo's only objective in meeting Simone at this point was to try to understand why the French left-wing intellectuals had not reacted to Stalin's purge. Was it because they didn't know what was happening at the time, or was it because they chose to ignore the events, she wondered. When she and Tania arrived at Simone's hotel room, they had an enjoyable few minutes of chatter over tea about family and children. And then, Jo began to tell Simone about Oskar. "I couldn't know, but I quickly understood that I had badly chosen my moment. Simone describes this scene in her book, *La Nostalgie*. She was worn out with fatigue and nervous tension. Perhaps for the first time in her life as an actress she didn't feel that she was up to doing this performance."

Simone had already explained that she could not think about anything except her role. So when Jo started her story, she cut her off with an insensitive question, referring to the years when Jo and Oskar had fled to the United States during the Nazi occupation: "Do you believe that in New York, if you had stayed there, your husband, being communist, wouldn't have likely been confronted with the same sort of fate?" Stunned, Jo didn't answer, and when Simone asked her to continue telling the story, "I told her that it seemed to me to be totally useless. I asked her to excuse me, I signaled to Tania to get up, and we left. All that happened with very few words, but enough however for her to feel how I judged her to be a valueless interlocutor."

Now, Simone believed that this debt to her second cousin had to be repaid and decided that the best way to do so was to translate *Convictions* into French. In 1980, Simone took a year off to finish her work, cringing when she had to translate the sections about herself. But she was determined to remain faithful to the text. When the French translation was ready for publication, she refused to write an introduction or preface to the book, believing that writing an introduction for a work she had translated and was so personally involved in was too "ambiguous." Instead, she used an interview with Jean-Claude Guillebaud, a journalist who questioned her about her motivation for the translation and her thoughts on the book itself. Simone admitted sins of ignorance: "I want this book to be known, because it's my way to repay by my work the debt I owe her. But I'm not a masochist. I translated this book because I found it fascinating and surprising from beginning to end and sometimes even funny. . . . It's anything but a political book."[4] Re-titled *Une Saison à Bratislava*, the book was published in France in 1981 and was a bestseller. Simone and Jo Langer maintained their relationship, and Simone was anxious to learn as much as possible about her paternal grandmother's family, nearly all of whom had been murdered during the Nazi occupation. It was the beginning of Simone's journey to discover and acknowledge her Jewish roots.

By 1980, Simone was exhibiting early signs of macular degeneration, which caused blurring in the center of her vision field. She was drinking heavily during this period and had aged beyond her years. But her bloated face and bleary eyes were well hidden behind a pair of white-framed sunglasses that were so absurdly large, they dominated her face. However, even the glasses could not hide Simone's strained facial expression. To compensate for her weight, Simone had long before adopted a sort of uniform: blue slacks or a skirt with a matching tunic-style vest over a white blouse, sometimes one that was flecked with tiny flowers. She wore little jewelry. Her only adornments were her plain gold wedding band, tiny earrings, and the diamond necklace she had received as a memento when she won the Oscar. The necklace was rarely taken off.

She made two films back to back in 1981: *Guy de Maupassant* and *Etoile du Nord* (*The Northern Star*). But during the filming of *Etoile*, Simone suffered a severe gallbladder attack and was rushed to the hospital. Initially, the doctors thought that she had cancer. Instead, they decided that her diseased gallbladder merely needed to be removed. But in reality, this attack was a symptom of undetected cancer. Her doctors admonished her, insisting her condition was alcohol-related, and that she must stop drinking immediately before it was too late. Simone heeded the warning and took the next six months off to rehabilitate; it was apparently the second time that she entered rehabilitation, but little is known about her prior treatment.

When she returned to the set, she was refreshed, energized, and ready to rejoin *Etoile*. However, it would be her last feature film. Her focus from this point forward was on made-for-television mini-series, productions that could be filmed closer to home, without the need for a lengthy stay on location. She began losing weight at this point, slowly. And it appeared that she was regaining her health, though in reality the weight loss was a sign of trouble ahead.

Friends noticed that Simone, now free of alcohol, had returned to her old self. Even her relationship with Montand improved considerably. "It wasn't easy for either of us to go from Casque d'Or to Madame Rosa," he explained to his biographers. "To be Casque d'Or's lover was simple, but it took a lot of love to love Madame Rosa." He approved of the change Simone had made after surgery. "She pulled herself together and began to take care of her husband again. I had my old Simone back, in blue with a white collar, very beautiful, less cutting."

With the exception of a benefit concert for Chileans in 1974, Montand had taken a thirteen-year break from singing. But in 1981, he decided to return to the stage, and after a successful re-entry at the Olympia in Paris, he scheduled a tour. Simone returned to her role as "groupie" and accompanied him to Poland.

CHAPTER 34

Adieu, Volodia

MONTAND'S DECISION TO BOOK THE METROPOLITAN OPERA HOUSE for four performances of "An Evening with Yves Montand" in September 1982 was a tremendous risk, one the press had a field day with. "Frank Sinatra may have conquered the Pyramids, but can Yves Montand fill the Metropolitan Opera House all by himself," asked Moira Hodgson, contributor to the *New York Times*. "And can he—alone in front of an enormous auditorium—hold that stage which is large enough to accommodate the elephants in *Aida*?" No solo performer had ever tried.

However, Jane Hermann, the presentation director for the Met, had seen Montand perform in Paris and was confident that the singer could not only dominate the stage, but also fill the auditorium with a diverse audience. Remarkably, Montand's international tour was attracting a younger generation of eighteen- to twenty-five-year-olds, who competed with older fans for tickets. When he booked the Met from Tuesday September 7 through Saturday, September 10, advance tickets sold quickly, and charter flights from Paris were due to arrive for opening night.[1]

Simone planned to attend the opening night performance but did not accompany her husband to New York. She was still recovering from gallbladder surgery and arrived a day or two ahead of Montand, who was on tour with Catherine and Jorge Semprum. Catherine was recruited to assist with Montand's international tour and had designed the posters and brochures. Montand had also hired a young woman, Carol Amiel, as an assistant for the technical aspects of the show.

While a guest at this event, Simone was still in her element. By the time Montand, Catherine, and Semprum arrived at the Le Parker Méridien hotel in Manhattan, they found that their suite had been transformed

into another version of the movie "trailer" environment of Place Dauphine and Autheuil, where artists gathered to talk, relax, and create.
The newspapers Simone had scanned for commentary on Montand's anticipated performance and any residual commentary on Marilyn were
strewn everywhere. The phone rang incessantly, and a steady stream of
visitors stopped by to say hello. Simone's sight was failing, and she was
using a magnifying glass to see the crossword puzzle she was working on
in the midst of it all. Seeing her, relaxing on the bed, dressed in white,
Semprum was reminded of "an old, regal cat." She had "marked her
territory" and reigned supreme over it, directing the flow of everything
around her as a center of activity.[2]

Simone had not visited America in years and was enjoying this opportunity to reunite with old friends—and in the manner she was accustomed to. But she had decided to take a back seat role, so as not to deflect
publicity Montand was entitled to have for this historic event. And, this
was her intent on opening night, when she worried that her presence
might distract from Montand's grand entrance on this momentous and
historic occasion. So, when she arrived at the Met, she hid offstage until
the audience settled down. Nearly four thousand people attended this
sold out opening night performance, with scalped tickets selling for a
minimum of 120 dollars apiece. When the lights finally dimmed, Simone began to work her way to her seat next to Catherine in the eighth
row, the place she always sat regardless of the venue. She was confident
that she could move there unnoticed, but her plan failed. When the
audience caught sight of her, the auditorium erupted in thunderous applause as they rose to their feet for a standing ovation that lasted five
minutes. Simone, taken off guard and embarrassed, tried to wave the
applause down. Catherine was impressed and proud of her mother, but
also worried about Montand, who was, at that very moment, waiting
behind the curtain.

He was so unnerved by the audience reaction to Simone that when
they finally quieted and the curtains parted, he felt weak-kneed. Although his concentration was broken for the moment, Montand quickly
regained his composure, and the evening was ultimately his, an unprecedented success. But the incident was instructive for Montand's biographers. Was it Montand's concern that Simone's popularity was infringing
on his own; that she might be more popular?[3] Regardless, Montand was
so shaken by the reaction to his wife that he was sure the audience could
see his pant legs quivering.

There was one technical glitch during the show, unperceived by the audience: The wireless mic was not working properly at one point, restricting Montand's movements. He glanced offstage, hoping to see his new assistant, Carole Amiel, a twenty-two-year-old who was assigned to address such issues. But she was nowhere to be found. When the show ended, Montand had every intention of addressing her absence. But as he bellowed out her name, he suddenly stopped short, surprised to find Simone waiting outside his dressing room door. She had slipped backstage before the end of his performance, hoping to be the first to congratulate him on his success.

Montand could see immediately that Simone had misread his calling out for Carole. She was stunned and jealous, he thought, as he tried to explain the technical problem and need for his assistant. But her pained expression was unnerving, and he stumbled, grasping for words. He never explained the incident, something he regretted later on. However, Simone had not completely misread the singer. Carole Amiel was Montand's assistant, but she was also his lover, and they would maintain a "secret" relationship for the next five years.

≈∿

There was a certain sense of urgency to the projects Simone took on after her surgery. Her failing vision was certainly at the root of this exigency, but it was not the only driving force. Even though Simone had not yet been diagnosed with cancer, she behaved as if she knew, instinctively, that time was not on her side. Over the next three years, she tackled four major projects almost simultaneously and with passion. In retrospect each project had special significance, as though she were attempting to tie up loose ends by repairing "sins of ignorance," and patching up the fissures she had created between herself and her past. She was also making one more attempt to fulfill a long desired dream.

As an actress, Simone had always maintained a cardinal rule: She never asked for a role; she had to be "chosen." The director had to envision her as the only actress possible for the role. Such was the case throughout her career until the later part of 1982, when she discovered that the director Marcel Bluwal was planning to film a television mini-series about Thérèse Humbert, the famous con artist who single-handedly created a financial crisis in France at the turn of the nineteenth century. Simone jumped at the opportunity, and contacted Bluwal. Although she did not have to convince him, Simone explained that at sixty-one, she was the perfect age for the character. And she knew a great deal about Humbert, because her grandmother Signoret used to enjoy telling stories about this famous woman, who borrowed over forty million francs with no intention of ever repaying them.

Thérèse Humbert claimed to be the heir to an imaginary American millionaire, Robert Crawford, a man she claimed she met on a train and saved by administering smelling salts while he was having a heart attack. According to Humbert, Crawford was so grateful that he told her she would be rewarded as a beneficiary of his fortune. When he died in 1881, she allegedly received a letter naming her as his beneficiary and entrusting her with his family fortune, which she was required to keep in a safe with its seal unbroken until her younger sister married one of Crawford's two nephews.

Of course, the letter was a forgery and the entire story a ruse—but it was a good one, because Thérèse was able to use the letter as collateral for substantial loans. And she made good use of the funds, living in a luxurious house, while being waited on by servants as she hosted lavish parties and enjoyed notoriety and respect. What made the story so incredible was that she was able to maintain the ruse, with variations on the theme, for twenty years without engendering suspicion. It wasn't until her debt exceeded the amount of the alleged inheritance that creditors became wary. She attempted to satisfy them by having her brothers play the part of Crawford's nephews and arranged a marriage for her sister. This plan was difficult to pull off, because her sister didn't want to marry her brother, even as a ruse.

The tide turned in 1901, when Humbert's frustrated creditors began to examine the situation more closely and discovered that she had lied about her investments. They demanded that the safe be opened for proof of financial security and that she repay her debts. Thérèse and her family fled to Madrid, as an angry mob of ruined creditors stormed her house and broke open the safe, only to discover that it was empty. At first, the mob turned on her housekeeper, who happened to be the mother-in-law of artist Henri Matisse. She was accused of stealing the money from the safe. But, when this high profile case was investigated by the police, it was finally determined that Thérèse was a formidable con artist. She was finally arrested in Madrid in 1902, tried and sentenced to five years of hard labor. Her husband also served time, but her sister was exonerated as a victim. After she served her time, Thérèse Humbert moved to the United States and lived in Chicago until her death in 1918.

Simone loved the possibilities of the story. It was noteworthy from a historical perspective because it occurred during the same time period as the Dreyfus Affair, when "France was at its most rich and most poor, most vain, most blinkered, most bigoted," she explained. But the character was also a unique and complex blend, a woman with "a side that is deeply vulgar, but at the same time is full of invention, imagination and fast thinking;"[4] a woman who takes advantage of the times and almost succeeds. It was a perfect role, and one she had to play now, she insisted, as she pressed Bluwal to move forward with the production least she became "too old" for the part. *Thérèse Humbert* aired on French television in 1983.

᠅

Simone had regrets that weighed heavily on her mind, particularly in these last years. She had always regretted her lack of participation in the Resistance movement during the Nazi occupation, and then her "sins of ignorance" in supporting the Communist Party. There was one thread of guilt that ran between the two: She had never acknowledged her Jewish roots. This was a failing she felt a need to address. And she began to do so in 1983 with her participation and support for Mosco Boucault's controversial documentary, *Terrorists in Retirement.*

Simone and the French actor Gérard Desarthe narrated the story of illegal immigrants—Jewish, Armenian and Polish—who fled to Paris as Hitler advanced. They formed a two-hundred-member assassination team known as the FTP-MOI (Immigrant Workforce Sharpshooters and Partisans), and although they were laborers without combat experience, they were responsible for many of the most violent and successful attacks against the Nazis in Paris. The Gestapo declared them "Jewish, Armenian and other stateless terrorists," plastering a red poster around the city announcing that they had captured and killed twenty members of the group. During the war, that red poster would become a badge of honor. However, after the war, the surviving members of the group were seemingly forgotten.

Simone became involved in the project when Mosco Boucault discovered seven elderly retirees who had remained in Paris after the war and resumed their trades. His initial intent was to prove that Jews had fought against Hitler and that they were not his only victims. He set up interviews, and Simone accompanied him to the shops where the retirees worked. She observed the interviews, which provided an otherwise overlooked perspective about the Resistance movement. Boucault was so fascinated by their accounts that he asked the men to act out their memories as they shared them, bringing the events to life with action. When it came to discussion about the round-up and execution of the twenty-two who were assassinated, the majority of the participants concurred that the Communist Party had sacrificed them by refusing to help them flee the country after it became apparent the Gestapo was on their trail. There was also a feeling that after the war the French government had failed to recognize this groups' accomplishments as resistors because their last names were too Jewish-sounding or not "French" enough.

The film was produced for the French government's public television station, Antennae-2, but when the production was complete, no airdate was scheduled. The film was so controversial that the Communist Party objected and exerted enough influence to delay airing. The real controversy began when the government banned the film, prompting Simone, among others, to launch a protest against censorship. *Terrorists in Retirement* aired two years later, in June 1985. By then, Simone was enjoying the unexpected success of *Adieu, Volodia.*

Though she had long dreamed of writing fiction, Simone didn't think she could. "I felt I was only good at describing what I knew about personally," she explained. After the success of her two books, she was often asked if she'd consider fiction. "I would reply, 'I have no imagination.'"[5] So when she began writing in April 1983, she intended to produce another memoir, a "fictionalized" version that focused on her rediscovery. The first ten pages flowed with little effort, but Simone became bored. Tossing the pages out, she started anew, thinking about the MOI survivors she had met during the filming of *Terrorists in Retirement*, which brought to mind the paternal side of her family, a side she knew little about beyond what she'd learned from her cousin, Jo Langer. She wondered which Polish ghetto her grandfather Kaminker had lived in, and about the life he and her grandmother had led when they immigrated to France. Suddenly, images began to flow, and the characters she created took on a life of their own as a story unfolded. "What's so exciting for an actress," Simone explained later on, "is suddenly feeling you're the master of everything. Writing a book, you become your own director, your own set designer, your own make-up artist, your own costume designer—and above all, your own film director."[6]

"There were no legends about their first meeting. They had never actually met, because they'd always known each other," Simone wrote, introducing two of her main characters, who were infants in 1925 when the story begins. Maurice Guttman was the only child of Elie and Sonia Guttman from the Ukraine. And, Elsa "Zaza" Roginski was the only child of Stépan and Olga Roginski, from Poland. Both families had fled their native countries to escape the brutal anti-Semitic pogroms of Simone Vassilievitch Petilura after the Russian revolution.

When the families settled in Paris and became neighbors, a steadfast friendship evolved. They lived across the hall from each other in an apartment building on the Rue de la Mare in the twentieth arrondisement, a working class neighborhood that was attractive to immigrants. Although the adults did not speak the same national language, Yiddish was an equalizer and their past a common thread that bound them together. The couples so feared Petilura they made a pact that they would never speak of the horrors of the past or utter his name in front of their children. "As parents, they would be the young amnesiacs . . . they would forget, or at least pretend to. They wouldn't be like their parents or grandparents, who had fed them the details of the pogroms of their day by the terrifying light of tallow candles."[7]

In spite of their desire to forget their past lives, the Guttmans were always seeking ways to contact their cousin, Volodia, who remained in Russia after the Revolution. Though the title of the novel suggests he is a central character, he makes only one brief appearance. But his existence becomes a metaphor for the Guttmans, who struggle with competing desires: to reconnect with their past, and to forget it completely.

Maurice and Elsa would become assimilated as French, but they would not be spared the prejudice that is awakened in Paris in the course of a saga that spans twenty years and unfolds against the backdrop of historical events—from the birth of the Popular Front to the Nazi occupation to the end of the war in 1945. Simone wrote with passion and intimacy about Paris. "Her sense of place is so strong and sure that if Paris were destroyed, *Adieu, Volodia* could serve as guidebook for its reconstruction," wrote Deirdre Bair for the September 14, 1985, issue of the *New York Times*.

Simone borrowed from her past and the pasts of others. When Stépan and Elie come home with tears in their eyes as they proudly display their new naturalization papers, it was a scene she had "pinched" from Montand's family. But unlike *Nostalgia*, this was not a story about Montand. It was a story about her life—with a little of Montand and her friends and her father's family, which she could only imagine. She injected herself into the characters of both Elsa and Maurice, though she is most often discovered in Maurice's story. She shared details of her childhood and reinvented important people that had impressed her in her youth. Her high school teacher, Lucie Aubrac, known then as Madame Samuels, became Monsieur Florian, Maurice's teacher, who brings history to life and allows his students to borrow his books. The girls didn't have that opportunity, reading fan magazines instead.

The Guttman and Roginski parents would never see the Nazi occupation. Simone was so fond of them that she couldn't bear the prospect of their ultimate imprisonment and death in a concentration camp. Instead, she decided to end their lives before the fall of France, in a tragic train accident she based on an actual event. After the fall of France, Maurice and Elsa became involved in the French Resistance. Elsa eventually travels with the children of deportees, taking them to safety in the mountains, where she waits for Maurice, who flees Paris after successfully fulfilling a bombing mission. They would remain in the mountains until Liberation.

When the house was quiet, Maurice would often slip downstairs to sit in the dark and drink. "He didn't go downstairs so that he could drink in secret," Simone explained. "He drank so that he could think in secret. It was a habit he formed to enable him to survive." Fearful that he might forget his parents as they had been in the full flower of their lives, he created a little exercise in which he pieced together memories until he created a full picture. This exercise was similar to the one Simone used to search her memory for *Nostalgia*. Maurice "undertook these dives, which he was now perfectly able to control—like a deep sea diver who knows where to find the ancient treasures whose exact location he has verified." However, in *Nostalgia*, the deep-sea diver brings all the coral and flotsam to the surface. Maurice must leave them where he found them, "because such treasures couldn't survive in the open air."[8]

"I put a fantastic amount of my own life in this book, yet I didn't realize it until much later," Simone explained. And, if it were up to her, she might have gone on and on with the saga and all its complexities. "But I would have liked my characters to go on living,"[9] in a book that others would read. So she brought the story to an end after the Liberation, when Maurice waited patiently at the station where Holocaust survivors were arriving in passenger trains. He decided that it was best to "forget," just as Simone had chosen to forget a part of her life that couldn't be explained. Simone wrote the novel over the course of eighteen months, from April 1983 to September 1984.

During those eighteen months, her eyesight gradually failed. In February 1984, when Catherine gave birth to her second child, Clementine, Simone had to ask Benjamin to hold the baby in the light so she could see the shadow of her granddaughter with her peripheral vision. By the time she finished writing her novel, Simone was using thick glasses and a magnifying glass to see her pages. "The day I sent the parcel of proofs back to my publisher that was it: I couldn't see any more, at all," she told the journalist, Catherine David. Simone made this sequence sound like a triumph, David explained—as though she had "fixed things," holding off blindness until she finished writing. *Adieu, Volodia*, published in France in January 1985, was a best-selling novel, which was as much a surprise to Simone as it was to the critics. The novel was translated and released on the international market in 1986. However, Simone would not live long enough to enjoy her success.

CHAPTER 35

"All I Ever Really Had in Mind"

"WE HAD A HABIT OF GLANCING AT EACH OTHER WHEN WE WERE with a group of people and we heard stupid remarks . . . just a quick glance was all it took and sometimes that was all it took to set off wonderful, uncontrollable giggles,"[1] Montand explained. It was something he and Simone did instinctively and took for granted, until one night at a dinner party, when "someone made a really idiotic remark." Montand looked at Simone but couldn't catch her eye. "And she was looking for me, my glance, and she couldn't find it. Then I felt so devastated. I felt so bad."

Simone's blindness was a bitter blow and took its toll, emotionally, as did the death of her mother in early 1985. Simone never spoke of her adult relationship with Georgette. Catherine explained that while Simone had always provided for her mother's needs, their relationship was distant. In part, the breech seems to have grown out of Georgette's dislike of Montand, whom she thought of as a "clown." But Simone never discussed her adult relationship with her mother. When Georgette was elderly and required care, Simone sent Catherine to tend to her grandmother's needs. Catherine complained that she sometimes felt herself a victim of her grandmother's mood swings. Simone, for her part, had already retreated to Autheuil when Georgette died.

Betty Marvin, Simone's longtime friend since the Hollywood years, did not know about Simone's blindness or health issues when she was in France for a visit and called in the hopes of getting together. While she and Simone had talked on the phone over the years, they hadn't seen each other in a while, and Betty was looking forward to reuniting. But that was not to happen, Betty recalled. "It was a sad conversation.

She told me she was completely blind." When Betty expressed her desire to see her, Simone declined, explaining, "But I can't see you."² She was otherwise gracious, inquiring about the family and Betty's new ventures. "She was very loving as always," Betty said. But Simone would not change her mind about their getting together. "It was the last time we spoke."

Yet, by spring Simone had regrouped and was already involved in her next venture, which she took on with passion—perhaps suspecting that it would be her last role. Marcel Bluwal had created another mini-series for television with Simone in mind. *Music Hall*, a two-part drama, was set in Paris in 1938, as Jewish refugees and communists were fleeing to France during Hitler's first purges. In the mini-series, Yvonne Pierre is the boisterous director of a music hall that has fallen on uncertain times as audiences turn to the cinema and theater for entertainment. Unbeknownst to others, Yvonne is Jewish, the daughter of a rabbi, a fact she has not only kept hidden, but has refused to acknowledge. She must come to terms with her identity as she struggles to keep the music hall alive and deal with the refugees who turn to her for work. Though she tells her workers, "I don't give a shit about Hitler," Yvonne visits her father and encourages him to flee France before it's too late. She returns to the music hall for what she knows will be the last show, because she, too, must try to flee before it's too late. The role, written exclusively for Simone, was perfect, piecing together the past and bringing it to closure. She agreed to take it on, even though someone would have to work with her, reading the script aloud, until she memorized her lines. She was determined to keep going, which was the "one big thing . . . all I ever really had in mind."

Shortly before filming began, Simone had to address another health issue that weighed heavily on her mind. Rapid weight loss, weakness, fatigue, and severe stomach pain were ominous signs that could no longer be ignored. "I went to see my dear doctor here," she told her friend Jean-François Josselin, referring to her physician in Normandy. "I said to him, 'Don't beat around the bush, this time, I'm in real trouble?' He answered, 'Yes, Madame Signoret.'"³ They suspected colon cancer; surgery would be required. Simone made it perfectly clear that she did not want a colostomy bag, and the doctor agreed, promising to use another form of drainage, if possible. She also did not want to drag things out with chemotherapy. She wanted to delay surgery until the end of *Music Hall*, so it was set for August 1, 1985. "So we sat down to figure out how we were going to tell this to Montand, to Catherine and my friends."⁴ She chose not to share her condition with the cast and crew of *Music Hall*. On the set, only Bluwal, his wife, and Catherine's second husband, the actor Maurice Vaudaux, who had a role in the series, were privy to her health issue. No one suspected how serious they were, because beyond her blindness, it was difficult to tell that she was suffering. Her performance was remarkable. "As soon as I say, 'let's roll,' she sees better than the others," Bluwal explained. "I have her do very difficult things. She still has a great career ahead of her."[5]

On screen, it is clear that Simone's condition is weakened. She is thin, her shoulders are rounded and hunched a bit. But there are also signs of the former Simone as she was before her alcoholism and weight gain. The author Susan Hayward wrote, "[W]e forget her blindness. She moves gracefully around the set as if she were fully sighted. When she takes cigarettes from her pack, we have to look very attentively to see the slightest fumbles . . . . By now, her voice has become very smoky indeed: deep, husky, dusty even."[6]

During the last weeks of filming, they had to alter the schedule a bit because Simone was tiring easily and in tremendous pain. Her role required a little singing and a great deal of shouting, which helped her push past the pain. And then, on August 1, when filming was completed, with her hospital bag packed and waiting, "Simone Signoret discretely eclipsed,"[7] Bluwal explained poetically, describing the grand actress leaving quietly, with no fanfare or goodbyes.

Catherine described Simone's surgery as "brutal and final."[8] Though it would not be diagnosed at the time, Simone had pancreatic cancer; the disease had spread throughout her body and was inoperable. The moment Simone woke from surgery, she knew the outcome before anyone gave her an official prognosis. When she felt for the drain the doctor had promised and did not find it, she turned to Catherine, who was standing at her bedside.

"The drain, they put it in?"

"No, Mama, it wasn't necessary," Catherine explained.

"It was no longer necessary," Simone responded, her voice trailing off.

"No, Mama, you didn't need it," Catherine confirmed, without elaborating.

"If only I could catch some filthy quick disease that would make everything so much simpler."

It was the first and last time that Simone spoke directly of death. From that point forward, she chose not to speak of it except in the most oblique way and did not tell her friends. So it was only in retrospect, when friends thought about their visits to Autheuil, that they recognized the little hints she had given. She had a healthy appetite at first, Jean-François Josselin noted during a lunchtime visit. Marcelle had served langoustines with homemade mayonnaise, and Simone dipped pieces of bread into the sauce to test it before commenting. "'It's good,'" she says approvingly, gaily enjoying her food (or giving me the impression of doing so.) 'If the appetite returns, so does health.'" Believing that she was recovering from cancer, Josselin encouraged her. "'But you are not sick anymore. . . . You were sick, but now, that's over.' She looked at me with a mischievous little grin. 'Well, yes.' And then she dipped a fourth little piece of bread in the mayonnaise."

The decision had been made not to tell Montand that Simone was dying. At the time, he was filming *Jean de Flore*. Perhaps Simone and Catherine did not want to distract him, but the reason for his ignorance remains unclear. He would visit during filming breaks, believing, like their friends, that his wife was making a slow recovery from cancer surgery. Catherine, who was staying at Autheuil with her family at the time, would help her mother primp for Montand's visits, guiding Simone into the shower and a fresh nightgown. The visits with Montand were not always pleasant. After one particular episode that did not go well because "Montand was terrible,"[9] Catherine explained (though she did not elaborate), she and her husband, Maurice, decided that it was time to tell Montand the truth. She waited until he was back on location before calling so that he wouldn't overreact at home, causing further distress. Montand was stunned, and from that point forward, he made sure that his visits were pleasant experiences. Apparently, he and Simone never discussed her condition.

When she and her mother spent time together, Catherine had a chance to discuss some of the misgivings she harbored about their relationship over the years, especially during childhood. Simone understood completely. But there wasn't enough time to discuss everything, and there was no sense of closure for Catherine. As she helped her mother, she realized the irony of their role reversal: She had become the mother to the woman who had never fulfilled this role for her. Although Simone would not directly address her impending death, during one of their conversations she told Catherine where she kept her jewelry, which she intended her daughter to have, "just in case." On another occasion, she expressed the hope that there might be some type of gathering, with pretty flowers, for friends. But these were rare comments, and the words "death" and "funeral" were not mentioned.

As Simone's condition worsened, Leon Schwartzenberg, a physician and friend of the family, moved into Autheuil to care for her. Catherine's friend, Marina, a nurse, also moved in to assist. At first, Simone was able to entertain guests, but by late September, she was too tired and slept much of the time. She had one final burst of energy and was able to get out of bed, walk around, and eat. She and Montand visited that day. It was her last burst of energy before her condition deteriorated rapidly. Her closest friends understood then, without being told, that Simone was dying.

She worried about them and felt the need to apologize for her inability to entertain in a manner they were accustomed to. But more than anything, she wanted them to know that she had come to terms with her life and death, and that now she sought release from the pain of her disease. Her friend and neighbor, Yvette Etiévant, an actress who had begun her career with Simone as one of the citizens of Thebes on stage at the Theatre des Mathurins, and had read her first draft of *Adieu, Volodia*, was a frequent visitor. After Yvette's last visit, Simone called her. "I felt you were sad. I don't want you to be,"[10] she told her.

During Josselin's last visit, he found her tired and ready for sleep. "She moved her hand in recognition and said, 'I'm sorry, but I believe I'm about to go under.' Just as I was leaving her bedroom she stopped me. Her cat's eyes, her sea-green eyes, were looking lovingly at me." And then, she said only a few words, which left an indelible impression: "I am at peace."

Dr. Schwartzenberg left Autheuil to take care of business for a few hours on September 29, expecting to return the next morning. At that point, Simone was stable, and he felt comfortable asking a young country doctor to care for his patient during his absence. However, before leaving him, the young doctor was apparently made aware of Simone's expressed desire that, when the time came, she did not want her daughter to see her die. And so, in the early morning hours of September 30, 1985, when Simone began struggling for breath, Catherine was asleep in her room, undisturbed.

Loneliness, cancer, and the prospect of a lingering death were Simone's worst fears. But, in the end, as she faced them all, she asked for no one and relied entirely on her doctor and nurse for support. At one point, in her struggle for breath, she asked the doctor to set her on the floor so she could have a firm surface to prop herself against instead of the soft mattress. The doctor declined but offered to prop her up in bed and held her back to support her. At 7:10 a.m., when their housekeeper,

Marcelle, began work and discovered that Simone was dying, she rushed to Catherine's room on the second floor to wake her. But by the time Catherine arrived at the bedside, Simone's blank stare was an unmistakable sign that it was too late, though her mouth continued to move involuntarily seeking breath, "like a fish out of water." The young doctor, who continued to prop Simone up, looked as horrified as Catherine felt when she closed her mother's eyes.[11]

Catherine now faced the prospect of calling Montand. Fearing that rumors would leak out, she tried calling him, but her efforts were in vain. When she finally reached him, she learned that he was on his way back to Autheuil. Her son, Benjamin, was at school in Paris, and she arranged for the actor, Jean-Claude Dauphin, a close family friend, to pick Benjamin up and drive him to Autheuil. Then she contacted the press and gave a statement: "She died as bravely as she lived."

During the drive to Autheuil, Benjamin, who was fifteen years old, listened to countless news reports of his grandmother's death on the radio. Up to that point, like most children, he never viewed his grandmother as an adult with a life of her own—and certainly not as a celebrity. In his world, she was "Mamie," always adoring and affectionate, not Simone Signoret. It occurred to him then that he would never have the opportunity to get her to know her as an adult and he felt guilty because he had never finished reading her novel, *Adieu, Volodia*—though Simone had encouraged him, explaining that the book was about their family. He tried to read it to please her, but as a teenager, it did not interest him and he never told her that he didn't finish it. After her funeral, he would bring the book to the gravesite and read the last chapter aloud.[12]

News of Simone's death at the age of sixty-four was staggering to friends who knew she was ill, but never expected the loss. Even those who suspected were still stunned by the suddenness and finality of Simone's death. The general public had not even been aware that she was ill until they heard the news and stopped at stands to read banner headlines: "*Adieu, Casque d'Or.*" Mary Blume, a journalist and friend, noted that photographers had gathered outside 15 Place Dauphine, wandering aimlessly about waiting for something to happen, even though Simone had died in Normandy. For the first time, there would be no public statements or signs of life from the famous apartment that had been a stage for so much activity. "The French knew that they had admired Simone Signoret; they learned that they had also loved her," Blume wrote. "The afternoon of her death, *Le Monde* gave her a front-page headline, and then wrote at great length that it was impossible to know what to say about her. In its awkwardness, it was the most heartfelt obituary I have ever read in France."[13]

Simone's life was so elaborate that it was often described as multiple lives. What aspect of it should reporters write about: acting, writing, social activism? Each article struck a different chord. In the *Quotidien de Paris*, on October 1, 1985, the novelist Marguerite Duras wrote about Simone as a "queen." "People will speak of the 'Era of Signoret' to describe the times from the fifties until the present. The great French Ambassador of the 20th Century. She shook up France and made it international. She speaks out for human rights everywhere. Impossible to replace Signoret."

The woman who had so wholeheartedly rejected Russia's communism and had made public efforts to repair her "sins of innocence," was responsible for deflecting attention away from preparations for a historic visit by Soviet leader Mikhail S. Gorbachev, who was expected in Paris for a summit. The French and Soviet flags lining the Champs Élysées went largely unnoticed on October 1, as dignitaries, friends, family, and onlookers gathered at Père Lachaise cemetery for Simone's funeral. CBS anchor Dan Rather, who was in Paris for the summit, reported on her funeral and provided perhaps the most poignant and all-encompassing obituary, which appeared against the backdrop of a photomontage:

> Simone Signoret, the actress, who died yesterday, was to many as much a symbol of France as the monuments and dignitaries . . . . [A]s a teenager [she] survived the dark days of the Nazi occupation of Paris and blossomed on film young and beautiful . . . and endured beyond youth and beauty to be old and wise. Like so many of their countrymen, she and her husband, Yves Montand flirted with communism in the Post War years, but moved gradually away, disillusioned with Moscow's repression and rigidity. They became important voices in French affairs, representing to several generations French independence, skepticism and pride. Montand once told Signoret, "You know, we're survivors." Today he and many other survivors of the great war and the Cold War, place flowers on her grave."[14]

Her death was such a sensitive subject with friends that they could not speak of it. Instead, they spoke of the day "Simone left us," as though she had taken a trip and might be returning at any moment—or worse, that she had abandoned them. Montand did feel that Simone had abandoned him, and he wavered between anger and sorrow. It was impossible to ignore her "presence" at Autheuil and the Place Dauphine. The mementos she accumulated were everywhere, and he was apt to find scraps of paper with notes for a new idea that she had written and stuffed in drawers. In her closet, Montand was surprised to discover the stiletto shoes that were ruined by the soft asphalt streets of New York during their first visit to the United States. She had kept them as a memento of a time when the future held boundless opportunities and was untouched by scandal. He in turn kept them, along with a favorite raincoat and other belongings of hers that he was fond of. He left her office on the upper level of Autheuil just as she had, with her vest draped across the back of the chair, as though she planned to return. Place Dauphine became a shrine for a while. At first, Montand would go there alone and lie on their bed where he could grieve in silence, surrounded by memories. When he stopped going, he left the apartment intact, just as she had left it, and moved on with his life. He apparently purchased another house and had set up one room there to simulate Simone's office, though he did not go in.

But his grieving was as complex and at times as incomprehensible as their relationship, because moving on for Montand meant resuming the affair he had been having with his young assistant, Carole Amiel, for the previous five years. She would eventually move into Autheuil, which created friction. It was no doubt her influence that prompted Montand to tell Catherine and her family they could not visit there as often or as freely as they had in the past. It wasn't their home, and Montand was not a blood relative, after all, as he made perfectly clear when he explained to Benjamin, "I am not your grandfather,"[15] and asked him to refrain from using the word. In time, Montand resumed his relationship with Catherine and her family with more freedom. But the tensions that were created during this period by his new love, a relationship that became public in 1987 at the Cannes Film Festival, left a bitter aftertaste with the family.

After the death of her father, Yves Allégret, who died January 31, 1987, Catherine was legally adopted by Montand, who gave her his last name. She then hyphenated her own surname as Allégret-Livi. Although Simone had not prohibited contact with Allégret, she never encouraged it, and Montand was the only father Catherine had ever really known, so the adoption brought a sense of closure for her, giving their relationship an appropriate definition.

On December 31, 1988, Montand had another heir when Carole Amiel gave birth to their son, Valentin. "He did not want a child, but more because of his age than from any deep-seated reluctance,"[16] Amiel explained. "Admittedly, I made the decision, not Montand . . . . It was the only thing I could give him that he had never had before, and also the only way of being with him my whole life long." However, contrary to popular belief, Montand never legally married Carole Amiel. She was the mother of his child and his lover and companion, but never his wife, a term of endearment that he reserved for remembering and speaking of Simone.

In early May 1988, Montand began filming *Three Seats for the 26th*, a musical adaptation of his life directed by Jacques Demy. "There will be the scene where I met Simone Signoret," Montand explained to *New York Times* reporter Mervyn Rothstein. "'But it will be very discreet. You will hear *Autumn Leaves*—his theme song—softly in the background.' He hummed the refrain—La di da di, la di da da da . . . . 'It was very tough to do this,' Montand explained. 'It was easy to talk about Piaf in the film. But Simone—it was very delicate.' Suddenly, after being so very much present, he was elsewhere. His eyes seemed to be focused inside, thinking, remembering. He closed them. 'Simone,' he said. 'I think she would be very happy if she were to see it.'"[17]

The original lyrics of *Autumn Leaves*, adapted from the poem written by Jacques Prévert, are far more compelling than the Americanized version in Montand's world. They tell the story of lovers and of "memories and regrets." The song easily becomes a story about Simone and Montand: "You loved me and I loved you. . . . And we lived together . . . . You loved me, I loved you. . . . But life separates those who love . . . . Gently, without making a sound . . . . And the sea erases from the sand the foot prints of separated lovers."

There is a verse that Montand did not sing at concerts, though it tells a story that is equally compelling:

The dead leaves gather on the rake,
As do the memories and regrets,
But my love, quiet and loyal,
Always smiles and is grateful for life.
I loved you so much,
You were beautiful.
How can you expect me to forget you?
In those times, life was more beautiful,
And the sun shone brighter than today.
You were my kindest friend,
But I only created regrets.

And the song that you used to sing, I hear always,
Always.

In mid-October 1991, Montand was enjoying a birthday dinner at Catherine's when he noticed that she had the mohair blanket Simone had crocheted for their bed at Place Dauphine. Catherine rescued it after Montand stopped visiting the apartment, because it was becoming dusty, and she thought it a pity that the beautiful creation might be ruined for lack of care. Montand was happy to see it in use, but had a favor to ask: When he died, he wished to be buried with the blanket covering him. Catherine agreed, but the reference to his death did not cause immediate concern, because at the time she was unaware that Montand was being treated for a heart condition, a fact he had chosen not to share with her. Two weeks later, on November 9, 1991, Yves Montand suffered a massive heart attack on the set of the film *IP 5* on the last day of filming. He was rushed to a hospital in Senlis, France, where he died the same day. He was seventy years old. Ironically, his role in the film was that of an old man who suffered the same fate. Catherine did not forget her promise: Before the casket was closed, she covered Montand with Simone's blanket.

Montand's funeral was a massive event, filling the streets of Paris with mourners who followed his casket on the journey to Père Lachaise cemetery. The *New York Times* reported on his funeral on November 13, 1991:

> Such was his following in France that in 1988 he was mentioned as a possible presidential candidate. By then, the man who for 25 years had been a darling of the French left had swung dramatically to the right, as ready to denounce Communism as to praise Ronald Reagan and Margaret Thatcher. His popularity survived his travels through passion and politics because his ability to charm the French—and a good many foreigners—never faltered. In recent years, his hair thinning and his face wrinkled, he exuded the air of a favorite uncle who would always be around.

Yves Montand was laid to rest beside Simone, his wife of thirty-six years, the woman who believed until the end that "individual courage is the only interesting thing in life."

ACKNOWLEDGMENTS

I wish to thank the following institutions for their contributions and assistance:

The Peter Glenville Foundation; Harry Ransom Center, University of Texas at Austin; the Margaret Herrick Library, Academy of Motion Picture Arts & Sciences; Dorothy and Lewis Cullman Center, New York Public Library for Performing Arts; the Mémorial de la Shoah in Paris; and the staff at the Algonquin Hotel in New York City.

I owe a debt of gratitude to many people for their assistance, support, and interest in this, my first biography. It was a great honor to meet and correspond with Jean-Pierre Kaminker, Simone's youngest brother, who patiently provided invaluable insights and information over the course of four years. Jean-Pierre brought me closer to Simone than I ever imagined possible, and I will always cherish our friendship and association.

Thanks to Jean-Pierre, I was introduced to author Nanon Gardin, who served as our translator as we toured Neuilly-sur-Seine. She opened her home to us, offering hospitality and a treasured friendship. Our visit to the Lycée Pasteur was a memorable adventure. I also extend a thank you to Robert Kaminker, Simone and Jean-Pierre's cousin, for sharing information about his family and relationship with André Kaminker.

My heartfelt appreciation goes to Barbara Greenwood, who provided French translation services for the project over the course of four years, as we waded through countless documents, articles, and books. She also provided encouragement and friendship.

It was a great honor to interview Robert Meeropol, youngest son of Julius and Ethel Rosenberg, who brought me closer to a dark and embarrassing period in our history. I am also grateful for his referral to David Alman, who provided invaluable information.

Although we corresponded, I never had an opportunity to meet Dominique Desanti, author, French historian and former member of the French Resistance. She was too ill to see me during my visits to Paris and passed away before I had a chance to meet her. Although Dominique did not know Simone during the Occupation years, she was well aware of the budding actress who turned heads in the cafes and later, in the jazz "caves" of Paris. Just as Simone consulted with her on historical facts when she was writing *Nostalgia Isn't What It Used To Be*, I took full advantage of Dominique's remarkable memory and perspective. I owe her a debt of gratitude, which sadly, I can never repay.

With grateful appreciation, I want to thank Deirdre Bair, who served as a mentor through the arduous process of writing a book proposal and then beyond. She always provided helpful advice and referrals, as I attempted to overcome obstacles and learn the intricacies of writing a biography. I value our friendship.

I send a thank you to Susan Dalsimer for initial editing services. Dee Speese-Linehan and Barbara Greenwood served as trusted "readers," and helped to solve many a dilemma during our "chicken wing emergencies" at Archie Moore's in New Haven.

Katja Koehnlein, Daniel Diaz, and Mary Lawrence Test assisted with translation in German, Spanish, and French, respectively. I also extend a thank you to Myrna Bell Rochester, Mike Brecher, and my attorney, Karen Shatzkin, for their assistance.

It was a pleasure to correspond with Betty Marvin, who I have remained in touch with through the years. Alvin Sargent and Jacques Zanetti provided valuable insights and referrals to new sources of information as my work progressed.

I extend a special thank you to my family, who never wavered in their encouragement, support, and patience. I thank my mother, Helen, for her inspiration and my father, Jim, for his encouragement. A thank you to my sisters, Laura Kaufman and Cynthia Dugay; my brother-in-law, Marco Dugay, Sr.; and my nieces and nephews: Melissa Kaufman and Emily Dugay, Marco Dugay, Jr., James Vitello, Arthur Vitello III, and his wife, Dr. Sarah Vitello, who all listened patiently throughout the years and offered unwavering encouragement.

Friends who provided encouragement from the moment I conceived the project, through to the end—and who no doubt know as much about Simone as I—will never know how much I appreciate their support and patience. These include: Leslie Bartholomew, Mark Graham, Dr. Robert Henry, Patricia Krause, Betsy Mase, Barbara Parks, Dr. M. L. McLaughlin,

John Prokop, Crystal Pilon, Helene Robbins, Cynthia Sanchez, Annette Solevo, Ann Tracz, and Michele Wade.

NOTES

CHAPTER 1

1. Simone Signoret, *Nostalgia Isn't What It Used To Be*. English translation. Harper & Row, 1978, p. 32. Originally published in French under the title, *La nostalgie n'est plus ce qu'elle était*, Éditions du Seuil, 1976.

2. *Studio Magazine*, "Tribute to Simone Signoret." Quoted from French radio program, *Radioscopie*, 1973.

3. Author interview with Simone's youngest brother, Jean-Pierre Kaminker, PhD (JPK), retired professor of semiotics and language sciences at the University of Perpignan, France. I corresponded with JPK in French, from 2009–11. In 2011, we also met in Paris and toured key points of interest in Neuilly-sur-Seine with our translator, the French author Nanon Gardin.

4. Jean-Pierre Kaminker.

5. Simone Signoret, p.32.

6. JPK.

7. Simone Signoret, p.17.

8. Ibid., p. 17.

9. Ibid., p. 16. Jean-Pierre explained that he was too young to recall the aesthetics and could not provide commentary on the apartment.

10. Simone never elaborated beyond this statement. Throughout her life, she was very careful when speaking about her parents, their relationship, and her own relationship with them. However, in the quote that follows, JPK provided invaluable insight.

11. JPK's revelation about their father's request for a divorce provides new information about the fragility of the marriage and Georgette's emotional state during this period. The marriage ended during World War II.

12. Ibid.

13. Ibid.

14. Both Jean-Pierre Kaminker and his cousin, Robert Kaminker, son of André's younger brother, Georges, provided the information in this section. Robert Kaminker became a conference interpreter and worked with his father and uncle at the United Nations. The author corresponded with Robert Kaminker in the early stage of book development.

317

15. JPK.

16. Although he did not enjoy success toward the end of his life, Charles was a gifted artist who sometimes used wood panels as a medium instead of canvas, considered a unique method at the time. He received prizes for his art at the peak of his career, years before Simone's birth, and his art frequently sells at auction.

17. JPK recalled that his mother kept olive oil in the house as a staple. Olive oil was not a staple in bourgeois households, and its use was frowned upon.

CHAPTER 2

1. Simone Signoret, p. 9.

2. Emmanuelle Gilcher, *Signoret, Une Vie*. Éditions Privé, France, 2005, p. 27.

3. Interview with Betty Marvin, first wife of actor Lee Marvin. Although Lee met Simone in 1960, Simone and Betty did not meet until 1963, during filming of *Ship of Fools*. The two women remained friends until Simone's death in 1985.

4. *Time*, October 31, 1932.

5. *L'Écran Française*, May, 1948.

6. *Redbook*, p. 51. A recorded dialogue between Simone and actress Arlene Francis, taped in New York, March 1962. Simone's description of the birth of Jean-Pierre, also quoted from this article, provides the most in-depth and instructive version of events, in contrast to the condensed version Simone generally shared about this turning point in her life.

CHAPTER 3

1. International Association of Conference Interpreters. History of the organization is outlined on the website: www.aiic.net, Fiftieth Anniversary Timeline. André Kaminker was a founding member and served as president of this worldwide professional organization for conference interpreters.

2. *Redbook*, March 1962, p. 110.

3. Robert Kaminker correspondence with the author, 2008

4. During a visit to the school in 2010 with Jean-Pierre Kaminker and our translator, Nanon Gardin, we met with an administration official in hopes of obtaining a copy of Simone's academic record. However, the official explained with great embarrassment that records for all of their famous pupils and staff—Signoret, Chris Marker, Jean-Paul Sartre, and others—had been stolen, allegedly by a former staff person. The school continues to watch for evidence of these records at auction.

5. Chris Marker was born Christian François Bouche-Villeneuve on July 20, 1921. He changed his name to Chris Marker and became a prominent French writer, photographer, documentarian, and film essayist. He maintained a lifelong relationship with Simone and with Alain Resnais, who would enter Simone's life during her last year of high school in Vannes. During the Nazi occupation, Marker joined the Marquis FTP. Later in life, he rented an apartment from Simone at 15 Place Dauphine and often hosted spaghetti dinners to help raise funds for living expenses and his art. His most prominent

films include: *La jetée* (1962), *A Grin Without a Cat* (1977), *Sans Soleil* (1983), and the essay *AK* (1985), based on the Japanese filmmaker, Akira Kurosawa. Chris Marker died July 29, 2012.

    6. Emmanuelle Gilcher, p. 37.

    7. JPK, 2009.

CHAPTER 4

    1. Alain Resnais was born on June 3, 1922 in Vannes, in the province of Brittany. He developed an interest in filmmaking at the age of ten, so that by age twelve, his parents gave him the 8 mm camera as a birthday present. Resnais was influenced by the surrealist movement in Paris and is closely associated with directors of the French New Wave, though he did not consider himself New Wave. He attempted acting before fully pursuing his interest in filmmaking. Resnais focused on two important themes in his writing and films, memory and time, themes also investigated by Chris Marker. Simone shared their interest in memory themes. Although his career spanned six decades, he is best known for early films: *Night and Fog* (1955), *Hiroshima Mon Amour* (1959), and *Last Year at Marienbad* (1961).

    2. Gilcher, p.39.

    3. Signoret, p. 27.

    4. Gilcher, p. 39–40.

    5. Signoret, p. 9.

    6. JPK.

CHAPTER 5

    1. Signoret, p. 3. Pétain was reassuring when he requested an armistice with Germany, though public opinion began to shift when the country was then divided into two governments. He set up the Vichy government, became head of state, and ruled the Vichy government as collaborator and dictator. In 1945, Pétain was convicted of treason and sentenced to death. His sentence was commuted to life in prison.

    2. Journalist John Freeman interviewed Simone for his BBC television program, *Face to Face*, which aired the interview on November 13, 1960. The interview took place shortly after the Marilyn Monroe affair and immediately after Simone signed the Manifesto of the 121 against the Algerian War.

    3. Robert Kaminker relayed a story about his family's journey as they joined the throngs of Parisians who clogged the roads leading out of Paris toward the Unoccupied Zone, where his family remained throughout the war.

    4. John Freeman/BBC, November 13, 1960.

    5. Signoret, p. 30. Over twenty-five years after Simone's death, various interpretations of her life continue to glamorize her role as tutor. Simone was never a teacher.

    6. Alan Ridding, *And The Show Went On*. Alfred A. Knopf, New York, 2010, p. 199.

    7. Oliver Barrot and Raymond Chirat, *La vie culturelle dans la France occupée*. Gallimard, Paris, 2009, p. 49.

8. Bernard Weinraub, *Saturday Evening Post*, February 25, 1967, pp. 39–41. Weinraub interviewed Simone over the course of two to three days in London and Paris. Simone was completing her performance as Lady Macbeth.

9. Ibid.

10. I corresponded with Dominique Desanti, French author, historian, and former member of the French Resistance. During the Occupation years, she was closely associated with Jean-Paul Sartre and Simone de Beauvoir. Although Desanti did not know Simone personally at the time, she recalled seeing her in the cafes, where everyone commented on the young girl's beauty. Later in life, Simone consulted with Dominique while writing *Nostalgia*. Dominique died in Paris on April 8, 2011.

11. Alistair Horne, *La Belle France*. Vintage Books, June 2006, p. 356. Originally published in Great Britain under the title *Friend or Foe* by Weidenfeld and Nicolson, London, 2004. Dominique Desanti also explained that the Nazis used the public address system regularly, providing chilling messages that warned citizens of rules and the consequences of breaking them.

CHAPTER 6

1. Signoret, p. 39. Jacques Fath was a French fashion designer. Ava Gardner, Greta Garbo, and Rita Hayworth wore his designs.

2. Laura Bergquist, *Look*, "The Lives and Loves of Simone Signoret," August 30, 1960.

3. Signoret, p. 40.

4. The theater could not confirm the date of the opening night performance. According to staff, records from the Nazis occupation are in storage in the basement and never been sorted through. They could not confirm a date, and the author could not find newspaper advertisements for the performance.

5. Claude Jaeger was born on April 2, 1917, in Geneva, Switzerland. He became a notable French actor, most known for *Diary of a Chambermaid* (1964), *Mademoiselle* (1966), *The Discreet Charm of the Bourgeoisie* (1972). Jaeger died on September 16, 2004, at the age of eighty-seven, in Paris, France.

6. Simone wrote the majority of articles for *Cinémonde* magazine's special edition, "Ombre et Lumière, le prochain film de Simone Signoret," 1952. In addition to articles about her personal life and career, she also wrote from the perspective of her character, telling the story of this woman's anguish and dysfunctional relationship with her older sister, who tormented her.

7. Ibid., and *Look*, August 30, 1960.

8. Roger Blin was born on March 22, 1907, in Neuilly-sur-Seine, France. By the time he met Simone, he was already a well-respected stage actor, associated with the October Group. He was a close friend of Antonin Artaud and Samuel Beckett. Blin directed the initial performances of Beckett's *Waiting for Godot* and *Endgame*. As an actor, Blin starred in *Le Coreau* (1943), *Orpheus* (1950), and *The Hunchback of Notre Dame* (1956) and appeared with Simone Signoret in *The Adolescent* (1979).

9. Gestapo/French Police arrest records, Memorial de la Shoah, Paris, France.

10. *Cinémonde* magazine special edition, 1950.

11. Dominique Desanti explained that Simone would often bring gossip or news she heard at the newspaper, which was sometimes useful information.

12. Otto Abetz became German ambassador to Occupied France.

13. *Redbook*, March 1962, p. 112.

14. Signoret, p.9.

15. Laura Bergquist, *Look*, August 1960, p. 68.

16. Signoret, p. 47

17. Ibid.

18. Ibid.

CHAPTER 7

1. Signoret, p. 54.

2. Jean-Pierre Kaminker, *La Persecution Contrarié*. Editions Lambert-Lucas. Limoges, France, 2007.

3. Marcel Carné and Jacques Prévert formed a successful liaison during World War II with *Les Visiteurs du Soir*, and then again in *Les Enfants du Paradis* (*The Children of Paradise*). Carne worked primarily in the Unoccupied Zone and was known to buck the system by hiring Jews for his production team. During the New Wave, Carné was dismissed as old school and his career faded. He and Prévert teamed up one more time in the post-war era on *Les Portes de la nuit*, one of Yves Montand's early film efforts. The film was not well received, and its production was considered one of the most expensive in the history of French cinema. Carné did not receive recognition as a director until the 1990s, when *Les Enfants du Paradis* was lauded as a masterpiece and a film classic.

4. JPK interview.

5. Signoret, p. 58.

6. Daniel Gélin was born on May 19, 1921, in Angers, Maine-et-Loire, France. His first wife was Simone's close friend, the actress Danielle Delorme. He became a popular French character actor and had roles in three films with Signoret: *La Ronde*, *The Sleeping Car Murders*, and *Is Paris Burning?*

7. Daniel Gélin, *Deux ou trois vies qui sont les miennes*. Julliard, Paris, 1977, p. 61.

8. Art Buchwald, *New York Herald Tribune*, 1959. Article included in press book for *Room at the Top*, part of author's collection.

9. *Daphnis et Chloé* is a ballet with music composed by Maurice Ravel.

10. Marcel Duhamel, born in 1900, became a notable French actor and screenwriter, and was the founder of the Série noire publishing imprint, Notable Films. By the time he met Simone, he had already launched a successful film career, starring in *The Crime of Monsieur Lange* (1936).

11. Signoret, p. 59.

CHAPTER 8

1. Yves Allégret was born October 13, 1905, in Asnières-sur-Seine, Hauts-de-Seine, France. As a director, he was best known in the film noir genre for: *Dawn Devils* (1946); *Dédée d'Anvers* (1948); *Manèges* (1950); *Mam'zelle Nitouche* (1954); *Oasis* (1955); and *Kong Yo* (1962). His French television series credits include: *Orzowei, il figlior della savanna*

(1977); *Les enquêtes du commissaire Maigret* (1979–81). Yves Allégret died on January 31, 1987.

2. Signoret, p.61,

3. In the documentary, *Henri Langlois: The Phantom of the Cinémathèque*, written and directed by Jacques Richard (2004), Simone was sighted pushing a baby carriage. It is the only reference and unconfirmed.

4. Ibid. Simone is on camera reading a letter she has written for a tribute to Langlois. She is at the height of her alcoholism, and her appearance has suffered. The documentary suggests through visuals that Simone and Montand were among many celebrities who were not generous financial supporters of Langlois and the Cinématèque at the time of his death in 1977, when he was living in abject poverty. The author was unable to establish the cause—rife or concern—between Langlois and the Montands, who were normally generous supporters of the arts.

5. Signoret, p. 67.

6. Serge Reggiani was born on May 2, 1922, in Reggio Emilia, Italy. He and his family moved to France when he was eight years old. Reggiani starred with Simone Signoret in *Casque d'Or*, a film that nearly ended his career. He performed on stage in Jean-Paul Sartre's play *Les Séquestrés d'Altona* in 1959. In 1965, with the financial backing of Simone and Montand, Serge launched a successful singing career. He suffered alcoholism after his son's suicide and died on July 23, 2004. He and Simone remained close friends throughout their lives and appeared in the film *Is Paris Burning?* with Yves Montand.

7. Danièle Delorme, her stage name, was born Gabrielle Danièle Marguerite Andrée Girard, on October 9, 1926, in Levallois-Perret, Hauts-de-Seine, France. Her father, André Girard, was an artist. He served as a resistance fighter during the Nazi occupation and was arrested with his wife. Danièle began her career as an actress in the French production of *Gigi* in 1948. She was eighteen years old when she joined Simone and Yves Allégret in 1944. Delorme met Daniel Gélin that year, and they married in 1945. Ten years later, she divorced Gelin, married the filmmaker Yves Robert, and began producing films. Delorme considered Simone a "big sister" and mother figure. They remained close friends until Simone's death in 1985.

8. BBC news, August 26, 1944.

9. Signoret, p. 75.

10. Catherine Allégret, *Les Souvenirs et Les Regrets, Aussi*. Éditions Fixot, Paris, 1994, p. 23. Catherine often assumed that Simone preferred boys to girls. She also explained that her parents, Simone and Yves Allégret, had "bad luck" with their male children. Patrick died nine days after his birth in 1944. Giles, Yves's son from his first marriage, died in a car accident at age twenty.

CHAPTER 9

1. Hervé Hamon & Patrick Rotman, p. 119.

2. Simone Signoret, *Adieu, Volodia*, pp. 413–14.

3. Simone Signoret, *Cinemonde Vécu*, 1950, pp. 8–9.

4. Laura Bergquist, *Look*, August 30, 1960, p. 68.

5. Alan Riding, p. 333.

6. Jean-François Josselin, *Simone*. Éditions Grasset & Fasquelle, Paris, 1995, p. 67.

7. Signoret, p. 64.

8. *Cinémonde*, April 4, 1954.

9. Signoret, p. 64.

10. CBS, *Small World*, CBS television transcript, December 6, 1959. The show was moderated by Edward R. Murrow. His guests included Simone Signoret, Agnes DeMille, and Hedda Hopper. The transcript is available at the Margaret Hennick Library, Academy of Motion Picture Arts & Sciences. The taped program is available for viewing at the New York Library for Performing Arts, Agnes DeMille collection.

11. Catherine Allégret, p. 22.

12. Bernard Blier, born on January 11, 1916, in Buenos Aires, Argentina, became one of France's great character actors. Early in his career, he was typecast because of his premature baldness and stocky frame and often played the role of a cuckolded husband. He was a versatile actor who could easily transition from drama to comedy. Notable films include: *Dédée d'Anvers* (1948), *Manèges* (1950), *Les Miserables* (1958), *High Infidelity* (1964).

13. Ibid.

14. Paris-Presse, September 7, 1948.

15. Harry Ransom Center, University of Texas at Austin, David O. Selznick Collection

16. *Cinémonde*, 1950.

17. Simone was interviewed in April 1963 for the television series *Cinépanorama*, directed by Frederic Rossif. Excerpts from this interview are contained, as supplemental material, on the Criterion Collection's re-mastered re-release of *Casque d'Or*.

18. Laura Bergquist, August 30, 1960.

CHAPTER 10

1. Hervé Hamon, Patrick Rotman, p. 187.

2. Signoret, p. 82.

3. Harry Ransom Center, University of Texas at Austin, David O. Selznick Collection.

4. Hervé Hamon, Patrick Rotman, p. 186.

5. Signoret, p. 83.

6. Hervé Hamon, Patrick Rotman, p. 192.

7. Signoret, p. 84.

8. Laura Bergquist, *Look*, August 30, 1960.

9. Ibid.

10. Art Buchwald, article included in press book for *Room at the Top*, September 1959.

CHAPTER 11

1. Catherine Allégret, p. 15.

2. Signoret, p. 91.

3. *Cinémonde: Le Film Vécu*, 1950, p. 4.

4. AIIC Fiftieth Anniversary Timeline.

CHAPTER 12

1. Signoret, p. 100.
2. Ibid., p. 94.
3. JPK interview.
4. *Redbook*, March 1962, p. 100.
5. Transcript: House of Representatives, eighty-second congress, first session; Boston Library: 3 9999 05445 2493

CHAPTER 13

1. Jacques Becker was born on September 15, 1906, in Paris, France. He began his film career as an assistant to director Jean Renoir. He dabbled with independent films and in 1935 co-directed the short *Pitiless Gendarme* with Pierre Prévert, brother of Jacques Prévert. He spent the year 1941 in a German prisoner of war camp. On his return to Paris in 1942, Becker launched his career as a director. Though his output was limited to thirteen films, his work was highly regarded by New Wave directors. These works include: *Antoine et Antoinette* (1947), *Edward and Caroline* (1951), *Touchez Pas au Grisbi* (1954), *Ali Baba and the Forty Thieves* (1954). *Casque d'Or* (1952) and *Le Trou* (1960) are considered his most important cinematic contributions. Becker died on February 21, 1960, in Paris. *Casque d'Or*, which failed when it was initially released in France, was re-released after his death and lauded as a masterpiece.
2. Signoret, p.106.
3. Serge Reggianni interview for television program *La France en Films*, 1995.
4. Signoret, p. 108.
5. Joëlle Montserrat, *Simone Signoret*. Editions, PAC, Paris, 1983, p. 267.
6. Signoret, p.114.
7. *Wages of Fear*, considered a masterpiece of the suspense genre, earned Clouzot the Golden Bear Award at the Berlin Film Festival (1953), the Palm d'Or (1953), and the BAFTA Award for Best Film From Any Source. When the film was first released to American art houses, critics felt that its portrayal of the US-owned oil company was "anti-American," and the offensive scenes were cut. The film was re-mastered and re-released by the Criterion Collection in 2009.
8. Emmanuelle Gilcher, p. 128.
9. Hervé Hamon and Patrick Rotman, pp. 198–99.

CHAPTER 14

1. Jeanne Moreau, considered one of France's greatest actresses, began her career in 1947 on stage before transitioning to film. She was a popular actress in the French New Wave, starring in François Truffant's *Jules et Jim*, which garnered international attention. She has worked with Orson Welles, Elia Kazan, and other notable directors. A versatile artist, Jeanne ventured into singing and released several popular albums before turning to screen writing and directing. In 1979 Simone appeared in a film written by Moreau,

L'Adolescente. Throughout their lives, Jean Moreau and Simone remained close friends. However, Simone did not provide any insights into their friendship.

2. Rex Reed, *New York Times*, January 12, 1969.

3. Signoret, p. 113.

4. The dates Montand suggests concerning Simone's miscarriages imply she experienced one in 1950 and another in 1952. However, the second miscarriage date conflicts with accounts that have it occurring after *Thérèse Raquin*.

5. *Tribune de Genève*, February 28, 1983.

6. Hervé Hamon and Patrick Rotman, p. 223.

7. Signoret, p. 117.

CHAPTER 15

1. When writing to appeal against the death penalty, American ambassador to France C. Douglas Dillon articulated the strength of this public sentiment in France on May 15, 1953, in a letter to Secretary of State John Foster Dulles, citing four reasons that the death penalty was perceived as excessive:

[F]act of the matter is that even those who accept guilt of Rosenbergs are overwhelmingly of opinion that death sentence unjustifiable punishment for offenses as revealed by trial, particularly when compared with prison terms meted to British scientists Allan Nunn May and Klaus Fuchs.

In addition to this, following important factors have combined to reinforce sentiment that even though guilty Rosenbergs should not (repeat not) get death: (1) marital and parental status Rosenbergs; (2) family connection to Greenglass without whose testimony charges could not (repeat not) have been brought home; (3) protracted delays; and (4) latest doubts aroused as to reliability Greenglass testimony by publication statement—allegedly in Greenglass handwriting— whose authenticity not (repeat not) yet denied. (Press here has run Photostats of statement in which Greenglass writes that what he told FBI may not have been true .... Department has informed Embassy such a statement "may well exist.") Substantial segment of French opinion also makes a distinction between degree of guilt of Rosenberg as the principal, and his wife as an accessory.

We should not (repeat not) deceive ourselves by thinking that this sentiment is due principally to Communist propaganda or that people who take this position are unconscious dupes of Communists. Fact is that great majority of French people of all political leanings feel that death sentence is completely unjustified from moral standpoint and is due only to political climate peculiar to United States now (repeat now) and at time when trial took place, even though trial itself conducted with fullest protection rights individual.

While over here, Mr. Cohn of Senator McCarthy's staff publicly sought to convince European opinion of his maturity experience in spite of his youth by claiming that he prosecuted Rosenbergs. In the light of highly unfavorable reaction of European opinion in mission and views of Messrs. Cohn and Schine, nothing could be better calculated than this claim to convince waverers that Rosenbergs if executed will be victims of what European press freely terms "McCarthyism."

But the US government's "peculiar climate" prevailed, and every attempt was made to deny death sentence reprieves. Most outrageous to many was that the Rosenbergs were offered the opportunity to avoid the death penalty if only they would admit their guilt. Julius and Ethel categorically refused, maintaining their innocence until their last hours, when they wrote a heartfelt farewell letter to their children, Michael and Robert, who were aged ten and six respectively: "Always remember that we were innocent and could not wrong our conscience."

2. Arthur Miller, *Time Bends: A Life*. Penguin, 1987, p. 347.

3. Signoret, p. 127.

4. Emile Zola, *The Dreyfus Affair, J'Accuse and Other Writings*. Yale University Press, 1998, p. 34.

5. Arthur Miller, "Again They Drink From the Cup of Suspicion," *New York Times*, November 26, 1989.

6. HUAC transcript: Ronald Reagan testimony, October 3, 1947. Tennessee Wesleyan College.

> *Stripling*. As a member of the board of directors, as president of the Screen Actors Guild, and as an active member, have you at any time observed or noted within the organization a clique of either communists or fascists who were attempting to exert influence or pressure on the guild?
>
> *Reagan*. Well sir, my testimony must be very similar to that of Mr. (George) Murphy and Mr. (Robert) Montgomery. There has been a small group within the Screen Actors Guild which has consistently opposed the policy of the guild board and officers of the guild, as evidenced by the vote on various issues. That small clique referred to has been suspected of more or less following the tactics that we associate with the Communist Party.

When asked if he had ever been approached by an organization associated with communism, Reagan related a story about providing sponsorship to a fundraising event for a hospital in Los Angeles. At first, when he learned that the African American singer and actor, Paul Robeson (who had not yet been blacklisted, but was on a watch list as a radical activist), was scheduled to perform at the gala event, Regan stopped short: "I hesitated a moment, because I don't think that Mr. Robeson's and my political views coincide at all; and then I thought I was being a little stupid because, I thought, here is an occasion where Mr. Robeson is perhaps appearing as an artist, and certainly the object, raising money, is above any political consideration: it is a hospital supported by everyone."

Reagan gave permission to use his name, only to learn weeks later that the event was sponsored by the Joint Anti-Fascist Refugee Committee (JAFRC). Though the organization was formed during World War II to provide humanitarian relief to refugees of the Spanish Civil War and to anti-fascist fighters trapped in Vichy France and North Africa, its members were suspected of ties to the Communist Party. And while they raised funds for the hospital in question, it later became evident that the event was a political rally. Reagan felt duped.

Reagan's experience validated the need for the House Un-American Activities Committee, its chair, J. Parnell Thomas explained. Americans were being duped into supporting communist causes, and in his opinion, it was necessary to purge communists "to make America just as pure as we can possibly make it." To Reagan's credit, he was taken aback by Thomas's reaction. "Sir, I detest, I abhor their philosophy," he responded, "but I detest more than that their tactics, which are those of the fifth column, and are dishonest, but at the same time I never as a citizen want to see our country become urged, by either fear or resentment of this group, that we ever compromise with any of our democratic principles through that fear or resentment."

7. "Be alert to the dangers of Communism. Report your information immediately and fully to the F.B.I. Avoid reporting malicious gossip or idle rumor. The FBI is interested in receiving facts. Don't attempt to make private investigations. Leave that to trained investigators. Don't circulate rumors about subversive activities or draw conclusions from information you furnish to the FBI." *U.S. News & World Report*, "How Communists Operate: An Interview with J. Edgar Hoover," August 11, 1950.

CHAPTER 16

1. Miller, Timebends, p. 349.
2. Hervé Hamon and Patrick Rotman, p. 264.
3. Ibid.
4. Ibid.
5. Ibid.

CHAPTER 17

1. Hervé Hamon and Patrick Rotman, p. 271. All un-annotated quotations from this text.
2. Laura Bergquist, *Look*, August 30, 1960.
3. Signoret, p. 179.
4. Ibid., p. 204.

CHAPTER 18

1. Signoret, pp. 216–17.
2. Telegram from Glenville to Rex Harrison explaining why he could not have the role. Glenville Collection, Harry Ransom Research Center, University of Texas at Austin. Used with permission from the Peter Glenville Foundation. Box 4.12.
3. Letter outlined all progress made to date on production issues before discussion turns to filling the role of Marianne. Glenville Collection, Harry Ransom Research Center, University of Texas at Austin. All correspondence in this chapter is taken from this collection, box 13.9 and box 28.6.
4. Dany: French version of the nickname Danny.
5. CIMURA MCA, the premiere talent agency in France during the 1950s.
6. Judith Crist, *New York Herald Tribune*, April 1959. The article was used in a promotional booklet for film. Author's collection.
7. Signoret, p. 127.
8. Art Buchwald.

CHAPTER 19

1. Signoret, pp. 237-42. All quotes in this chapter are taken from this text.

CHAPTER 20

1. The Continental Distributor campaign booklet containing articles quoted in this chapter is part of author's collection.

2. Signoret, p. 239.

3. Ibid.

4. Ibid.

CHAPTER 21

1. *HUSH-HUSH*, September 1960.

2. Hervé Hamon and Patrick Rotman, p. 325.

3. Taped interview with choreographer Agnes De Mille. Dorothy and Lewis Cullman Center, New York Public Library for the Performing Arts.

4. Miller, *Timebends*. Penguin, 1995, p. 440.

5. FBI Hedda Hopper files, document 100-359945-2. Unannotated quotations are taken from documents in this file.

6. The telegram is part of the Hedda Hopper Collection, Margaret Herrick Library, Academy of Motion Picture Arts and Sciences. Permission to reprint Simone's telegram was not granted by her estate. However, Simone refers to the "last line" in her autobiography, quoted in this chapter. During editing of the program, the segment Simone referred to as the "last line" was moved up in the segment so that the program did not end on that note. Simone noted in her autobiography that Hopper was wearing one of her famous hats. However, this recollection was not correct. As Murrow notes, Hopper made a rare appearance without a hat.

CHAPTER 22

1. Hedda Hopper file, Margaret Herrick Library, Academy of Motion Picture Arts & Sciences.

2. Peer Oppenheimer, *Sarasota Herald Tribune*, April 3, 1960.

3. Signoret, p. 268.

4. George Cukor, *Little Women* (1933), *Dinner at Eight* (1933), *David Copperfield* (1935), *The Philadelphia Story* (1940), *Adam's Rib* (1949), *Born Yesterday* (1950), *A Star Is Born* (1954), and *My Fair Lady* (1964).

5. Hervé Hamon, Patrick Rotman, p. 317.

6. While searching for a copy of the televised program, which I was unable to find, I had the pleasure of communicating with Alvin Sargent, who won Academy Awards for *Julia* and *Ordinary People*. He wrote the screenplays for the successful *Spiderman* film

series. Mr. Sargent was responsible for putting me in contact with Betty Marvin, first wife of actor Lee Marvin.

7. Hervé Hamon, Patrick Rotman, p. 317.

8. Signoret, pp. 291–92.

9. *They Shoot Horses, Don't They?* The story is based on a novel of the same name by Horace McCoy. It was adapted as a film directed by Sydney Pollack in 1969, with Jane Fonda and Michael Sarrazin in lead roles. Jane Fonda was nominated for an Academy Award for her performance.

10. Simone, p. 293. Unannotated quotes taken from this text.

11. Hedda Hopper, *The Whole Truth and Nothing But.* Double Day, 1962, 1963, p. 71.

12. Barbara Leaming, *Marilyn Monroe.* Three Rivers Press, 1998, pp. 348–49.

13. Signoret, p. 296.

14. *New York Times*, March 25, 1960.

15. *Black Orpheus*, a film adaptation of the Greek myth of Orpheus and Eurydice is set during a carnival in Rio de Janeiro and directed by French film director Marcel Camus.

CHAPTER 23

1. Catherine David. *Simone Signoret.* Translated by Sally Sampson. Overlook Press, 1993, p. 117. Originally published in France, Editions Robert Laffont & Sons, SA, Paris, 1990.

2. Peers Oppenheimer, *Sarasota Herald Tribune*, April 3, 1960.

3. Bosley Crowther, "Simone Signoret Toughs it in Rome," *New York Times*, May 8, 1960.

4. Hervé Hamon, Patrick Rotman, p. 329.

5. Barbara Leaming, *Marilyn Monroe.* Three Rivers Press, 1998, p. 357.

6. Hedda Hopper and James Brough, *The Whole Truth And Nothing But.* Doubleday, 1962, 1963.

7. Laura Bergquist, *Look*, August 30, 1960.

8. Hedda Hopper and James Brough, p. 42.

9. Signoret, p. 302.

10. Anthony Summer, *Goddess: The Secret Lives of Marilyn Monroe.* Gollancz, 1985, p. 197.

11. Hervé Hamon, Patrick Rotman, p. 329.

CHAPTER 24

1. Simone Signoret, "The Private Life of Simone Signoret," *Cine Universal*, February 15, 1963.

2. Signoret, p. 328. Simone Signoret's French translation of *The Little Foxes* is available at the Harry Ransom Library, University of Texas at Austin. According to French author Emmanuelle Gilcher, the Hellman estate has issued specific instructions prohibiting the use of that translation. I was unable to verify that information.

CHAPTER 25

1. Anthony Quinn with Daniel Paisner, *One Man Tango*. HarperCollins, 1995, pp. 315–51, 359.

2. Pauline Kael. *Kiss, Kiss, Bang, Bang*. Little, Brown, 1965, p. 213.

3. The mood of the country was brought to life in the techniques Stanley Kramer used to bring his actors together and prepare them for the themes portrayed in *Ship of Fools*. He arranged for a mini-bus to take them all to the summer Olympics held in LA that year. According to Simone, John Birch Society members were at the entrance handing out leaflets to protest the Russian athletes, who they claimed were Soviet spies. Simone was convinced that Kramer had brought his cast to this event so they could ponder the situation. Kramer also accompanied Simone and Oskar Werner to Synanon, a drug-rehab center in LA, where they could witness addicts in detox. Simone was disturbed by the youth of the patients, who ranged in age from sixteen to eighteen years of age.

4. Jane Fonda, *My Life So Far*. Random House, 2005, pp. 138–39.

5. Betty Marvin, *Tales of a Hollywood Housewife*. iuniverse, 2009, p. 185.

6. Author interview with Betty Marvin.

7. Refers to characteristics in the works of Luigi Pirandello, an Italian dramatist and poet known for creating dramas in which actors become inseparable and indistinct from the characters they play.

8. Hervé Hamon, Patrick Rotman, p. 344.

9. Ibid.

CHAPTER 26

1. Bernard Weinraub, *Saturday Evening Post*, February 25, 1967.

2. Signoret, p. 339.

3. *Cinémonde*, November 11, 1969, p. 14.

CHAPTER 27

1. Jo Langer, *Une saison a Bratislava*, with translation from English and preface by Simone Signoret. Editions du Seuil, 1981. Originally published as *Convictions: My Life with a Good Communist*. Andre Deutsch, 1979. Reprinted by Granta Publications, 2011.

2. Hervé Hamon, Patrick Rotman, p. 223.

3. Signoret, p. 354.

4. Rex Reed, *New York Times*, January 12, 1969. Mr. Reed declined an interview but gave permission to quote from his article.

5. Hervé Hamon, Patrick Rotman, p. 223.

6. Vanessa Redgrave, *Vanessa Redgrave, An Autobiography*. Random House, 1991, p. 168.

CHAPTER 28

1. *Redbook*, March 1962, p. 50.

2. Jean-Pierre Grumbach (October 20, 1917–August 2, 1973). During the Nazi occupation, he joined the French Resistance and changed his name to Jean-Pierre Melville, a

tribute to his favorite author, Herman Melville. Other notable films include: *Le Silence de la Mer* (1949); *Les Enfants Terribles* (1950); *Le Samoura* (1967).

3. Interview for documentary *L'invite du dimanche* on the making of *Army of Shadows*, included as supplemental material in the Criterion Collection re-release of the film. The interview originally aired March 1969. Gaumont-Pathé archives, France.

4. Hervé Hamon, Patrick Rotman, p. 341.

5. Ibid.

CHAPTER 29

1. Hervé Hamon, Patrick Rotman. p. 336.

2. Ibid., p. 388.

3. David Thomson, *The New Biographical Dictionary of Film*. Knopf, 2004, pp. 311, 830.

4. Catherine Allégret. *Un Monde à l'envers*. Librairie Arthème Fayard, 2004, pp. 92-93. All unannotated quotes in this chapter are taken from this text.

5. As shared with me by Charlotte Sheedy, who represented author Bernice Rubens.

6. Benjamin Castaldi, *Maintenant, il faudra tout se dire*. Albin Michel, 2004, p. 82.

7. Hervé Hamon, Patrick Rotman. p. 389.

8. Ibid., p. 390.

CHAPTER 30

1. Liz Smith, *Dishing: Great Dish—and Dishes—From America's Most Beloved Gossip Columnist*. Simone & Schuster, 2005. I had email correspondence with Ms. Smith. Although she did not have any insight to share about Simone, she was kind enough to provide contact information for Rex Reed and granted permission to use her story about Mario Puzo.

2. Signoret, p. 321.

3. Joëlle Monserrant, *Simone Signoret*. Editions PAC, 1983, p. 272.

4. *Le Monde*, June 12, 1973.

5. Hervé Hamon, Patrick Rotman, p. 388.

6. *Le Monde*, June 12, 1973.

CHAPTER 31

1. Catherine David, *Simone Signoret*. Editions Robert Laffont, SA, 1990, p. 201. First English translation by Sally Sampson, published by Overlook Press, 1993.

2. Hervé Hamon, Patrick Rotman, pp. 345–46.

3. Patrice Chéreau is a French actor, director of both theater and opera, filmmaker, and producer.

4. *Marie Claire*, September 1979.

5. Régis Debray is a French author, journalist, and intellectual. After joining Che Guevara in Bolivia in 1967, he returned to Paris. In 1981, he served as foreign affairs advisor to French president François Mitterrand.

6. Simone Signoret, *Le lendemain, elle était souriante*. Editions Du Seuil, 1979, pgs. 36–37.

7. Simone Signoret, *Nostalgia Isn't What It Used To Be*. Preface. English translation, Harper & Row, 1978. Originally published in French as *La nostalgie n'est plus ce qu'elle était*. Éditions du Seuil, 1976. Simone did not write the preface in the original, French edition. This preface was written by Maurice Pons.

8. Hervé Hamon, Patrick Rotman, p. 391.

CHAPTER 32

1. Simone Signoret, *Le lendemain, elle était souriante*. Editions Du Seuil, 1979. All unannotated quotes are taken from this text. This supplement to Simone's autobiography has not been translated into English. It was widely believed that Simone should not have written the book because her tone— bolstered by alcohol—was sarcastic and biting. In *Nostalgia*, Simone made a point of mentioning that she was not settling old scores with her memoir. However, that was not the case with *Le lendemain*. Her intent, at least in the first part of the book, was to settle a score with those who doubted her authorship of *Nostalgia*. *Le lendemain* is not widely quoted from in French biographies. As already mentioned, in spite of Simone's initial intent, the book provides valuable insight and information about a little-known period in her life.

2. Hervé Hamon, Patrick Rotman, p. 392.

CHAPTER 33

1. Simone Signoret, *Le lendemain, elle était souriante*. Editions du Seuil, 1979, p. 146.

2. Pamela Andriotakis, "It's Useless to Hang Onto The Branches of Youth." *People*, June 12, 1978.

3. Simone Signoret, *Nostalgia Isn't What It Used To Be*, p. 194.

4. Jo Langer, with translation and preface by Simone Signoret. *Saison à Bratislava*. Editions du Seuil, 1981, pp. 7–19. Originally published as *Convictions: My Life with a Good Communist*. Andre Deutsch, 1979. Reprinted Granta Publications, 2011.

CHAPTER 34

1. Moira Hodgson, *New York Times*, September 5, 1982.

2. Huguette Bouchardeau, *Simone Signoret*. Editions J'ai Lu, 2007, p. 296.

3. Hervé Hamon, Patrick Rotman, p. 401.

4. Télérama interview with Simone Signoret, November 9, 1983.

5. Danièle Heyman, *L'Express*, January 25, 1985.

6. *Los Angeles Times*, August 10, 1986.

7. Simone Signoret, *Adieu, Volodia*. Random House, 1986, p. 9. Originally published in France by Librairie Arthème Fayard, 1985. First translation published in Great Britain by Macmillan Publishers, 1986.

8. Ibid., pp. 373–74.

9. *Elle*, January 21, 1985.

CHAPTER 35

1. *Studio*, June 1990.

2. Author interview with Betty Marvin.

3. Jean-François Josselin, *Simone*. Éditions Grasset & Fasquelle, 1995, p. 16.

4. Ibid.

5. Ibid.

6. Susan Hayward, *Simone Signoret: The Star as Cultural Sign*. Continuum, 2004, p. 236.

7. *Tele Poche*, "Le Dernier Role de Madame Signoret," April 28, 1986.

8. Catherine Allégret, *Les Souvenirs et Les Regrets, Aussi*. Éditions Fixot, 1994, p. 262.

9. Ibid.

10. Hervé Hamon and Patrick Rotman, p. 433.

11. Catherine Allégret, pp. 272–73.

12. Benjamin Castaldi, *Dans les yeux de Simone*. Edition Albin Michel, 2010, p. 13.

13. Mary Blume, "Simone Signoret, A Memory," in *A French Affair: The Paris Beat, 1965–1998*. Free Press, 1999.

14. CBS News, October 1, 1985. Vanderbilt Television News Archive, Nashville, TN.

15. Benjamin Castaldi, *Maintenant, il faudra tout se dire*. Éditions Albin Michel, 2004, p. 86.

16. Hervé Harmon and Patrick Rotman, p. 436.

17. *New York Times*, April 25, 1988.

FILMOGRAPHY

1941
Le Prince Charmant, directed by Jean Boyer
Bolero, directed by Jean Boyer

1942
Le Voyageur de la Toussaint, directed by Louis Daquin
Les Visiteurs du soir, directed by Marcel Carné
L'Ange de la nuit, directed by André Berthomieu
Dieu est innocent (theater), directed by Marcel Herrand

1943
Adieu Léonard, directed by Pierre Prévert
Service de nuit, directed by Jean Faurez
Le Mort ne reçoit plus, directed by Jean Tarride
Beatrice devant le désir, directed by Jean de Marguenat
La Boîte aux rêves, directed by Yves Allégret

1945
Le Couple idéal, directed by Bernard Roland
Les Démons de l'aube, directed by Yves Allégret

1946
Macadam, directed by Marcel Blistène
Fantômas, directed by Jean Sacha

1947
Dédée d'Anvers, directed by Yves Allégret
Against the Wind, directed by Charles Crichton

1948
L'Impasse des deux-anges, directed by Maurice Tourneur

1949
Manèges, directed by Yves Allégret
Four Days Leave, directed by Leopold Lindtberg

1950
Gunman in the Streets, directed by Frank Tuttle and Boris Lewin
La Ronde, directed by Max Ophuls
Sans laisser d'adresse, directed by Jean-Paul Le Chanois
Ombre et Lumière, directed by Henri Calef

1951
Casque d'Or, directed by Jacques Becker

1953
Thérèse Raquin, directed by Marcel Carné

1954
Les Diaboliques, directed Henri-Georges Clouzot
Les Sorcières de Salem (theater), directed by Raymond Rouleau

1955
Mother Courage, directed by Wolfgang Staudte
Les Sorcières de Salem, directed by Raymond Rouleau
Death in the Garden, directed by Luis Buñuel

1958
Room at the Top, directed by Jack Clayton

1960
Don't You Remember? (television, GE Theater), directed by Leslie H. Martinson
Adua e le Compagne (Adua et ses compagnes), directed by Antoni Pietrangeli
Les Mauvais Coups, directed by François Leterrier

1961
Les Amours célèbres, directed by Michel Boisrond

1962
Term of Trial, directed by Peter Glenville
The Day and the Hour, directed by René Clément
The Little Foxes (Les Petits Renards; theater), directed by Pierre Mondy

1963
Dragées au poivre, directed by Jacques Baratier
Le Joli Mai (documentary), directed by Chris Marker

1964
Ship of Fools, directed by Stanley Kramer
A Small Rebellion (television), directed by Stuart Rosenberg
Compartiment tueurs, directed by Constantin Costa-Gavras
Aux grands magasins (documentary), directed by William Klein

1965
Is Paris Burning?, directed by René Clément

1966
The Deadly Affair, directed by Sidney Lumet
Games, directed by Curtiss Harrington
Macbeth (theater), directed by William Gaskill

1968
The Seagull, directed by Sidney Lumet
The Jewish Wife (television), directed by Alain Dhénaut

1969
Army of Shadows, directed by Jean-Pierre Melville
L'Américain, directed by Marcel Bozzuffi
L'Aveu, directed by Constantin Costa-Gavras

1970
Compte à rebours, directed by Roger Pigaut
Le Chat, directed by Pierre Granier-Deferre
Un Otage (television), directed by Marcel Cravenne

1971
The Widow Couderc, directed by Pierre Granier-Deferre

1972
Les Granges brûlees, directed by Jean Chapot

1973
Rude journée pour la reine, directed by René Allio

1974
La Chair de l'orchideé, directed by Patrice Chéreau

1975
Police Python 357, directed by Alain Corneau

1976
Madame le juge (six-part television series), directed by Edouard Molinaro, Nadine Trintignant, Claude Chabrol, Claude Barma, Philippe Condroyer

1977
Madame Rosa (*La Vie devant soi*), directed by Moshe Mizrahi

1978
Judith Therpauve, directed by Patrice Chéreau
L'Adolescente, directed by Jeanne Moreau

1979
I Sent a Letter to my Love (*Chère Inconnue*), directed by Moshe Mizrahi

1981
Guy de Maupassant, directed by Michel Drach
L'Étoile du Nord, directed Pierre Granier-Deferre

1982
Thérèse Humbert, directed by Marcel Bluwal

1983
Des Terroristes à la retraite (documentary), directed by Mosco Boucaut

1985
Music-Hall (two-part Television series), directed by Marcel Bluwal

BIBLIOGRAPHY

BOOKS

Allégret, Catherine. *Les souvenirs and les regrets, aussi.* Paris: Editions Fixot, 1994

Allégret, Catherine. *Un Monde à l'envers.* Paris: Librairie Arthème Fayard, 2004.

Bair, Deirdre. *New York Times Book Review.* September 14, 1985.

Barrot, O., and R. Chirat. *La vie culturelle dans la France occupée.* Paris: Gallimard, 2009.

Blume, Mary. "Simone Signoret, A Memory." In *A French Affair: The Paris Beat 1965–1998.* New York: Simon & Schuster 1999; Free Press, 2000.

Bouchardeau, Huguette. *Simone Signoret.* Paris: Editions J'ai Lu, 2007.

Castaldi, Benjamin. *Dans les yeux de Simone.* Paris: Edition Albin Michel, 2010.

———. *Maintenant, il faudra tout se dire.* Paris: Edition Albin Michel, 2004.

David, Catherine. *Simone Signoret.* Paris: Editions Robert Laffont, SA, 1990.

Fonda, Jane. *My Life So Far.* New York: Random House, 2005.

Gelin, Daniel. *Deux ou trois vies qui sont les miennes.* Paris: Julliard, 1977.

Gilcher, Emmanuelle. *Signoret, Une Vie.* Paris: Editions Privé, 2005.

Hammond, Hervé, and Patrick Rotman. *You See, I Haven't Forgotten: Yves Montand.* New York: Alfred A. Knopf, 1992.

Hayward, Susan. *Simone Signoret: The Star as Cultural Sign.* New York: Continuum, 2004.

Hellman, Lillian. *Pentimento.* Boston: Little, Brown, 1973.

Hopper, Hedda, with James Brough. *The Whole Truth and Nothing But.* New York: Doublday, 1962.

Horne, Alistair. *La Belle France.* New York: Vintage Books, 2006.

Jones, Colin. *Paris: The Biography of a City.* New York: Penguin, 2005.

Josselin, Jean-François. *Simone.* Paris: Éditions Grasset & Fasquelle, 1995.

Kael, Pauline. *Kiss, Kiss, Bang, Bang.* Boston: Little, Brown, 1968.

Kaminker, Jean-Pierre. *La Persecution Contrariée.* Limoges: Editions Lambert-Lucas, 2007.

King, Carol, with Richard Havers. *Peter Glenville.* London: Peter Glenville Foundation, 2010.

Langer, Jo. *Convictions, My Life with a Good Communist.* London: Granta, 2011.

Leaming, Barbara. *Marilyn Monroe.* New York: Three Rivers Press, 1998.

MacLaine, Shirley. *My Lucky Stars: A Hollywood Memoir.* New York: Bantam, 1996.

Marvin, Betty. *Tales of a Hollywood Housewife.* iUniverse, 2009.

Meeropol, Robert. *An Execution in the Family*. New York: St. Martin's Press, 2003.

Montserrat, Joëlle. *Simone Signoret*. Paris: Éditions PAC, 1983.

Miller, Arthur. *Timebends: A Life*. New York: Penguin, 1995.

Périsset, Maurice. *Simone Signoret*. Paris: Editions J'ai lu, 1988.

Quinn, Anthony, with Daniel Paisner. *One Man Tango*. New York: HarperCollins, 1995.

Redgrave, Vanessa. *An Autobiography*. New York: Random House, 1991.

Ridding, Alan. *And the Show Went On*. New York: Knopf, 2010.

Signoret, Simone. *Adieu, Volodia*. New York: Random House, 1986. Originally published in France by Librairie Arthème Fayard (Paris), 1985.

————. *Le lendemain, elle était souriante*. Paris: Editions Du Seuil, 1979.

————. *Nostalgia Isn't What It Used to Be*. New York: Harper & Row, 1978. Originally published as *La nostalgie n'est plus ce qu'elle était*. Paris: Éditions du Seuil, 1976.

————. *Saison à Bratislava*. Translation and Preface. Paris: Editions du Seuil, 1988.

Smith, Liz. *Dishing: Great Dish—and Dishes—From America's Most Beloved Gossip Columnist*. New York: Simone & Schuster, 2005.

Summer, Anthony. *Goddess: The Secret Lives of Marilyn Monroe*. London: Gollancz, 1985.

Thomson, David. *The New Biographical Dictionary of Film*. New York: Knopf, 2004.

Zola, Emile. *The Dreyfus Affair, J'Accuse and Other Writings*. New Haven, CT: Yale University Press, 1998.

MAGAZINES & NEWS ARTICLES

Andriotakis, Pamela. "It's Useless to Hang onto the Branches of Youth," *People*, June 12, 1978.

Bair, Deirdre. "Adieu, Volodya," *New York Times Book Review*, September 14, 1986.

Bergquist, Laura. "The Lives and Loves of Simone Signoret," *Look*, August 30, 1960.

Blume, Mary. "Simone Signoret, A Memory." In *A French Affair: The Paris Beat 1965–1998*. New York: Free Press, 1999.

Cine Universal, "The Private Life of Simone Signoret," February 15, 1963.

Cinémonde, April 4, 1954; November 11, 1969.

————. November 11, 1967.

————. Special Edition. "Le Film Vécu, Simone Signoret," 1950.

Crowther, Bosley. "Simone Signoret Toughs It in Rome," *New York Times*, May 8, 1960.

Démeron, Pierre. *Marie Claire*, September 1979.

Elle, January 21, 1985.

Heymann, Danièle. *L'Express*, January 25, 1985.

Hodgson, Moria. *New York Times*, September 5, 1982.

HUSH-HUSH, September 1960.

Le Monde, June 12, 1973.

L'Écran Française, May 1948.

L'Express, January 25, 1985.

Los Angeles Times, August 10, 1986.

Marie-Claire, September 1979.

Miller, Arthur. "Again They Drink trom the Cup of Suspicion," November 26, 1989.

Oppenheimer, Peer. "America Discovers a Unique Couple," *Sarasota Herald Tribune*, April 3, 1960.

Paris-Presse, September 7, 1948.

Redbook, March 1962.

"Simone Signoret Denies Being a Red," *New York* Times, April 7, 1960.

"Simone Signoret Discusses Films," *New York Times*, March 25, 1960, p. 21.

Reed, Rex. "I've Lived My Friend," *New York Times*, January 12, 1969, Arts & Leisure D1.

Studio, June 1990.

Tele Poche, "Simone Signoret's Last Role," April 28, 1986.

Tribune de Genève, February 28, 1983.

Time, October 31, 1932.

U.S. News & World Report, "How Communists Operate: An Interview with J. Edgar Hoover," August 11, 1950.

Weinraub, Bernard. *Saturday Evening Post*. February 25, 1967.

OTHER SOURCES

AIIC: International Association of Conference Interpreters, "Fiftieth Anniversary Timeline;" www.aiic.com.

Casque d'Or (film). "La France en Films," Serge Reggianni interview for television, aired 1995. Segment contained on the Criterion Collection re-release of film.

CBS News footage: Dan Rather reports on funeral of Simone Signoret, October 1, 1985. Vanderbilt Television News Archive, Nashville, TN.

Cinépanorama television series, April 1963; excerpts contained on the Criterion Collection re-lease of *Casque d'Or*.

Continental Distributor campaign booklet for *Room at the Top* (film), containing articles and interviews with cast. Author's collection.

Continental Distributors Press Book for *Room at the Top*. Dorothy and Lewis Cullman Center, New York Public Library for Performing Arts.

FBI, Hedda Hopper files, document 100-359945-2.

Freeman, John. BBC Interview, November 13, 1960.

Harry Ransom Center, University of Texas at Austin, David O. Selznick and Peter Glenville Collections.

Henri Langlois: The Phantom of the Cinémathèque. Documentary, written and directed by Jacques Richard, 2004.

House of Representatives transcript, Eighty-Second Congress, first session. Boston Library: 3 9999 05445 2493.

House Un-American Activities Committee transcript, October 3, 1947. Tennessee Wesleyan College.

L'invite du dimanche interviews on the making of *Army of Shadows*, aired March 1969; Gaumont-Pathé Archives, France; contained on the Criterion Collection re-release of the film.

Margaret Herrick Library, Academy of Motion Picture Arts & Sciences, Beverly Hills, CA.

Télérama, November 9, 1983.

Vanderbilt Television News Archive, Nashville, TN.

INDEX